The Dunlop Book of Rugby Union

THE DUNLOP BOOK OF RUGBY UNION

by

DAVID GUINEY

Cartoons By

EASTLAND PRESS

LAVENHAM   SUFFOLK

1974

Published in the United Kingdom by
EASTLAND PRESS
ISBN 0 903214 06 7

Printed in Great Britain by
THE LAVENHAM PRESS LIMITED
LAVENHAM   SUFFOLK

CONTENTS

FOREWORD

I would like to make it quite clear that this book does not purport in any way to be a history of rugby football. To suggest that would be an impertinence on my part. It is purely a collection of short stories, anecdotes, facts and some statistics about a wonderful game that we all love. Some of the stories may be well-known; others I hope will be new to my readers.

In compiling this book I owe a tremendous depth of gratitude to many people, particularly to Edmund van Esbeck of the *Irish Times* who answered query after query with an incredible patience . . . . to Paul MacWeeney of the *Irish Times* for the valuable books he lent me . . . . to Alex Potter in Paris who taught me so much about French rugby . . . . to Tudor James in Wales . . . . to the many Dunlop officials in South Africa, Australia and New Zealand, who provided so much material for me . . . . to Sean Diffley and Mitchel Cogley of the *Irish Independent* . . . . to Ann Sinclair who painstakingly transcribed over 30 hours of tape-recordings . . . . and to my family who refrained from talking to me for almost six months . . . . and finally to all the great writers on rugby whose books I read for reference purposes.

"HEAVENS! DO WE LOOK LIKE THAT?"

ENGLAND

THE BEGINNING

When legend becomes more entertaining than fact, then print the legend. So a famous newspaper editor once advised his staff . . . and so it is with the noble game of Rugby Football. In the winter of 1823, for reasons best known to himself and which will never be fully known, one William Webb Ellis, a native of Manchester and a pupil of Rugby School, caught a football in his hands and ran forward with it. His action is now recalled in a plaque at Rugby School; "This stone commemorates the exploit of William Webb Ellis, who with a fine disregard for the rules of football as played in his time, first took the ball in his arms and ran with it, thus originating the distinctive feature of the rugby game. A.D. 1823". That legend is now fact. William Webb Ellis entered the church and his death remained a mystery until October, 1959 when my good friend Ross McWhirter traced his grave to the Cimetiere du Vieux Chateau at Menton in south-east France. The inscription on the headstone is "The Reverend William Webb Ellis, late Rector of St. Clement Danes Church, London. Died February 24, 1872".

AND SO IT BEGAN

The first rugby club in England was established at Cambridge University in 1839 and the famous Blackheath Club came into existence in 1858. Subsequently clubs began to flourish in England and eventually on 26th January, 1871, the English Rugby Union was formed in London with Mr Algernon Rutter as the first President. A year later the first international game between England and Scotland was played at the Academy Ground in Raeburn Place, Edinburgh and was for a duration of two 50-minute periods. Four years later England played the first international against Ireland at the Kennington Oval and in 1881 England met Wales for the first time on Mr Richardson's Field at Blackheath London.

ALL ON HIS OWN

When Reginald Halsey Birkett (Clapham Rovers) trotted on to the pitch at the Academy Ground, Raeburn Place, Edinburgh, on 27th March, 1871, he set off on a record which is unique in the history of English rugby. To add to the distinction of representing England against Scotland in the first ever international rugby game, he also wound up with the honour of scoring England's first try. In all he won four international rugby caps between 1871 and 1876 and then, having accomplished that, he switched his full attention to soccer. Three years later, in 1879, he became the first of three English rugby internationals to win double honours. He was capped for England at soccer against Scotland at the Kennington Oval and scored in a 5-4 victory. There was, however, more to come. A year later he became the only English rugby international to win an English F.A. Cup medal when Clapham Rovers defeated Oxford University by 1-0 in the final. For extra measure, his brother Louis Birkett also played rugby for England with three caps between 1875 and 1877 and later he had the satisfaction of seeing his son, John Guy Birkett, win 21 international rugby caps for England between 1906 and 1912.

THE FIRST SIX-FOOTER

The Honourable Marshall Brooks, who went up to Oxford University in 1873 had the distinction of being selected to play for England against Scotland at the Kennington Oval on 23rd February, 1874 and was one of the 20 to engineer a good win by a goal to a try. However, after making one appearance for Oxford and that one appearance for England, he devoted himself totally to athletics and on 4th April, 1876, he was to be involved in one of the first great feats of modern athletics. At Lillie Bridge in London he became the first man to clear 6' in the high jump and he did it with a remarkable leap for the time of 6' 2½". This was to remain as a world record until the American William Byrd Page broke it in America in 1887 by clearing 6' 3" and later 6' 4". Brooks, who lived to be eighty-nine, died in 1944.

TOO TRIVIAL

The learned Dean of Trinity College, Oxford University in 1875 was not enamoured of rugby and was not at all impressed when two of his students, Edward Nash and Charles Crosse, approached him to look for leave of absence. They had been invited to play for England against Scotland at Edinburgh and were most anxious to turn out. The Dean, however, would not listen and refused to tolerate the reasons and arguments they put forward. Permission for even one night's absence was refused. Possibly he had a change of heart later for both Nash and Crosse turned out in the next international game against Ireland at the Kennington Oval, but then, of course, that did not involve any great travelling.

IN ANOTHER SPORT

Walter Slade loved rugby but was never good enough to move beyond club class. He was, however, a famous runner of his time and in Dublin in 1876 when he represented England in the international athletics match against Ireland at Lansdowne Road, he raced through the 880 yards in one minute 59.5 seconds—and thus became the first man in history to break two minutes for the distance. Before leaving Ireland to return home, he took part in another local meeting in Dublin and reduced his world record to 1 minute 58.2 seconds. Slade, who also set a world record for the mile of four minutes 24.5 seconds, was to be the first Honorary Secretary of the English Rugby Football Union.

THREE BROTHERS

James Hunt, Robert Hunt and William Hunt were the first three brothers to represent England in international rugby, but, unfortunately, never appeared together on the English side. William Hunt was the first to be capped with three against Scotland (1876) and Ireland (1877-1878). James Hunt also won three against Scotland and Ireland in 1882 and against Wales in 1884. Robert Hunt won two caps against Scotland and Wales in 1881. Their record was subsequently equalled by the three brothers, Charles, George and Thomas Gibson, but like the Hunts, the three Gibsons never appeared together on an international side. Between them they won five caps. Charles Gibson played against Wales in 1901, George Gibson appeared against Wales in 1899 and against Scotland in 1901 and Thomas Gibson won his two caps against Wales and Scotland in 1905. The Hunts and the Gibsons are the only sets of three brothers to play international rugby for England.

A BRAVE FORWARD

In one way, at least, Harry Garnett of Bradford, who won his only international cap for England against Scotland at Raeburn Place, Edinburgh, on 5th March, 1877, could, perhaps be described as one of the bravest forwards to play for his country. In accounts of the time, Garnett, who captained Bradford from 1874 to 1881, is described as "a typically heavy forward who used to charge about the field in great fashion". One, however, cannot imagine that the same Mr Garnett was ever invited to take any kicks at goal. He played throughout the 1877 international in his bare feet! Throughout his rugby career he was never known to wear boots, stockings or shinguards. Subsequently Harry Garnett became the tenth President of the English Rugby Union.

THE CALCUTTA CUP

The Calcutta Rugby Club having ceased to exist, the honorary secretary of the club, one James Rothney, despatched a letter to the secretary of the English Rugby Union on 20th December, 1877 with the suggestion that the remaining funds of the club should be utilised to create a challenge trophy to be competed for annually. The offer was accepted and the trophy, made from silver melted down from rupees, turned out to be a delightful affair of magnificent workmanship and the inscription on it now reads; "The Calcutta Cup. Presented to the Rugby Football Union by the Calcutta Football Club as an international challenge Cup to be played for annually by England and Scotland. 1878". The trophy was first awarded in 1879 and at the end of the 1973-1974 season, England had won the Cup on 39 occasions and Scotland on 30 occasions with 11 draws. In the case of a draw the Cup remains in the possession of the holders.

A WORLD RECORD

One of the first great players of the Sunderland club was threequarter Henry Kayll, who was capped for England against Scotland in 1878. Kayll, however, was one of the most versatile athletes in England at the time and, in fact, is the first recorded holder of the world's pole vault record. Having won the British A.A.A. title in 1877 with an effort of 10' 3", he cleared 10' 9" some weeks later and finally on 11th August, 1877, he set a British and world record of 11' 1"—the first time that 11' had ever been cleared in an official competition.

A CAP BY ACCIDENT

Ernie Woodhead, a native of Huddersfield, who had been at Edinburgh University for some years where he had gained a remarkable reputation as a sprinter, decided on a trip to Ireland in 1880 to finish his studies at Dublin University. During his time at Edinburgh, he had played quite a lot of rugby and was noted as a fast wing-threequarter. However in Dublin, he failed to find a place on either Trinity's first or second team. At that particular stage of Irish rugby history Trinity invariably provided the backbone of the Irish side and finding a place on either of their sides was quite a problem. But Woodhead was to become an international in most extraordinary circumstances. When the England team arrived for their international game of 1880, one or two of the players had taken ill on the rough sea crossing and on the day before the game it became evident that at least one replacement would be needed. The English captain, Fred Stokes had words with one or two of the Trinity players and they came up with a suggestion. Ernie Woodhead was in the College and he might be prepared to lend a hand. And so it happened that the 25-year old Woodhead played international rugby for England. It is hardly necessary to add that it was his one and only cap.

AT THE RIGHT MOMENT

Being in the right place at the right time brought Frank Thurlow Wright his one and only international cap for England. Shortly after they had left London by train for Edinburgh with the team to play

Scotland in 1881, the English selectors found themselves with an embarrassing problem on their hands. H. H. Taylor of Blackheath, then recognised as one of the finest half-backs in England, had failed to show up for the train and they were left without a replacement. Their only hope was to look for an Englishman in Edinburgh who might be able to fill the vacancy. Some enquiries after they arrived in Edinburgh led them to Frank Wright—and, fortunately for them, he fitted the bill. He was a native of Manchester and was, at the time, playing rugby with Edinburgh Academicals. Better still, he was a back and had been tried at half-back on a few occasions. So Wright went in to the English team but, alas, he was not an overnight success. The newspaper accounts of the time say that he played pluckily and well but was totally unequal to the task of facing such experienced halves as Campbell and Wauchope. Taylor was restored for the next game against Ireland and Frank Thurlow Wright, English international for a day, went back to his law studies and disappeared into sporting obscurity.

THE FIRST FOUR

Wales's first entry into international rugby was a chastening experience. They went to Blackheath on 19th February, 1881 and were routed by England to the tune of seven goals, a drop goal and six tries to nil. Under present-day scoring this would be a 69-0 defeat. The English forward Henry Vassal became the first man in rugby history to score three tries in an international game but his record had a short life. In this same game, England's half-back G. W. Burton eventually went on to score four tries, which was then a record by an English player in an international game. Burton's total of four was subsequently equalled by Ronnie Poulton-Palmer in England's 39-10 win over France at Stade Colombes, Paris on 13th April, 1914.

NOT CRICKET, OLD BOY!

Apart from the trouncing that Wales took from England at Mr Richardson's Field in Blackheath on 19th February, 1881 when the English won by seven goals, a drop goal and six tries to nil the other significant feature of the game was that Dr Lennart Stokes tried an innovation for which the umpires duly reprimanded him. England won a throw-in and Stokes, noticing that his fellow doctor Robert Hunt was standing alone in the middle of the field, decided to fling the ball over the forwards and straight out to Hunt, who duly collected the ball and ran unopposed for a try. The umpires were livid. This had never happened before and by their judgement would never happen again. They gave Dr Stokes a sharp ticking off, penalised him for offending against the proper conduct of rugby—and, of course, disallowed the try. This was the first time Wales had met England and it was also the first time that Blackheath had been used for an international game. At the time the Blackheath Club had the ground on rent from Mr Richardson for the princely sum of £10.

ENGLAND'S FIRST

England became the first winners of the Triple Crown with three successive wins over Wales, Ireland and Scotland in the 1883-1884 season. They went to Leeds on 5th January, 1884 to take on Wales and won convincingly with tries from A. Rotherham (Oxford University), H. T. Twynam (Richmond) and G. C. Wade (Oxford University) and a conversion by W. N. Bolton (Blackheath). On 4th February, they were in Dublin and won with a try from Bolton which was converted by A. M. Evanson (Oxford University). Their final game was against Scotland at Blackheath, where they won by a goal to a try. The try, which was hotly disputed and which, subsequently, was to lead to a rift between England and Scotland, was scored by R. S. Kindersley (Devon) but the name of the man who kicked the conversion has not been recorded. Including their three wins in 1884, England have now won the Triple Crown on a record 13 occasions. Their other wins were in 1892, 1913, 1914, 1921, 1923, 1924, 1928, 1934, 1937, 1954, 1957 and 1960. In 1892, in beating Scotland, Ireland and Wales, England went through their internationals without having a score registered against them. They beat Scotland by a goal to nil, Ireland by a goal and a try to nil and Wales by three goals and a try to nil.

FIVE-A-SIDE

When the Hancock brothers of Wiveliscombe in Somerset wanted to play rugby, it was quite a simple matter. They divided themselves into two teams of five and went hard at it in their own front garden. Five of them were eventually to play for Somerset and they did, of course, create a most unusual record when P. F. "Baby" Hancock went on to play for England and his brother F. E. Hancock won his international honours with Wales. P. F. Hancock was absolutely dedicated to rugby and, so that he might play with the famous Kent Club, he frequently made the round trip of 170 miles from Somerset to London in a day to play a game. That also involved walking home a distance of 10 miles at night on his return from the games in London. He was, of course, also to tour with the Lions in South Africa in 1891 and 1896.

I'D RATHER NOT

Charles Luis Fernandes of Leeds, described as one of the greatest forwards of his time, won three caps for England against Scotland, Ireland and Wales in 1881 and having achieved his objective, then decided to retire from the international game. But seven years later, in slightly extraordinary circumstances he was again invited to play for England. On 15th December, 1888, he went down to the station at Wakefield to bid good luck to the North team which were travelling to play the South in a trial game in London and was persuaded to come along for the fun. However, when the players got to Blackheath, it was discovered that one of the North players was missing. The game started without him. After 20 minutes Fernandes was talked into turning out and in borrowed kit he did so and thus qualified for a "North" cap seven years after he had retired. He put on such a startling display that some of the English selectors watching the game suggested that he might be interested in playing for England again. However, he declined politely. As far as he was concerned that one game was enough.

A CAP TOO MANY

All the records show that Andrew Edward Stoddart, who captained the first Lions touring side of 1888, won 11 international caps for England. But did he? It is true that he was, in fact, selected to play for England against Wales at Newport on 3rd January, 1891, and, according to the record books, he is credited with having played in that game. For reasons, however, which he did not explain at the time, he did not turn up for this game which England won by two goals and a try to a goal. Obviously someone overlooked this significant fact subsequently when the list of international players for that year were being added to the international roster. And to this day, Stoddart is shown as having won 11 caps for England. Before his death, Stoddart regularly pointed out this mistake but apparently no one has ever since taken the trouble to amend the official record of England's capped players.

DOUBLE INTERNATIONAL

England, having withdrawn from games against Scotland, Ireland and Wales in 1889, ended up with just the one international match, against the touring New Zealand Native side, at Blackheath on 16th February, 1889. That was fortunate for wing-threequarter J. W. Sutcliffe (Heckmondwike) who made his one and only appearance on an England side and celebrated the occasion with a good try which helped the English to their win by a goal and four tries to nil. A year later, Sutcliffe became a professional soccer player and joined Bolton Wanderers as a goalkeeper. Subsequently he was England's goalkeeper in five internationals, against Scotland in 1895 and 1901, against Wales in 1893 and 1903 and against Ireland in 1895. He also played for Bolton Wanderers in the 1893-1894 English F.A. Cup final but was on the losing side against Notts County, Sutcliffe is one of three English rugby internationals to win England soccer international caps. The others are Reginald Halsey Birkett and Charles P. Wilson. Capped at rugby in 1881 against Wales, Wilson, who played soccer with the Casuals and Corinthians, won his soccer caps against Scotland and Wales in 1884 He also played for Casuals in their defeat by Old Carthusians in the first English F.A. Amateur Cup final.

A CAP FOR YOU

Fred Bonsor and Jim Wright were the best half-backs in both the Bradford Club and in Yorkshire in the late 1880s and Bonsor won six caps between 1886 and 1889 and in the latter year had the distinction of playing against the New Zealand Native side—the first touring side to play in Britain and Ireland. But while Bonsor was winning his international caps, Wright was languishing in the background. The tendency in those days by the English selectors was to name one half-back from the north of England and the other from the south and while Bonsor was in form, there was never any hope that Wright would be fitted in. Bonsor, however sorted out the matter neatly. He was selected to play against Wales on 15th February, 1890 and then at the last moment he cried off—and, of course Wright came in to the English team to play at Cardiff Arms Park where he teamed up with F. H. Fox of Marlborough. Wales won by a try to nil—a 1-0 win in those days when a try was worth just a point—but at least Wright had won his one and only English cap and Bonsor was satisfied.

A GREAT NAME LOST

With the breakaway of the 20 Northern clubs which led to the establishment of the game now known as Rugby League, England lost one of their great wing-threequarters of the 1890s. Jim Valentine, born in 1866 was capped as a wing-threequarter against Wales in 1890 and then came back to win three further caps against Ireland, Scotland and Wales in 1896. One of the most prolific scorers of the time with his club Swinton, he had probably his greatest season in 1889-1890 when he was credited with scoring 61 tries and kicking 35 goals. When Swinton moved over to Rugby League in 1896, Valentine went with them and became one of the early great players of the new code. Unfortunately, while on holiday at Barmouth in 1904, he was struck by lightning during a sudden storm and was killed instantly.

A VALUABLE MAN

Could there have been a more valuable man on the first Lions tour of South Africa in 1891 than half-back Arthur Rotherham of Cambridge University. He played in 16 of the nine games including the two international games against South Africa and he wound up as the top scorer by collecting 78 points from 36 conversions, two penalty goals and a placed goal from a mark, and for good measure he also went in for two tries. But what happened to him when he returned to England? Some accounts say that he devoted himself to his studies at Cambridge, others say that he just lost interest in the game. Certainly after his inter-Varsity appearance against Oxford in 1891, he never again played with Cambridge. But, suddenly, out of the blue and now playing with Richmond, he shot back on to the international scene in 1898—seven years later—and went on to win five caps for England within the next two years. He was a cousin of Alan Rotherham, who also played with Richmond but who had won his colours with Oxford and had played for England 11 times between 1883 and 1887.

IT'S THAT MAN AGAIN

When Ireland's fifteen lined out against England for their international fixture at Manchester in 1892, quite a few of them had the distinct feeling they had seen England's wing-threequarter John Marsh on a previous occasion. And so they had. Marsh had, in fact, already won an international cap against Ireland . . . but not for England! Three years earlier, while a student at Edinburgh University, he had been on Scotland's winning side against Ireland at Belfast and during that season had also helped Scotland to their win over Wales at Edinburgh. On his graduation Marsh had moved to Swinton, joined the local rugby club and now, here he was, back again in international football but this time with England and Ireland, quite understandably, took a dim view of all this and took up the matter officially. Marsh's unique necessity of playing for two countries against Ireland, strengthened the distinction for an International Rugby Football Board, who subsequently ruled that nothing similar could ever again take place.

THE BREAKAWAY

Allegations of semi-professionalism, particularly the payment of expenses for time off work, among rugby union clubs in the North of England, finally came to a head at a meeting of the Rugby Union committee at the Westminster Palace Hotel, London on 20th September, 1893. A proposal was put forward by the Yorkshire delegates that players should be allowed compensation for bona fide loss of time in playing rugby. An amendment that such a proposal was contrary to the true interests of the game and therefore should not be sanctioned, was carried by 282 votes to 136. Two years later, 22 of the Northern clubs met at the Mitre Hotel, Leeds and they decided to form the Northern Football Union with the principle that payment should be made for bona fide loss of time. Following the meeting, all of these Northern clubs resigned from the English Rugby Union. Three years later unrestricted professionalism was permitted in the Northern Football Union, which was eventually to become the Rugby League as we know it today. Among the famous clubs to secede from the English Rugby Union were Batley, Bradford, Halifax, Wakefield Trinity, Leeds, Rochdale Hornets, Wigan, Warrington, St. Helen's, Leigh and Oldham.

A LITTLE TOO CAREFUL

The Reverend Edward Baker, capped seven times for England between 1895 and 1897, had a few "prayers" said for and about him at the Rectory Field, Blackheath on Saturday, 28th January, 1896 when Ireland won for the second time on English soil. During the second half when the scores were level at a goal each, Baker, a first-class three-quarter from Oxford University, was presented with the chance of a lifetime when a pass was delivered to him and there was not an Irishman in front of him. He duly raced for the line, crossed it and then decided to turn in towards the posts to provide the chance for an easy conversion. But in his care to do just the right thing, he went just a little too far and, in fact, ran over the dead-ball line and his try, of course, was promptly disallowed. Ireland subsequently struck back for a second try which was converted and it brought them their second victory over England in England in two years. The said Reverend Baker, however, was forgiven and continued to play for England for another season.

A DIFFERENT FIELD

His father James Shaw had played international rugby for England against Scotland and Wales in 1898 and for quite a long time, his son cherished ambitions of emulating his Dad. The youngster turned out for his local club in Cornwall, played for the county at eighteen and with his speed—he set an English schoolboy 220 yards record of 21.4 seconds—he looked set to have quite an interesting rugby life ahead of him. Gradually, however, he drifted away from the game. He had become an actor and success in this field came quickly for him. To this day, he still retains a passionate interest in the game, never misses an international game if the opportunity presents itself and is one of the most entertaining conversationalists on the game. Nowadays, however, he is better known as one of the most famous writer-actors of the present time and one of the stars of the Oscar-winning "The Sting" in 1974. And his name . . . . Robert Shaw.

NOT A WIN!

The 1898-1899 season was to be a sad one for England. They went first to St. Helen's, Swansea to take on Wales and got a sound beating by 3-26. Their centre-threequarter, G. C. Robinson was the contributor of the sole English try. There was a further surprise in store for them when they headed off to Lansdowne Road a fortnight later on 21st January, 1899 and failed to get a score as Ireland with a try from G. G. Allen and a penalty goal from full-back John Fulton put on six points. The final straw came at Blackheath where they met Scotland and again failed to score. Scotland won with a try from J. I. Gillespie and a penalty goal from the full-back H. Rottenburg and that left England with a scoring record that season of 3 points, while conceding 38. It also marked the first time that England had ever lost all three international rugby games in the one season!

A LITTLE CONFUSED

David Robert Gent grew up in Swansea and like every other Swansea youngster his one ambition was to play for Wales. And that became a healthy prospect when as a nineteen-year old student at Cheltenham College in 1904, he was invited to play for the Probables in the final Welsh trial. But the best he could manage was reserve to Dicky Owen and he travelled with the Welsh side for all three internationals that season against Ireland, England and Scotland. The following season he played in a Welsh trial in October and then became a little confused when out of the blue, he got an invitation to play in an English trial. He was now playing with the Gloucester club and was thus qualified. After some long thought, he decided to throw in his lot with the English. And, of course, he went on to become one of the most gifted English scrum-halves in the history of the game. At 5′ 2½″ and 9st 13lbs, he was also one of the smallest. He went on to win five English caps in all and played in England's first international against New

Zealand. When he retired from rugby in 1910 "Dai" Gent became rugby correspondent of the *Sunday Times* and up to his death in 1964 was one of the game's most gifted writers.

IN TWO CAMPS

G. A. Vickery, from the Aberavon Club, won his first and only cap for England against Ireland at Cork Park in 1905 and, according to the newspaper accounts of the time, had a "useful drive" in an English pack that was badly beaten by the Irish forwards. Ireland won the game by a goal and four tries (17) to a try (3). Vickery disappeared from the international scene after his debut in Cork but the Vickery name came back into the international scene in 1938 when his son, W. Vickery, also with the Aberavon Club, won four caps. This, however, was not just another instance of a father and a son playing international rugby. His son, in fact, was capped for Wales and they are the only father and son in rugby history to play for different countries.

A HAPPY MISTAKE

Arnold Alcock, then a twenty-four-year old doctor at Guy's Hospital, was more than mildly surprised when he received a letter from the Rugby Union towards the end of November, 1960. He was, in fact, quite astonished and, indeed, so too were all his friends and team-mates at Blackheath. While he was a sound and reliable forward, no one, and that included himself, believed that he was anywhere near international class. But the letter said plainly and clearly that he had been invited to play for England against the South African international touring side at Crystal Palace on 8th December, 1906. However, duly armed with his football gear, Dr Alcock reported to Crystal Palace for the game and at the first opportunity introduced himself to the Union secretary, Percy Coles, whose reaction, to say the least of it, was one of blank astonishment. He had no idea that Dr Alcock was due to play for England. In time, it was all sorted out. Due to a clerical error, the invitation to play for England had been sent to Arnold Alcock instead of the great Liverpool forward Andrew Slocock for whom it had been intended. At that stage there was no possibility of rectifying the error and so Dr Arnold Alcock went out to play international rugby for

England against South Africa. It was, however, his first and last cap. The next time no clerical errors were made. Slocock was brought on to the side for the next international game and subsequently went on to win eight caps for England.

JUST THIS ONCE

Freddie Brooks, a native of Rhodesia, who had been educated at Bedford Grammar School, came back to England in 1906 for a long holiday, most of which was spent in Bedford. Being a keen rugby man and anxious to keep himself fit he decided to have a few outings in club football with the local club. Much to his surprise he was invited to play for the South against the North in the annual trial games of that time. And he put on quite a performance in the South's 33-3 win at Blackheath by scoring three good tries. On the strength of that, he was invited to play for England in the international game against the touring South Africans at Crystal Palace, London on Saturday, 8th December, 1906. The Springboks scored in the first half with a try from W. A. Millar but England struck back in the second half to draw the game with a fine try from one Freddie Brooks. Having achieved that Brooks disappeared back to Rhodesia and that was the end of his brief but spectacular international rugby career.

MOVING AROUND

Edward Hackett, who won 13 caps for England between 1906 and 1909, joined the exclusive company of the few who have played for a Lions touring side and against a Lions touring side. Having won an Olympic silver medal with the United Kingdom in the 1908 Games in London, he toured in Australia and New Zealand with A. F. Harding's Lions and subsequently having settled down in South Africa, where he was in the Transvaal team, he played against Dr Tom Smyth's Lions in South Africa in 1910.

ONCE ONLY

Henry Vassall was just nineteen when he made his first appearance in the Oxford team which beat Cambridge by 12-8 in the Inter-varsity match of 1906 at the Queen's Club. Subsequently he played in the

Inter-Varsity matches of 1907 and 1908 and was capped as a centre for England in 1908 in their 13-3 win over Ireland at Richmond. Vassall was one of the tremendous successes of A. H. Harding's Lions side which toured in Australia and New Zealand in 1908 and as he was then only twenty-one, there appeared to be a glowing future ahead for him with England. But on his return from down under, Vassall decided enough was enough. He retired from rugby and that was that. That cap against Ireland in 1908 was the only international cap he won for his country.

THE SCOURGE OF THE FRENCH

In the light of what he did to them in their first uneasy years of international rugby, Douglas Lambert of Harlequins, known to all and sundry as "Daniel" became a second Scarlet Pimpernel to the French. He made his debut against them at Richmond on Saturday, 5th January, 1907 and as England hammered them into a 41-13 defeat, the well-built Lambert, who was to be killed in the First World War raced in for five tries, which is still a record for an English international. But there was even worse to come. Lambert, who was to finish his career with seven England caps, played his final international against France on Saturday, 28th January, 1911 and this time, did even better. In England's 37-0 win, by five goals, two penalty goals and two tries, the twenty-eight-year old Lambert scored the two tries, kicked the five conversions and kicked the two penalty goals for a total of 22 points, which, of course, is still the greatest individual performance by an English player in an international game and the highest total of points ever amassed in an international game by a player from any of the five countries in the International Championship in this century. In the only other international he played against France in 1908, Lambert converted two tries for a total of 41 points in his three appearances against the French. His only other score in his international career was a conversion against Wales at St. Helen's, Swansea on Saturday, 21st January, 1911.

THE CABBAGE PATCH

A certain gentleman, by name William Williams, with an amazing foresight and a sound head for business took it upon himself to purchase 10 and a quarter acres of ground for the sum of £5,572.12.6

and this fine area of ground near London, to be known for quite some time as "Billy Williams's Cabbage Patch" was eventually to become . . . . Twickenham. Williams was the man who discovered the ground and then urged the English Rugby Football Union to buy the market garden site which today has become the most famous international rugby ground in the world. The first match was played there on Saturday, 2nd October, 1909 between Harlequins and Richmond and the first kick-off was made by Gordon Carey, who incidentally was again to make the kick-off when Harlequins opened the Adrian Stoop Memorial ground in 1959! The first try on the new ground was scored by the English international J. G. G. Birkett. The first international match to be played there was between England and Wales on Saturday, 15th January, 1910. Wales were beaten by 6-11, and the first try scored on the ground was by Frederick Ernest Chapman of Hartlepool Rovers. Ireland played at Twickenham for the first time in 1910, and Scotland and France made their debut there in 1911. England's first defeat on the ground was on 4th January, 1913 when the touring South Africans won by 9-3.

A FIRST AT TWICKENHAM

With five successive victories behind them against England from 1905, Wales went to London in January, 1910 with high hopes of beating England in the first international game ever played at Twickenham. They were firm favourites to do so, but England struck first with a try from Fred Chapman and that was the stepping stone to an unexpected English win by 11-6. This particular try had a special significance for John Guy Birkett who shared in this historic first international fixture at Twickenham. Thirty nine years earlier in England's first international fixture with Scotland at Raeburn Place, Edinburgh on 26th, January 1871, his father Reginald Halsey Birkett had scored England's very first try in international rugby.

AND THAT WAS THAT

Bert Solomon from Redruth, made the debut that every wing-three-quarter dreams about at Twickenham on Saturday, 15th January, 1910. It was the opening day of Twickenham for international rugby and

Wales had the honour of facing England. Within two minutes Solomon was in action and with a delightful pass he sent Fred Chapman streaking over for a try. And he added one himself as England went on to win by 11-6. The English selectors were delighted with Solomon's performance and promptly invited him to play against Ireland but he declined. Then they invited him to play against France and again he declined and when they finally invited him to play against Scotland he declined again. For reasons best known to himself, Bert Solomon, a winner of an Olympic silver medal with the United Kingdom in 1908 in London, was satisfied with just that one cap for his country. Always a great club man with Redruth and recalled as one of the greatest "dummy" sellers of his time, he was involved in a well-remembered incident at a club game in Redruth in 1907. He took a pass, made ground and then feinted superbly with a "dummy" pass to his wing-threequarter and ran on to score a try. The referee was so baffled with what had happened that he blew his whistle and penalised Solomon for a forward pass!

THAT IRISH FULL-BACK

Until Bob Hiller turned out for England against the President's XV in England's Centenary game in 1971, England's most capped full-back was . . . an Irishman. When Hiller won his 17th cap that afternoon in 1971—he was to add two more to the record before he retired—the English record for a full-back stood to William R. Johnston from Bristol, who was Irish-born. Johnston was an automatic selection for England between 1910 and 1914 and won 16 caps at full-back.

A DOUBLE INTERNATIONAL

His father had worn the All-Blacks jersey on one occasion and when young James Watson arrived at Edinburgh University to study, he went straight out to try for his place on the rugby side. He made it, of course and in 1912 gained a fame in another sport by representing Scotland in international athletics. At the time he was regarded as one of the top sprinters in Scotland, capable of touching 10 seconds for the 100 yards. He eventually came to the eyes of the Scottish selectors who invited him to play in a series of trials but he just did not strike form and that was that. In 1913, having graduated from Edinburgh University he went to London and joined Blackheath and, having been given a trial by England he made his international debut for them against Wales at Twickenham on Saturday, 17th January, 1914. He missed the match against Ireland because of injury but returned to play against Scotland and France. It looked certain that he had a bright international future ahead of him but then came the war and he, sadly, was one of the England internationals to die.

THE THIRD TRIPLE CROWN

England's visit to Cardiff Arms Park to take on Wales on Saturday, 18th January, 1913, really set them up for the season. Vincent Coates started the ball rolling with a try which was converted by John Eric "Jenny" Greenwood. Then Charles "Cherry" Pillman scored another try and Coates finished it all off with a superb drop goal for a 12-0 victory. It was England's first victory at the famous Cardiff Arms Park. But there were even better things to come. They took off for Dublin and with Ronnie Poulton-Palmer showing the way with a splendid try, they raced away to a 15-4 win. So they took on Scotland at Twickenham and it was to be a bitterly fought battle all the way and at the final whistle there was just three points between them—a try scored for England by Vincent Coates. England took the Calcutta Cup . . . . and they became Triple Crown champions for the third time.

JUST THE ONCE

William John Abbott Davies, who answered to the name of "Dave" had quite a remarkable career in international rugby. Born in 1890, he learned the rudiments of the game at the Royal Navy Engineering College and having gained quite a reputation as a scrum-half with the Navy in inter-Services games, he was given a trial by the English selectors in 1912 and then made his international debut against Wales at Cardiff Arms Park on Saturday, 18th January, 1913 and early in the game put Vincent Coates over for the first English try at Cardiff Arms Park in 20 years. This was England's first win at Cardiff and from there on Davies was a regular on the side—and regarded as England's lucky mascot. Ten years later, almost to the day, Saturday, 20th January, 1923, he finally bowed out of international rugby and again it was against Wales at Cardiff Arms Park and again it was a victory for England. And Davies was certainly a lucky mascot. In his 22 appearances for England, he was on the losing side only once—and that was against the touring South Africans at Twickenham on 4th January, 1913. And he also captained England to victory on 11 occasions!

A SAD TOTAL

England, the Triple Crown champions of 1913, got a most unexpected fright when they took on Wales in their first championship match of the 1913-14 season at Twickenham on Saturday, 17th January, 1914. With less than five minutes left in the game Wales were ahead by 9-5 and defeat for England looked almost certain. But in one last fierce breakaway Charles "Cherry" Pillman launched himself over for a try and out-half Frank "Tim" Taylor, winning his one and only cap, kicked the easy conversion for a 10-9 win. Ireland, at Twickenham on 31st January, were a somewhat easier proposition. Under the shrewd prompting of W. J. A. Davies at out-half and a dazzling opening try by Ronnie Poulton-Palmer, England made sure of a Triple Crown decider with Scotland by winning 17-12. That decider turned out to be one of the most memorable games between the two countries at Murrayfield and was on a razor's edge right up to the final few moments when W. R. Johnston, the England full-back kicked the conversion of W. J. A. Davies's try for a 16-15 win. This gave England the Triple Crown for the second season in succession, a feat that had only been accomplished once previously by Wales in 1908 and 1909. But that game at Inverleith was to have the saddest of sequels. Of the 30 players who appeared in it, eleven were to die in the First World War.

THREE TWICE

Cyril Lowe, one of the few English internationals to span the First World War years—he established a record for the time by making 25 appearances on the wing for England between 1913 and 1924—had two unforgettable outings in 1914, which gave him another English record. Against Scotland at Inverleith on Saturday, 7th March, 1914, he scored three tries for England in their 16-15 win over Scotland—and he did it again by scoring another three against France in a 13-4 win in the last international game to be played at Twickenham before the outbreak of the First World War. His record of 25 caps on the wing stood as an English record until overtaken by Jeff Butterfield and then by Mickey Weston who holds the present record of 29 caps in the threequarter line.

A HAPPY PARTNERSHIP

Captain Cecil Kershaw of the Royal Navy came safely through the First World War and when he resumed playing rugby with the Navy, he had the good fortune to team up with "Dave" Davies, who had been an international before the war. Kershaw made a losing international debut for England against Wales on Saturday 17th January, 1920 but, unfortunately, did not have the injured Davies as his partner at half-back. However, they got together for the next game and in all they were to play together for England on 14 occasions—and not one of those games was lost. Significantly when Davies was unable to play against Wales in 1922, this was only the second time in his 16 appearances for his country that Kershaw had figured on a losing side. Kershaw was also one of the outstanding swordsmen of his time and fenced for Britain in the 1920 Olympics at Antwerp and also for Britain against America in 1921.

AN ALL-ROUND MAN

Stanley Harris, a native of South Africa, won just the two caps for England against Scotland and Ireland in 1920 but would probably have collected far more but for his extraordinary versatility in sport. He just did not have the time to cope with all the sports in which he was in international class. During 1924, he toured with Cove-Smith's Lions and had the unusual distinction of playing against his own countrymen. While he was there, Harris, who had previously won the South African light-heavyweight boxing championship was invited to box for his native country in the Olympic Games in Paris and that posed quite a problem for him. He had already been invited by Britain to compete for them in the same Olympic Games in the Modern Pentathlon. Later he turned to serious tennis and having played four times at Wimbledon he represented South Africa in the Davis Cup of 1931.

THE LAST MINUTE CHANGE

Saturday, 17th January, 1920 began as a memorable day in the life of the twenty year old wing-threequarter Wilfrid Lowry of Birkenhead Park. He had been selected for his first international game against Wales at St Helen's, Swansea, and he duly went to the dressing room, togged out and went to have his picture taken with the English team. A few moments later, however, when England ran out onto the muddy ground at St Helen's, Lowry was missing. In his place was H. L. V. Day of Leicester, who was also in the English party for the first time. Apparently the English selectors, having taken a look at the state of the ground, decided that the heavier Day would be a better proposition against the Welsh than the lightly-built Lowry. Not that in the end it made any difference. Day did manage to score a try on his debut but England were trounced by 19-5. There was, happily, to be consolation for the broken-hearted Lowry. At the end of the season he was given his one and only England cap against France.

THE LEGENDARY "WAKERS"

Born at Beckenham in Kent on 10th March, 1898 William Wavell Wakefield became one of the most versatile sportsmen of his time and one of the enduring giants of English rugby. A brilliant athlete at school over the 100, 220 and 440 yards and hurdles, he went on to become 440 yards champion of the R.A.F. and after a distinguished service in the First World War, he was capped for England against Wales at St Helen's, Swansea on 17th January, 1920 and over the next seven sesaons was to achieve a legendary place in the game. At the end of his international career, against Scotland and France in 1927, he had taken his total of caps to 31 which was to endure as a British record until it was overtaken by D. P. "Budge" Rogers in 1967. Later famous as a politician, he was also the 42nd President of the English Rugby Union and is now Lord Wakefield of Kendal.

A LITTLE LION CUB

Barry Cumberlege was just thirty when he won the first of his eight caps for England as a full-back in 1920 and his debut at Swansea on Saturday, 17th January, 1920 was not an auspicious one, although he did mark it with two points by converting England's only try in their defeat by Wales. The sad feature, however, about Cumberlege, who was to become one of the game's outstanding referees, was that but for the war he might have won a record number of caps for England. As far back as 1909, he had been invited to tour South Africa with Dr Tom Smyth's Lions but as he was still at school, neither his parents nor his headmaster were overly interested, so he had to decline.

CHAMPIONS AGAIN

England, with wins over Wales by 18-3, over Ireland by 15-0 and over Scotland by 18-0, took the Triple Crown for the fifth time in 1921 and then with a 10-6 win over France at Colombes Stadium, Paris, also collected the Grand Slam of the championship also for the fifth time. But a shattering defeat by 6-28 ruled out any hope of the Triple Crown in 1922. England, however, came back in 1923 with one of their greatest Triple Crown years. Scoring directly from the kick-off at Twickenham with a try from Bert Price, followed by a sensational drop goal from Alistair Smallwood, they survived an epic fight back by Wales to win by 7-3. Ireland, at Leicester on Saturday, 10th February, 1923, were never a problem. England, with a drop goal from Davies, a try from Smallwood, a try from Corbett and a try from Price which Conway converted, raced into a 15-0 lead after 35 minutes and then in the second half after McClelland had scored a try for Ireland which Crawford converted, Lowe with a try and Conway with a conversion and a penalty goal, left England in front by 23-5 at the finish. So the Triple Crown decider was at Inverleith, Edinburgh on Saturday, 17th March, 1923. Scotland had already beaten Wales and Ireland, and indeed had also beaten France, so that the Grand Slam was also involved. This, by the accounts of the time was a tremendous battle and in the end it was decided by just one kick. England took the lead after 23 minutes with a try from Small-wood but McLaren brought the scores level before half-time with a try. Gracie with a try put Scotland ahead early in the second half and they held their 6-3 superiority until eight minutes from time. Then Voyce got England's second try and now it all came down to the attempt at conversion. Ernie Gardner held the ball and Bill Luddington, England's prop forward took the kick—and although it was quite close to the sideline, it went dead centre between the posts. This 8-6 victory which gave England their sixth Triple Crown, was also their sixth in succession over Scotland. From Inverleith, England headed to Colombes Stadium on Monday, 2nd April, 1923 and duly collected the Grand Slam with a 12-3 win.

A FAST BIT OF WORK

The twenty-three-year old Bert Price of Leicester, a powerfully built forward, found himself in quite a predicament in 1922. Into his post box one morning came two letters, one an invitation to play rugby for England against Scotland and the other an invitation to play hockey for Scotland. He would have been delighted to accept both but for one small thing—the two matches were on the same Saturday afternoon. Price chose to play rugby and so he won his first English cap against Scotland on Saturday 23rd March, 1922 at Twickenham. He was, of course, to go on to share in England's Triple Crown victory of 1923 when he won the last of his four caps. He did, however, later in the 1923 season manage to play against Ireland at rugby and at hockey on successive Saturdays.

THE OLDEST CROWN WINNER

With the retirement of Bill Johnston just before the outbreak of the First World War, England found themselves in a predicament about a full-back when international rugby came back after the cessation of hostilities. Several were tried but none more unusual than F. G. Gilbert of Devenport Services at the start of the 1922-1923 season. Gilbert had been around quite a time in rugby at that stage and his selection after the final trial in which he had played on the Possibles was a shock to most people. Gilbert made his debut against Wales at Twickenham on Saturday, 20th January, 1923 and with an English win by 7-3 he was retained for the next game against Ireland which was won by 23-5 at Leicester where he had the distinction of kicking two conversions. Unfortunately, before the game against Scotland, he was injured in an inter-services game between the Army and the Navy and had to be replaced by T. E. Holliday for the trip to Murray-field. But at least Gilbert shared in England's Triple Crown win of that season and is certainly the oldest man in the history of rugby to play in a Triple Crown year. According to the newspaper accounts of the time he was just a month short of his fortieth birthday when he played against Ireland and indeed one newspaper was unkind enough to remark that he was of "an extraordinary age". He is, without any question, the oldest full-back to play in international rugby.

THE FASTEST

There can hardly have been a more sensational start to a rugby international than the score that put England into the lead against Wales at Twickenham on Saturday, 20th January, 1923. Wavell Wakefield kicked off for England and Bert Price, the England wing-forward, tore forward to gather the ball. For reasons best known to himself, Price tried for a snap drop at goal but the ball swung wide of the posts and while the Welsh backs stood around to watch the ball go over, Price raced forward at a tremendous pace and dropped on the ball before it reached the dead-ball line for a try. Accounts of the game vary in the time it took for England to score with a minimum of 10 seconds and a maximum of 14. It remains as the fastest score ever achieved in international rugby football. And there was to be quite another shock for Wales that afternoon. Len Corbett on the wing found himself completely closed in by Welsh forwards and in a moment of inspiration passed the ball back between his legs to his other wing-threequarter Alistair Smallwood, who promptly proceeded to drop a goal from almost 50 yards out. Those two extraordinary scores were enough to beat Wales by 7-3.

THE CENTENARIES

To celebrate the historic run of Master Webb Ellis in 1823, the English Rugby Union arranged a Centenary match at Rugby School in 1923 and the game was played between England-Wales v Ireland-Scotland. The teams consisted of seven Englishmen, eight Welshmen, eight Scots and seven Irishmen and the two captains were England's international W. J. A. Davies and Scotland's W. E. Bryce. The two teams represented 30 of the finest international players of the time and they put on a delightful exhibition which in the end was won by

England-Wales, 21-16. On Saturday, 3rd October, 1970 the Centenary game of the English Rugby Union was played at Twickenham between England-Wales v Ireland-Scotland and the teams comprised eight English, seven Welsh, eight Irish and seven Scots—all internationals. The game ended in a 14-14 draw.

SIXTY NINE POINTS

The story of England's Triple Crown and Grand Slam wins in 1924 is simply told by the matter of scoring. They totted up 69 points in four games and conceded 17, of which nine were scored by Wales. England began with a 17-9 win over Wales at St Helen's, Swansea, on Saturday, 19th January, 1924, followed this with a 14-3 win over Ireland at Ravenhill, Belfast and walloped Scotland by 19-0 at Twickenham before winding up their season with a 19-7 win over France. With this season, England equalled Wales's record of seven Triple Crown wins, became the first and still the only country to take the Crown twice in successive years—they had done it earlier in 1913 and 1914—and also became the only country to do the Grand Slam twice in successive years.

REJECTED

Although he had been born in India, Stanley Ulick Considine had all the qualifications he needed to play for Ireland. His father was Irish and most of his relations lived in Ireland. And he told the Irish selectors in 1920 that he would be happy to travel from Bath if they would consider him for an Irish trial. The selectors were happy to do so and they gave him not just one, but two trials. And they decided he just was not good enough to displace men like Denis Cussen, George Stephenson, Harry Stephenson or A. R. Foster in Ireland's threequarter line. So Mr Considine went back to Bath and continued to play club rugby. Out of the blue in 1924 came an invitation to play in the English trials and it is now on record that the man rejected by the Irish selectors was selected by England to play against France in 1925.

AGAINST IRELAND

Harold Periton (Waterloo), known to everyone in rugby as "Joe", won 21 caps for England against Scotland, Wales, France, Ireland and New South Wales between 1925 and 1930. Perhaps the most significant one he collected was at Lansdowne Road, Dublin in 1930 when Ireland met England. This was a win for Ireland but only just. They won by a drop goal to a try. For Periton, however, it was a special afternoon. He led the English side and that appearance at Lansdowne Road marked the only time that an Irishman has ever captained England.

ENGLAND'S YOUNGEST

When he took his place at out-half on the English side which met Ireland at Twickenham in January, 1927, Henri Colin Laird became the youngest Englishman to be capped in international rugby. He was then 18 years and four months. Subsequently he went on to win 10 caps for England but his international career ended after the game against France on 1st April, 1929. At that time he was twenty years and six months.

ENGLAND MOVE AHEAD

England took over the lead in the Triple Crown race in the 1927-1928 season with a record eighth win. And in addition to taking the Crown, they also carried off the Grand Slam and created a record which they have never since been able to equal of winning all their five international matches that season. They began with an 18-11 win over the "Waratahs" at Twickenham but after that their path to both the Triple Crown and the Grand Slam was laborious. They were fortunate to beat Wales by 10-8 at Swansea on 21st January, 1928, were even luckier to scrape through by 7-6 against Ireland at Dublin, then beat Scotland by 6-0 at Twickenham and came with a late rush to defeat France by 18-8 in London.

A LATE CALL-UP

In the matter of age, the Gloucester foreward L. E. Saxby remains as one of the great mysteries of international rugby. He had been in club rugby for well over 20 years when he was invited to play for England against the South African touring side of 1931-1932 at Twickenham. Although all efforts to trace his birthday have failed, it was known at the time that he was well over forty. It is now generally accepted that Saxby, who won a second cap against Wales in 1932, is the oldest player to be capped in English or international rugby.

GADNEY'S WIN

Under the captaincy of Bernard Gadney, who was to win 14 caps for his country, England swept to yet another Triple Crown victory in 1933-1934. They began convincingly with a 9-0 win over Wales at Cardiff Arms Park on Saturday, 20th January, 1934, and a fortnight later, were never seriously troubled by Ireland in a 13-3 win at Lansdowne Road. They held out for a 6-3 win over Scotland at Twickenham to take the Triple Crown for the ninth time.

THE LONG SERVICE MAN

Jack Heaton of Waterloo won only nine caps for England and it took him quite a long time to achieve that meagre total. Capped for the first time in 1934-1935, he won three caps that season against Scotland, Ireland and Wales and then disappeared from the international scene. Four years later, he was recalled to the English side and collected his second group of three caps, against Scotland, Ireland and Wales. International rugby disappeared with the war years but eight seasons later, in the 1946-1947 season he popped up again on the England side and this time he got his third group of three caps by playing against Scotland, Ireland and France. No one in English rugby has had a longer span between his first and last international cap.

NO ENTRANCE

Cyril Gadney, who was to become the 55th President of the English Rugby Football Union in 1962-1963, was one of the most talented international referees of his time and between 1936 and 1948 handled 13 major games. There was, however, one that he almost missed. He was named to referee the Wales v Ireland game at Cardiff Arms Park on Saturday, 14th March, 1936, which, as it happened, was one of the most extraordinary fixtures ever played in Wales. This was an afternoon when Ireland were going for the Triple Crown and Wales were hoping for the international championship and thousands turned up to see the battle. Unfortunately that battle began in the streets outside Cardiff Arms Park when over 75,000 people tried to get in to watch Wales take on Ireland. The police were unable to cope with the crowds, the fire brigades were called out to drench the crowd with water in a bid to avert a disaster. But it was all to no avail. Far too many people fought their way into Cardiff Arms Park and by kick-off time the crowds had spilled out on to the sidelines. In the middle of all this chaos and confusion, Mr Gadney duly arrived at the ground and presented himself at the entrance, only to be told, in no complimentary terms, to take himself off. He patiently explained that he was the referee. But that did not do any good either. He was told, "Think of a better one than that. We have six referees already". Eventually, with the help of Welsh officials he was able to get in. All in all it was not the happiest of days for him. He brought down the wrath of both the Irish players and Irish spectators by awarding a penalty against Mike Sayers and Vivian Jenkins duly kicked the goal that took the Triple Crown from Ireland.

A VITAL DROP GOAL

A South African led England to their 10th Triple Crown Championship in 1937. Harold Geoffrey Owen-Smith, known to all and sundry as "Tuppy", won 10 caps for England but that 1937 year was to be his greatest. He had already played on the English Triple Crown team of 1934 but was elevated to captain for the 1936-1937 season and that set the seal on a remarkable career. He had already played cricket for South Africa in 1929 and had also won the British inter-Varsities welterweight boxing title in 1931. All of England's victories in this

10th Triple Crown win were tight. And they owed most of their success to the English wing-threequarter Hal Sever. Presented with a gift chance against Wales with a chance to run either for a certain try or attempt a drop at goal, he elected to try for the goal and he got it. It was the first time in his career that he had ever dropped a goal in any sort of a game. It was to be the vital score in that international and enabled England to hold out for a 4-3 win. Sever was again in the news with a sensational try against Ireland in London which brought a 9-8 victory, although to this day the Irish swear that a try by Freddie Moran which looked perfectly legitimate should never have been disallowed. The English clinched the title at Murrayfield and again it was touch-and-go all the way in a 6-3 result.

THE MYSTERIOUS MR COOK

Beyond the brief note in the England v Scotland programme for their meeting at Twickenham in 1938, to say that this was his first cap, very little is known of J. G. Cook, who played for England on that particular day, Saturday, 17th March, 1938. He was a member of the Bedford club and quite obviously was made to shoulder a little of the blame for England's 16-21 defeat that day. He never again played for England; yet he deserves a little place to himself in sports history. He was a double international . . . he also played cricket for Ireland!

A LATECOMER

Cyril Holmes was a latecomer to international rugby and was, in fact, thirty-two when he made his first appearance on the wing for England against Scotland in 1947. He was to make two further appearances the following year against Ireland and France and at thirty-three was one of the oldest wing-threequarters to play in international rugby. There was, however a good reason for his late adventure into international rugby. He had been extremely busy in another field. He had represented Britain in the 100 metres at the Berlin Olympic Games in 1936 and two years later had won both the 100 and 220 yards in the British Empire Games at Sydney, Australia. He had also represented England internationally in athletics and before the outbreak of the war had won three British A.A.A. titles in the 100 and 220 yards.

THE LAST FOUR POINTS

The late N. M. "Nim" Hall, who won 17 international caps for England between 1947 and 1955, finished his rugby career with one unusual record in his possession. He dropped the last two four-points goals in international rugby. He got the first of the two against Wales at Cardiff Arms Park on 18th January, 1947 and the second against Scotland on Saturday, 15th March, at Twickenham.

A VETERAN CAPTAIN

The thirty-six-year old Eric Evans from Sale, who was to win 30 caps for England and to become the first English international to appear against successive touring sides from overseas—the Australians of 1947-48 and the Australians of 1957-58—led England to their 12th Triple Crown victory and to their seventh Grand Slam win in 1957-1958. Evans, all of whose caps were won in the front row, took his men to a fortunate 3-0 win over Wales with a penalty goal from Fenwick Allison of Coventry and then to a 6-0 win over Ireland at Lansdowne Road, to a 16-3 win over Scotland at Twickenham and to a 9-5 win over the French also at Twickenham.

AN OLYMPIC GOLD—ALMOST

For 24 glorious hours at London in 1948, two rugby internationals, Jack Gregory (England) and Ken Jones (Wales) were the holders of Olympic gold medals—and then they had to give them back and have them exchanged for silver ones. Representing Britain in the 4 x 100 metres relay they had finished second but the Americans who had won the race were disqualified. Later, however, a film showed that the U.S.A. team should never have been disqualified and Britain were ordered to return their Olympic gold medals. However, both Gregory and Jones were to get Olympic silver medals.

FOR ENGLAND AND IRELAND

Jack Gregory, who had served in the British Army from 1941 to 1947 kept himself fit by playing a little Rugby League in the immediate post-war years—but purely as an amateur. He duly applied for reinstatement to the rugby union game but this was turned down. However he applied again and the final decision was that he should stand suspended until April, 1948. Gregory immediately returned to rugby with the Wanderers Club in Dublin and during his time in Ireland, he won six Irish national championships over 100 yards and 220 yards and represented Ireland in international athletics on two occasions. He was eventually capped by England for the games against Wales at Cardiff Arms Park on 15th January, 1949 but failed to score from the wing threequarter position in England's 3-9 defeat. Although he continued to play rugby for another six years, this was to be his one and only cap for England. Gregory also represented Britain in the Olympic Games of 1948 at London and of 1952 at Helsinki and won a silver medal in the sprint relay at London in 1948. His final honours at rugby were to play for Western Counties against the Springboks of 1951-1952 and for Gloucester and Somerset against the All-Blacks of 1953-1954.

A DUBIOUS HONOUR

John Kendall-Carpenter of Oxford University was one of England's greatest forwards in the immediate post Second World War era and by the time he ended his international career in 1954 he had collected 23 caps. One of his dubious honours, the one he does not like to remember was that he captained the first England side to lose at Twickenham to France in 1951. France won that afternoon, Saturday, 23rd February, by 11-3.

THE 11TH TRIPLE CROWN

England had been without a win over Wales since 1939 when the two teams ran out at Twickenham on Saturday, 16th January, 1954 and for 79 minutes it looked ominous that the pattern would continue. The score was then 6-6 with Ted Woodward having scored two tries for England and all of Wales's points coming from Gwyn Rowlands with a try and a penalty goal. Then with barely seconds to go, Chris Wynn, the Rosslyn Park winger, finished off a threequarter movement with a last-gasp try in the corner. And that was to be a very vital score that season for England. It really won them their 11th Triple Crown.

After that narrow shave, they beat Ireland easily by 14-3 at Twickenham and went off to Edinburgh to score a 13-3 win over Scotland. France, however, stepped in to deny England the Grand Slam by winning 11-3 at Colombes Stadium, Paris.

A LION FIRST

Although he had not been capped for England Dickie Jeeps was selected for the Lions tour of South Africa in 1955 and was, in fact, the only non-international in the party. For all that he played his first international game for the tourists against South Africa in the first international match of the tour and he held his place for the four internationals which ended all square 2-2 with the Springboks. Jeeps could hardly fail to be recognised by the England selectors after that and he was given his first international cap the following season against Wales but, somewhat surprisingly, was dropped for the next game. A year later, he returned to help England to the Triple Crown and Grand Slam for the first time in 29 years. He made a second Lions tour to Australia and New Zealand in 1959 and a record third tour with the Lions to South Africa in 1962. In all, in addition to his 24 caps for England, he made 13 international appearances for the Lions which, at the end of the 1973-1974 season was still a record for an England player and, at the time, equalled only by Ireland's Willie John McBride and Syd Millar.

THE THIRTEENTH

A new star came brilliantly into the English rugby sky in 1959-1960 when the twenty-one year-old Richard Sharp was brought into the international side to substitute for the injured Beverley Risman in the opening game of the season against Wales at Twickenham on 16th January, 1960. His was a sensational debut and his glorious display sent England into a 14-0 lead at half-time and a 14-6 win at full-time. Sharp retained his place in the side to meet Ireland who went down by 5-8 and he put on another scintillating performance as England romped home against Scotland by 21-12 at Murrayfield. This was England's 13th and up to the end of the 1973-1974 season, their last Triple Crown win. France, however, ruined their hopes of the Grand Slam with a

3-3 draw at Colombes Stadium. Sharp's subsequent career was to be marred by a succession of injuries, including a quite serious one against Northern Transvaal in his Lions tour of South Africa in 1962 and he never really recaptured his glorious form of the 1959-1960 season. Having won 13 caps between 1960 and 1963, he made his final appearance for England against the Australian tourists of 1967-1968.

WESTON'S RECORD

Mickey Weston of Richmond and Durham City made his international debut for England against Wales on Saturday, 16th January, 1960 and it was a happy afternoon for him. He put on quite an impressive performance as England scored 14 points in the first half at Twickenham and eventually went on to win by 14-6. Over the next eight years Weston was to become one of the best-known names in English rugby and went on two Lions tours, to South Africa in 1962 and New Zealand and Australia in 1966, during which he won four international caps for the tourists against the Springboks and two against the Wallabies. His career finally came to an end in 1968 with two very vital caps for England against France and Scotland. One brought him level with Jeff Butterfield as England's most capped back in international rugby and the other brought him the record all on his own which he still holds. His total number of caps was 29.

THE FIRST DOWN UNDER

England made their first tour of Australia and New Zealand in 1963 and, in all, played six games, won one and lost five and scored 54 points while conceding 91. The touring side was captained by Mickey Weston and of the six games, three were international fixtures with two against New Zealand and the final game against Australi.a During the tour which lasted 17 days, England opened up with a 14-9 win over Wellington but went down in their second game by 9-4 and then it was into Eden Park, Auckland, on Saturday, 23rd May, 1963 for the opening international against the All-Blacks. And, unfortunately, it was never a game that was in any doubt. In front of 50,000 spectators England flattered to deceive in the first half when Roger Hosen, their full-back kicked them into a 6-0 lead at half-time with two penalty goals. Don Clarke reduced the leeway with a penalty goal in the second half but England tore back into the lead with a try from their wing-threequarter John Ranson to lead by 11-3. But that was the end of it for the tourists. Don Clarke joined in on a threequarter movement and scored a great try which he then converted. Ralph Caulton added another try which Clarke again converted and just a few minutes later the same two collected another five points. Clarke duly ended the proceedings by dropping a goal from 50 yards out and the final score was 21-13 for the All-Blacks. Their 10 points margin was their greatest over England since the first meeting of the two countries in 1905 at Crystal Palace, London when New Zealand won by 15-0.

A DRUBBING

Three days after their defeat by New Zealand, England took a severe drubbing from Hawkes Bay and were fortunate to get away with a 3-20 defeat. All-Black Ian MacRae ran in three tries, Kel Tremain had another, all four were converted, and after that Hawkes Bay eased up. With this display England dropped even lower in the betting for their second meeting with New Zealand at Lancaster Park on Saturday, 1st June, 1963. Yet they came up with quite a startling performance and in the end, it was left to Don Clarke to rescue the All-Blacks with one of his massive kicks. D. W. McKay gave the All-Blacks the lead with a try but England's full back Roger Hosen struck back with a fine penalty goal before Pat Walsh went in for the try that left New Zealand in a 6-3 lead at the break. Entirely against the run of play England came level early in the second half and centre M. S. Phillips, with a glorious run to the corner flag was the man who brought the vital try. The scores stayed level and with time running out, England looked set to survive for a draw. Then came disaster and once again Don Clarke, the scourge of so many international sides against the All-Blacks, had the final say. From a bad kick ahead by England he marked the ball 10 yards inside his own half. His brother Ian Clarke lay down to hold the ball for him and then the England forwards charged too soon. The referee waved them back, Clarke was now allowed to place the ball and from almost 60 yards out he kicked the goal that won the day. It was New Zealand's fifth win over England in their six meetings since 1905. One of the other interesting features of this game was England's decision to play F. D. Sykes on the wing. He had won his first two caps for England against France and Scotland in 1955, had to wait until 1963 for his third cap against Scotland and in this, his fourth international appearance for his country, he was over thirty-five years old. He was the oldest man ever to play for England in their threequarter line and it is now generally accepted that he is also the oldest international back in the history of rugby.

TO AUSTRALIA

With four losses and one win to their credit, the 1963 England tourists crossed over to Australia for just the one game—a full international against the Wallabies at the Syndey Sportsground. From a weather point of view it turned out to be an appalling afternoon. Torrential rain swept Sydney on the day of the game and at kick-off time, with only 7,864 spectators there to see an England team in Australia for the first time, the Sydney Sportsground was almost covered with water. Nothing could have suited the Australians more and within 30 minutes they went tearing into a lead of 18-0 with four tries from Peter Jones, Keith Walsham, Gred Davis and Ted Heinrich and full-back Peter Ryan convered three of them. England, however, put on a brave showing in the second half and, with tries from Phillips, Clarke and Godwin, managed to leave the final score at 18-9. This win was Australia's first against a major country in Australia for 29 years and their captain that afternoon was John Thornett, who had been first capped for Australia in 1955 and whose international career was not to end until 1967.

IT'S BEEN A LONG, LONG TIME

Saturday, 16th January, 1965 was wet and cold and stormy at Cardiff Arms Park but there was warmth from the Welsh crowd for one English player as he ran out on to the pitch. It had been a long, long time since they had seen him before and they gave him a special welcome. For Johnny Williams was back at scrum-half for England that afternoon and it had been exactly 10 years since he had made his only other appearance against Wales. It would have been a nice send off to the thirty-three-year old Williams's international career that day had

England won. But he was in against the wily Clive Rowlands and with the Welsh scrum-half dictating the game Wales went on to win by 14-3. So ended the remarkable career of Johnny Williams who over 11 seasons had won just nine caps for England. First capped in 1954 against France, he played in all four championship games in 1955 and then went to South Africa with Robin Thompson's Lions. He won a further three caps in 1956 against Scotland, Ireland and France . . . and that was the end. Then came the era of Dickie Jeeps for England and Johnny Williams disappeared from the international scene. Then came that day in 1965—and nine years after his eighth appearance for England came his ninth cap and the second against Wales. That nine year gap is still one of rugby's most extraordinary records.

HILLER AND FRIENDS

England's full-back Bob Hiller represented his country on 19 occasions and had the satisfaction and distinction of scoring in all 19! Hiller made his debut for England against Wales on 20th January, 1968 at Twickenham and celebrated the occasion with a penalty goal and a conversion. Between then and his final cap for England against Ireland in 1972, he eventually reached a total of 138 points, made up of three tries, 12 conversions, 33 penalty goals and two drop goals. Perhaps his greatest feat was in 1971. Dropped for the game against Wales, he was brought back for the fixtures with Ireland, France and Scotland and scored 49 of the 55 points England obtained in these three games. Of these 49 points, 32 were consecutive. Hiller, who toured with the 1968 Lions, was top scorer in South Africa with 104 points from two tries, 19 conversions, 18 penalty goals and two drop goals. On his second tour with the Lions in 1971, he was second top scorer in New Zealand with 102 points from 24 conversions, 14 penalty goals and two dropped goals.

GOSFORTH DISASTER

During their tour in Britain in 1970, the touring Fijians took on the Barbarians at Gosforth Park, Newcastle and the Barbarians selectors gave them the respect they deserved by fielding a side of 14 current internationals—with only Derek Quinnell, later to become a Lion in the New Zealand tour of 1971, as the odd man out. The world of rugby was astonished by the result. After 3-3 at half-time the uninhibited Fijians ran riot in a glorious second half and sparked off by scrum-half Isimeli Batibasaga, who converted four tries and scored one himself, they eventually won by four goals and three tries to two tries and a penalty goal . . . 29-9. It was the Fijians' finest hour in Britain.

FOUR IN A ROW

For the first time in their international history, England lost all four games to Ireland, Scotland, Wales and France in the 1971-1972 season —and the worst day of all for them was at Colombes Stadium on Saturday, 26th, February 1972 when they took on the French. Prior to that afternoon, England's greatest defeat by a French side had been 13-35 two seasons earlier but this time the French were to improve on that performance by just a point. Things looked bright for the English early on and they were still there with a chance up to 10 minutes after half-time. Then the French opened up with a vintage display of the champagne rugby they can turn on so often. They ran England into the ground and the keeper of the scoreboard had a busy afternoon. In the end when he had totted up all the scores, France, with two tries from Bernard Duprat, one each from Pierre Biemouret, Jean Silliers, Jean Paul Lux and Walter Spanghero and five conversions and a penalty goal from Pierre Villepreux had 35 points on the board and England with a try from Mike Beese and two penalty goals and a conversion from Alan Old had 12. It was England's worst defeat by France since the two countries had met for the first time at Parc des Princes in 1906, a day on which, incidentally, England had scored 35 points to France's eight.

A GREAT DAY FOR ENGLAND

England had their worst season in the history of the International Championship in 1971-1972 when for the first time they lost all four games in the Championship and their dismal performances promised little success in the summer of 1972 when they flew out to South Africa for a seven-match tour, including a full international against the Springboks at Ellis Park, Johannesburg. But, somewhere along the line, England found a new strength and courage and the tour turned out to be a remarkable success. They wound up by winning six of their seven games, they drew the other and finished with 166 points while conceding 58. Their top points scorer was Sam Doble with 47 points from seven conversions, 10 penalty goals and a drop goal and their top try scorer was A. A. Richards with four. Their greatest margin of victory was the 60-21 beating of Griqualand West and their only draw was 13-13 with Northern Transvaal.

A FINE START

Under the captaincy of hooker John Pullin, England opened their 1972 tour of South Africa with a decisive win over Natal at Durban on 17th May. Natal were outclassed in every phase of play and a stream of scores, two tries by Peter Knight, another from Fran Cotton and two conversions and a penalty goal from Sam Doble sent England to a comfortable 19-0 victory. Three days later, however, they came up against Western Province at Capetown and they just barely got through against one of South Africa's best sides. With two penalty goals from Ian McCallum, the Springbok full-back, Western Province led 6-3, England having had a penalty goal, led until well into the second half. Then Peter Knight with a swift kick ahead, went streaking through the Western Province backs and won the race to touch down for a try. Doble kicked the conversion for a 9-6 win. After that the England side stayed on in Cape Town to play a South African Rugby Federation XV at the Athlone Stadium and this, of course, marked an historic milestone in South African rugby history. It was the first meeting between an all-White international touring side and a non-White South African side.

STILL UNBEATEN

The England side duly beat the Coloured XV at Athlone Stadium, Capetown on 22nd May but it was not the gentle training outing that everyone had expected. In the end the tourists won by 11-6 with tries from Palmer and Watkins and a penalty goal by Whibley to two penalty goals kicked by the Coloured's wing threequarter Errol Tobias. With the sobering lesson of that tight win, England really opened up in full force in their fourth game of the tour against the South African Rugby Board's XV at Port Elizabeth on 24th May. They beat the Bantu side by 36-3 and the first Africans to play against White opposition were never mapped in a one-sided affair. Outhalf John Wani had the Bantus' only score with a penalty goal and England's total was compiled with two tries from Richards, one each from Old, Larter, Boddy and Morley and Sam Doble kicked three conversions, a penalty goal and also dropped a goal.

A FIGHT BACK

England faced their first real test of the 1972 tour of South Africa when they came up against the powerful Northern Transvaal side at Loftus Versfeld on 27th May and they were in trouble right from the start. Led in tremendously strong fashion by the South African international full-back Toni Roux, Northern Transvaal raced into a 13-3 lead with tries from Muller and Stapleberg and a conversion and a penalty goal by the wing-threequarter Luther. But Sam Doble with three penalty goals and Andy Ripley with a magnificent try brought the score to 13-13 and England's unbeaten record was saved. And they had no trouble at all in keeping it when they took on Griqualand West in the sixth match of the tour at Kimberly on 30th May. Griqualand West took the worst hiding in their history up to then, as the English went on the rampage for a record win by 60-21. This at the time was the greatest total ever achieved by any touring side from these islands in South Africa, adding 15 points to the previous record set by the Lions of 1910 who beat Transvaal Country by 45-4. And there was also to be a record for England's Alan Old, who dropped a goal, kicked a penalty and converted all nine tries for a personal total of 24 points. This, at the time, was the highest score ever set against a South African side by a player from England, Ireland, Scotland or Wales. England's tries came from Spencer and Richards with two each and from Morley, Stevens, Spencer, Janion and Cowell with one each. For Griqualand West, Smith kicked two conversions and three penalty goals and their two tries come from Fourie and from Piet van Deventer who had toured with the Springboks in Britain and Ireland in 1969-1970. There could hardly have been a better warm-up for the seventh and final game of the tour—the international against South Africa at Ellis Park, Johannesburg on 3rd June.

A DAY TO REMEMBER

With Piet Greyling as captain and with a backbone of famous Springboks, Gert Muller, Joggie Jansen, Toni Roux, Joggie Viljoen, Jan Ellis and Albie Bates, South Africa went in against England at Ellis Park on 3rd June with all the confidence that this meeting, the seventh between the two countries since 1906 would bring revenge for the 8-11 defeat they had endured at Twickenham during the 1969-1970 tour. They were, however, to be shocked and stunned as England beat them on their own sacred soil at Ellis Park—and decisively at that. It was one of the major upsets of modern international rugby. Right from the start the Springboks were in trouble up front in the forward battle where, traditionally, down through the years they had always been strongest. England took the game to them and beat them hands down. In the final count-down there was just one try in the game, a brilliant effort by Alan Morley, who followed up Jan Webster's kick ahead and outpaced the Springboks defence for a score that was converted by Sam Doble. All the other points in the game came from penalty kicks. Doble kicked four for England and and Dawie Syman kicked three for South Afrcia. With his 14 points Doble set a record for a game between England and South Africa. The best previous individual performance in a meeting between the two countries had been Doug Morkel's six points with two penalty goals in South Africa's 9-3 win at Twickenham on Saturday, 4th January, 1913. It was also South Africa's biggest defeat by England in their seven games and with this result the record between them now stood at four wins for South Africa, two for England and one drawn. England had scored 38 points in the seven games and South Africa had scored 49. This final win also gave England the honour of being the first unbeaten tour side in South Africa since W. E. Maclagan's side of 1891 which had won all their 19 games.

THE ALL-BLACKS BEATEN

With the cancellation of England's tour to Argentina in 1973—Argentinian guerillas had threatened the kidnap of some of England's players —there was quick consolation for England's rugby players when it was announced that there would be a four-match tour of New Zealand, with the high spot a full international game against the All-Blacks at Eden Park, Auckland on Saturday, 15th September, 1973. And this

" HE'S EVEN BETTER AS A
BRAIN SURGEON "

short tour, arranged without much notice, was to bring England a remarkable triumph. Under the captaincy of John Pullin, the tour began badly with three successive defeats. They went down 3-6 to Taranaki on 1st September, crashed 16-25 to Wellington at Athletic Park on 5th September and were beaten 12-19 by Canterbury at Lancaster Park, Christchurch on 8th September. Then on Saturday, 15th September, exactly a fortnight after their first game, they went into Eden Park to tackle the All-Blacks. The odds at that particular moment were heavily in favour of the All-Blacks who had gone through their 1972-1973 tour of Britain, Ireland, France and Canada with 25 wins in their 32 games in which they had scored 640 points and they had beaten England 9-0 at Twickenham on 6th January, 1973.

STEVEN'S FIRST

Little Grant Batty gave the All-Blacks an early lead in their international game against England at Eden Park on 15th September, 1973. He grabbed a loose ball on the wing and ripped England's defences apart with a glorious try. England, however, struck back with a shock try. Alan Old went racing into the All-Blacks "25" and with Peter Preece and Peter Squires backing him up strongly he put Squires over for a try which Peter Rossborough converted for a 6-4 lead. But with half-time looming up, the All-Blacks came storming through and Ian Hurst went over for a try which Bob Lendrum converted and at the break New Zealand had 10 points. That was the end of the All-Blacks' supremacy. In a titanic second half in which John Pullin's pack dominated a relentless forward battle, England jumped into the lead with a try from "Stack" Stevens which Rossborough converted and then wing-forward Tony Neary sealed an historic victory with a try to give England a 16-10 margin at the final whistle. It was England's second victory over New Zealand in 68 years—their last one had been 13-0 at Twickenham in 1936—and it also marked the first time that prop-forward C. B. "Stack" Stevens had scored a try for England. He could hardly have picked a better occasion to do it.

SQUIRES IN FRONT

In their four match tour of New Zealand in 1973, which lasted for an exact fortnight, England played four games, lost three, won one and scored 47 points while conceding 60. Their top scorer was Peter Squires with three tries which gave him a total of 12 points. Peter Rossborough contributed 11 points from a penalty goal, a try and two conversions. Their other scorers were Tony Jorden with eight points from two penalty goals and a conversion and Peter Knight, Chris Ralston, "Stack" Stevens and Tony Neary had a try each.

NOW AT 331

England have played official international games against Scotland, Ireland, Wales, France, Australia, New Zealand, South Africa, the New Zealand Native side, New South Wales—and against the R.U. President's XV in their Centenary Year of 1970-71. England, with their win over Wales at Twickenham on 16th March, 1974, had played 331 international games, and their record is 166 won, 125 lost and 40 drawn.

AGAINST THE SCOTS

Including the special Centenary match at Murrayfield in 1971—they had already met Scotland at Twickenham that season in the International Championship—England have played Scotland on 90 occasions and have won 43, lost 33 and drawn 14. In the process, they have scored 842 points against the Scots. England's record margin of victory is 19 points which they achieved at Twickenham in 1924 (19-0) and again at Twickenham in 1947 (24-5). England's longest span of supremacy over the Scots is 13 seasons. They beat Scotland at Twickenham in 1913 and with the First World War years intervening, remained unbeaten until the Scots won in Edinburgh in 1925. They put up an even better record by beating Scotland at Twickenham in 1951 and were not beaten again until the Scots won at Murrayfield in 1964.

HEADING FOR 1,000

England took on Ireland for the first time in 1875 and of their 86 games have now won 59, lost 29 and drawn eight and by the end of the 1973-1974 season, had scored 939 points. Their longest unbeaten sequence against Ireland began with the 1875 game and lasted until Ireland won by two goals to nil at Lansdowne Road in 1887. Their highest win over Ireland was at Lansdowne Road in 1938 when they scored six goals, a penalty goal and a try (36) to the home side's one goal and three tries (14).

THE WELSH CONFRONTATION

In their 79 international games against Wales, of which they have won 33, lost 35 and drawn 11, England's longest spell of domination began with the first meeting at Blackheath on 18th February, 1881, when Wales failed to score against England's seven goals, a drop goal and six tries, and ended at Dewsbury in 1890 with Wales's first win by a try to nil. England's greatest victory over the Welsh was in 1881 when their total, under present-day scoring, amounted to 69 points. England's grand total of points in their 79 games against Wales is 831.

THE FRENCH CONNECTION

England had their first international meeting with France in Paris in 1906 and won by the overwhelming margin of 35-8. They have now played France on 49 occasions in the International Championship and have won 29, lost 14 and drawn six. Under present day scoring they have collected 705 points and have failed to score in only four games (1927, 1948, 1962, 1966). England's longest unbeaten run lasted from 1906 until 1927 at Colombes Stadium, where France won for the first time by a try to nil. England's greatest winning margin was in 1911 when they scored five goals, two penalty goals and a try (37) to nil.

TO A RECORD

The young man who began his international career with England in their 6-11 defeat by Wales at Twickenham on Saturday, 15th January, 1966, was not what one might term an immediate hit with his selectors. He was dropped . . . and did not appear again in the England side until Saturday, 20th January, 1968 and again it was at Twickenham and this time it was a draw against Wales on the score of 11-11. From that day onwards, however, he was to become England's top hooker, and the hero of two epic wins against the Springboks in South Africa and against the All-Blacks in New Zealand. And when he stepped off the pitch at Twickenham on Saturday, 16th March, 1974, celebrating England's first win over Wales at the ground for the first time in 11 seasons, John Pullin, his country's captain from Bristol, had become England's most capped forward and player with 35 international caps —one more than the record held up to that day by the famous "Budge" Rogers.

THE ENGLISH TOTAL

From Frederick Stokes who captained the English team in their first ever international game against Scotland at Raeburn Place, Edinburgh on 27th March, 1871 down to W. H. Hare of Nottingham, who played full-back for England against Wales at Twickenham on Saturday, 16th March, 1974, 1,024 players have been honoured by the English selectors in international rugby.

SCOTLAND

AND SO IT STARTED

Rugby was played in Scotland prior to 1850 and in 1858 with the founding of the Edinburgh Academical F.C., the first club came into being. That year, they played a game with Merchiston Castle School, which has become an annual fixture ever since. In 1871, a group of Scottish rugby enthusiasts, aggrieved at Scotland's defeat at association football during the previous year, challenged the English to a game under the new code at Raeburn Place and won it. At this time in Scotland the leading clubs were members of the English Rugby Union but in 1873, the Scottish Rugby Union was established. In 1971, they celebrated 100 years of rugby between Scotland and England in even better form than they had started. At Murrayfield, they trounced England by 26-6—a little better than the goal and a try to a try that had marked their first win back in 1871. In those 100 years, Scotland have now met England on 90 occasions.

A TREASURED POSSESSION

One of the most valuable documents in the possession of the Kilmarnock Rugby Club is a copy of their fixture list for 1869—and it makes interesting reading. Its first rule is that the length of the field should be 200 yards, the breadth 100 yards and the distance between the goalposts, 15 feet. Another of the rules quoted in their fixture list is that any attempts to strangle or throttle were, of course, opposed to the principles of the game! All of which leaves one with the feeling that the early days of the Kilmarnock club must have been quite entertaining.

OPENED THE SCORING

Scotland scored the first points in international rugby with their win, by a goal and a try to a try, over England at Edinburgh in 1871. As previously stated, they have now played England on 90 occasions, have won 34, lost 42, drawn 14 and, under present day scoring values, have collected 755 points in the 90 games. Their widest margin of victory was at Murrayfield in 1971 in the Special Centenary game, which they took by four goals, a penalty goal and a try to a penalty goal and a drop goal. Only twice have Scotland managed four wins in succession over England. They won at Leeds in 1893 and went undefeated by England until the 1897 match at Manchester. They equalled this record by winning in Edinburgh in 1970, then had two wins in 1971 which included the Centenary game and had their fourth in a row at Murray-field in 1972.

THE SCOTTISH TOTAL

From F. Moncrieff of Edinburgh Academicals, who captained Scotland in their first international against England at Raeburn Place, Edinburgh on 27th March, 1871, down to M. D. Hunter of Glasgow High, who played in the Scottish threequarter line against France on Saturday, 16th March, 1974 at Murrayfield, Scotland have capped 786 players in international rugby.

SCOTLAND'S FIRST FAMILIES

The first three brothers to play for Scotland were the Irvines of Edinburgh Academicals and the first three brothers to play on the same Scottish side together were the Finlays, also of Edinburgh Academicals. R. W. Irvine played his only international in England's first meeting with Scotland at Raeburn Place in 1871 and his brother D. R. Irvine followed him on to the Scottish team in 1879 to win three caps. T. W. Irvine was capped for the first time in 1885 and went on to win 10 caps for Scotland. Both N. J. Finlay and A. B. Finlay were capped for the first time for Scotland against England in 1875 and they joined their brother J. F. Finlay on the side that played a scoreless draw. This game, however was A. B. Finlay's only international, and it also marked the final of J. F. Finlay's four caps. Their younger brother Ninian J. Finlay went on to win nine caps which included five successive appearances against England.

HIGH JINKS

Scotland and England played a scoreless draw at the West of Scotland ground at Partick, Glasgow on 13th March, 1873. It began with a mild controversy between the Scots and the English and ended that night with a hilarious celebration that almost ended in the local courts. Prior to the game the English players took one look at the ground which was in a sodden condition and on the instructions of their captain, Frederick Stokes, they made straight for the nearest shoemaker to have special bars put on their boots. The cobbler, apparently a strong Scottish supporter, managed to mislay some of the boots and England subsequently had more than a little difficulty in finding suitable footwear for the game. However, their little dispute with the Scots was patched up later that evening in one of the local hostelries in Glasgow and things became quite merry. It is recorded that late that evening, one of the English players was found driving one of Her Majesty's post-office carts at a furious pace through one of the main streets in the city, with several Scottish and English players as passengers. They were eventually halted by the police, who on discovering that they were dealing with the pride of England and Scotland's best international rugby players, duly escorted them all back to their hotel—and promptly forgot about the matter.

A COSTLY BITE

L. M. Balfour-Melville, barely over seventeen and just out of school was invited to turn out in the first international rugby game ever played at Raeburn Place in 1871. The Scottish selectors had seen him play while he was still at school and were highly impressed with him. He, of course, was delighted to accept and there is the possibility that had he been able to play he would now be the youngest man to have played in international rugby. Unfortunately, some days before the game he was, of all things, bitten by a dog and in the fear that there might be complications, his parents had him removed to hospital. He did, however turn out for Scotland the following year and won his only cap against England. He was then just eighteen years old.

SCOTLAND'S FIRST

Lieutenant H. W. Rennie-Tailyour of the Royal Engineers played in the first international rugby game in England, played in the first international soccer game in England, played in the first English F. A. Cup final and eventually became the first and only Scottish rugby international to win an English F. A. Cup winners medal. For extra measure, he won his rugby and soccer caps and his Cup medal all on the same ground! Rennie-Tailyour, described as "a forward of fine stature and one of the keenest of players, following up splendidly and never sparing himself and very quick on his feet", was capped for Scotland at rugby against England in the first international game at the Kennington Oval, London on 4th February, 1872, when Scotland lost by two goals and two tries to a goal. Just over a year later, on 8th March, 1873, he was capped for Scotland against England in soccer, again at the Kennington Oval and again he was on the losing side with England winning 4-2. Rennie-Tailyour appeared for Royal Engineers against Wanderers in the first English Cup final but was out of luck as Wanderers won by 1-0. Subsequently he was on the losing Royal Engineers side against Oxford University in the 1873-1874 final but he eventually won his Cup medal when Royal Engineers beat Old Etonians, 2-0 in the 1874-1875 final at the Kennington Oval. He is, of course, the only Scot to be capped at both rugby and soccer.

JUST ENJOYMENT

In 1931, the historian, E. D. H. Sewell asked Ninian J. Finlay for his recollections of the 1875 international game between Scotland and England and was told; "I was too young then to do anything more than enjoy the game keenly but I now remember being struck by Hay-Gordon's play. My admiration of his play may have been partly due to his being new to me. He played his club matches in England, while most of the others who played for Scotland in 1875 were familiar to me either as Edinburgh Academicals or as opponents whom we often met in club matches. Of the names, the most familiar to me, apart from my two brothers, is Irvine, familiarly and universally known as 'Bulldog'. I am sure he contributed more to Scotland's holding her own than would appear from the *Scotsman* report of the game. Malcolm Cross, who played at half-back, now called threequarter back, was a familiar figure beside me in later internationals. He was magnificent". At the time he played in this game against England which ended in a scoreless draw at Edinburgh, Ninian J. Finlay was seventeen years, one month and eight days old. At the time he was the youngest to play in international football but he lost this record six years later to his countryman, Charles Reid, who was 15 days younger when he wore Scotland's jersey for the first time.

A DECISIVE START

Scotland showed no mercy to Ireland when they met in their first international game at Belfast in 1877 and ran out the easiest of winners by six goals and two tries, which, under present-day scoring values would be 44-0. This is the most decisive victory Scotland have had over Ireland in their 84 games since 1877. Scotland have won 42, lost 39 and drawn three and in the process, again by present-day scoring values, have totalled up 857 points. Scotland's longest spell of unbroken supremacy was from their 1882 win at Glasgow to their defeat by Ireland at Lansdowne Road in 1894.

THE "HIPPO"

When Charles Reid made the last of his 20 appearances for Scotland against Ireland, he had become the world's most capped international —and he was still only twenty-four! Reid, a powerfully-built youngster who towered well over 6′ 2″ and weighed over 16 stone, made his debut for Scotland against England in 1881 at the age of seventeen and went on to play six successive games against England, eight successive games against Ireland and six successive games against Wales. Because of his size Reid was known as "Hippo" but, unquestionably, he was one of the great forwards of his time.

STILL AT SCHOOL

In his record of the Scotland v England international game at Edinburgh on 19th March, 1881, the Scottish historian Arthur Budd singled out one player for special attention. In his report on this drawn game, he wrote; "C. Reid of Edinburgh Academicals made his first appearance against England. This player through his magnificent physique and clever play may fairly claim the title of 'champion forward' of Scotland. At the line out and in the scrummage he has had no equal while his tackling was a terror to his opponents. Few will deny his claim to be considered the finest forward that ever played for Scotland". What Mr Budd omitted to add was that Charles Reid was then a schoolboy at Edinburgh Academy and was aged seventeen years and 22 days. Reid, who went on to win 20 caps for Scotland, remains to the present day as the youngest player to take part in an international rugby game.

A DOUBLE INTERNATIONAL

The entire history of rugby is marked with men who have achieved international honours in more than one sport but none can claim to be in quite the same class as Thomas Anderson, the young Scot from Merchiston. In 1882 he played full-back for Scotland against Ireland at rugby and that year he also played international cricket for Scotland against the touring Australians and what makes it really interesting is that Master Anderson was still a schoolboy at Merchiston at the time!

AN AWAY WIN

When the Scots took on the English at Manchester on 14th March, 1882, the situation between the two countries was quite unusual. Since the beginning of international rugby 11 years earlier Scotland had always won at home and had never been able to record an away victory and England were in exactly the same boat. So it was a first for international rugby when the Scots beat England with two tries to nil. But there were other first as well. A. N. Hornby was England's captain and it marked the first time that the side had been led by a man who was also England's current cricket captain. It was also the first time that an international game had been handled by a neutral referee. Unfortunately his name has not been recorded and thus his place in international rugby history is lost.

THE SCOTS GET ANGRY

Scotland's game against England at Blackheath on 1st March, 1884 ended in a defeat for Scotland by a goal to a try—and that really made the Scots mad. They claimed that the try scored by N. S. Kinderley of Exeter had not been a try at all and that England should, therefore, not have been given the opportunity to convert a goal. The Scots pointed out that one of their players had knocked the ball back and that Kinderley had been there to collect it and cross the Scottish line. The English contended that it was legal to knock back and that even if it were illegal to do so the Scots could claim no advantage from an illegal act committed by one of their side. Apart from that they maintained that the referee had awarded the try and his decision was final. There were more disputes and counter disputes, arguments about the laws and the controversy went on and on. Eventually the Scots conceded the victory—but not for some years later until the International Board had been set up to deal with such matters. England, in the meantime, became just as angry as the Scots and the general result was that England did not play any international games against Ireland, Scotland or Wales for the next two years.

A RICH HARVEST

George Lindsay made his international debut for Scotland against Wales at Rodney Parade, Newport on Saturday, 12th January, 1884 and, sadly, it was not an auspicious debut. He was promptly dropped for the next game and although he was invited to play in the Scottish trials of the following year he declined. He was then living in London and playing with London-Scottish and did not relish the idea of the long trek back home with only the very faint possibility of a second cap to entice him to Edinburgh. He did, however, get that second cap in somewhat fortuitous circumstances. He was back home in Scotland on a holiday in 1887 and when one of the Scotland players had to cry off with an injury, Lindsay was called in to play at the back. And it was quite a return. Scotland walloped Wales by a score, which under modern values would be 56-0—four goals and eight tries to nil. In crossing the Welsh line 12 times, eight Scots contributed the tries . . . and the substitute Lindsay collected five! He was the first man to score five tries in an international rugby game, is still the only Scottish international to do so and only one other player since then— Douglas Lambert of England against France in 1907—has managed to equal his record in international rugby. They share a world record with their five tries each. The sad sequel to Lindsay's career was that he was given a third cap against England on Saturday, 5th March, 1887 and was found wanting. According to the accounts of the time he was "nervous and did not show international class!"

THE SEVENS MAN

Ned Haig, although he was one of the great scrum-halves in Scotland at the time never managed to win an international cap for his country. But for all that, he has his own place in the history of Scottish football as the originator of "sevens". While he was playing with Melrose, and with the club funds in a bad way, he conceived the idea of the tournament on its present lines as the ideal solution to pull in paying customers who would in turn make Melrose's treasurer a little happier. The experiment, at the Greenyards in 1883, was an immense success and perhaps fittingly, Haig led the Melrose team which beat Gala in the final by a try to nothing. One of Melrose's finest characters, he lived to 1939 and died at the age of eighty-two. One of his proudest boasts was that he had watched Scotland in international rugby in every year they had played from 1880.

THE FIRST SCOTTISH TOURISTS

The first brothers to travel with a touring side from these islands to New Zealand and Australia in 1888 were the two Scots, William and Robert Burnett, both of the Hawick club, but, neither was ever capped in international football for Scotland. William Burnett played as a half-back and Robert, described as "a powerfully-built man with more than a useful turn of speed" played in the forwards.

A GOLF ENTHUSIAST

Patrick Hamilton Don Wauchope, brother of the famous "Bunny" Wauchope, played five times for Scotland between 1885 and 1887 . . . but had another interest which was to benefit golfers from all over the world in the years since then. A tremendous golf enthusiast, he was largely responsible for the alterations which turned a certain golf course into a course where championships could be staged . . . and its name is . . . Muirfield.

" HE'S ONLY PICKED FOR HIS "
PUB SINGING AFTER THE GAME

WRONG SPORT

J. G. Tait of Edinburgh Academicals won two international caps for Scotland against Ireland in 1880 and again in 1885 but he always felt that his younger brother F. G. Tait was a much better rugby player. He tried hard to get the brother to devote himself to rugby but the younger Tait showed far more interest in golf which, of course was then as it is now the most popular game in Scotland. F. G. Tait devoted himself to golf with quite a dedication which eventually paid off handsomely in 1896 when he defeated the legendary Harold Hilton to win the British Amateur Championship in 1896. Hilton had previously won the British Open title and was later to win the British amateur title and American amateur titles. Tait was also British amateur champion in 1898, but it is on record that he never did get around to progressing beyond club rugby.

FIRST AND LAST

The Scottish forward, David Morton, who won nine caps between 1887 and 1890, kicked the first drop goal from a mark in international rugby during the game against Ireland at Belfast in 1887 when the Scots won by two goals and two tries to nil. The last man to achieve this score in the Home Championship was also a forward and the score came again in a game between Ireland and Scotland. At Lansdowne Road in 1939, Mike Sayers dropped a goal from a mark in Ireland's 12-3 win. Sayers, who played with the British Army, Aldershot Services and Lansdowne, won 10 caps for Ireland between 1935 and 1939.

UP AND DOWN

Scotland and Wales have now met on 78 occasions in international rugby and the Scots have won 33, lost 43 and drawn two and, by present-day scoring values, have reached 702 points. Scotland's most convincing win over the Welsh was in 1887 at Edinburgh where they came out on top by a margin of four goals and eight tries to nil, which on present day values would be 56-0. Scotland's best years against Wales were in the 1920s. After their win in Edinburgh in 1920, they remained unbeaten until Wales won at Edinburgh in 1928.

A COLD SET OFF

Scotland started their 1894-1895 season on a bleak, frosty afternoon at Raeburn Place, Edinburgh on Saturday, 26th January and for a long time there were fears that the game would not go on. The Welsh did not like the frozen state of the ground and wanted to have the fixture postponed. However, after long discussions it was agreed to go ahead and the Scots with a try from Jim Gowans which a full-back converted eventually pipped the Welsh for whom the great Arthur Gould had dropped a goal. The Irish were the next visitors to Raeburn Place that season and they arrived on Saturday, 6th February. But even with the two Magees, Joe and Louis and the famous Tommy Crean in the side, Ireland were never a match for the Scots and failed to score. Scotland had tries from their two centre threequarters G. T. Campbell of London-Scottish and R. Walsh of Watsonians for a comfortable 6-0 win. Now only England, who had hammered Wales by 25-6 and lost 4-10 to Ireland, stood between Scotland and their second Triple Crown. And this was a battle that raged all the way to a dramatic ending. England took the lead with a penalty goal by full-back John Byrne but early in the second half Alan Smith brought the sides level. Then in a glorious finish, the Scottish forward G. T. Neilson of West of Scotland battered his way over for a try to win the day. With this victory Scotland took over from Ireland as Triple Crown champions.

THE TWO LEADERS

Mark Morrison, first capped for Scotland in 1896 and who was to win 23 caps before he retired, shares a record with Arthur Smith, who was first capped for Scotland in 1955 and who had 33 caps to his credit when he retired from international football in 1962. Both had the honour and the record of captaining Scotland on 15 occasions. They also share the honour of having captained a Lions touring side. Morrison led the 1903 Lions to South Africa where they won 11 of their 24 games and drew three and Arthur Smith led the 1962 Lions to South Africa for a record of 15 wins in 24 games with four drawn.

THE THIRD TRIPLE CROWN

Scotland won the Triple Crown for the third time in 1900-1901 and their half-back J. I. Gillespie of Edinburgh Academicals had the distinction of scoring in all three victories with a total of four tries. Against England on Saturday, 19th January, 1901 at Blackheath, the Scots, with a powerful display up front and smart running by their back division had no bother in sweeping England out of their path. With tries from Gillespie, W. H. Welsh, A. B. Timms and A. N. Fell, three of which were converted by Gillespie, they won as they pleased by 18-3. And the Scots ran up the same total against Wales at Inverleith on Saturday, 9th February. This time Gillespie scored two tries, Turnbull and Fell added another each and Gillespie converted two and A. B. Flett of Edinburgh converted a third. The final score was 18-8 for Scotland and they were firm favourites when they took on Ireland in the final game of the season at Inverleith on Saturday 2nd March. By all accounts this was a tempestuous affair and "Darky" Bedell-Sivright, who was later to lead the 1904 Lions to New Zealand and Australia, came in for special attention from a strong Irish pack. Ireland led 5-3 at half-time with Scotland's try coming from W. H. Welsh, who added a second in the second half to put Scotland ahead by 6-5. Towards the end, Gillespie broke clean through for his fourth try of the season which gave Scotland a 9-5 win and their third Triple Crown. Gillespie, of course was Scotland's top scorer that season with 22 points from four tries and five conversions.

A STRONG RETURN

Champions in 1901, Scotland suffered the indignity of going through the following season without an international win, but in 1902-1903 they came fighting back to win the Triple Crown for the fourth time since 1891. England were taken on at Richmond, London and were beaten by 10-6 with their tries coming from J. D. Dallas and E. D. Simpson and A. B. Timms topped it off with a magnificent drop goal. Wales put up a much sterner battle at Inverleith on Saturday, 7th February, 1903 and after forward W. E. Kyle had scored a try, Timm, with a penalty goal, brought the Scots a 6-0 win. Ireland were to provide Scotland with their toughest opposition that season and the sides had a titanic battle when they met at Inverleith, Edinburgh on Saturday, 28th February. Jack Coffey, George Hamlet, Joe Wallace and Sam Irwin waged an all-out attack on the Scots who were led up from by Mark Morrison and "Darky" Bedell-Sivright and for most of the game there was stalemate. But with time running out, Scotland's

J. E. Crabbie stole away on the wing and nipped over at the corner for a try and the only score of the game. Accounts of the game say that the gallant fight on the field of play was later enjoyed at a most convivial banquet that evening.

EARLY RETIREMENT

When K. G. McLeod made his debut against the New Zealanders at Inverleith in 1905, he joined his brother L. M. McLeod on the Scottish team and they became the first brothers to play against a touring side in Britain and Ireland. Both played for Cambridge University in the centre and they appeared together for Scotland against New Zealand, Wales and Ireland in 1905. They continued to play for Cambridge up to 1908 and at this time K. G. McLeod had collected 10 Scotland caps before the age of twenty-one. That year, however, his brother died suddenly of appendicitis and Kenneth G. McLeod, at his parents' wishes, decided to retire from all forms of sport. One of the most elegant of players, he still remains in the exclusive few of those who have been capped on 10 occasions before reaching their majority.

IN AGAINST NEW ZEALAND

When the Scottish selectors heard about the startling young centre-threequarter at Fettes School, they went along and took a good look at him. One look was enough to convince them that he was the young man they wanted for Scotland's game against Wales at Inverleith, Edinburgh on Saturday, 7th February, 1903. The problem was to get permission for him to play from Dr Heard, then the Headmaster of Fettes. Dr Heard listened politely to the request of the selectors and promptly refused permission. Young McLeod was only fifteen! Under no circumstances would he be allowed to play international rugby. However the Scottish selectors kept their eye on the youngster and two years later they named him to play against Wales at Inverleith on Saturday, 4th February, 1905. This time Dr Heard was really indignant. He had not even been consulted and he refused point-blank to let McLeod play. McLeod left Fettes that summer and went to Cambridge University and he let it be known quickly that if Scotland needed him, he was ready. And so, on 18th November, 1905 at

Inverleith, K. G. McLeod made his debut for Scotland against the New Zealand touring side. In the *Daily Mail* account of the game, F. T. Prall wrote; "On the Scottish side the two outstanding successes were K. G. McLeod and E. D. Simson, although all the forwards worked with unflagging zeal". McLeod, destined to become one of Scotland's great personalities of the early part of the century was then a few months after his seventeenth birthday. He was to go on to win 10 caps for Scotland before his twenty-first birthday.

DOWN TO DEFEAT

Before 32,000 people at Hampden Park, Glasgow on Saturday, 17th November, 1906, the South Africans played their first international on foreign soil when they took on Scotland. On this tour the South Africans had already reeled off 15 wins in succession and were confidently tipped to whip the Scots. Scotland, however, provided a most unexpected opposition and at half-time neither side had scored. Early in the second half Grant McLeod (Cambridge University) opened the scoring for Scotland with a try and just before full-time A. L. Purves (London-Scottish) clinched a great victory for the Scots by 6-0. In all, Scotland have now played South Africa on eight occasions and won three. Their biggest win was the 6-0 of 1906 and their worst defeat was the 0-44 game at Murrayfield in 1951.

ONE OF THE GREATEST

The season 1906-1907 is still regarded as one of the greatest in the history of Scottish rugby. It began with that epic victory over the touring South Africans at Hampden Park, Glasgow on Saturday, 17th November, 1906 when tries from K. G. McLeod and "Darky" Bedell-Sivright brought a 6-0 win and the Springboks only international defeat of the tour. And from that victory came a great championship season. With tries from Alan Purves and E. D. Simpson, one converted by D. G. Schulze, Scotland defeated England at Blackheath by 8-3 and a fortnight later at Inverleith, after Wales had led 3-0 at half-time, Scotland came back with tries from Purves and H. G. Monteith to win 6-3. The final game against Ireland, also at Inverleith on Saturday, 16th February, promised to be the highpoint of the season but this was a day when Ireland were never in the reckoning. G. A. Sanderson gave Scotland an early lead with a try, Purves added another and G. M. Frew had a third and with Schulze converting all three, Scotland romped to a 15-3 win and their fifth Triple Crown. It was to be 14 years before they added another.

AGAINST THE FRENCH

Scotland took on France for the first time in Edinburgh in 1910 and two years later, again in Edinburgh had their record win over the French by five goals, a penalty goal and a try to a try, which, by present-day scoring values would be 37-4. Scotland have now played 44 matches against France, winning 23, losing 19 and drawing 2. In the 44 matches, by current scoring values, they have scored 521 points. Scotland's longest undefeated record against France is from 1925 in Edinburgh until they were beaten in Paris in 1930.

CONFLICTING REPORTS

New Year's Day, 1913 when the Scots took on France at Parc des Princes, Paris in their fourth international meeting, was hardly the type of day to promise good things for the coming 12 months. The accounts of what happened that day at Parc des Princes are conflicting. The Scottish accounts agree that it was a rough game with the French getting totally out of hand and the French accounts allege that most of the trouble began when the referee Mr John Baxter showed favouritism to the Scots by starting the second half while most of the French side were still in their dressing room! However, we can take it that it was an infamous game. H. D. Sewell, the great historian, records in his book *Rugby Football Today,* published in 1931, that; "Perhaps some of my readers did not know that after the riot match in 1913, a squadron of cuirassiers galloped across from behind the in-goal on the right of the grandstands to form a barrier between the occupants of those stands, some of whom had struck at Scottish players on their way to the dressing room and thus prevented a very serious ending to the afternoon". It is possible, of course, that the scoring of the Scots during the game may have had some effect on the French players. Scotland left Paris with a 21-3 victory—and the definite promise that they would never again meet France in an international game. However, peace was restored after the First World War and Scotland returned to Parc des Princes in 1920 and won this time by 5-0 and, apparently everything passed off tamely.

FROM COLOMBO

He was born in Colombo on 15th October, 1896, the son of a Scotsman . . . and he was to become one of the best-remembered heroes of Scottish international rugby. After his arrival in England in 1907, he went to Eltham College and it was there that Archibald Leslie Gracie saw a rugby ball for the first time. From school, where he had achieved a sound reputation as a wing threequarter, he went up Oxford but in November, 1916, he was commissioned in the 60th Rifles and after service in France, returned to the University in 1920. Exactly a week after his demobilisation, Adrian Stoop, the famous English international invited him to turn out for Harlequins seconds but when a vacancy came on the first team he was promoted to turn out against Old Merchant Taylors at the Old Deer Park. After that game, his fame spread in London and somehow or other it got to the ears of the Scottish selectors who felt that with a name like Gracie, this young man had to have a little Scottish blood in him somewhere. A year later, he made his debut for Scotland against France and between then and 1924 when he won his 13th cap, his tremendous understanding and partnership with Eric Liddell, turned Scotland into one of the finest international sides of the post-war years. For business reasons, he retired from football in 1924.

NOT TO BE WASTED

The international career of Jock Wemyss lasted for nine seasons but produced only seven caps. He was unfortunate that his first cap came in 1914 against Wales and on the strength of a tremendous performance in this game held his place for the next game against Ireland. Then came the First World War and Wemyss spent the next four years in France. He was badly wounded, lost an eye and no one really expected him to return to rugby. The irrepressible Wemyss, one of the memorable characters of Scottish rugby, plunged straight back into club rugby, won back his place in the Scottish pack against England and France in 1920 and wound up his career by playing against Ireland, Wales and France in 1922. One of his favourite stories was that when he was recalled to play against France in 1920, he went along to the selectors on the morning of the game, New Year's Day, at Parc des Princes, Paris and asked for an international jersey. They gave him one but only reluctantly. As one of them pointed out to him; "You shouldn't need one. You got one before the war!"

A FAIR START

There was quite a surprise when Scotland announced their team for the opening international of 1923-24 against France at Inverleith on Saturday, 20th January, 1924. H. H. Forsyth of Oxford University had been the national full-back for two seasons and no one believed that there was any serious challenger around to displace him. But the Scottish selectors announced that D. Drysdale would replace him for this game. And the young man from Heriots took the chance in flying style. He was a sensational success and kicked two conversions to open his scoring tally for his country. Five years later Drysdale made his final appearance for Scotland against France at Murrayfield and he ended his career in another victory and also by scoring, this time a penalty goal. With this last game, he became Scotland's most-capped full-back with 26 appearances and his record was to last until Ken Scotland brought the mark to 27 in 1965. Drysdale, however, played his 26 games in succession and that still endures as a record for a Scotland full-back. The unusual feature was that Drysdale began his career as an out-half, was shifted to centre and finally was persuaded to try his hand at full-back.

A DIFFERENT STADIUM

Ireland, England and Wales have played at two venues in France— Parc des Princes and Colombes Stadium. Scotland, however, can claim to have played at three. When they arrived in Paris in 1924 to take on France, the city had been under constant rain for a week and there was the distinct possibility that the game which was to be played at the Olympic Stadium at Colombes would have to be cancelled. Colombes was under several inches of water and up to late on the Friday hight, the general feeling was that the Scots could catch the train the following morning and head for Calais and home. However, some enterprising French officials suddenly remembered the new Stade Pershing just outside Paris and a visit there at midnight showed that the ground was playable. And there, in front of a small crowd the following afternoon it was duly carried out with France winning an exciting game by 12-10.

A MAN OF PRINCIPLE

Eric Liddell was a man of deep principle and deep integrity. He would not run nor play football on a Sunday and that subsequently was to cost him a second Olympic gold medal. Fortunately all of Scotland's rugby internationals are played on a Saturday and, although he was to win only seven caps for Scotland, he became his country's greatest wing-threequarters of the early 1920s . . and certainly the fastest. He gave up international rugby at the end of the 1922-1923 season to train seriously for athletics and he had his proudest moment at Paris in 1924 during the Olympic Games when he took the gold medal in the 400 metres with a new Olympic and world record of 47.6 seconds. He might easily have added a further Olympic gold medal to his collection but for the fact that the final of the 100 metres for which he was the favourite, was to be staged on a Sunday and because of this, he withdrew from the event. In 1923, he set a record in London by winning the British A.A.A. 100, 220 and 440 yards championships on the same afternoon. Liddell, who was to work in the foreign missions died in a Japanese prisoner-of-war camp during the Second World War.

IAN SMITH'S AFTERNOON

France had a rude and shattering experience when they opened up their 1924-1925 season against Scotland at the Inverleith Ground, Edinburgh on Saturday, 24th January, 1925. Within six minutes, Ian Smith with a try and A. C. Wallace with another, both converted by full-back Drysdale, who then dropped a goal had put Scotland 14 points up. From there on it was a procession and in the end with Smith running in three further tries, one of which was converted by Drysdale,

Scotland finished on top by 25-4. And Smith continued his record-breaking spree with three first half tries against Wales at St Helen's, Swansea, on 7th February, 1925 A. C. Wallace added two more, Smith had a fourth and with Drysdale dropping a goal and converting a try, Scotland had 25 points on the board at the finish to Wales's 14. The battle against Ireland at Lansdowne Road, however, was a much sterner affair. The first half was a dour, unrelenting struggle but just on half-time Wallace broke away for a try and Drysdale converted to leave Scotland 5-0 ahead at the break. In the second half in which almost every member of the Scottish team, with the surprising exception of Ian Smith, handled the ball, the visitors ran the length of Lansdowne Road for a try by Douglas McMyn which Drysdale again converted. Ireland came surging back with a try from Harry Stephenson and a penalty goal by Ernie Crawford left the Scots with just a 10-8 lead with five minutes to go. But in the last seconds, just as the referee was looking at his watch, Herbert Waddell dropped the neatest of goals and it was 14-8. Scotland now needed to beat England and the Triple Crown would be theirs for the sixth time.

EIGHT ALTOGETHER

On Saturday, 24th January, 1925 Scotland played their last international game on the historic ground at Inverleith, Edinburgh and made it a fitting goodbye by beating France 25-4. On Saturday, 7th February, 1925, Scotland went to St Helen's, Swansea and had another convincing victory with a 24-14 win over Wales. Both of these were red-letter days in the career of Ian Smith, the Scottish wing-threequarter. He set an all-time rugby record by scoring four tries in each game and even more remarkable was his other record that six of them came in succession. He scored the final three tries at Inverleith in the second half and went over for the first three at St Helen's in the first half.

THE SCOTS AGHAST!

Had Ireland beaten Scotland at Lansdowne Road on Saturday, 21st February, 1925, there would have been, as the late "Horsey" Browne, of Ireland, said afterwards—"holy, blue, bloody murder". It all revolved around one particular incident in the game. Ireland were awarded a line-out and wing-threequarter Harry Stephenson motioned the Irish forwards to stand well back. Then he threw the ball forward, grabbed it himself and dashed over the Scottish line for a try that made the Scots recoil in horror. But the try was legitimate and the incident subsequently led to a change in the laws of rugby. It was ruled that the ball would have to be thrown in at least five yards. Fortunately the Scots recovered from this try and went on to win by 14-8 but that particular incident, the sharp thinking of Harry Stephenson, was to remain a lively topic of conversation for the rest of the season.

A MURRAYFIELD OPENING

Saturday, 8th March, 1925, was of special significance in the history of Scottish rugby. It marked the opening of the new Murrayfield Stadium and what better game could there be to mark this historic day than Scotland v England, for not only the Calcutta Cup but also the Triple Crown. And the match fitted the glorious afternoon. England opened the scoring with a penalty goal but within a matter of minutes Scotland's dapper scrum-half, J. B. Nelson, slipped over for a try which Drysdale converted. But England never let up in attack and again within a matter of minutes they were ahead with a splendid try from their flying wing-threequarter Hamilton-Wickes. The try was converted and Scotland were threepoints down at half-time. Wakefield added to Scotland's misery early in the second half by crashing through a wall of Scottish forwards for a try but once again the Scots lifted themselves and Wallace ran 50 yards for a try in the corner which Gillies converted. With only minutes to go, England still held on grimly to their 11-10 lead. And then it was Herbert Waddell's turn to come on the scene. He tried for a long drop at goal but the ball soared inches wide. From the drop-out, the ball went loose and Waddell snapped it up and for the second time in 60 seconds he tried for a drop and this time there was never any doubt about it. It dropped neatly between the posts and Scotland were Triple Crown champkons—and Grand Slam champions. In their four games, they had scored 77 points and conceded 37. Ian Smith, of course, was their top scorer with 24 points from his eight tries.

THE FLYING SCOTSMAN

Ian Smith, born in 1903, wore the Scotland jersey for the first time against Wales at Inverleith, Edinburgh on Saturday, 2nd February,

1924 and helped to make it quite a day for Scotland. They trounced Wales by 35-10 and Smith on the wing had three tries on his debut. On that particular afternoon, Oxford University provided the entire Scottish threequarter line with Smith, G. P. S. Macpherson, the New Zealander G. G. Aitken and the Australian, A. C. "Joe" Wallace, who was later to captain the 1927-1928 "Waratahs" in their tour of Britain and Ireland. Smith, who was selected for Scotland on 39 occasions but had to drop out of seven of these games through injury or illness and also toured with Cove-Smiths Lions in South Africa in 1924, finished his international career with the remarkable world record of having scored 23 tries in international rugby—a Scottish record of 18 in his 32 appearances for the country and five more in his two international appearances for the Lions against South Africa in 1924.

TO RUGBY LEAGUE

The twenty-year old centre-threequarter Roy M. Kinnear was uncapped when he was chosen to travel to South Africa with Cove-Smith's Lions of 1924 but he made four successive international appearances against the Springboks and played in eight games against the provincial sides. The following year, still playing with Heriot's F.P., he was capped against Ireland, Wales and France and these were to be his only three international outings with Scotland. Before the following season opened he had joined Wigan and, in fact, had become the first Lions player to go over to Rugby League. Kinnear, regarded as one of the finest centres of his time, died tragically, while playing in a Services game at Uxbridge, London on 22nd September, 1942.

THIRD TIME UNLUCKY

Murrayfield was opened in March 1925 and the Scots celebrated the occasion by beating England, and then going on to take the Triple Crown and Grand Slam. A year later Wales made their first appearance at Murrayfield and they suffered the same fate as the English. So, on a wet and muddy day at Murrayfield in February, 1926, Scotland tried for the hat-trick of wins over the three home countries. And nothing could have been more dramatic. With only two minutes to go Scotland were still holding on to their record of an unbeaten record at Murrayfield. There was no score. Then Ireland's "Horsey" Browne crashed headlong into Herbert Waddell, Scotland's out-half and both were knocked unconscious. Waddell who tried to crawl along the ground was led off with severe concussion and whipped straight off to hospital. Following the stoppage, which lasted for over four minutes, George Stephenson launched an attack which ended with Jack Gage making history for himself and Ireland by dashing over at the corner for a try. The whistle went just after the attempt to convert by Ernie Crawford failed . . . and Scotland had lost their first game at Murrayfield.

37 IN SUCCESSION

The twenty-nine-year old J. MacDonald Bannerman finished with international rugby at the end of the 1928-1929 season with three happy memories—his first game for Scotland, the Triple Crown win of 1924-1925—and the win over Wales on Saturday, 3rd February, 1923. Bannerman was just twenty when he wore the Scottish jersey for the first time against France at Paris in 1920 and it brought a 6-0 win. He was, of course, the towering lock-forward of Scotland's four successive triumphs of 1924-1925 when they took the Grand Slam for the only time and the Triple Crown for the sixth time with wins over France, England, Wales and Ireland. But, by general agreement, his greatest game for Scotland was against Wales in 1923. That was the afternoon when the Welsh supporters chaired Scotland's Archibald Leslie Gracie from the field at the end of an historic game. Bannerman was at his greatest that afternoon and many a Welshman suffered under his tremendous drive to get a win for Scotland in this game. Eventually, with a try in the closing moments by Gracie, Scotland won and Bannerman was happy. It was the first time that Scotland had beaten Wales at Cardiff Arms Park since 1890! Bannerman never missed a game for Scotland during his international career and his 37 consecutive games were to stand as a record until overtaken by Hughie McLeod in 1962.

A RECORD EQUALLED

On Saturday, 8th April, 1933 at Lansdowne Road, Dublin, Scotland's right wing-threequarter Ian Smith won his 32nd cap for his country in the defeat of Ireland by 8-6. On Saturday, 24th February, 1962, Scotland came again to Lansdowne Road and this time won by 20-6. By an odd coincidence on that afternoon, Scotland's right wing-threequarter, another Smith, this time Arthur, also collected his 32nd cap for Scotland and thus equalled Ian Smith's record as his country's most capped back. Arthur Smith was subsequently to win one more cap for his country that season against England to set the present Scottish record at 33 for a wing-threequarter.

ONE IN, ONE OUT

D. I. Browne (Cambridge University) made his debut at full-back for Scotland in 1933 and played in all three games against Ireland, England and Wales. Unfortunately, Scotland can hardly have had a full-back who collected so many injuries. Shortly before the start of the 1933-1934 season, he picked up an injury and was forced to cry off Scotland's side to play Wales, and subsequently he had to call out of the games against Ireland and England. That provided K. W. Marshall of Edinburgh Academicals with his chance to come in as a replacement full-back and he played in all three games. For the following season Browne went down with injury again—and once again Marshall stepped in to collect another three caps. As it happened Browne was never again to play for Scotland and Marshall, who collected his first six caps as a replacement, went on to win two more before he ended his international career in 1937.

THE DELAYED MATCH

Scotland, with a narrow win by a try to nil over England and an 11-3 win over Wales, arrived in Dublin on Friday, 24th, February, 1933 to take on Ireland—and found Dublin caught in a violent snowstorm. Lansdowne Road was covered in several inches of snow and there was never the slightest hope that the game on the following day could be played. So Scotland, with the Triple Crown at stake, had to wait until 18th March that year to return to Dublin for their vital last game of the season. But it was worth the wait. Although Ian Smith was injured early on and remained a passenger for most of the game on the wing and the Scottish forwards were well outplayed by a spirited Irish pack, they eventually scraped home by 8-6 with two drop goals from K. L. T. Jackson and D. I. Brown. This was Scotland's seventh Triple Crown win since 1891.

A LONG TIME WITH US

W. C. W. Murdoch of the Hillhead High School Former Pupils Club wore his first Scottish jersey against England in the 1934-1935 season and proved himself to be an able full-back. He was capped later that year against the touring New Zealanders at Murrayfield and with two further caps that season against Ireland and Wales, he disappeared from the international scene for three years. He surfaced again in 1939 to play against England and, then, of course the war years brought an end to international football. International rugby came back in 1945-1946 with the "victory" games and a season later, the official games were renewed. And who arrived back in the international scene in 1948 to play in all four games against Ireland, England, Wales and France? None other than the same W. C. W. Murdoch. He won only nine caps for Scotland but on a matter of long service no Scottish international can equal his record, particularly not a full-back.

THE FINAL CROWN

Scotland won a controversial game against Wales on Saturday, 5th February, 1938 at Murrayfield—and as it turned out it was to be the most vital victory they had that season. They were being led 5-6 by Wales with barely a minute to go when one of the Welsh forwards was penalised for lying on the ball right in front of his own posts and the referee Cyril Gadney promptly gave Scotland the kick which wing-forward W. H. Crawford of United Services booted over the bar for an 8-6 win for Scotland. It was an incident that provoked quite an amount of controversy. The Welsh asserted that the player in question had been kicked on the head and was concussed at the time and was in no condition to release the ball. However, Scotland had won and in the light of what was to follow, it was their most important victory of the season. They trounced Ireland by 23-14 at Murrayfield on 19th February and a fortnight later they went to Twickenham and downed

England by 21-16. So for the eighth time Scotland had won the Triple Crown and to this day it remains as the last time they managed to beat all three countries in a season.

A DAY FOR MEMORY

Wales were the Triple Crown and Grand Slam champions of 1949-1950 and they opened up their 1950-1951 season with a shattering victory by 23-5 over England at St Helen's, Swansea. And when John Gwilliam led his men out at Murrayfield on Saturday, 3rd February, 1951 to face Scotland, there could be only the one result—another decisive win for the Welsh. What else could there be? But this was to turn out to be one of the most memorable afternoons in Scottish rugby, one that is still remembered vividly. The Scottish captain Peter Kininmouth, with the finest drop goal of his life, made the first score and from there on it was a "massacre" of a proud Welsh side. By the time it was all over, with two tries from Gordon on the wing, one from prop-forward J. C. Dawson and conversions from H. M. Inglis and full-back H. M. Thomson who also dropped a goal, it was a 19-0 win for Scotland. It was the first time since 1927 that Wales had failed to score against Scotland in an international game.

THE FIRST OF 40

When they ran out on to the pitch at Murrayfield on Saturday, 13th February, 1954, Scotland had 13 successive defeats behind them and few gave them any chance of halting this sad run. Changes had been made on the side and one of the interesting ones was that of Hugh McLeod, the twenty-two-year old prop-forward from Hawick. He had taken up rugby when he was sixteen and in no time at all had made the first side. Known as "The Abbott", this powerfully-built youngster was making his debut that day, and although Scotland after a fierce battle went down to their 14th successive defeat, it was a near thing. Only a fortunate penalty goal by the balding Bob Scott had saved New Zealand. Young McLeod had acquitted himself well and most people felt that he deserved another chance in Scotland's colours. He got it, of course. For the next nine seasons he was on every Scottish side that played in an international game and when he finally called a halt to his career in 1962 he had established a Scottish record of 40 international caps—all of them in succession. After two tours with the Lions to South Africa in 1955 and to Australia and New Zealand in 1959, he was invited to make what would then have been a record third tour with the Lions of 1962, but he said "no". It was time, he said, to concentrate on the family business.

AND SO IT ENDED

When Scotland beat Wales at Murrayfield on Saturday, 5th February, 1955, there was almost as much rejoicing as when Scotland had last won the Triple Crown in 1938. This time, however, the elation was for a different reason. In beating Wales by 14-8, the Scots had ended the most dismal sequence in their rugby history. Prior to that win, they had lost to France in 1951, 1952, 1953, 1954, 1955, to Ireland in 1951, 1952, 1953, 1954, to England in 1951, 1952, 1953, 1954 and to Wales in 1952, 1953, 1954 and had also been routed 44-0 by the touring South Africans at Murrayfield in 1951. In all they had gone 17 successive internationals in defeat.

SCOTLAND BY NAME, TOO

As John Ireland of Windsor had achieved for Ireland in 1876 against England, Ken Scotland in 1957 achieved the honour of playing for a country of his own name. Scotland, of Heriots and Cambridge University, won his first caps in 1957 against England, France, Ireland and Wales and from there on until 1965, he was Scotland's top full-back. By the time he ended his career, he had become Scotland's most capped full-back, one ahead of Dan Drysdale who had 26. Selected for the Lions tour to New Zealand, Australia and Canada in 1959, he played in five international games for the tourists and his scoring record from 22 games during the tour was 72 points from six conversions, five dropped goals, three penalty goals and 12 tries. Those 12 tries are still a record for a Lions touring full-back.

THE LATE-COMER

He wanted to be a soccer player and up to the age of nineteen he played nothing else. Then he was persuaded to try his hand at rugby with the Howe of Fife Club and five years later he did them proud by becoming the first member of the club to win an international cap for Scotland. His debut was against England in 1959 at Twickenham and he was left with a reminder of it—a badly broken nose. But, in his opinion, it was all worth it as Scotland held England to a 3-3 draw. That was the first of David Rollo's games for Scotland and a long, long way from the last. That was to come in 1968 and by then his total of caps had reached 40 which now makes him joint holder with Hughie McLeod of the all-time record in Scottish rugby. He did have a chance to make the record his own. He was chosen to play against England in 1968 but was forced to call off because of an injury. Rollo, one of Scotland's greatest forwards, toured with the British Lions in South Africa in 1962 but surprisingly did not play in any of the international games.

SCOTLAND IN SOUTH AFRICA

Under the captaincy of Gordon Waddell, Scotland made a short tour of South Africa in 1960, during which they played three matches, won two and lost one, scoring 61 points and conceding 45. They opened with the first international game ever played by South Africa at the Boet Erasmus Stadium in Port Elizabeth and faced a Springbok side that contained no fewer than 10 new caps, including Jan Engelbrecht, John Gainsford and Doug Hopwood, all of whom were to become world famous in the years that followed. The South Africans were never in any serious trouble against the Scots and, sparked off by two magnificent tries from Hugo van Zyl, they romped home by 18-10 with Scotland's scores coming late in the game from wing-threequarter Arthur Smith. Smith, unquestionably the outstanding man of this Scottish touring side, finished up as top scorer in the three games with 29 points from five tries and seven conversions and was also the top try scorer.

A DISTANT CONNECTION

Franz ten Bos's qualifications to play international rugby for Scotland were, to say the least about them, tenuous. He had been born in England of Dutch parents and when his family settled in Scotland, he went to Fettes where he played rugby for the first time. Later, after winning three Blues at Oxford, he joined London-Scottish and that brought him firmly to the notice of the Scottish selectors who wrote to him, asking him to confirm that his mother had been Scottish. Ten Bos replied honestly that he had tried hard to locate some Scottish blood in his family tree but had failed; there was not even a drop. However, he added that he had been educated in Scotland, reared in Scotland and had served in the Argyll Regiment. Apparently that was enough for the selectors. They gave him his chance in 1959 against England and after a scoreless draw at Twickenham, he became quite a regular from there on. Now remembered as one of the best second row forwards of his time, he won 17 caps for Scotland and ended his international career with the game against England at Twickenham in 1963.

AWAY UP THERE

Peter Stagg of Scotland was the bane of every wing-threequarter's life during his international career with Scotland. At a throw in the opposing wing-threequarter had the problem of either throwing short to avoid Stagg or throwing high and long to get the ball out of Stagg's reach. Just to make things just a little more complicated for the wing-threequarters. Stagg varied his position in the line out and probably did as much as anyone else to popularise the short-line out. Capped first for Scotland in 1965 against England and France, he went on to win 28 caps and also appeared in three of the Lions international games of 1968 in their tour of South Africa. Quite an impressive record but Peter Stagg, at 6' 10", will probably be remembered more for the fact that he is the tallest man ever to play in international rugby than for his great prowess in Scotland's second row.

11 NEW CAPS

During the 1967-1968 season, Scotland used 26 players with 11 new caps for their games against Ireland, France, England and Wales. But they were in the best of company that season. England used 28 players including 11 new caps, Ireland used 22 players with five new caps and Wales hit the jackpot with 30 players who included 13 new caps. Altogether that season 137 players took part in the championship, which stands as one of the game's unusual records in these islands.

UP AND UP—AND UP

Ian Smith from Dundee was playing with the London-Scottish thirds at the start of the 1968-1969 season and might have stayed there as an obscure full-back but for the fact that an injury to one of the players on the seconds gave him a chance of promotion. He was noticed then and was elevated further to the firsts and on the strength of a few sound displays, he was invited to play for Hampshire against Surrey on 12th November. And that was where the Scottish selectors saw him. What they saw impressed them for just ten days later he was in the Scottish side which faced South Africa in the international game at Murrayfield on Saturday, 6th December. And he left quite a mark on the game. South Africa were beaten and Scotland's six points in their 6-3 win all came from young Smith. Subsequently he was to win eight caps for Scotland at full-back between then and 1971.

ARGENTINA 1969

Scotland made a short tour to Argentina and discovered, like Ireland and Wales before them, that rugby in Argentina was not quite the "push-over" that most people had anticipated. They beat Argentina "C" by 19-9, beat the Interiro Union by 11-6, lost the unofficial international against the Pumas by 3-20, beat Rosario by 20-6, beat Argentina "B" by 9-5 and finally beat the Argentinians in the second unofficial international by 6-3.

ALL ALONE

Scotland's outstanding back row forward Nairn McEwan, who came on to the international side in 1971 and who had taken his international cap total to 16 at the end of the 1973-1974 season has, apart from his undoubted rugby talent, another tiny claim to fame in the annals of Scottish rugby history. It is hardly likely that any other Scottish international was born in . . . Dar-es-Salaam!

SCOTLAND IN AUSTRALIA

Having beaten England by 14-5 in the Calcutta Cup game at Murray-field on 21st March, 1970, Scotland took off at the end of the season for their second short overseas tour—this time to Australia for a six-match programme. And they opened it convincingly with a crushing win over Victoria by 34-0 at Melbourne on 20th May. Three days later, however, they went down 14-28 to New South Wales at Sydney. On 27th May, they beat New South Wales Country by 18-15 at Bathurst but again three days later they lost narrowly by 13-16 to Queensland at Brisbane. In their final warm-up game for the full international against Australia, they took on Sydney at Sydney on 3rd June and scored a decisive win by 27-12.

A FIRST FOR LAUDER

Wing-forward Wilson Lauder had the unique experience of winning his first international cap for Scotland in Australia in 1971, but, sadly for him and the rest of the Scottish side, it was not to be a memorable occasion. John Hipwell opened the scoring for the Wallabies with a try which Arthur McGill converted and Dick Batterham added another to put the Australians eight points up and then Lauder celebrated his new cap by kicking a penalty goal for Scotland. And that was to be Scotland's only score. The Australians added four more tries in the second half, two from John Cole and one each from Bob Rosenblum and Batterham and Arthur McGill ended the rout with a penalty goal. That 23-3 still remains as Scotland's worst defeat by the Australians. With the completion of this match, Scotland had played six, won three and lost three and had scored 109 points while conceding 72.

AFTER YOU, BROTHER

Of all the brothers who have played international rugby for Scotland since 1871, none have a more unusual claim to fame than the two Browns, Peter and Gordon of West of Scotland. Peter, who was first capped for his country in 1964, was named to play for Scotland against Wales at Cardiff Arms Park on Saturday, 7th February, 1970 and he duly turned out in a game that Wales won by 18-9. But he took a knock in this game was forced to retire . . . and, of course, a replacement had to come on. The reserve who trotted out on to the field to take over was none other than his younger brother Gordon. This case of a brother replacing a brother during the course of an international game is unique in the history of rugby.

THE EIGHTH HERIOT

Andy Irvine of Heriots FP made quite an impact on Saturday, 15th December, 1972 by kicking two penalty goals in his international debut for Scotland against the All-Blacks at Murrayfield, Edinburgh. And he also set quite an astonishing record for his club. He was, in fact, the eighth member of Heriots to play at full-back for Scotland. The other seven were Dan Drysdale with 26 caps between 1923-1929, J. M. Kerr with five caps between 1935-1937, T. Gray with three caps in 1950-1951 and I. H. M. Thompson with seven caps between 1951 and 1953, Ken Scotland, with 27 caps between 1957-1965, Colin Blaikie with eight caps between 1963-1969 and Ian Smith with eight caps between 1969-1971. At the end of the 1973-1974 season, Heriots eight Scotland full-backs had collected a total of 94 international caps between them.

ARGENTINA IN SCOTLAND

The 1973 Argentinian touring side, having lost two games in Ireland, drawn one and won one, completed their visit to Europe with four games in Scotland and wound up with the same tally of losing two, drawing one and winning one. But their game against a Scottish XV at Murrayfield on Saturday, 24th November, 1973 turned out to be quite an explosive affair, so much so that one newspaper the following morning carried the headline—"Too soon to Let the Pumas out of their Cage". The surprising feature was that most of the game was played in the happiest of spirits. The last five minutes however were little short of brutal and the Scottish hooker, Duncan Madsen, was kicked on the head and an ugly gash had to have three stitches. Fighting flared up and after the final whistle had gone, Gordon Brown, the Scottish second row forward on his way to the dressing room was chopped down from behind by one of the touring players. Subsequently the police suggested that there might be an inquiry into the affair but in the end it was allowed to peter out without any charges being preferred. Scotland, with three penalty goals from scrum-half D. W. Morgan won 12-11 with a late drop goal by Colin Telfer.

ON THE DEBIT SIDE

Scotland have played official international games against England, Ireland, Wales, France, Australia, New Zealand, South Africa, New South Wales and SRU President's XV. At the end of the 1973-1974 season, they had played 317 international games of which they have won 140, lost 155 and drawn 22.

IRELAND

THE IRISH START OFF

It is generally accepted that the game of rugby was introduced into Ireland by some English students who enrolled at Trinity College, Dublin prior to 1850.. The first indication that the game was thriving within the College came with an announcement in the Dublin *Daily Express* of Saturday, 1st December, 1855 that a match would be played that afternoon between the "original and new members of the club". It was signed by one Robert Henry Scott who is recorded in Trinity's rugby history as the secretary and treasurer of the football club between 1854 to 1856. However, it was not until November, 1874 that the Irish Football Union was formed and it was significant that Trinity were represented on the new Committee by five members—G. H. Stack, the brothers Robert and Edward Galbraith, A. P. Cronyn and H. D. Walsh. All five were to play in Ireland's first international game against England at Kennington Oval, London in 1875. Unfortunately for the new Irish Football Union, some of the Northern Ireland clubs were not too enamoured of it and in a certain pique, went ahead and formed the North of Ireland Union. In 1879, however, a happy end was reached and the unity was restored.

WHERE DID THEY GO?

Ireland's first expedition to London in 1875 to take on England in the first ever international rugby game was not quite the serious affair that the Irish Rugby Football Union would have liked. They named 20 men to play and included were H. B. Robinson, a native of London and W. B. "Darky" Smyth, both of whom were students in Dublin University at the time. But, despite the fact that their names appeared on the programmes, which were sold outside the Kennington Oval, inside the ground there was no sign of either Robinson or Smyth. They just did not show up for this historic game and thus lost the chance of playing for Ireland. Neither was ever invited again to play.

One of the theories put forward at the time was that Robinson availed himself of the trip to visit his family in London and took Smyth along with him for a leisurely week-end. Jacques McCarthy, the noted rugby historian of the time described Ireland's first international as; "Such an enterprise and such a twenty. The 20-a-side game was unknown in Ireland and some of the team did not turn up at all". What is not recorded are the names of the two players who played in place of Robinson and Smyth.

THE FIRST TOURIST

Wanderers' M. Barlow, who played in Ireland's pack in their first international rugby game against England in February, 1875, subsequently became Ireland's first tourist and the first Irishman to play against New Zealand. Sometime after winning his only cap for Ireland Barlow settled down in Australia and in 1882 was invited to tour with New South Wales in New Zealand. This was the first rugby tour of New Zealand. The New South Wales side played seven games against local sides and won four.

A TRIFLE SHORT-SIGHTED

R. B. Walkington of N.I.F.C., who played on the Irish team that met England in their first ever international against England at Kennington Oval, London in 1875 and later went on to win 10 caps for his country, was followed on to the Irish international side by his brother D. B. Walkington, also of N.I.F.C. And in his eight appearances for Ireland, he turned out to be every bit as good a full-back as his older brother. He must, however, go down in rugby history as one of the most unusual full-backs of all time. He was inclined to be a little short-sighted and on the occasions when he did not wear spectacles on the international field, he wore a monocle! And it is on record that on many occasions before taking a penalty kick, he would delay matters for perhaps a minute or so while he carefully cleaned and polished his monocle. Jacques McCarthy, the famous Irish rugby historian of the time, wrote of him; "He is as good as he can be on a bright day, but in the dark, his sight tells terribly against him. He has a magnificent kick into touch and very often drops goals as he did from full-back against Wales some years ago".

THE REMARKABLE MR GORDON

5th February, 1877 at the Kennington Oval, London, was a significant milestone in the history of rugby football. The teams involved were England and Ireland, the result was a victory for England by two goals and a try to nil and rugby's great historian, the Reverend F. Marshall records that it was a game that "was fast and brilliant from start to finish". What he did not record, however, was that this game also marked the debut for Ireland of one Thomas Gisborne Gordon, who appeared in the threequarter line. And the said Mr Gordon must surely be granted a special niche in the history of international football. Educated at Rugby School, where he first played the game, he then returned home to the North of Ireland where he joined N.I.F.A. and developed into one of the finest running backs of his time. He made his international debut against England in 1877 and also played in the next international against England in 1878, in which year he also won a third cap against Scotland. The astonishing feature of Thomas Gisborne Gordon was that at an early age, he had lost his right hand in a gun accident and played throughout his international career with only his left hand. Gordon, who subsequently won a second sporting fame in breeding horses and in horse racing, died in July, 1935.

THE FIRST TRY

When the nineteen-year old John Loftus Cuppaidge went up to Dublin University in 1875 to study medicine, he was, on the strength of a certain schoolboy sporting reputation at Rossall, invited to try his paces with the Trinity second side. The only trouble was that the selectors wanted him as a forward and the powerfully-built Cuppaidge fancied himself as a back. Young Cuppaidge won the argument. He played as a back on the Trinity seconds in 1875 and 1876 and eventually won promotion to the senior side in 1878 and 1879. However, when the Irish selectors picked him for the international game against England at the Kennington Oval on 24th March, 1879, they put him in the forwards. And he was still a forward when he made his second international appearance, again against England at Lansdowne Road on 30th January, 1880 and this was the day when he added a significant first to Irish rugby history. Midway through the first half, following a line-out near the English line, Cuppaidge took a pass from his captain,

H. C. Kelly, and crashed over for a try. It was Ireland's first try and also the first time that Ireland had gained any sort of a score in international rugby. Cuppaidge, who won his third and last cap that year against Scotland, went to Queensland after his graduation and, apart from a few years before the turn of the century when he practiced at Totnes in Devon, he remained in Australia until his death at the age of seventy-six in 1934.

SOMEWHAT UNSATISFACTORY

The proceedings at Lansdowne Road on 22nd January, 1882, must, to say the least of them, been somewhat unruly and possibly a little hilarious. Wales were in Dublin for the first time to play Ireland and what went on during the game surely set a pattern which, on more than one or two occasions, since then, has been carried on in memorable fashion. It would appear that the Irish team took grave exception at some of the rulings of the Welsh umpire, one Mr Richard Mullock, who at the time, was secretary of the Welsh Rugby Union and that plus the fact that Wales were administering some most unexpected punishment in the way of scoring, did not put the local heroes in a happy frame of mind. The match created one record in that Ireland finished with just eleven men, two having been carried off with injuries and the other two had stalked off the pitch in high dudgeon. The newspaper accounts of the game, using a commendable discretion, do not list the names of the four Irishmen who did not finish the game, but they are all in agreement that the entire affair was most unsatisfactory. The Irish Rugby Union were obviously in agreement. The fixture with Wales was forthwith discontinued and the next game between the two countries did not take place until 1884.

ENGLAND'S IRISHMAN

The first Irishman to share in a Triple Crown victory was Wilfred Nash Bolton—and the sad part of it from an Irish point of view was that he achieved it with England and in doing so scored against the country of his birth. Bolton, a wing-threequarter, who won 11 caps for England between 1882 and 1887, was later to become a major in the British Army in the Boer War and subsequently he settled down in

South Africa where he died in 1930. During the 1883-1884 season, he was on the three English teams which in turn defeated Wales, Ireland and Scotland to win the mythical Triple Crown for the first time. Against Wales, Bolton converted one of England's three tries, against Ireland he scored a try and he was prominently involved in the disputed try which gave England their win over Scotland in the final match of the season.

THE SWALLOW

Ernest H. Greene, who played for Dublin University and Wanderers and for Ireland was never known as anything else but "Swallow Green". The Irish 100 yards champion of 1885, he first came on to the Irish international rugby team in 1882 and won five caps over the next four seasons. Apart from being a glorious runner, Green had the most beautiful swerve on the football field and, sometime after Jacques McCarthy had written that Green reminded him of the flight of a swallow, the name stuck and to the end of his days—he died in November 1937 at the age of seventy-five—he was known ever after as the "Swallow Green".

ENGLISH TRIALIST

Victor le Fanu of Cambridge University and later of Lansdowne, was the first Irishman to play in the Cambridge v Oxford inter-Varsity match and on the strength of his outstanding displays in college games, he was invited to play in several trials for the England team. He did so but obviously the English selectors did not feel he was quite up to the standard they required. On his return to Ireland, le Fanu, the son of the famous novelist Sheridan le Fanu, threw in his lot with Lansdowne and with his 12 caps between 1886 and 1892, was to become one of the most memorable Irish internationals of his time.

A WORLD CHAMPION

One of the entertaining personalities of the Irish side which beat England in a rugby international for the first time at Lansdowne Road in February 1887 was Ned Walsh, who was to win seven caps for his country between 1886 and 1892. He could justifiably claim to be a champion of the world at the time. Having won the 120 yards hurdles championship of Ireland for two years he went to America in 1885 and during his visit there he challenged Malcolm Ford, then the reigning world's athletic all-round champion to a contest and defeated him decisively. Educated at Blackrock College, he subsequently became Accountant-General of the Supreme Court of Ireland and was seventy-five when he died in March 1939.

WIMBLEDON CHAMPION

F. O. Stoker of Wanderers, one of two brothers to play for Ireland between 1886 and 1891, had the distinction of playing in the Irish side against the first international tourists side, the New Zealand Native team, in 1888 but after his final international against Wales, he devoted himself to tennis. And with rewarding results. In partnership with J. Pim in 1890 they were declared Wimbledon Doubles champions when the Renshaw brothers did not defend their title, but they came back in 1893 to take the title after a challenge, against the reigning champions H. S. Barlow and E. W. Lewis.

THREE BY FOUR

The record number of tries by an Irish player in one international game is three and this is shared by four men. The first to achieve three tries was R. Montgomery (N.I.F.C. and Cambridge University) in Ireland's game against Wales on 12th March, 1887. In a bid to reduce travelling expenses, it was agreed to play this international at the neutral venue of Birkenhead and although Ireland scored three tries to Wales's try and a drop goal, the result was a victory for Wales. Under the present day scoring values Ireland would have won by 12-7 but in 1887 a goal of any kind was equal to three tries. The second man to get three tries for Ireland in an international game was J. P. Quinn (Dublin University) in Ireland's 24-0 win over France at Cork in 1913. Eugene Davy (Lansdowne) got three tries in Ireland's 14-11 win over Scotland at Murrayfield in 1930 and Seamus Byrne (U.C.D. and Lansdowne) became the fourth to do so against Scotland at Murrayfield in 1953.

THE DAY HE MISSED

Joseph B. Allison was just eighteen and a half when he played international rugby for Ireland in 1888-1889 and remains as Ireland's youngest man to win a Triple Crown. Unfortunately having played against England in the first match of that season, he was unable to turn out for the second against Wales. At the time he was suffering from . . . mumps! Allison, eventually to win 12 caps for Ireland, was educated at Campbell College, Belfast but, in fact, at the time of his first international appearance he was a first-year student at Edinburgh University. With that first cap he turned the Edinburgh University back division into an all-international one. The full back A. Duncan, and the other three in the threequarter-line, W. H. Welsh, A. B. Timmins and A. N. Fell were all Scottish internationals.

THE ACCUSED

It had been a good game and a good day at Lansdowne Road on Saturday, 1st March, 1890 and both the Irish and the Welsh players were happy with the result. A magnificent game had ended in the first draw between the two countries. R. Dunlop, Trinity's wing-threequarter scored an early try for Ireland which Roche of Wanderers converted and shortly before time Thomas went over for a try for Wales which Bancroft converted. A fair result and the celebrations which began subsequently in one of Dublin's better-known hotels of the time were fast, furious and lengthy. Late that night, however, as a group of Irish and Welsh players were heading on towards a party, their singing and indeed their general behaviour, brought them to the notice of the local constabulary, who, apparently, had neither heard of the result of the game nor were interested in the noble game of rugby. The upshot was that nine members of the group were led away gently but firmly to the local police station on the south side of the Liffey, duly summonsed and told to report to the Dublin district court on the following Monday morning. The judge, however, must have had a little leaning towards rugby. The offending gentlemen were given a nominal fine each, gently reprimanded and that was that.

THE FIRST DROP

The international game between Ireland and Wales at Stradey Parl, Llanelli on Saturday, 7th March, 1891 was not an affair that brought any lasting joy to the 10,000 people who came along to see a dour and somewhat dreary battle. But at least it did provide a "first" for Ireland. Full-back D. B. Walkington of N.I.F.C., with Ireland being outplayed, took a pass just inside the Welsh half and tried for a pot at goal. Much to everyone's astonishment on a dark and muddy day, it went straight between the posts and gave the said Mr Walkington, the first of two brothers to play for Ireland, the honour of dropping Ireland's first goal in international rugby.

THE TRIPLE CROWN LEADERS

E. G. Forrest (Wanderers) captained Ireland to their first Triple Crown victory of 1894 by beating Wales by a penalty goal to nil at Ballynafeigh, Belfast on Saturday, 10th March, 1894, and Louis Magee (Bective Rangers) was the captain when Ireland took the Crown for the second time by beating Wales in the final game at Cardiff Arms Park on Saturday, 18th March, 1899. The third Triple Crown captain was Karl Mullen of Old Belvedere, who led Ireland to the vital win by 6-3 at Ravenhill, Belfast on Saturday, 13th March, 1948 and he was the leader again the following year when Ireland took the Triple Crown for the fourth and last time with a win by 5-0 over Wales at St Helen's, Swansea, on 12th March, 1949.

A LYTLE EFFORT

With 25 minutes gone in the first half of Ireland's final match of the season at Ballynafeigh, Belfast on March 10, 1894, the Welsh forwards were penalised for offside. Without the slightest hesitation, Ireland's captain E. G. Forrest (Wanderers) singled out John Lytle (N.I.F.C.) to try for a shot at goal. Under the appalling conditions that afternoon, Ballynafeigh, never the best of grounds, was at its worst and with a hailstorm sweeping over the pitch, Lytle's hopes of landing a goal from 40 yards out looked remote. But Lytle, one of the strongest men in Ireland's pack, pulled out the most memorable kick of his career and with a mighty effort he sent the ball soaring between the posts. As it transpired this was the only score of the game—and it brought Ireland the Triple Crown for the first time. Furthermore it gave Lytle the proud distinction of having scored in all of Ireland's Triple Crown game wins that season. Against England at Blackheath he had scored a try in Ireland's 6-5 win and against Scotland at Lansdowne Road he had converted the try by C. M. Wells (Bective). Ireland have now won the Triple Crown on four occasions—1894, 1899, 1948, 1949.

A SHORT CAREER

Michael Gilbert Delaney of Blackrock College and Bective Rangers had an international rugby career with Ireland that lasted for less than half an hour. Chosen to play in the centre for Ireland against Wales at Cardiff Arms Park, on 16th March, 1895, the general opinion that the twenty-two-year old Gilbert had a glittering international life ahead of him. Unfortunately he was taken down in a hard tackle by the Welsh defence within the first 30 minutes and carried off with a fractured leg and a broken collar bone. He was never again to play rugby at any level. Subsequently he became one of Ireland's best-known club referees and was active up to just a few years before his death in 1938.

IN TWO CENTURIES

The three Doran brothers of Lansdowne, Eddie, Gerry and Bertie, were all capped for Ireland between 1890 and 1904 and Gerry and Bertie managed to achieve a distinction that is unique in the family history of rugby. Against Wales at Cardiff Arms Park on Saturday, 18th March, 1899 Gerry Doran scored the try that brought Ireland their second Triple Crown. On Saturday, 23rd February, 1901, Bertie scored a try against Scotland at Inverleith and although it was converted it did not help Ireland very much in their 5-9 defeat. But, at least it gave the Doran family, a very special place in the story of Ireland's rugby. They are the only brothers to have scored in two centuries!

THE SECOND CROWN

Despite the fact that Ireland got their 1898-1899 season off to a good start by beating England at Lansdowne Road by 6-0 with a try from G. G. Allen of Derry and a penalty goal by John Fulton of N.I.F.C., the Irish selectors made sweeping changes for the second game at

Inverleith against Scotland. Four old caps were restored to favour and one of the four new men to be capped was one G. P. "Blucher" Doran of the Lansdowne Club. And he was to play a major role in Ireland's rugby story that year. The Scots were duly beaten by 9-3 with the Irish tries coming from Edward Campbell of Monkstown, Charles Reid of N.I.F.C. and John Sealy. Then it was on to Cardiff Arms Park to take on Wales. And that turned out to be quite a game. A record crowd turned up, broke through the railings and spilled on to the pitch before the kick-off. The spectators were eventually pushed back and the game began fifteen minutes late. And the first memorable feature of the game was a tackle on W. J. Bancroft by Jack Ryan of Rockwell. Bancroft, the prince of Welsh full-backs in those days had never missed a match for his country up to then but this was one he was destined not to finish. Ryan tossed him into the crowd and his injuries prevented him from taking any further interest in the proceedings. Then just before half time G. P. Doran went charging in for a try and as it turned out it was to be the only score of the game. With his score Ireland had won the Triple Crown for the second time. It was to be 49 years before they won it again.

AN OLYMPIC MEDAL

James Cecil Parke, born at Clones, Co. Monaghan on 26th July, 1881 was one of the most versatile sportsmen of his time. He won his first trophy, a challenge cup at the Clones tennis club in 1900 and between then and the outbreak of the first World War he pursued an astonishing sporting career that took him all over the world. He was a scratch golfer, an Olympic silver medal winner at London in 1908 in tennis, champion of Europe, Australasia, England and Ireland in tennis, a member of a winning Davis Cup side, a magnificent track and field athlete—and he won 20 international rugby caps for Ireland! He captained Ireland on three occasions and collected his 20 caps against England, Scotland, Wales, France, New Zealand and South Africa over a period of six years. At the end of the 1909 season, however, he decided to quit rugby completely so that he could concentrate on tennis. Parke went on to win the Irish Singles Chapimonship in 1910, 1911, 1912, 1913 and also shared in the Doubles and Mixed Doubles on five occasions. He also won the Singles Championship of Europe, shared in the all-England Mixed Doubles in 1910, 1912 and 1913 and in 1912, also won the Australian Singles title. In international tennis, he represented Ireland against England in 1912 and 1913 and then represented England against America, France, Belgium and Australia and played for Britain in the Davis Cup against America and Australasia and appeared on two winning sides. His Olympic career was brief. He won a silver medal in the Doubles in 1908 but passed up the 1912 Olympics in Stockholm so that he could go on a tour of Australia with a British team. He scored his only try for Ireland against Scotland in a 6-13 defeat at Lansdowne Road, Dublin in 1906.

A LITTLE CONSOLATION

Ireland went down by 0-15 to New Zealand in the first game between the two countries at Lansdowne Road, Dublin on 25th November, 1905 but there was just a little consolation for them in the fact that Dave Gallaher, the captain of the tourists, was an Irishman from Belfast and that Billy Wallace, who converted the three All-Blacks tries at Lansdowne Road was the son of an Irishman. Indeed, Wallace's big regret that day was that his grandfather was then too old to travel down from Derry for the game in Dublin. New Zealand's tries were scored by R. G. Deans and A. McDonald. At Limerick on the following Tuesday, 28th November, the All-Blacks played Munster in their 23rd game of the tour and won by 33 points to nil. This gave Basil MacLear, the Irish wing-threequarter, a record of having played four times against the All-Blacks that season. Earlier he had played for Blackheath and Bedford and in all four games not a score had been registered against the tourists.

KID GLOVE STUFF

It is doubtful if international rugby has ever thrown up anyone quite so fastidious as Basil Maclear—the British Army officer who played for Ireland on 11 occasions between 1905 and 1907. Maclear, an Englishman from Bedford, who on one famous occasion converted 12 tries in a club game for Bedford, was given several trials by the England selectors but they promptly forgot about him when he was posted on Army duty to Ireland. Maclear went first to Cork, where he played with Cork County and later he was a member of the Monkstown

Club in Dublin. After a few club games he was quickly snapped up by the Irish selectors who gave him his chance against his native country at Cork in 1905 and he repaid their faith in him with a splendid try in a 17-3 victory. A year later he got his second try of international rugby and again it was against England who went down by 6-16 to the Irish. MacLear also scored a try against Wales that season and collected his fourth and final try for Ireland against the South Africans in Belfast. The intriguing feature of Maclear, who was to be killed in the First World War was that he always wore white kid gloves while playing rugby. For international games he always insisted on two pairs so that he could make a change at half-time!

THE FINAL HURDLE

Ireland's hopes of a Triple Crown in 1905 were pinned solidly on their two wing-threequarters, the elegant Basil Maclear, then playing with Monkstown and the powerfully-built and hard-running J. E. Moffatt of Old Wesley. They had been at their best in a rout of England at Cork where Moffatt had scored two tries and Maclear one in a 17-3 win. Then against Scotland at Inverleith, Edinburgh, Moffatt had opened the scoring with a magnificent try and sparked Ireland off to an 11-5 win. Now just Wales at St Helen's, Swansea, on Saturday, 11th March, 1905, stood between Ireland and the Triple Crown. But Wales had also beaten England and Scotland and for the first time Ireland and Wales were meeting with both sides in line for the Triple Crown. For this game Maclear was moved into the centre in a switch with Harry Thrift of Trinity but it was all to no good. The Welsh singled out both Maclear and Moffatt and both were remorselessly policed and tackled out of the game. Ireland went down by 3-10 with the only Irish try coming from outhalf T. H. Robinson of Trinity. It was the first time that Wales had robbed Ireland of the Triple Crown. Unfortunately it was to be the first of many.

THE FIRST SCORE

Ireland went down to South Africa in the first international between the two countries at Ravenhill, Belfast on Saturday, 24th November, 1906, but in doing so they set a record which to this day has yet to be equalled by England, Scotland, Wales or France during a Springbok tour to this part of the world. They scored 12 points, three tries and a penalty goal, which remains as the highest international score put up against South Africa during a tour of Britain, Ireland and France. Scrum-half D. C. Jackson put South Africa into the lead with a penalty goal and Sugars levelled the scores with a try. The South Africans moved into a half-time 12-3 lead with two tries from J. A. Loubser and a third from centre threequarter Japie Krige. In the second half Cecil Parke kicked a penalty goal for Ireland, Sugars had a second try and then Basil Maclear went over for a try to make it 12-12. Just on time wing-threequarter A. C. Stegmann scored the winning try for South Africa. Since then, the highest score put up against the South Africans in an international game during a tour of Britain, Ireland and France is 11 points by England in 1969-70. France also scored 11 points against the South Africans during the Springboks short tour of France in 1968.

TWO AGAINST SOUTH AFRICA

Harry Sugars of Dublin University was to win only three international caps for Ireland, against the touring New Zealand side of 1905-1906 and against Scotland and the touring South Africans of 1906-1907. But in that short space of time, he achieved a distinction that no Irish international player has since managed to equal. Against the South Africans at Belfast in 1908, when Ireland went down 12-15, he scored two tries and remains as the only Irish international to do so against the Springboks. And he is in an exclusive company for only four players in the long history of rugby have managed to get more than one try against the Springboks in an international game between two nations. The other three to do so were J. L. Sullivan of New Zealand in 1937, Ian Smith of New Zealand in 1965 and Benoit Dauga of France in 1968.

THOMPSON'S TWO TRIES

By the time they had assembled all their players in Paris and had then set off for Dublin by coach, rail and sea, it took the French over five days to arrive in Dublin for their match against Ireland at Lansdowne

Road in 1909. They complained of fatigue before the game and they complained of even more when the final whistle was blown. It had not been a profitable trip. Charles Thompson the wing threequarter from Belfast Collegians struck the first blow for Ireland with a try, John O'Connor of Garryowen added a second and Frank Gardiner had a third before Thompson went in for his second. G. J. Henebry, one of three Garryowen men on the Irish side kicked a penalty goal and also converted two of the tries and Ireland eventually romped to a 19-8 victory. This game marked the first visit of France to Ireland, the first international game between the two countries and by the end of the 1973-1974 season Ireland had completed 23 wins to France's 21, with three drawn in their 47 meetings.

THE LAST STRAW

Dr Tom Smyth, who had led the Lions on the tour of South Africa the previous year, got Ireland off to a promising start in the 1910-1911 season with the only try of a 3-0 win over England at Lansdowne Road. Then in a shock result at Inverleith, with tries coming from C. T. O'Callaghan (Old Merchant Taylors), A. R. Foster (Queen's), C. Adams (Old Wesley), and J. P. Quinn (Trinity), Ireland ran rings around a strong Scottish side to win by 16-10 with all of the Scottish scores coming in the final 10 minutes. So once again Ireland were in the hunt for the Triple Crown and once again they had to travel to Cardiff Arms Park to face Wales on Saturday, 11th March, 1911. Sadly it was never a close battle. Ireland gambled on seven forwards and eight backs, with S. B. Campbell (Derry) being taken out of the pack to play as an extra back—and the outcome was disastrous. Wales, without the slightest trouble, romped away to a 16-0 win.

AN UNEXPECTED CAP

With 18 international caps under his belt since 1900, Lansdowne's Jack Coffey, surely one of the lightest forwards to play for Ireland—he rarely weighed in at more than 10st 6 lbs!—decided it was time to retire at the end of the 1907-1908 season. And for almost two years he thoroughly enjoyed himself as a spectator. Then, in somewhat dramatic fashion, he became a player again and in the process collected a most unexpected 19th international cap. In 1910 he decided to treat himself to a week-end in Paris for Ireland's match against France at Parc des Princes and travelled with the official Irish party. On the Saturday when he arrived at the ground and made his way to the Irish dressing room to wish the team luck, he found the selectors with a major problem on their hands. One of the Irish players had reported ill and there was no substitute available. Coffey's appearance in the dressing room provided the happy solution. After all, he had been out of rugby for only two years and he was still extremely fit. Furthermore he was the only Irishman available! It took a little persuasion but in the end he agreed. He duly togged out in borrowed kit—and the team picture for that game shows that he was the only man of the Irish fifteen whose jersey did not carry the official shamrock emblem—and, by all accounts, he played a noble role in Ireland's win by a goal and two tries to two tries. This game gave Coffey the distinction of having won his 19 caps against six countries—England, Scotland, Wales, New Zealand, South Africa and France. Two years later he became an Irish selector, an honour which was also accorded to his son, another Jack Coffey, in 1964.

THE ONE HE DIDN'T PLAY

Dickie Lloyd, the Dublin University and later Liverpool out-half, was one of the durable Irish internationals to span the years of the first World War. He won 17 international caps for Ireland between 1910 and 1914 and then came back after the War to add another two against England and France. But although Lloyd won 19 caps, he appears in 20 pictures of Ireland's international sides! At Belfast in 1914, he togged out for the game against Wales and then went out to have his picture taken with the rest of the Irish side. A few minutes later, however, he was back in the dressing room and out of the game. In the run around before the start of the game he broke down with a muscle injury and had to be assisted from the field. His place went to H. W. Jack (University College, Cork) who went into the game as scrum-half with Victor McNamara, his club-mate, who took over at out-half.

DEAD ON THE DROP

Ireland's scrum-half Harry Read, who was to partner his Trinity out-half Dickie Lloyd in most of their international appearances from 1910-1914, claimed that the diminutive Lloyd was the greatest expert in kicking of the particular era. And he was probably right. In the 1911-1912 season for Trinity Lloyd dropped a goal in every club game from October to Christmas and, in fact, dropped two within five minutes against Cambridge in the inter-Varsity match at Cambridge. Lloyd carried that prowess into the international field as well. In his 19 appearances for Ireland he scored a total of 27 points and 24 of these came from drop goals which at the time were valued at four points. He kicked two against England in 1913 and 1914, one against Scotland in 1912, another against Wales in 1912 and two against France in 1911 and 1920. His total of six drop goals is still a record by an Irish international.

BUT HE PLAYED!

Trinity's scrum-half Harry Read, who won 13 international caps for Ireland, did not feel well on the morning of the game against Wales at Balmoral, Belfast in 1912 and his first reaction was to cry off the side. Unfortunately there was no substitute available and after a long chat with his club-mate and Irish captain, Dickie Lloyd, he agreed, albeit a little reluctantly, to turn out. According to the newspaper accounts of the game he played magnificently and his superb understanding with Lloyd was the major contributing factor to Ireland's great win by 12-5. Within 24 hours, however, Read was delirious and promptly whipped away to hospital where it was diagnosed that he had played against Wales . . . with measles!

AN UNHAPPY DAY

Ireland, who had shared the 1911-1912 International Championship with England, were given more than a fair chance of upsetting the South African touring side at Lansdowne Road on Saturday, 30th November, 1912. A week earlier at Inverleith, with two tries coming late in the game, the South Africans had not been particularly impressive in beating Scotland by 16-0. Ireland, on the other hand, were in the happy position of being able to call on most of the men, including their great half-back partnership of Harry Read and Dickie Lloyd, who had taken them to convincing victories over Scotland, Wales and France during the previous season. But it turned out to be a sad unhappy day for Ireland. Within a matter of minutes, the South African wing-threequarter J. A. Stegmann went over for an easy try and this was followed by another from the other wing-threequarter E. E. McHardy. From there on, it was all one-way traffic, with the Springboks piling on score after score. Stegmann and McHardy each wound up with three tries, an individual try-scoring record for a South African in an international game, which has since been equalled by only two other Springboks—Tom van Vollenhoven (1955) and Hennie van Zyl (1961). In all, the South Africans scored 10 tries, four of which were converted, to leave the final score 38-0. It was and still is Ireland's worst defeat in an international game.

TEN OF THE BEST

During the 1912-1913 club season in Ireland, Dublin University were in the extraordinary and happy position of being able to field 10 Irish internationals on their side and it probably goes without saying that they were the Leinster Senior Cup champions in both 1912 and 1913. Dickie Lloyd and Harry Read were the half-backs, A. W. P. Todd was full-back, C. B. V. MacIvor, G. W. Holmes, G. H. Wood and J. P. Quinn were in the threequarter line and F. G. Schute, R. B. Burgess and Robin Hemple were in the pack. All at one time or another had turned out for Ireland.

AGAINST FRANCE

Ireland travelled down to Cork in 1913 to take on France in the fifth meeting between the two countries and came away with a win by three goals and three tries to nil. This 24-0 win, or 30-0 by modern values, is Ireland's most decisive margin of victory over the French. Ireland have now played France on 47 occasions and have won 23, lost 21, drawn three and, by present-day scoring values have scored 459 points in the 47 games. Ireland's longest unbeaten record against France is six—from the first win in Lansdowne Road in 1909 until France won at the same place in 1920 and again from the win at Lansdowne Road in 1924 until France won at Belfast in 1930.

A HARSH DEBUT

There could hardly have been a more searing baptism of international fire for the young centre-threequarter from Queen's University than that afternoon against France at Lansdowne Road in 1920. Just a year earlier he had been playing on Queen's University third team but by the end of the 1918-1919 season he had improved sufficiently to make the first side. Now with Ireland crashing to successive defeats in the 1920 season, he had been drafted into the Irish side. His debut was not spectacular but then neither was Ireland's performance that afternoon. They crashed to their first defeat by France in international rugby and Ireland's rugby stock was at its lowest for years. But the Irish selectors had faith in the youngster from Queen's and George Stephenson was again selected for Ireland the following year. He went on, of course, to become one of the greatest personalities of international rugby and in 1930 when he finally put away his boots, he had become the most capped international in the world with 42 appearances for Ireland. His record was to stand for 27 years until it was overtaken by Wales's Olympic sprinter Ken Jones and it remained as an Irish record until Jack Kyle equalled it in 1958 and then went on to leave the record at 46.

THE STEPHENSON BROTHERS

George Stephenson, who was to set a world record of 42 caps between 1920 and 1930 was joined on Ireland's team against Scotland in 1922 by his brother Harry and together that season they played in three matches. In 1924 they came together for four games and a year later they played five together in the four championship games and the outing against Cliff Porter's New Zealanders. Only twice after that were they to play again together on an Irish side and that was in 1928 against England and New South Wales. In all, they played together on 14 Irish international sides—a record for brothers in Irish international rugby.

ALL FOUR DOWN

Losing all three games in the one international season happened for the first time for Ireland in 1884 when they went down by a goal to nil against England in Dublin, lost by two goals and two tries to a try against Scotland at Edinburgh and tumbled to Wales by a goal and two tries to nil at Cardiff. But 1920 was to bring an even more chastening experience when Ireland for the first time crashed to defeat in all four games and it was all the more bitter by reason of the fact that the final defeat came from France, the last to join in on the International Championship and who at the time were looked on as the poverty-stricken relations of international rugby. Ireland went down by 11-14 to England at Lansdowne Road, took severe punishment from Scotland at Edinburgh with an 0-19 defeat, had salt rubbed into their wounds by taking a hammering at Cardiff Arms Park by 4-28 and the final blow was losing to France 7-15 at Lansdowne Road. Ireland scored 22 points that season and had 76 scored against them, a sad record which remains to the present day.

OLYMPIC GOLD

Noel Mary Purcell, a Dublin solicitor, capped four times in 1921 against England, Scotland, Wales and France, is the only Irish rugby international to win an Olympic gold medal. In 1920, at the Antwerp Games, he played on the British waterpolo team which defeated Belgium in the Olympic final. Purcell, who was also capped for Ireland at waterpolo in 1910, subsequently became the first man to represent two countries in the Olympic Games. Having played for Britain in 1920, he played for the newly independent Irish Free State at the Paris Games in 1924. Because of this, he was responsible for a major change in the rules of the Olympic Games.

A FAMILY TRY

Ireland beat Wales in Wales for the first time in 25 years at Cardiff Arms Park on 8th March, 1924 and it was a tight shave, by 13-10. Tom Hewitt gave Ireland the lead with a try which Ernie Crawford converted but Cliff Richards and Charlie Pugh came back with tries to take the lead at 6-5. Ireland went ahead again with a try from George Stephenson which Crawford converted and Charlie Pugh promptly dropped a goal for Wales to level affairs. But Ireland came through with yet another try, this time from Frank Hewitt, making his debut for Ireland that afternoon. And those two tries from Tom and Frank Hewitt added up to another celebration and a record for Ireland. It was the first time that two brothers had scored tries for Ireland in the same international game.

THE SCHOOLBOY INTERNATIONALS

In Ireland's 100 years of international rugby, there have been at least five schoolboy internationals and of these the youngest is Frank Hewitt who was seventeen years, five months and five days when he made his debut against Wales at Cardiff Arms Park on Saturday, 8th March, 1924. He had already been a reserve that season for both the games against France and Scotland. Just slightly older at seventeen years and six months was Johnny Quirke, who was still at Blackrock College when he won the first of his three caps in 1962. The others were G. McAllan of Dungannon High School who was capped in 1896, Aidan Bailey, who was eighteen years, two months and five days and was still at Presentation College, Bray when he was first capped in 1934 and F. M. W. Harvey of Ellesmere College, Salop, who was eighteen years and seven months when he was first capped in 1907. And Harvey, of course, was later to win the Victoria Cross in the First World War. J. B. Allison was still at Campbell College, Belfast and was aged eighteen years and eight months, when he made his first appearance for Ireland in 1899.

THE IRISH SPRINGBOK

Queen's University wing-threequarter, J. H. Gage, had the honour of scoring Ireland's first try at Murrayfield, Edinburgh in 1926. This was Ireland's first visit to the ground which had been opened the previous year and his try was the only score of the game. Gage, who was capped four times for Ireland, against Scotland and Wales in 1926 and against the same two countries in 1927, has, however, an even greater claim to distinction in the history of Irish rugby. He collected a fifth international cap with the Springboks! Following his graduation from Queen's University, he went to live in South Africa, where he continued to play rugby for the Orange Free State. He figured in the trials for the Springbok tour of Britain and Ireland in 1931 but failed to win selection. Two years later he was capped for South Africa against Australia and is, of course, the only Irishman to represent two countries in international rugby.

WALES AGAIN!

After a lapse of 15 years Ireland were back in line for a Triple Crown in 1926 and they looked to have the team to win it. Ernie Crawford, at full-back, was the captain, Denis Cussen, the Irish and Olympic sprint star was on one wing and J. H. Gage, the only man to represent both Ireland and South Africa in international rugby was on the other. In between them were George Stephenson and Tom Hewitt and at half-back there was the solid and spectacular partnership of Eugene Davy and Mark Sugden. And the pack had men like Jammie Clinch, "Horsey" Browne, M. J. Bradley, Jim McVicker, Jimmy Farrell and Charlie Hanrahan. Before they took on Wales at St Helen's, Swansea on Saturday, 13th March, 1926, they had beaten England by 19-15 at Lansdowne Road and had just pipped Scotland at Edinburgh by a try to nil. But Ireland were really out of luck against Wales. With just 30 seconds left on the watch, Wales were ahead by 11-8, having come back from being 3-8 down at half-time. Charlie Hanrahan had opened the scoring with a try which George Stephenson converted. Wales, with tries from Harding and Hopkins, one converted by Tommy Rees, then moved to an 8-5 lead but Stephenson with a penalty goal had levelled the scores. Ron Herrera, the Welsh prop-forward, then went in for a try and Wales held their lead almost to the full whistle. But with time running out Tom Hewitt snapped up a pass from Eugene Davy and tried for a drop at goal. The ball rose magnificently, headed straight for the posts but at the last moment the wind caught it and the ball just shaved the posts on the wrong side. This was the third time that Wales had foiled Ireland in a Triple Crown bid.

THE MURRAYS

Between them the Murray family provided internationals in four sports! Paul F. Murray began his international rugby career against

France in 1927 and went on to win 19 caps in somewhat versatile fashion. Seven of them were won at centre threequarter, six at out-half and six at scrum-half! Paul's wife Rachel represented Ireland in international golf in 1952 and their son John was later to follow his father on to Ireland's rugby team with his appearance against France in 1963 and he then, of course, went on to become one of Ireland's top internationals in tennis. And there was his sister Oonagh. She played on Ireland's international hockey team in 1965!

THAT ONE KICK

No one who watched Ireland's international campaign of 1927-1928 will forget the name of James Vere Richardson in a hurry. In one split second and with less than a minute to go in England's international game with Ireland at Lansdowne Road on Saturday, 20th January, 1928, he destroyed Ireland's Triple Crown and Grand Slam hopes for that year. Ireland were later to go on to beat Scotland and Wales and France but in that split second in Dublin Vere Richardson, who won five caps for his country, wrecked what would have been a great record for that year. Time was almost out, the referee had already consulted his watch and with Ireland in a 6-3 lead, it seemed as though nothing could catch them. Then Richardson, who had not been prominent at wing-threequarter, snapped up a stray ball almost 35 yards out and seeing that his path to the line was well defended, he elected to try for a pot at goal. His drop was spot on, sailing dead and true between the posts and a certain victory a second before had been turned into a depressing 6-7 defeat at the final whistle. While it was not a memorable afternoon for Ireland, at least it provided a moment to remember for Vere Richardson. He had never dropped a goal before in his career—and he never did again.

VICTORY IN LONDON

Back in 1910 Ireland had met England for the first time at Twickenham and the game had ended in a scoreless draw. Nineteen years later Ireland were still trying to improve on that performance at Twickenham and the great day finally arrived on Saturday, 9th February, 1929. Led by George Stephenson, then making his ninth successive appearance against England, the Irish got away to a striking start with a try from Eugene Davy within two minutes and Stephenson with a soaring kick from close to the touchline just missed the conversion by inches. The English came back strongly and with a try from Bob Smeddle which Guy Wilson converted, they led 5-3 at the break. Midway through the second half and it was a moment of irony for the English, Mark Sugden broke away and with a dazzling run, shot over for a try and Ireland were 6-5 ahead with a try from an English born player. It was Ireland's first victory at Twickenham and they were to repeat it two years later with an identical score, 6-5. And in 1931, with a second win over Scotland at Lansdowne Road, 8-5, Ireland were chasing the Triple Crown again. Unfortunately they were never in with a chance, despite the fact that the deciding game was in Ireland for a change—at Ravenhill, Belfast. Ireland lost Morgan Crowe early on, and Eugene Davy was concussed for most of the proceedings and in the end Wales eased away to a 15-3 win. It was the fifth time that Wales had halted Ireland at the last hurdle to the Triple Crown.

JACK ARIGHO'S NO-TRY

Ireland had beaten England 6-5 at Twickenham in 1929 and the crowd that turned up to see the Irish take on the Scots at Lansdowne Road on Saturday, 18th February, that year was unprecedented. The spectators barged their way into the ground, spilled out on to the sidelines and eventually on to the field. And this was the afternoon that Ireland's wing-threequarter Jack Arigho went shooting through the Scottish defences for a certain try and then found himself with a wall of spectators between him and the Scottish line. He grounded the ball in front of the spectators but the referee Mr B. S. Cumberlege disallowed it. He subsequently stopped the game and refused to continue until the offending spectators moved back. In the end Scotland went on to win by 16-7 but how different it all might have been had Arigho been able to get around the wall of spectators to ground the ball behind them and over the Scottish line.

STEPHENSON BOWS OUT

Ireland's bid for the Triple Crown in 1930 began with a drop goal by Eugene Davy—and it ended with another drop goal by Eugene Davy. He beat England by 4-0 at Lansdowne Road and then Ireland went off to Murrayfield and pipped the Scots with a 14-11 win. But Wales once again were there to put the damper on what would have been a magnificent farewell for Ireland's captain George Stephenson. They met on Saturday, 8th March, 1930 at St Helen's, Swansea, and with a penalty goal from Eugene Davy and a drop goal from Davy, Ireland took a 7-6 lead early in the second half, but it was not to last for long. Jack Bassett kicked a penalty goal for Wales and Tom Arthur sealed the afternoon with a late try for a 12-7 win. When it was all over George Stephenson walked off an international field for the last time. It was his 42nd and final appearance for Ireland and his number of caps was then a world record that was to last as an Irish record until the great years of Jack Kyle in the 1950s. Stephenson had made 10 successive international appearances against England, 10 successive appearances against Wales and 11 successive appearances against France. He had played eight times in succession against Scotland but missed out on the 1929 match because of injury but came back for the 1930 game. His other two international caps were against New Zealand and New South Wales. In all he made 36 consecutive appearances for Ireland until he had to drop out of the game against Scotland in 1929—and this too, was a world record at the time.

WAIDE'S HOUR OF GLORY

Wales had beaten England 12-5 at Cardiff Arms Park and had chalked up another win by 6-0 against Scotland at Murrayfield. Only Ireland stood between them and an eighth Triple Crown. They were to meet at Cardiff in 1932 and the game brought in a capacity crowd who had plenty to cheer about as Wales dominated the proceedings for most of the way, and led by 7-3 at half-time—a try and a drop goal to a try. The Welshmen got over for another try and moved to 10-3 and then the Irish in a sudden burst came fighting back to get two tries and with just minutes to go the Welsh were hanging on to their 10-9 lead. But the Irish had run out of steam and the Welshmen were camped deep in the Irish "25" and looked certain to crack the now desperate Irish defence. Wales attacked strongly and Ireland's full-back Ernie Ridgeway was driven back over his own line. He miskicked and his weak effort went heading straight for the waiting arms of the Welsh threequarter J. C. Morley of Newport, who had the Irish line at his mercy and less than 10 yards to run in. But as he reached out to take the catch, the wind that had marred the game, suddenly swung the ball just a few feet away from him and into the arms of Ireland's wing-threequarter S. L. Waide who had been heading across in his bid to bustle Morley. Waide paused for a split second in astonishment and then, seizing this gift of the wind he ran for the Welsh line and made it all the way to collapse gratefully at the corner flag. It was Ireland's fourth try and Wales's dreams of that eighth Triple Crown had disappeared on the wind.

A GIFT FROM THE BLUE

If Dermot Morris had chosen to walk through a wicket gate to retrieve a ball during Ireland's pre-match practice for the international game against Scotland in 1932, Ernie Ridgeway of Wanderers might never have won a cap for Ireland. Morris, however, decided to vault over the railing and in doing so rapped his knee on it so badly that he was ruled out of the side. A telegram to Dublin to Ridgeway was first treated as a joke by the Wanderers full-back but once he was persuaded that the request was genuine he travelled by boat from Dublin to Glasgow which left him with a train journey to Edinburgh and just a scant few hours to prepare for his debut. He played a noble role in Ireland's win, was retained against Wales when another good win was recorded and eventually ended his international career with five caps. Morris recovered and won six caps for Ireland before he ended with his game against the touring New Zealanders of 1935-1936.

THE FIRST SCORE

Apart from being one of the youngest players to represent his country, Aidan Bailey, winner of 13 caps for Ireland between 1934 and 1938, had the distinction of getting Ireland's first score against a New Zealand international side. On 7th December, 1935, with the All-Blacks leading by 8-0 after 15 minutes, Bailey kicked a penalty goal. Shortly before half-time Charles Beamish, winner of 12 caps and brother of George Beamish who played on 25 occasions for Ireland, scored the first Irish try in an international game against New Zealand. Prior to this, in their two international games against New Zealand in 1905-1906 and 1924-1925, Ireland had failed to score and before the 1935 game the tally against them was 17 points. In their six games against New Zealand to date, Ireland have lost five, drawn 1, have scored 27 points and conceded 68.

HE STEPPED IN

There was just one vital person missing when the final arrangements were being made for Ireland's international game against the touring All-Blacks at Lansdowne Road on Saturday, 7th December, 1935. The referee, Mr M. A. Allen of Scotland, had not shown up. He had decided to travel by boat from Glasgow to Dublin but a sudden storm and heavy seas had delayed the arrival and shortly before the game it became apparent that he had no hope of getting to Lansdowne in time for the kick-off. The suggestion was then put forward to the New Zealanders that R. W. Jeffares, then Secretary of the Irish Rugby Football Union and an international referee, should take charge. The request was a little unusual but there was little else that could be done at such short notice and, in the circumstances, the All-Blacks were quite happy to agree. Mr Jeffares duly took over the whistle—and this is still the only time in modern rugby history that a major international game has been refereed by a non-neutral. For the record Jeffares, later described by theNew Zealanders as "sternly just", did an excellent job of handling the game. Indeed, the only criticism levelled at him came from the 35,000 Irish crowd in the second half when the Ulster forward Jack Siggins burst over the New Zealand line but was whistled back for a previous infringement. At the time the All-Blacks were leading 11-6. The final score was 17-9 against Ireland.

AND IT WENT WIDE

A sad history was to be repeated for Ireland on Saturday, 14th March, 1936 when they took on Wales at Cardiff Arms Park with the Triple Crown again at stake for the Irish. A year earlier Ireland had won the international championship outright for the first time in 35 years and with a 6-3 win over England at Lansdowne Road, followed by a 10-4 win over Scotland at Murrayfield, the game to decide it all was once again against Wales, who had beaten Jack Manchester's All-Blacks that season. It turned out to be a dogged, dour battle all the way and it ended with a win for Wales with a penalty goal kicked by Vivian Jenkins. But in the closing minutes Victor Hewitt whipped up a pass outside the Welsh "25" and tried for a drop at goal. The ball went straight for the posts but at the last vital moment, the wind took it just away from the posts and Ireland were denied a 4-3 win. Ten years earlier, almost to the day, 13th March, 1926, Ireland had been in line for the Triple Crown against Wales at Swansea and with the score at 11-8 for Wales, Victor Hewitt's brother, Tom, had tried for a drop goal in the last 30 seconds and on that occasion, too, the ball had been caught by the wind and had gone inches wide.

THE O'FLANAGANS

Kevin O'Flanagan was one of the most versatile sportsmen Ireland has ever produced—and his younger brother Michael was little behind him. Kevin was first capped for Ireland at soccer in 1937 at the age of eighteen and between then and 1947 was to win 10 in all. During this time, he was also broadjump champion of Ireland on two occasions and also Irish 100 yards champion. Having qualified as a doctor, he went to London where he played with Arsenal and Brentford and at the beginning of 1946 was selected to play for Ireland in the unofficial rugby internationals. He had the unique distinction of playing for Ireland at rugby on one Saturday, soccer for Ireland against Scotland the following Saturday and would, in fact, have played international rugby again the next Saturday, but for the fact that he missed the game when fog delayed the boat-train from London to Holyhead and he was unable to get to Dublin in time to turn out against England. Subsequently he was to get one official international cap for Ireland at Rugby against Australia in 1948. In the meantime, his brother Michael had played international soccer for Ireland against England in 1946 and two years later, in Ireland's third Triple Crown year since 1894, he played in the centre for Ireland against Scotland. They are the only two brothers in sporting history to win international caps in both rugby and soccer.

IN THREE SPORTS

Ireland produced the fastest wing-threequarter of the countries in the international championship in the 1930s—Freddie Moran. Capped for the first time against England in 1936 he was to win nine caps before the outbreak of the Second World War, he also represented Ireland internationally in athletics and in 1938 as the Irish 100 yards record holder, held jointly with a former Irish rugby international, Denis

"SAY WHAT YOU LIKE ABOUT HIM, THE
NEW WING THREE QUARTER HAS STYLE"

Cussen, he competed in both the 100 yards and 220 yards against Scotland and England. After the war he became an international in a third sport, clay-pigeon shooting and, in fact, in addition to winning the Irish championship, also took the British Open Championship. But for the advent of the War, Moran would almost certainly have gone on to win many further caps for Ireland and also to represent his country in the Olympic Games.

MORAN'S EPIC TRY

Clontarf's Freddie Moran, who just a season before had won the Irish 100 yards sprint championship in 9.8 seconds, gave the Welsh crowd just one glimpse of his superb speed at St Helen's, Swansea, on Saturday, 12th March, 1938 and it ended with an epic try. With the Welsh backs passing and attacking in the Irish "25", the burly Moran intercepted a bad pass from Wilf Wooller to Billy Cleaver and broke away. Gathering speed he raced away from every Welshman on the field and after his run of over 70 yards, he still had time to amble around and ground the ball between the posts to give Harry McKibbin an easy convert. Unfortunately Ireland lost George Cromey with injury shortly after the start of the second half and, despite Moran's sensational try, the Welsh eventually recovered to win by 11-5.

THE WRONG MOMENT

As far as Ireland were concerned Wales's fly-half Willie Davis could not have picked a worse moment to drop the first goal of his rugby career. He did it at Ravenhill, Belfast on 11th March, 1939 and then to rub salt into Ireland's wounds, he scampered over for a try. Both of his scores came in the last five minutes and they put paid to Ireland's dreams of their first Triple Crown since 1899. Already that season Ireland had beaten England at Twickenham by a goal to nil and then had beaten Scotland at Lansdowne Road by a penalty goal, two tries and a goal from a mark by Mike Sayers to a try. The Triple Crown hung on the last game against Wales at Belfast and there had been no scores up to five minutes from time. Then Willie Davis, taking a pass outside the Irish "25", found himself in an open space and with a smart drop kick put the ball between the posts. It was the first successful drop kick of his career and it upset the Irish so much that three minutes later they allowed Davis to slip through for a try to clinch the game. This drop goal was the last one for Wales in international rugby that counted for four points. Their next drop goal in international rugby came against Scotland at Swansea in 1950 by which time the drop goal had been devalued to three points.

A BRILLIANT FUTURE

The compiler of the "Who's Who on the Irish XV" for the programme for the unofficial international game between Ireland and England at Lansdowne Road on Saturday, 9th February, 1946, had his own look into the future. "The discovery of the season"—he wrote—"He was on the Ulster Schools XV two years ago and proved himself to be in top class by his great display for Ulster against the Kiwis in November, subsequently confirming that form against the Army. A particularly straight, strong runner, he looks to have a brilliant future. Age 19". The young man he was referring to was . . . Jack Kyle.

NOT WALES AGAIN

With the resumption of official internationals in the 1946-1947 season, Ireland got their post-war hunt for the Triple Crown off to a sensational start by humiliating England with a 22-0 win at Lansdowne Road. But they just barely scraped through with a 3-0 win against Scotland at Murrayfield and so once again it was to be St Helen's, Swansea, for a Triple Crown decider on Saturday, 8th March, 1947. Unfortunately, that was the year of the big freeze and the game had to be delayed until Saturday, 29th March and those three weeks made all the difference. By the time the game was played, the drive had gone out of Ireland and Wales, with a try from Evans and a penalty goal from Tamplin won far more easily than the final score of 6-0 would suggest. This was the eighth time that Wales had tumbled Ireland in their bid for a third Triple Crown since 1894. But, as the next few years showed, the balance of power was about to turn.

EIGHT YEARS WAIT

The longest gap between international appearances by an Irish player is the eight years by Lansdowne's full-back Con Murphy. He was capped for the first time in 1939, when he made appearances against England, Scotland and Wales. Then, having spanned the Second World War years, he came back in 1947 to win two further caps against England and France. Ireland's longest-serving international, however, is Tony O'Reilly (Old Belvedere, Leicester and London-Irish) who was capped for Ireland against England, Scotland, Wales and France in 1955 and won the last of his 29 caps against England in 1970. O'Reilly, of course, shares with Syd Millar (Ballymena) and Kevin Flynn (Wanderers) of having played with Ireland in three different decades.

THE THIRD CROWN

Ireland's start to the 1947-1948 season was hardly a promising one. They met the touring Australians at Lansdowne Road and were given a thorough trouncing by 16-3. The first day of 1948, however, a bleak cold New Year's Day at Colombes Stadium, Paris, brought the hope of brighter things to come. The French were beaten by 13-6 and then it was on to Twickenham for the game against England. And this was one that was almost thrown away. Ireland led up to five minutes from time by 11-5 and then England's wing three-quarter Dickie Guest was let clean away and ran the length of the field to score a magnificent try that was converted to leave the score at 11-10. Ireland, with a little luck, survived a final assault by England and went on to take on the Scots at Lansdowne Road. Des McKee, the Irish sprint champion, sent Barney Mullen away for a try early in the second half and Jack Kyle eventually added another to give Ireland a 6-0 win. Now all that remained was Wales at Ravenhill, Belfast. Ireland were in with a chance of a third Triple Crown and perhaps even of their first Grand Slam in the International Championship.

DALY'S AFTERNOON

John Christopher Daly of Cobh, Co. Cork, who had just come back from serving in the Second World War and who had graduated from the local Cobh Pirates Club to Cork Constitution and then to Munster and Ireland, scored the only try of his short international career at Ravenhill, Belfast in 1949—and it remains as the try that will never be forgotten in Ireland. Ireland took the lead against Wales in front of a capacity crowd when Jack Kyle slung out a long pass to Barney Mullen on the wing and the Clontarf man shot over for a try. The great Bleddyn Williams brought matters level for Wales with a try after a glorious run and it was 3-3 at half-time. Shortly after the start of the second half Bertie O'Hanlon kicked ahead for Ireland and Des O'Brien and Daly brought the ball at their feet right up to and then over the Welsh line. And Daly crashed down on it for the try that was to bring Ireland their third Triple Crown. Of even greater importance it also brought Ireland their first and still their only Grand Slam of France, England, Scotland and Wales in the International Championship. In Ireland's four internationals in the championship that season, they scored 36 points and conceded 19.

TWO IN A ROW

At the beginning of the 1948-1949 season only England and Wales had ever managed to win the Triple Crown two years in succession and England had achieved it twice in 1913-1914 and again in 1923-1924. But after an uncomfortable start to the season which brought a shock 9-16 defeat at the hands of the French at Lansdowne Road, Dublin, Ireland were to join them in March of 1949. Ireland recovered from that defeat by France to beat England by 14-5 at Lansdowne Road and then with a young man named Noel Henderson making his international debut at Murrayfield, Scotland were removed from the path by 13-3, with wing-forward Jim McCarthy, two tries and George Norton, a conversion and a penalty goal, contributing Ireland's total. The next step was to St Helen's, Swansea to meet Wales and that promised little reward. Ireland had not beaten the Welshmen at St Helen's since 1889 when they won by two tries to nil. This time, Ireland were to score only one try which was converted and that was enough to win the Triple Crown for the second year in a row. Once again the Irish try was scored by wing-forward Jim McCarthy, who thus had the distinction of scoring three successive tries for his country and George Norton added the conversion.

UNBEATEN IN 1951

Ireland went through the 1950-1951 season unbeaten and yet failed to win the Triple Crown. They beat France by 9-8 at Lansdowne Road, England by 3-0 at Lansdowne Road and Scotland by 6-5 at Murrayfield.

But once again, the Welsh game at Cardiff Arms Park, while it gave Ireland the international championship outright for the seventh time since 1894, robbed Ireland of the Triple Crown. Wales took the lead with a penalty goal and held their lead for quite some time until Jack Kyle with a sensational burst of speed, spreadeagled the Welsh defence for a superb try. Unfortunately Angus McMorrow's attempt to convert from close to the sideline went inches wide. After the two Triple Crown victories of 1947-1948 and 1948-1949, Ireland were back in the old trouble with Wales. This was the ninth time in the history of meetings between the two countries that the Welsh had halted Ireland in their bid for the Triple Crown.

A DOUBLE HONOUR

The Rugby League Challenge Cup final at Wembley Stadium on Saturday, 19th April, 1952 carried a special significance for everyone associated with the game of rugby in Ireland. Played out before a crowd of 73,000, Workington Town, the favourites, survived some great early scoring by Featherstone Rovers and eventually pulled away to win by 18-10. The result was one of bitter disappointment to one of Featherstone Rovers forwards, who, by the reports of the game, gave an astonishing display of enthusiasm and power from start to finish. He got only a runners-up medal but at least this appearance at Wembley gave John Christopher Daly of Cobh, Co. Cork the distinction of having scored the winning try for Ireland in the 1947-1948 Triple Crown and of being the only Irish international to play at Wembley in a Rugby League Challenge Cup final.

ARGENTINA 1952

Ireland, under the name of "The Shamrocks" made their first tour to Argentina in 1952 under the captaincy of Des O'Brien and the management of Sarsfield Hogan. The Irish played nine matches over a period of five weeks and won six, drew two and lost one. The one defeat was in the first of the two unofficial international games against Argentina at Buenos Aires.

READING THE PAPER!

On the Friday night before Ireland's game against Wales on Saturday, 13th March, 1954, Ireland's Johnny O'Meara, surely one of the most elegant scrum-halves to play for his country, reported fit and well and ready to renew his great partnership with Jack Kyle. But when Ireland lined out the following day at Lansdowne Road, O'Meara was missing and, in fact, spent that afternoon listening to the game on the radio from a hospital bed. That morning, while reading a newspaper, he twisted his back in some unaccountable fashion and had to be taken to hospital. His place went to Herbie McCracken, whose only international appearance for Ireland this was to be. He is remembered, however, as one of the eight scrum-halves who played with Jack Kyle during the Ulsterman's 46 games with Ireland. The other seven were Ray Carroll, Ernie Strathdee, Tom Cullen, Sean MacDermott, John Burgess, Hugh de Lacy, John O'Meara, and the inimitable Andy Mulligan.

KYLE'S DROP

Ireland had not won a game against Wales since Swansea on Saturday, 12th March, 1949, when they lined out at Lansdowne Road on Saturday, 10th March, 1956 and there was a record crowd in Dublin that afternoon to see the balance of power change. Ireland, led by Noel Henderson, got away to a tremendous start and although the Welsh opened the scoring with a penalty goal, there was never any danger that Ireland would not win. By the final whistle they had put up 11 points to Wales's three, with a try from Marney Cunningham, which Cecil Pedlow converted and Pedlow also added a penalty goal. Ireland's only other score was a drop goal . . . from Jack Kyle! Strange as it seems, it was to be the only goal that Kyle ever dropped for Ireland in all his great years of service in the green jersey.

A LONG WAY OFF

Andy Mulligan, one of the irrepressible and memorable characters of Irish rugby of the late 1950s, won his first cap against France in 1956 but after his second appearance which happened to be the 0-20 defeat by England at Twickenham, he was promptly dropped and had to shoulder some of the blame for Ireland's crash. He bobbed up again the following year and, of course was subsequently selected for the Lions tour of Australia and New Zealand. Appointed captain of Ireland in 1960, he completed his international career with 22 caps for Ireland. Among his many claims to fame in the game must be the fact that he came a long, long way to play for Ireland. He was, in fact, born in Kasauli in India!

MILLIONS SAW IT

Noel Murphy, Ireland's most capped wing-forward with 41 caps between 1957 and 1969 had a striking debut in his international career and a striking end. In both games he took a punch on the jaw. Against the 1957-1958 touring Australians, he was laid low by a punch from the "iron man" of Wallaby rugby, Nick Shehadie and on 8th March, 1969 he was again laid low this time with a punch from Wales's Brian Price. The second punch got world-wide coverage. The game was being televised and millions saw what happened. Apart from that, the game was not memorable. Ireland were chasing the Triple Crown and although Mike Gibson scored a try and Tom Kiernan added a conversion and two penalty goals, Ireland finished 13 points behind on the score of 24-11. Murphy, whose career was marred by injuries, was the first Irish forward to win more than 40 caps and he also made six international appearances in his two tours with the Lions of 1959 and 1966. His father Noel had also played for Ireland and they came together in an unusual setting during Ireland's tour of South Africa when Noel Senior was the manager of the international side in which his son was playing.

THE END OF AN ERA

With Ireland's victory over Scotland by 12-6 at Lansdowne Road on Saturday, 1st March, 1958, one of the truly great personalities of Irish and world rugby bowed out of the international scene. Jack Kyle, then thirty-two, and with 46 Irish caps and six Lions caps to his credit, had played his last game. His 46 Irish caps then represented not only just an Irish record but also a world record and his total would have been greater but for the 1939-1945 war. In fact, Kyle wore the green international jersey of Ireland on 51 occasions but, sadly, five of these did not count as official internationals. With the last of the war-time internationals, an Irish XV v the British Army at Ravenhill, Belfast on Saturday, 15th December, 1945, he made his debut for his country and during the 1945-1946 season he appeared in Ireland's unofficial internationals against France, England, Scotland and Wales. For his record, however, his official international debut came against France in the 1946-1947 season. Except for injury, he was never again out of the Irish side for 11 seasons. At school at the Belfast Royal Academy and later at Queen's University, he had ambitions of becoming either a centre or a full-back and played his first game at out-half in a club game when the Queen's top out-half of the time was injured. That was the beginning. He went straight into the Ulster side as an out-half, then into the Irish XV and then into the Ireland team . . . and into the history of rugby football as possibly the greatest man of all-time in that position.

A GOOD VETERAN

Syd Millar of Ballymena, born on 23rd May, 1934 finished off his "second" international career with Ireland's sensational win over Wales at Lansdowne Road on Saturday, 14th March, 1970, when the Welsh, chasing the Triple Crown, were well and truly hammered by 14-0. Millar's "first" international career had begun in 1958 with a cap against France and he was a regular prop in the Irish pack up to the end of the 1963 season. In 1964, however, he played just the one match against France and disappeared from the international scene. He was, in fact, even dropped by his province Ulster in the inter-provincial championship. The general feeling then was that Millar was getting just a little too old for international football. He was then thirty and, in addition to playing for Ireland he had also toured with the Lions in 1959 and 1962. But Millar decided he was far from finished. He got back into training and early in the 1967-1968 season, after a brilliant series of performances in the inter-provincial championship with Ulster, he came back into the international reckoning again. He resumed against France in 1968 and kept his place on the Irish side right up to 1970 which gave him the distinction of having played for Ireland in three decades. He played so well in 1968 that he made what was then a record third tour with the Lions. Millar's last game for Ireland came shortly before his thirty-sixth birthday and he stands as one of the oldest men to be capped for his country.

THE TOP REFEREE

No Irishman has made a greater contribution to international rugby as a referee than Kevin Kelleher, who between 1960 and 1971 set a world record of handling 22 major games. He began in 1960 with the Wales v Scotland game, followed this with two in 1961, Wales v England and England v Scotland and had two more again the following year with Scotland v England and Wales v France. In 1963 he handled the Wales v England and the France v Italy games and in 1964 was in charge of England v France and Rumania v France. He had two again in 1965 with France v Scotland and Wales v England and in 1966 took charge of three internationals, Scotland v England, Wales v France and Wales v Australia. In 1967 he went one better with four games, England v Australia, France v Scotland, Scotland v Wales and Scotland v New Zealand. In 1968 he was in charge of Scotland v France and in 1969 handled Scotland v Wales and England v South Africa. In 1970 he had the whistle in the Wales v France game and after handling the France v Scotland game in 1971, he retired from international refereeing. His most remembered game, of course, is the Scotland v New Zealand game in 1967 at Murrayfield when he sent the legendary Colin Meads to the sideline. One of Kevin Kelleher's unusual possessions nowadays is the original of a cartoon that appeared in the following week's New Zealand newspapers. It shows a motorist filling up at a wayside garage with the caption; "With a name like yours Mr Kelleher, do you think it is wise to venture up into King Country".

IRELAND IN SOUTH AFRICA

Ronnie Dawson led Ireland to South Africa in 1961 for a four-match programme which opened up with a full international game against the Springboks at Newlands. It was not an auspicious start for the Irish and having run up a 13-0 lead at half-time the South Africans moved on comfortably to a 24-8 victory. Significantly, in the light of what he was to do in South Africa in the years that followed, Tom

Kiernan scored all of Ireland's points with a penalty goal and a try which he also converted. Two of South Africa's five tries in this game came from centre-threequarter Colin Greenwood and this, in fact, was to be his first and last appearance for South Africa. Immediately after the game he accepted an offer to join the English rugby league club, Wakefield Trinity and there was quite an astonishing reaction from the South African Rugby Board. They withdrew his international colours for this game against Ireland. However, they subsequently relented and Greenwood now appears in the official list of South African internationals. One of the other features of this first international by Ireland on South African soil was that the Springboks fielded four Van Zyls—Ben-Piet, who scored two tries, Hennie, Hugo and Piet. Of the four, only Hugo and Piet were cousins. Subsequently Ireland beat Southwest Districts at Oudtshoorn by 11-6, Western Transvaal by 16-6 at Potchefstroom and Rhodesia by 24-0 at Salisbury. Top points scorer for Ireland was Tom Kiernan with 38 points from a try, seven conversions, four penalty goals and three drop goals. The top try scorer was Niall Brophy with three.

DUGGAN'S THIRTEEN

The twenty-year old Alan Thomas Anthony Duggan made his first appearance in the Irish jersey against New Zealand on Saturday, 7th December, 1963 at Lansdowne Road, Dublin. On Saturday, 29th April, 1972, again at Lansdowne Road, this time against France he collected his 25th and final cap. That afternoon, too, he collected a try, which was to bring his total for Ireland in international games to 13—the highest ever by an Irish international.

THE MISSED GOAL

No one will ever know just what might have happened at Lansdowne Road on Saturday, 9th March, 1968 if Wales had beaten Ireland. For this was the afternoon that Mike Titcomb of Bristol made a snap decision that could have led to a riot by the Irish spectators at the end. At the time Ireland were leading 6-3 and then Gareth Edwards tried for a drop at goal. From the Press Box, it was quite obvious that the ball had gone wide, most of the spectators on one side of the field were fully aware that it had missed the posts and so too were both the Irish and Welsh players. The Irish players lined up for a "25" drop out, the Welsh players ranged themselves in front of them. But Mr Titcomb was pointing to the middle of the field—indicating that the drop at goal had been successful. That brought the score to 6-6 and the mood of the crowd was quite angry. The game eventually went on into the ninth minute of injury time when the ball was heeled close to the Welsh line and wing-forward Mick Doyle went through on the blind side for the try that won the game by 9-6. Nine minutes of injury time seemed a little long but as a certain Irish international said later . . . "In the light of what happened, I had the feeling that this game would go on and on and on until Ireland scored, even if it meant playing on until darkness fell".

THE ONE WHO CAME BACK

Terenure's Mick Hipwell was capped for Ireland against England, Scotland and Wales in 1962 and that seemed to be the end of his international career. But the tall Air Force officer soldiered on in club and provincial football and then out of the blue he was recalled to international action in 1968 to play against Australia at Lansdowne Road. He lasted for one more international game that season, against the French but the curtain came down again. In 1969 he won three caps but two of them were as replacements against France and Scotland and it was not until 1971 that he went through a full season by playing against France, England, Scotland and Wales. He won his final cap in 1972 against France . . . but, in between, the man who had been in the wilderness of international rugby for six years, went to Australia and New Zealand as one of John Dawes's Lions in 1971.

RAY McLOUGHLIN'S MEN

Ray McLoughlin, then playing with Gosforth, led his men out at Cardiff Arms Park on Saturday, 13th March, 1965 in yet another bid for the Triple Crown. For the first time in 54 years it was a real Triple Crown decider between the two countries. Both had beaten England and Scotland that season. Ireland had pipped England by 5-0 at Lansdowne Road, Dublin and had improved out of all recognition with a 16-6 win over the Scots at Murrayfield. Wales, on the other hand, had beaten England comfortably by 14-3 but only a last-gasp try had given them a 14-12 win over Scotland. The odds looked to be slightly in Ireland's favour and they lengthened more than a little when John Dawes had to leave the field in the first half after only five minutes of play. But Wales scored first with a try by David Watkins which Terry Price converted and Dewi Bebb put them into an 8-0 lead shortly after half-time. The dapper Kevin Flynn went over for an Irish try which Tom Kiernan converted and with Kiernan's penalty goal the score stood at 8-8. Terry Price, however, killed off Ireland's hopes with a magnificent drop goal and a penalty goal and it was 14-8 at the finish. For the 10th time since 1905, Wales had taken the Triple Crown away from Ireland.

TWICE IN FOUR MONTHS

Ireland set an unusual record in 1967 by beating Australia twice in the space of four months. During the Wallabies tour of Britain, Ireland and France in 1966-1967, they took on the Australians at Lansdowne Road, Dublin on Saturday, 21st January, 1967 and won by 15-8. Four months later Ireland took off on a short tour of Australia and at the famous Sydney Cricket Ground beat Australia by 11-5 before a crowd of 32,605. Ireland's scorers in Sydney were Gerry Walsh and Pat McGrath with a try each and Tom Kiernan with a conversion and a drop goal. Ireland opened their tour of Australia by trouncing Queensland by 41-8 at Brisbane but lost to New South Wales by 9-21 at Sydney. At Woologong they beat New South Wales Country by 31-11 and then after beating Australia at Sydney, lost their fifth game by 8-30 to Sydney. They wound up their 20-days tour by beating Victoria, 19-5 at Melbourne. Their full record on this short tour was; played six, won four, lost two and scored 119 points while conceding 80.

HIS SIX POINTS

When Mike Gibson cried off the Irish team before the international game against France at Colombes Stadium in 1968, young Billy McCombe, a student at Dublin University, was named to take over

"REMEMBER, I THROW THE BALL TO YOU, THEN
ALEC THROWS YOU OVER THE LINE .. "

at out-half. This turned out to be McCombe's only cap, and, apart from gaining it outside his own country, he also celebrated it by scoring all of Ireland's points. The Irish were beaten by 16-6 and McCombe collected the six points with his two penalty goals.

MORONEY'S MARK

Although he liked to play his rugby at out-half John Moroney, who made his debut for Ireland in 1968 won all of his six international caps at wing-threequarter. And in Ireland's 17-9 win over France at Lansdowne Road on 25th January, 1969, he left his indelible mark on the proceedings. He put Ireland into the lead with a penalty goal and then went over for a try which he converted. Then he went on to kick a further two penalty goals, with Ireland's other points coming from a penalty goal by Barry McGann (Cork Constitution), who was making his debut for his country in this game. Moroney's 14 points (15 under present day scoring values) stands as the top individual scoring performance by an Irishman in an international game.

AFTER YOU, ROGER

Between them, Roger Young and Colin Grimshaw set an unique record for Queen's University at Lansdowne Road on Saturday, 8th February, 1969. At the time, Young who had 14 caps to his credit was the No 1 choice scrum-half for Queen's and Grimshaw was his patient understudy. And for this international game against England they were again in similar roles with Young named to play on the Irish side and Grimshaw as his reserve replacement. As it happened, however, Young was a first half casualty and in the 33rd minute was forced to retire with a badly bruised hip. Grimshaw came on and played quite effectively in Ireland's win by 17-15. And so, for the first time in rugby history, one club had two scrum-halves capped in the same international game. This was Grimshaw's only appearance for Ireland—and, in fact, he was the first replacement to be used by his country in an international game—and his 47 minutes on the field represents the shortest international career of any Irish player against another country.

SOME CONSOLATION

Ireland went to Cardiff Arms Park on Saturday, 8th March, 1969 with high hopes of the Triple Crown and the Grand Slam of the international championship. They had beaten France by 17-9, England by 17-15 and Scotland by 16-11. And Ireland's hopes rose even further when captain Tom Kiernan kicked them into the lead with a penalty goal after five minutes. But after that, it was Wales all the way and Ireland eventually crashed to an 11-24 defeat. The only consolation for the Irish was that they had managed to set an all-time scoring record in that season. Their 61 points in an international season is still the highest achieved by an Irish side.

ARGENTINA 1970

Ireland's short tour of Argentina between 25th August and 22nd September, 1970 was hardly a success. Their record was played seven, won four, lost three, scoring 73 points and conceding 57. The two unofficial internationals against Argentina were lost by 3-8 and 3-6 and in addition Ireland took quite a beating from an Argentinian C Selection by 0-17. In the first unofficial international at the Ferrocarrill Stadium in Buenos Aires, Ireland's Phil O'Callaghan and Ronnie Foster of Argentina were sent off with just 20 minutes to go. Tom Kiernan was the top scorer of the tour with 21 points from five penalty goals and two conversions.

A LONG, LONG WAIT

Eight minutes after the start of Ireland's game against France at Colombes Stadium, Paris, on Saturday, 29th January, 1972, Ireland's scrum-half John Moloney sold a beautiful dummy to the French defences and went surging over for a try. Pierre Villepreux kicked a penalty goal for France but Tom Kiernan added one for Ireland and then with half-time looming up, Ireland's iron man of the front row, Ray McLoughlin, with Frenchmen hanging out of him, barged his way over for his first try in international rugby for Ireland. Midway through the second half Kiernan kicked a second penalty goal and France's only answer was a try in injury time by Jean-Paul Lux which was converted by Villepreux. A good win for Ireland—and a break-through after a long, long time. After 20 years they had finally beaten France at Colombes Stadium. Their last victory there had been as far back as 1952 when they got their 16th win over the French by 11-8. It was to be Ireland's last appearance at Colombes Stadium. The next time they played in Paris in 1974, the French headquarters had been moved back to Parc des Princes where Ireland and France had met for the first time in France back in 1910.

A THREE DECADES MAN

Kevin Flynn of Wanderers, one of the few Irish players to appear in three decades of international rugby, made his debut against France in 1959 and won 17 caps between then and 1966. Then, unfortunately, through a long series of injuries his international career came to an end—or so it seemed. Six years later Flynn popped up again for Ireland against England and no one could have made a more impressive return to the international field after an absence of six seasons. Ireland had not beaten England at Twickenham since 1964 and with just seconds to go on Saturday, 12th February, 1972, there appeared to be little likelihood that the situation might change. Then Flynn went scampering through the English defences for a try that changed the score from 12-10 for England to 14-12 for Ireland. Kiernan kicked the conversion in the last second of the game. Flynn went on to win a total of 22 caps for Ireland and made his last appearance against the touring New Zealanders at Lansdowne Road on Saturday, 20th January, 1973 when he had the satisfaction of sharing in Ireland's 10-10 draw—the best result Ireland have ever had against the All-Blacks.

THE FINAL GAME

The curtain came down for the last time in a remarkable international rugby career at Murrayfield, Edinburgh, on Saturday, 24th February, 1973, when Scotland met Ireland in the 83rd meeting between the two countries. This game marked Tom Kiernan's final appearance for Ireland. He had won his first cap against England in 1960 and had played international football for Ireland in every season up to 1973. It was also his 54th cap for Ireland which added to his record as Ireland's most capped player up to that time. He is still, of course, the most capped of all international full-backs, having won all of his 54 caps in the one position. Kiernan was also capped five times for the Lions against South Africa and holds the record of most consecutive points by a player in an international game. In 1968 he scored 35 in four international games for the Lions against South Africa. Kiernan, who captained Ireland on a record 25 occasions, also scored the most points by a Lions player in an international game when he kicked five penalty goals and a conversion against South Africa at Pretoria in 1968.

KIERNAN'S FAREWELL

Ireland's full-back Tom Kiernan, one of rugby's great record-makers, scored the second try of his long and proud international career against Scotland at Murrayfield on Saturday, 24th February, 1973—and this was to be his last score on the international scene. With this try he brought his total of points to an Irish record in internationals of 158 since his debut in 1960. Coupled with his 35 points for his four international appearances for the Lions against South Africa in 1968, his international total is second to that of Don Clarke's 207 for New Zealand—the present world record. This game against Scotland was to be Kiernan's 54th appearance for Ireland and his last and at the time it was an Irish record, which has been broken since by only Willie John McBride of Ballymena. In his two tours with the Lions in South Africa, 1962 and 1968, Kiernan scored a total of 91 points and in his other visit to South Africa with the Irish team of 1961 he scored 38 of Ireland's 55 points.

THE FIJIANS IN DUBLIN

The Fijians, who made their first entry into the world of international rugby in 1938 at a time when most of their top players had not become accustomed to wearing boots, paid their first visit to Ireland in 1973 and took on Leinster at Lansdowne Road on Saturday, 15th September. They were on a four match tour at the time and before arriving in Dublin had walloped Swansea by 31-0 and then had gone down to Leicester by 17-22. Despite the fact that they played some highly entertaining rugby at Lansdowne Road, they were never quite in the class of Leinster who won easing up by 30-9. In their final match of this tour the Fijians went down by 12-25 to Moseley.

ARGENTINA IN IRELAND

The Argentinians, in Ireland for the first time, opened their 1973 tour with a draw 12-12 against Munster at Limerick, lost to Ulster 12-23 at Ravenhill and then beat Connacht at Galway by 16-7 and none of the games were what one might term the friendliest of affairs. On Saturday, 10th November, 1973, they met Ireland in an unofficial international game at Lansdowne Road and despite all the gloomy forebodings, this was not the roughhouse that most people had anticipated. Leiros and Porta had tries for Argentina and Ireland cantered away to an effortless win by 21-8 with tries from Fergus Slattery, Mick Quinn, Tom Grace, Wallace McMaster, one conversion from Tony Ensor and a drop goal by Mick Quinn. This marked Ireland's second win over Argentina in five games since 1952.

OUTRIGHT CHAMPIONS

With the change in the International Championship programme in 1973-1974, Ireland completed their series of four games with a win over Scotland at Lansdowne Road on Saturday, 2nd March, 1974. They had come through the campaign with a narrow defeat to France at Parc des Princes, a draw against Wales, a fine victory over England and a decisive win over Scotland. Then they had to wait for a fortnight to know how they got on in the championship. It all hinged on the two games that were to be played on Saturday, 16th March, with France meeting Scotland at Murrayfield and Wales taking on England at Twickenham. The only way that Ireland could take the championship outright then was that France and Wales should be defeated. And England and Scotland duly obliged the Irish and for the first time since 1951, Ireland took the Championship outright. Ireland had previously been outright champions in 1894, 1896, 1899, 1935, 1948, 1949 and 1951.

McBRIDE'S 56th CAP

Willie John McBride of Ballymena made his first international appearance for Ireland at Twickenham in 1962 and his career got away to a somewhat depressing start when Ireland crashed by 0-16. Twelve years later, on Saturday, 16th February, 1974, Willie John McBride led Ireland out on to the pitch at Twickenham and this was an afternoon to remember for him. Ireland, with a glorious performance, raced into a 26-9 lead at one stage of the second half and eventually survived a spirited comeback by England to win by 26-21. With this performance McBride made his 56th appearance for Ireland, a new world record. The previous record had been held by his great friend and rival, Colin Meads of New Zealand. McBride, of course, went on to play against Scotland and at the end of the 1973-1974 season had carried his world record of international rugby caps to 57. He gained a 58th international cap on 7th September, 1974, when he captained Ireland in the game against the President's XV at Lansdowne Road which opened Ireland's Centenary Year.

McBRIDE'S SERVICE

With the final whistle of Ireland's victory over Scotland at Lansdowne Road on Saturday, 2nd March, 1974, Willie John McBride (Ballymena) completed a remarkable sequence of 47 consecutive international appearances for Ireland—another world record in international rugby. In compiling his 57 caps for Ireland—he missed only the game against Wales in 1964—McBride has now played 13 consecutive games against England, 12 consecutive games against Scotland, 14 consecutive games against France and of his 11 appearances against Wales, nine have been consecutive. He has also made three appearances against Australia, two against South Africa and two against New Zealand; and, of course, added a further consecutive appearance for Ireland against the President's XV on Saturday, 7th September, 1974.

THE HEWITT FAMILY

The astonishing Hewitt family have their own special place in the history of Irish sport. Frank and Tom were both capped for Ireland at rugby for the first time against Wales in 1924 and Frank, of course, is the youngest international ever to be capped for Ireland in rugby. He won nine caps until an injury ended his career before he was twenty. Tom also won nine caps for Ireland and then a third brother, Victor came on the rugby scene in 1935 to win six caps. Two other brothers, Hammie and Willie were capped for Northern Ireland in amateur international soccer, and yet another Norman was capped for Ulster at Rugby. But that was not the end of the Hewitts. Their nephew John Hewitt won four international rugby caps between 1954 and 1961 and another nephew, Gerry Gilpin won three caps in 1962. Then there was David Hewitt, a son of Tom, who was to win 18 rugby caps between 1958 and 1965 and he also went on a Lions tour. And just to complicate things a little more, Stanley Hewitt, a son of Frank, played international cricket for Ireland!

THE OUTSIDERS

From George Stack, who was named to captain Ireland in the first international game against England at Kennington Oval in February, 1875, to Pat Lavery, who was selected to play against Wales at Lansdowne Road in February, 1974, the number of players who have been capped for Ireland is 750. But there is the embarrassing evidence to show that at least 752 have played for Ireland in international rugby. For their game against Wales at Cardiff in 1884, Ireland could muster only 13 players on the morning of the game and, rather than call off the fixture, they made the unusual suggestion to the Welsh Rugby Union that two local players might be recruited to make up the side. The Welsh were agreeable and after a quick hunt around, D. J. Daniel (Llanelli) and F. Purdon (Newport) were invited to become Irishmen for the afternoon. Purdon had already won four caps for Wales and had, in fact, played against Ireland two years earlier. Daniel, who was uncapped at the time, subsequently made eight appearances for his country, two of which were against Ireland. Their contribution, however, did not help Ireland on that particular afternoon in 1884. Their names are not mentioned in any report of the proceedings which Wales won by a goal and two tries to nil. Apart from the known cases of Purdon and Daniel, there is the distinct possibility that other Welshmen were also pressed into service to play for Ireland. In those early days, international games against Wales did not enjoy the status of the games against England and Scotland and quite a few of Ireland's top players of the time showed a marked reluctance about travelling to Wales and it is known that on more than one occasion the Irish selectors had to search urgently for replacements.

DOHERTY ON HIS OWN

For the Centenary Year game between an Irish XV and the President H. P. McKibbin's XV at Lansdowne Road on Saturday, 7th September, 1974, the Irish Rugby Football Union's original intention had been not to award official international caps to the members of the Irish side. Later, however, they had a change of mind and, in doing so, provided Alan Doherty (Old Wesley) with an unprecedented honour in the history of Irish rugby. When Mike Gibson was injured in the second half and forced to leave the field, he was replaced by Doherty who was winning his first cap for Ireland. By winning it against the President's XV, Doherty became the first and only Irish player to gain international recognition while not playing against another country or an official touring side. He also became the 751st player to be capped for Ireland.

THE ONES WHO LASTED

The first Irishman to complete 10 seasons of international rugby was J. A. MacDonald (Methodist College, Belfast) who won the first of his 13 caps against England in 1875 and the last against Scotland in 1884. Since then 25 others have also achieved 10 or more seasons in the Irish jersey. They are; Niall Brophy (1957-1967), Jammie Clinch (1923-1932), Jack Coffey (1900-1910), Billy Collopy (1914-1924), Eugene Davy (1925-1934), Kevin Flynn (1959-1973), A. R. Foster (1910-1921), F. Gardiner (1900-1909), Mike Gibson (1964-1974), G. T. Hamlet (1902-1911), Noel Henderson (1949-1959), Mick Hipwell (1962-1972), Ronnie Kavanagh (1953-1962), Ken Kennedy (1965-1974), Tom Kiernan (1960-1973), Jack Kyle (1947-1958), Dickie Lloyd (1910-1920), Bill McBride (1962-1974), Ray McLoughlin (1962-1974), Louis Magee (1895-1904), Sid Millar (1958-1970), Noel Murphy (1958-1969), Tony O'Reilly (1955-1970), George Stephenson (1920-1930), Patrick Stokes (1912-1922).

A FRATERNAL AFFAIR

In the matter of brothers playing international rugby, Ireland holds an astonishing record. When Tom Doyle joined his brother Mick Doyle on the Irish side to play England at Lansdowne Road, Dublin on

Saturday, 10th February, 1968, they brought the number of brothers to represent Ireland to 41! Even more remarkable in that total is the number of sets of three brothers to represent Ireland. This comes to 10! The first three to do so were Fred, Malcolm and Frank Moore, between 1883-1886, and they were followed by the Rosses (1884-1886), the Pedlows (1882-1891), the Johnstones (1884-1886), the Forrests, (1880-1897), the Dorans (1890-1902), the Harveys (1900-1911), the Smyths (1908-1920), the McVickers (1922-1930) and the Hewitts (1925-1935). Pairs of brothers have played for Ireland from 1875 to 1967. The first were Edward and Robert Galbraith of Dublin University who played in Ireland's first-ever international game against England in 1875. The others are; Glynn and Elliot Allen (1896-1907), George and Charles Beamish (1925-1933), T. and H. Brown (1877), Michael and Larry Bulger (1896-1899), Seamus and Frank Byrne (1953-1962), Willie and Dickie Collopy (1914-1925), Morgan and Phil Crowe (1929-1935), Mark and Seamus Deering (1929-1936), Ian and Jim Dick (1961-1963), Mick and Tommy Doyle (1965-1968), William and Fred Gardiner (1902-1909), Lucius and A. P. Gwynn (1894-1895), James and William Heron (1877-1880), Ray and Larry Hunter (1962-1968), Ronnie and Paddy Kavanagh (1953-1962), J. M. and F. Kennedy (1880-1884), John and James Lytle (1889-1899), E. H. and J. E. McIlwaine (1895-1899), Harry and Des McKibbin (1938-1951), Louis and Joe Magee (1895-1904), R. and A. Montgomery (1887-1895), William and Hamilton Moore (1878), Kevin and Michael O'Flanagan (1948), V. J. and T. O. Pike (1927-1934), Mick and Jack Ryan (1897-1904), George and Harry Stephenson (1920-1930), Frank and Edward Stoker (1886-1889), R. B. and D. B. Walkington (1875-1891), Joe and James Wallace (1902-1906), and W. A. and A. K. Wallis (1881-1893).

DADS AND SONS

In the matter of sons inheriting their fathers' prowess in international rugby, the Irish wins hands down. No other country even approaches their list of father-and-son combinations in the history of the game. In all there have been nine sets with the latest coming in the 1973-1974 season. The first were the Schutes. F. Schute played for Ireland against England in 1878 and 1879 and his son F. G. Schute won three caps in 1913 against England, Scotland and South Africa. W. S. Collis, capped against Wales in 1884 was followed by his son W. R. F. Collis, who was to win seven caps between 1924 and 1926. George Collopy was first capped in 1891 and his two sons Dickie (1923-1925) and Willie (1914-1924) followed him into the record books. Sam Irwin (1900-1903) and Sinclair Irwin (1938-1939), A. D. Clinch (1892-1897) and Jammie Clinch (1923-1932), Noel Murphy (1930-1933) and Noel Murphy Junior (1958-1969), Paul Murray (1927-1933) and John Murray (1963), Seamus Deering (1935-1937) and Shay Deering (1974) bring the total to eight and the Hewitts, one of the most remarkable families in Irish rugby, complete the nine. Tom was capped between 1924 and 1926 and David, his son, won 18 caps for Ireland and was, of course, also a Lion.

THE TRIPLE INTERNATIONALS

The number of Irish rugby internationals who have also represented their country in another sport is quite large but Harry Read of Trinity, who won 13 rugby caps between 1910 and 1913, J. B. Ganly of Monkstown, who won 12 caps between 1927 and 1930 and Freddie Moran, with nine caps between 1936 and 1939, share the rare honour of having represented their country in three sports. Read and Ganly played rugby, cricket and tennis for Ireland and Moran won his three in rugby, athletics and shooting. The list of those who won double international honours encompasses some of the most famous names in Irish sport and they include George Morgan, Ham Lambert, Bob Alexander, Dickie Lloyd, Jack Notley, Kevin Quinn, Mark Sugden, Mick Dargan and Lucius Gwynn (rugby and cricket), Paddy Reid (rugby and hockey), Barney Mullan (rugby and shooting), Denis Cussen, Larry Bulger, Vincent Becker, Charles Reidy, Louis Crowe, Ned Walsh (rugby and athletics), Mick and Kevin O'Flanagan (rugby and soccer) James Cecil Parke (rugby and tennis) . . . and many, many more.

AGAINST THE OLD ENEMY

Despite the fact that they have failed to score in 24 of their games against England between 1875 and 1974, Ireland have now collected 604 points, by current values, against the English. Of the 86 games played, Ireland have won 29, lost 49 and drawn eight. Using either the scoring values of the time or the present-day values, Ireland's biggest win over England was at Lansdowne Road in 1947 when they scored two goals, a penalty goal and three tries to nil. Ireland's longest unbeaten spell against the English was from 1939 at Twickenham, where they won by a goal to nil to 1950, again at Twickenham where England broke the sequence of four successive victories by scoring a try to nil.

AGAINST WALES

In their 76 international games against Wales, Ireland have won 26, lost 45 and drawn five and have scored 542 points. Ireland's most decisive win over Wales was at Belfast in 1925 by a margin of two goals, a penalty goal and two tries to a try. Ireland have never scored more than three successive wins over Wales and achieved the hat-trick only in 1923, 1924, 1925 and again in 1966, 1967, 1968.

AGAINST SCOTLAND

Ireland have now played 84 games against Scotland and have won 39, lost 42 and drawn three and, by modern scoring values, have scored 681 points. Ireland's widest winning margin over the Scots came at Lansdowne Road in 1950 when Ireland won by three goals and two penalty goals to nil. Ireland's longest spell of domination over Scotland began in 1939 with the win at Lansdowne Road and lasted until Scotland won at Murrayfield in 1955—nine successive victories.

ON THE DEBIT SIDE

Beginning with the defeat by England at the Kennington Oval on 19th February, 1875 and ending with the victory over Scotland at Lansdowne Road on 2nd March, 1974, Ireland have played 314 official international games. International caps have been awarded against England, Scotland, Wales, France, New Zealand, South Africa, Australia, the New Zealand Native side of 1888-1889 and the New South Wales side of 1927-1928. Of the 314 games played, Ireland have won 122, lost 171 and drawn 21. Apart from New South Wales and the New Zealand Native side—only one game has been played against each and both were lost—Ireland have defeated all the major countries with the exception of New Zealand. Of the six games against the All-Blacks, five have been lost and one drawn. To open their Centenary Year in September 1974, Ireland played a special game against the President's XV and international caps were awarded to the Irish XV in the 18-18 draw at Lansdowne Road, Dublin.

WALES

AND SO IT BEGAN

By the early 1870s, rugby football had got a firm grip in Wales and four clubs, whose names were to become household words in the history of the game in Wales, had come into being. They were Cardiff, Newport, Llanelli and Swansea and later when they were joined by other clubs, they got the ambitious notion of playing in international football. A fixture was arranged against England at Mr Richardson's Field, Blackheath on 19th February, 1881, and that was hardly an afternoon to give hopes that Wales might ever become a power in rugby. They were "murdered" by seven goals, a drop goal and six tries to nil! But, out of this humiliation came the founding of the Welsh Rugby Union on Saturday, 12th March, 1881. England refused to play Wales in 1882, but they met Scotland for the first time in 1883 and Ireland for the first time a year earlier and from there, barring just a few little incidents over the years, Wales gradually progressed to become one of the great powers of world rugby.

GO SOMEWHERE ELSE

After the trouncing they had handed out to Wales in 1881, the English did not want to know about Wales again. The message was clear. Go somewhere else and find out how to play rugby. So the following year Wales were granted a match with the North of England at Newport and although the North won, Wales put up a good performance with a try coming from E. Treharne, so that England decided to renew their fixture with the Welsh. That year, too, it helped that Wales scored their first international victory by beating Ireland at Lansdowne Road in Dublin with tries from Baker-Jones, Tom Clapp, Willie Evans and John Bridie. Charles Lewis, in this game, became the first man to kick a goal for Wales by converting two of the tries. It took Wales until 15th February, 1890 to beat England and Billy "Buller" Stadden of Cardiff scored the famous try that clinched the game. Wales had their first win over Scotland on 4th February, 1888 at Newport by a try to nil and, of course, they won their first game against a full overseas touring side by beating Dave Gallaher's All-Blacks at Cardiff Arms Park on Saturday, 16th December, 1905. They had, of course, earlier, beaten the New Zealand Native side of 1888 at St Helen's, Swansea, on 22nd December, 1888 by a goal and two tries to nil.

DID HE OR DID HE NOT?

Wales travelled to Dublin in 1882 to play Ireland at Lansdowne Road and scored a comfortable win by two goals and two tries to nil. Their half-back R. H. Bridie (Newport) was one of the try-scorers. Subsequently that season Wales went to Raeburn Place, Edinburgh to play Scotland and again they had a comfortable win by three goals to a goal. Included in their line-out, according to the newspaper accounts of the time, was R. H. Bridie. This time, however, his club was given as Cardiff. As late as 1913, when L. M. Holden published his book on Rugby Union Football, his line-outs for both matches give R. H. Bridie as having played. Nowadays, however, the official list of Welsh internationals includes R. H. Bridie (Newport) as having played in only the one game against Ireland in 1882! So what happened in Edinburgh that season? In the Welsh Rugby Union Handbook, G. F. Harding (Newport) is credited with having played against Scotland; yet his name does not appear in the newspaper line-outs nor is he mentioned in Holden's book as having played against Scotland. The Welsh now accept that Harding did, in fact, play and that R. H. Bridie did not. The only assumption that can be drawn now is that Bridie, who lived and worked in Cardiff, did travel to Edinburgh and that Scotland refused to play against him, and that Harding came in to replace him. After all, Bridie was born and bred in Glasgow and it may have offended the Scots that he should choose to play against the land of his birth!

ARTHUR THE MONKEY

Arthur "Monkey" Gould, so nicknamed for his ability to climb trees and on occasions rugby posts, was probably the first great personality of Welsh rugby and in his long career which brought him 28 caps, he played with Newport, Richmond, Middlesex and Wales between 1885 and 1896. Under his leadership Wales were the first of the home countries to adopt the four threequarters system, which was to lead to some heated controversy in those far off days. At the end of his career, his admirers, and they were many, subscribed over £600 as a testimonial to his contribution to Welsh rugby and this eventually led to the famous "Gould Dispute". The money was used to purchase a house for Gould but when the other unions heard about it, they promptly pointed out that this was downright professionalism. This led to a direct cleavage between Wales and Scotland and Ireland and Wales did not have any games with either country in the 1896-1897 season. Gould resolved the controversy by announcing his retirement from the game.

IN OPPOSITE CAMPS

F. E. Hancock (Cardiff) fell out of favour with the Welsh selectors at the start of the 1886 season. Having played against Ireland in 1884 and against England and Scotland in 1885, he was not selected for the game against England at Blackheath on 2nd January, 1886, but reappeared again on the Welsh side for the match against the Scots. That he missed the game against England was always a deep regret to him—and to his brother P. F. Hancock, who played his club rugby with Blackheath. Had he been chosen, they would have played against each other! P. F. Hancock was capped that year for England against Ireland and Wales and subsequently won a third cap against Wales in 1890. They were the first brothers to play for different countries in international rugby. The only others to do so are R. L. Ashton who played for England and his brother F. T. D. Ashton, who played for South Africa and W. M. C. McEwan, who appeared for both Scotland and South Africa and his brother M. C. McEwan, who was capped for Scotland, and Rodney Webb, who played for England on 12 occasions and his brother, Richard Webb, who was in the Australian party which toured in Britain, France, Ireland, Canada and America in 1966-1967. Although Richard Webb is regarded as an international player in Australia, he did not play in any of the international games against the major countries.

THE YOUNGEST

Norman Biggs, still a schoolboy when he began his international career with Wales went on to win eight caps for his country but his first, against the New Zealand Native side of 1888 was to be a significant milestone in his short career. In this game played at St Helen's, Swansea, on 22nd December, 1888, which was a suitable date for young Biggs because he was on school holidays, he was seventeen years and four months and to this day remains as the youngest man ever to wear the Welsh jersey in international rugby. He was just twenty-three when he played the last of his eight games for Wales.

A FRUITLESS WAIT

Tommy England of Newport got the wonderful news at the start of February, 1890 that he had been selected as Wales's full-back for the international game against England at Dewsbury on 15th February. This was to be his first international cap and what greater honour could there be for a Welshman? But, in a club game just a week before the international, England injured a leg and despite treatment, he was eventually forced to tell the selectors that he would not be available to play. Still, it seemed to be only a temporary thing. Time would eventually bring that international cap. Unfortunately, it did not. The Welsh selectors took a good look around and after long deliberation decided to gamble on a youngster from the Swansea club—one W. J. Bancroft. And Billy Bancroft took his golden chance with everything he had to offer. Wales beat England with a try by W. H. Stadden of Cardiff and Bancroft, destined to become one of Wales's finest full-backs played the game of his young life. He became a permanent fixture on the Welsh side, went on to play 33 consecutive games for his country . . . and Tommy England, named as his understudy for many years, finally retired from rugby without ever gaining that one Welsh cap that back in 1890 had been so close.

THE JAMES BROTHERS

The James brothers, Evan and David, who were to collect nine Welsh caps between them, joined forces for the first time against Ireland at Stradey Park, Llanelli on 7th March, 1891 . . . and within a year were to become the most talked of brothers in rugby. Unfortunately, it was not because of their rugby prowess which was recognised by everyone, but because of the sad fact that they had gone north to play with Broughton Rangers and there was more than a faint suspicion that they were being rewarded in cash for their services. After their second appearance against Ireland in 1892, they disappeared from view completely but then, lo and behold, they reappeared in Wales and, quite surprisingly, were selected to play against England at St Helen's, Swansea. Over the protests of every English official in sight, they played and performed wonders in routing England by 26-3. This was something that the English could not condone. Some interesting correspondence followed between the English and Welsh rugby unions and that was that. The James brothers were not to play for Wales again. Not that it really mattered for by this time the two James boys had uprooted their entire families and taken them all back to the North of England where there was good money to be earned in the now fully professional rugby league.

THE CUP MEDALS

Dai Fitzgerald's rugby union career was short but impressively exciting. Midway through the 1892-1893 season he was just another undistinguished centre on Cardiff's second team. Then an injury to one of the men on the first team gave him his chance of senior football and from that moment he never looked back. In February of 1893 he helped Cardiff to end Newport's long run of invincibility and a year later he was on the Welsh team to play Scotland at Newport. And he had the perfect debut. Scotland were beaten by 7-0 and Fitzgerald collected all the Welsh scores with a try and a drop goal. Later that season he won his second international cap for Wales against Ireland and then as the great historian of Welsh rugby, W. J. T. Collins puts it, he left Wales for "a handful of silver" to play professional rugby in the North of England. He joined Batley, and had the distinction of playing on three winning sides in the Northern Union Challenge Cup finals between 1897 and 1901. He was, of course, the first rugby union international to win a Rugby League Cup final medal. Fitzgerald, the son of Irish parents, lived to seventy-nine and died in 1951.

A FIRST FOR WALES

Wales had lost all three games in 1892 and were given little hope of improving when they lined out against England, the Triple Crown winners of the previous season, at Cardiff on 7th January, 1893. And even that little hope seemed to have disappeared just after half-time when England took the score to 11-0. But the Welsh staged an extraordinary fight-back over the final 20 minutes and with two tries from Bert Gould and another from Norman Biggs, they brought the score to 11-9. Then, in the dying seconds of the game full-back W. J. Bancroft dropped a sensational goal to win the game. Wales then went to Edinburgh to beat Scotland by a penalty goal and three tries to nil and finally on 11th March, 1893 they faced Ireland at Llanelli. And even though Ireland fielded with seven substitutes, this turned out to be an extremely close affair. It was eventually decided by a try from G. H. Gould and so Wales became Triple Crown champions for the first time. They have now won the Triple Crown on 12 occasions—1893, 1900, 1902, 1905, 1909, 1908, 1911, 1950, 1952, 1965, 1969 and 1971.

DIFFERENT SCORING

With time running out at Cardiff Arms Park on Saturday, 7th January, 1893, Wales were trailing 9-11 to England and then came a penalty to Wales. Arthur Gould told Billy Bancroft to place the ball and try for a goal but the full-back refused to place the ball. He insisted to trying for a drop at goal. Gould, in anger turned on his heels and walked away. Bancroft, however kicked the goal and Wales had won by 12-11. The interesting feature of this vital game was that if the Welsh scoring values had been used, the result would have been a 14-14 draw. At the time a try was worth three points in Wales but the International Board's value was only two points and this was the factor that gave Wales their win. It was to be a valuable win. Wales went on to beat Scotland by 9-0 at Raeburn Place in Edinburgh, their first win in Scotland and on Saturday 11th March, with just the one try from Bert Gould, Wales beat Ireland . . . and won the Triple Crown for the first time.

FOUR UP

Wales had taken a beating from England in 1898 and their game at St Helen's, Swansea, on Saturday, 7th January, 1899, promised to be a close one. In fact, it turned out to be a rout of England and no one enjoyed the afternoon more than young Willie Llewellyn of Llwaynpia, who was making his international debut for Wales. As the Welshmen surged away to a 26-3 victory, with four goals and two tries and a try, Llewellyn crossed the English line four times. He was the first Welshman to score four tries in an international game.

THE SECOND TRIPLE CROWN

Led by Billy Bancroft from the full-back position, Wales began the 1899-1900 season with a resounding win over England by 13-3 at Kingsholm, Gloucester and their opening try that afternoon came from a young man, by name Billy Trew, who was eventually to become one of the truly famous names of Welsh rugby. This was the first of his 29 appearances for Wales and the first of 11 tries he was to score in international rugby. Scotland came next at St Helen's on Saturday, 27th January, and a record Swansea crowd saw Wales take another vital step towards the Triple Crown with a 12-3 win. The Welsh headed for the muddy pitch at Balmoral in Belfast to take on Ireland, the reigning Triple Crown champions. In a gruelling game in which no quarter was asked or given between two mighty packs, there was just the one score by the Welsh centre George Davies, who unfortunately did not know until after the game that he had scored and brought Wales the Triple Crown for the second time. He had taken a kick on the head, was concussed and had to be removed from the field immediately after he had scored.

THE BANCROFT BROTHERS

Possibly the two most remarkable brothers in the history of Welsh rugby were Billy and Jack Bancroft, who, between them, collected 51 international caps—at full-back! And it took them 24 years to do so! Billy made his debut when he came in as a substitute for Tom England against Scotland on Saturday, 1st February, 1890 and his international career ended in 1901. Eight years later, and he was also a substitute full-back, Jack made his debut for Wales against England at Cardiff Arms Park and he finished out in 1914. Billy was to win 33 caps for Wales and Jack added on another 18 and both of course were also prolific scorers. Billy collected 60 international points and Jack took the Bancroft total in the 51 games to 148 with his 88. Billy also had the distinction of dropping the first goal from a mark in the history of international rugby when his last-minute kick in 1893 at Cardiff defeated England by 12-11.

GWYN NICHOLLS' YEAR

The immortal Gwyn Nicholls, who had made his debut for Wales against Scotland in 1896, led Wales to their third Triple Crown victory in 1901-1902. They beat England at the Rectory Field, Blackheath by 9-8 and beat Scotland at Cardiff Arms Park by 14-5. W. J. T. Collins, the great Welsh historian recalling that game against Scotland, wrote; "How Scotland's captain Mark Morrison, who had won the toss, could persuade himself—or how he was persuaded—that it was good policy to play against a half-gale at Cardiff in 1902, is one of the mysteries of captaincy". Morrison later admitted that he had made a dreadful mistake. Wales raced into a 14-0 lead in the first half, defended stoutly for the rest of the game and all Scotland could offer in return was one goal. So once again, by reason of the set programme for international games which was to last until the 1973-1974 season, the decider for the Triple Crown lay in the match between Wales and Ireland at Lansdowne Road, Dublin on Saturday, 8th March, 1902. This was the first all-ticket game at Lansdowne Road and the large crowd got little value for their money. Gwyn Nicholls dropped a goal in the first minute and later scored a try and Wales surged away to an effortless 15-0 win—and their third Triple Crown.

THE GHOST TRY

Rhys Gabe, who played with London-Welsh and Cardiff, wound up his great career with Wales by scoring 11 tries in his 24 international appearances between 1901 and 1908. Gabe, whose partnership with the great Gwyn Nicholls was the backbone of Welsh sides during those golden years, had probably his greatest day with Nicholls when they led Cardiff to an astonishing win by 17-0 over Paul Roos's 1906 South African tourists at Arms Park. The try he is most remembered for is the one that no one really saw. On the foggy day at Bristol City's A.F.C. Ground in 1908, he arranged a strategic move with Percy Bush and with Bush acting as a decoy to draw England to one side of the ground, Gabe went flying off in the opposite direction to score his immortal "ghost" try. Gabe, who was born in 1880, died at the age of eighty-seven.

A CAPTAIN'S PART

Willie Llewellyn of Newport, who had made his debut as far back as 1899, led Wales to their fourth Triple Crown in 1904-1905 and he really played a captain's part by scoring twice against England and twice against Scotland. England provided no trouble at all for the Welsh that season. They met at Cardiff Arms Park on Saturday, 14th January, and the Welsh ran in seven tries, two of which were converted for a 25-0 win. Against the Scots, however, three weeks later at Inverleith in Edinburgh, they ran into unexpected trouble and after Arthur Little had given Scotland the lead with a try, it took a try from Llewellyn to bring the sides level just before the break. Time wore away rapidly and the game was into its final eight minutes before Llewellyn picked up a loose ball, started a passing movement and then when the ball came back to him, he went tearing in for the try that won the game. Ireland had also won both their games that season so the meeting of the two countries at St Helen's, Swansea, on Saturday, 11th March, 1905 was really a final. Gwyn Nicholls, now in the twilight of a great career was brought back into the Welsh side for this game. Ireland's out-half Thomas Robinson opened the scoring with a try but in the second half Wales got well on top and eventually ran out fairly easy winners by 10-3.

A LONG TIME AROUND

No one in rugby has had as long an international career as the legendary Tommy Vile of Newport—and yet he is not Wales's longest-serving international. Vile, regarded as one of the greatest half-backs of his time, joined the Newport club in 1902 and two years later was invited to become a member of the Lions touring side, captained by D. R. Bedell-Sivright, which travelled to New Zealand and Australia. During his trip down under, he played in three Tests, on the two winning sides against Australia and on the side that lost 3-9 to New Zealand. Four years later, in 1908, Vile was capped for the first time for Wales against England at Bristol and against Scotland at Swansea, where, surprisingly, he appeared in the Welsh pack. In all he went on to win seven caps for Wales before the outbreak of the First World War and he came back to win his final cap as captain of Wales against Scotland at Swansea in 1921. His international career thus extended over 18 seasons. The Welsh record, however, for long service is held by Hadyn Tanner (Swansea and Cardiff) who made his first appearance for his country against New Zealand in 1935 and won the last four of his 25 caps against England, France, Ireland and Scotland in 1949—an international career of 15 seasons.

THE FIRST RECORD

Hailed as one of the finest scrum-halves of his time Dickie Owen, who was born in 1877, won 35 caps for Wales between 1901 and 1912 and had the great honour of playing on four Welsh Triple Crown winning sides. His record of 35 caps for Wales stood as a record until it was broken by Ken Jones 40 years later. His most celebrated bit of games-manship was in the closing moments of Wales's game against England at the Rectory Field on Saturday, 11th January, 1902. At a scrum in front of the English posts he whispered to his forwards to hold the ball in the scrum. Then he rushed around, pretended to take the ball and was promptly tackled by the England scrum-half Oughtred. As he was without the ball, the referee awarded a penalty in front of the posts and Strand Jones kicked the goal that beat England by 9-8. He was, of course, one of the prime architects in the Welsh defeat of the All-Blacks at Cardiff Arms Park in 1905.

CRASH OF CHAMPIONS

On Saturday, 16th December, 1905 Welsh rugby had its greatest afternoon when Wales became the only side to beat Dave Gallaher's All-Blacks, who up to that international had scored 801 points in 27 games and conceded only 22. The Welsh were really on top of the world and they showed it by slamming England 16-3 on 13th January, 1906 and then beating Scotland by 9-3 at Cardiff Arms Park just three weeks later. Now came the formality of beating Ireland at Balmoral,

Belfast to take the Triple Crown for the fifth time—and to become the first side to win four international rugby games in the one season. It was to be a sad afternoon for the rampant Welshmen. They lost two players with injuries and Ireland produced all the fireworks with sparkling tries from Harry Thrift, Joe Wallace and Basil Maclear and Fred Gardiner converted one. Wales scored two tries but were never in with a chance. Ireland, for the first time, had robbed Wales of a Triple Crown—a happy revenge for what the Welsh had done to them the previous year.

AND WHO SCORED, PLEASE?

As far as the journalists who were covering the game were concerned, the meeting of Wales and England at the Bristol City F.C. Ground on Saturday, 18th January, 1908, was not a very satisfactory affair. To keep themselves abreast of things, they had to ask the players for the names of the scorers and also for the type of scores that had been made! Early on the morning of the game, a thick fog settled down over Bristol and by kick-off time it was impossible to see from one side of the ground to the other and as W. J. T. Collins, the Welsh rugby historian recalls; "Never was it possible to see all the players of either side. There was not one combined movement of which we saw both the beginning and end. A thickening and thinning of the fog made visibility variable, but at the best it was barely possible to see halfway across the field, at the worst figures moving through the fog ten yards from the touch line were but dimly seen . . . Who had scored we did not know". However, when it was all totted up at the end, Rhys Gabe had scored two tries for Wales, Percy Bush, Billy Trew and Reggie Gibbs had also collected one each. Full-back Bert Winfied had two conversions and had also kicked a penalty goal and Bush had rounded off his day with a conversion and a drop goal. England had been beaten by 18-28 and, in the light of what was to follow, this was an historic foggy afternoon for the Welshmen.

THE GOLDEN ERA

An unforgettable golden era began for rugby on a foggy pitch at Bristol City A.F.C. ground on 18th January 1908, when in a game where few people managed to see everything that was going on, they beat

England by 28-18. Scotland came next at St Helen's, Swansea, on Saturday, 1st February, 1908 and that was a cliff-hanger all the way with Wales winning eventually by 6-5 with tries from Billy Trew and John Williams. Then before Wales went to Balmoral, Belfast to take on Ireland in the final hurdle to the Triple Crown, they had a happy warm-up game by meeting France for the first time and that was an easy formality. Reggie Gibbs ran in four tries, Billy Trew and Teddy Morgan added two each and that led the way to a 36-4 win. But the unpredictable Irish caused trouble again in Belfast. Their big forward Henry Aston battered his way over for a try which James Parke converted and they led 5-0 at half-time. Reggie Gibbs opened the Welsh scoring with a try and Bert Winfield added the extra points to make it 5-5. And so it remained until six minutes from the end. Then came the Irish collapse. Gibbs was let in for an easy try and two minutes later John Williams set the seal on a shock victory with a try. Wales had now brought their Triple Crown successes to five—and there was another fine year looming up.

FIVE IN THE SEASON

Dr H. M. Moran brought his touring Australians to Cardiff Arms Park on Saturday, 12th December, 1908 and Wales with a late penalty goal from Bert Winfield recorded their second victory over an overseas side by 9-6. A month later at Cardiff Arms Park, they removed England with ease by 8-0 but had all the luck in the world when they faced the Scots at Inverleith on Saturday, 6th February, 1909. Billy Trew had scored a try which Jack Bancroft converted but Scotland's George Cunningham then kicked a penalty goal to leave matters at 5-3. That was still the score until two minutes from time when Wales were penalised in front of their own posts but Cunningham, normally a safe kicker, managed to drive the ball well wide of the posts. Once again Ireland stood between Wales and the Triple Crown and that, sadly for the Irish, was never a real battle. They met at Swansea on Saturday, 13th March, and Wales cruised away at their ease to win by 18-5. Wales had also beaten France that season by 47-5, so it had been quite a season. A year earlier they had won their first Grand Slam by beating England, Ireland, Scotland and France but this time they had gone one better by also beating Australia. It marked the first time that any of the home countries had won five international matches in the same season. It was also the first time that any country had completed the Triple Crown in successive years and also the Grand Slam.

FIVE ON THE TROT

By beating the 1908-1909 Australian touring side on Saturday, 12th December, 1908 at Cardiff Arms Park, Wales set off on one of their most memorable seasons of rugby. In the space of four months they were to win the Triple Crown, complete the Grand Slam of beating all four home countries and end the season with the proud distinction of five wins on the trot, and Billy Trew had the honour of captaining the side in all five games. They beat Australia with tries from G. Travers and P. Hopkins and a penalty goal by full-back Bert Winfield. Subsequently on 16th January, 1909, they beat England 8-0 at Cardiff Arms Park with tries from Hopkins and J. L. Williams, a conversion by Jack Bancroft and then went on to beat Scotland at Inverleith by a try by Billy Trew, converted by Bancroft and then it was Ireland's turn to go down by 5-18 at Swansea with the Welsh scores coming from tries by Hopkins, J. P. Jones, J. Watts and Trew and three conversions by Bancroft. Against France in Paris—and the game was played on a Tuesday—the Welsh ran riot and won by 47-5 with the scores coming from Trew and A. M. Baker (three tries each), Williams and Jones (two tries each) and John Watts (a try). Seven of the tries were converted by Bancroft. Wales's record for that season was; played five, won five, scored 69 points and conceded 14. Billy Trew, the Welsh captain played 29 times for Wales, six times on the wing, nine times at half-back and 14 in the centre.

A GALA AFTERNOON

France's visit to Cardiff Arms Park on Saturday, 2nd March, 1908 was historic but not profitable. It was their first international game against Wales and their first on the Cardiff Arms Park ground. They managed to get a drop goal from their wing-threequarter Claude Vareilles, but that did not make much difference to the result. Wales went off on a scoring spree. Dick Jones had a try but Teddy Morgan and Billy Trew topped that with two each . . . and wing-threequarter

Reggie Gibbs went even better. He shot over for four tries to equal the Welsh record that had been set by Willie Llewellyn back in 1899. For good measure, he also converted one of his own tries. Gibbs, who was to play 16 times for Wales before he retired in 1911 finished his career with another Welsh record of 17 tries in international rugby. This has since been equalled by Ken Jones who had 44 international games to get his 17 tries and Johnny Williams who took 17 international games to get his 17.

A 10 POINTS FLOURISH

Jack Bancroft, who came on to the Welsh team as a substitute full-back for the injured Bert Winfield at Cardiff Arms Park on Saturday, 16th January, 1909, began his international career with a conversion and ended it with a conversion five years later. Against England in his first game he kicked just the one conversion but against France on Monday, 2nd March, 1914 at St Helen's, Swansea when Wales won by 31-0, he kicked five conversions. And those last 10 points he scored for Wales were to take his international total to 88 in 18 games, from 38 conversions and four penalty goals and this was to endure as a Welsh record until Barry John, beginning his final Welsh appearance against France at Cardiff on Saturday, 25th March, 1972 with 78 points, kicked four penalty goals to lift the all-time record in Wales to 90 points.

TWICKENHAM START AND END

When Billy Trew led Wales out to play England on Saturday, 15th January, 1910, he and his men were breaking new ground in every sense of the word. It was Wales's first visit to Twickenham in London and they went there with a proud record behind them. Unfortunately, Twickenham on that particular afternoon was not to be a happy experience for the Welshmen. Englands Fred Chapman took a pass from Dai Gent and Wales were three points down in as many minutes. Fred Chapman converted the try and then came a further disaster for Wales. Chapman, who was playing on the wing dived over for a try and England were eight points clear. Wales never recovered from these sudden blows and although Reggie Gibbs and Jim Webb scored tries, Bert Solomon eventually put the issue beyond all doubt with a

153

soaring penalty goal and England were five points clear, 11-6 at the end. With this defeat, one of the greatest records in rugby history came to an end. From that foggy afternoon against England at Bristol in 1908, Wales had been unbeaten and had scored an unprecedented 11 wins in succession until they were beaten at Twickenham. It was the first time, too that England had beaten Wales in an international game since 2nd April, 1898 at Blackheath, London.

BILLY TREW'S YEAR

Under the captaincy of Billy Trew, who had been on the go since his first international game in 1900, Wales won the Triple Crown for the seventh time in 1910-1911. Their only difficult game was the one against England at St Helen's, Swansea on Saturday, 21st January, 1911 when they had to fight desperately to hold out against a fine English side led by Guy Birkett. They were held all the way and with a late try by Joseph Pugsley, they won by 15-11. But once England were out of the way, the Welsh really caught fire. They went to Inverleith, Edinburgh to shatter the Scots by a record score of 32-10, which gave Reggie Gibbs the astonishing record of having scored four tries in a match against France at Cardiff in 1908, three in another match against France at Swansea in 1910 and now three against Scotland in 1911. In between then and taking on Ireland, Wales whipped France by 15-0 and eventually at Cardiff Arms Park on Saturday, 11th March, 1911, they overran Ireland by 16-0. That season in completing the Grand Slam for the third time in four seasons, Wales scored 78 points and conceded only 21. But as subsequent events were to show it was to be a long, long time before Wales again accomplished the Triple Crown or the Grand Slam.

A LITTLE OLD

Only two men by the name of Uzzell—and they are related—have played for Wales in international rugby and both have their claim to fame. Harry Uzzell of Newport, was capped 11 times for Wales before the First World War and returned after the war to captain Wales in their four games of 1920 against England, Ireland, Scotland and France. He was then approaching his thirty-eighth birthday, is one of the oldest men to play for Wales and definitely the oldest man to captain the country. The younger Uzzell, John, also of Newport won only five caps, all in 1965 but he carved out a special spot for himself in Welsh rugby history at Rodney Parade, Newport on Wednesday, 30th October, 1963. He turned out for Newport against New Zealand and there was just the one score in the game—a drop goal by John Uzzell. It was to be the only defeat for Wilson Whineray's All-Blacks in their 34 games of the 1963-1964 tour of Britain, Ireland and France.

JERRY SHEA'S MATCH

It was the first official international rugby game after the First World War and it was played at St Helen's, Swansea on Saturday, 17th January, 1920 and it was a first cap for Jerry Shea of Newport. He was to play only three international games for Wales but that first one was enough to make him a hero in the valleys of Wales for many, many years after. Wales won by 19-5 but as far as the spectators were concerned Jerry Shea had beaten Scotland. That was close to the truth. With a remarkable display, after England had led by 5-0 at the break, Shea started off the second half by dropping a goal, then worth four points. Then he raced over for a try and did the conversion himself. Next he kicked a penalty goal, made a try for Wick Powell but failed to convert it. He wound up the game by dropping a second goal for a total of 16 points out of Wales's 19 . . . and, of course, he had collected his total with all the ways that one could score—a try, a penalty goal, a conversion and a drop goal.

THE ONE THAT GOT AWAY

Down in Wales they were talking about the seventeen-year old youngster in Cardiff, who had already shown that he might become one of the outstanding personalities of rugby union football. But Jim Sullivan was never to play rugby union for Wales. A certain gentleman from Wigan with shrewd foresight signed him as a professional in 1921 and young Jim went north. His rugby league was to last right from 1921 to 1946 and he did gain international honours with Britain with 25 appearances against New Zealand and Australia and he also made 25 appearances for Wales and six for Other Nationalities against England. But his scoring record deserves to be remembered. In all he scored 76 tries and kicked . . . 2,208 goals!

THE CROWD BEAT THEM

There was a record crowd of over 50,000 spectators at St Helen's, Swansea on Saturday, 5th February, 1921 to see Wales take on Scotland. They were there to cheer for a Welsh victory; in the end they managed to defeat Wales. A. R. Thompson opened the scoring for Scotland with a try which J. C. R. Buchanan converted—and then the crowd invaded the pitch. It took the Welsh players and a squad of police almost 10 minutes to push the spectators back to the sideline. And all during this time the Scots relaxed and had a rest. Once the game had started again G. H. Maxwell kicked a penalty goal for Scotland and with a try from Buchanan, Scotland led 11-0 at the break. Albert Jenkins then put Wales back into the picture with two drop goals and the score was 11-8 . . . and in their excitement, the spectators poured back on to the field again. This time, the Scots, who were getting the worst of the game at that stage, had the opportunity of a 15 minutes break while the Welsh team pushed and shoved, cajoled and pleaded with the crowd to move back. That was the rest Scotland needed. They came back with a try from Buchanan and Scotland had won in Wales for the first time in 29 years. W. J. T. Collins, the Welsh historian recalls in his famous book, *Rugby Recollections*; "I felt at the time and I think still that Wales were beaten that day not by Scotland but by the distracting effects of the crowd's invasion of the ground, at two critical stages when they seemed to have the Scots flagging and on the run".

A FAIR CLUB SIDE

For their final match of the 1920-1921 season against Bristol at Rodney Parade on 13th April, 1921, Newport found themselves in the happy position of being able to field their strongest and most representative side of that season. It included the Englishmen Reg Edwards, Bob Dibble, Ernie Hammett, the Irishman W. J. Roche, the Scot Neil McPherson and the Welshmen Len Attewell, Jack Whitfield, Harry Uzzell, Percy Jones, Jerry Shea, Jack Wetter, Reg Plummer, Tommy Vile, Archie Brown and Fred Birt. All fifteen were internationals and, of course, the four home countries were represented on the side. Because of injury, Tommy Vile had been able to play only six games for Newport that season but all of the others at one time or another had played 11 or more games for Newport. This, however, was the first time they had been able to field their 15 internationals together and they duly won comfortably by 17-0.

THE OLD CHESTNUT

One of the stories that has come down through rugby history—and it is often repeated—is that Albert Freethy, the Welshman, who sent Cyril Brownlie to the line in England's game against Cliff Porter's invincible All-Blacks of 1924-1925 at Twickenham on Saturday, 25th January, 1925, was never again invited to referee an international rugby game. This, of course, is totally untrue. Mr Freethy had the full support of all the Home unions in his action that afternoon and subsequently went to referee many more international games. Before he put away his whistle for good, he had, in fact, set a world record by refereeing 16 international games. One of the interesting features of that particular international game at Twickenham that afternoon was that there were three international teams present, England, New Zealand and Ireland. The Irish that year had played France on Thursday, 23rd January and on their way home to Ireland were invited to Twickenham as special guests of the English Rugby Union.

SENT HOME

B. O. "Ossie" Male of Cardiff set off for Paris in 1924 with the rest of the Welsh team to take on France at Colombes Stadium on Saturday, 27th March, 1924 but when the team lined out at Paris, Male was missing and his full-back spot was filled by M. A. Rosser of Penarth. In between, Male, first capped for Wales in 1921, had been sent back home under suspension. He had broken the cardinal rule of having played in a club game in a week before an international game and had made no secret of it. He freely admitted that he had turned out for Cardiff and as far as the selectors were concerned, there could be no excuse for that. He was promptly suspended and sent back home after the Welsh party had reached London. He was, however, eventually forgiven and restored to their good books. But not until 1927! He came back on to the Welsh side that year and eventually finished his career with 11 caps.

WHAT HAPPENED?

At half-time at Twickenham on Saturday, 17th January, 1931, the scoreboard read; England 6 pts—Wales 6 pts. Before the second half started, the same scoreboard read; England 8 points—Wales 6 pts. And from there on the game continued to end in an 11-11 draw, which from the Welsh point of view, subsequently had a great bearing on their Triple Crown hopes. But for that change on the board, Wales today might be on level terms with England in the matter of Triple Crowns with 13 wins each. What happened was that towards the end of the first half Don Burland, the English centre, had run in from almost 70 yards out to score a fine try midway between the posts and the touchline. When he had recovered from his exertions, he took the conversion attempt and neither touch judge raised a flag. This brought the score to 6-6 and when the Irish referee noticed this at half-time he called the touch judges together and ordered them to have the scoreboard changed immediately. He had been in a position to judge the conversion attempt and he was satisfied that it had gone over. With those two extra points added on, England eventually drew with Wales and the Welsh at a later stage that season were not overjoyed about the draw. They beat Scotland and Ireland and those two points had taken a Triple Crown away from them.

BEFORE AND AFTER

In their international game against Scotland at Cardiff Arms Park on Saturday, 7th February, 1931, Wales had the unique experience of scoring before the actual starting time . . . and of scoring again after the finishing time of the game. For some reason or other the game started four minutes before 3 o'clock and within a minute John Morley of Newport had launched himself over the Scottish line for a try which Jack Bassett converted. On the clock the game was over but in the fifth minute of injury time, Ronnie Boon raced in for a try to give Wales a 13-8 victory. Up to that moment the scores have been level at 8-8 but this late try converted by Jack Bassett gave Wales the unusual record of scoring before the 80 minutes had started and after the 80 minutes had ended.

IRELAND STEP IN AGAIN

A decade of defeat by England came to an end for Wales at St Helen's, Swansea, on Saturday, 16th January, 1932. With a try and a drop goal from Ronnie Boon, and a conversion and a penalty goal they beat Carl Aarvold's men by 12-5. This put a little heart into the Welsh who had already been beaten that season by the touring South Africans and they put themselves into line for the Triple Crown for the first time since 1911 by beating Scotland 6-0 at Murrayfield on Saturday, 6th February, 1932. So the final battle was at Cardiff Arms Park with Ireland on Saturday, 12th March and the Welsh were odds-on favourites. But Ireland opened up with a try from Lansdowne's wing-threequarter Eddie Lightfoot, and with two further tries from William McC.Ross of Queen's, they had nine points on the scoreboard. The Welsh, however, came storming back and with tries from Claude Davey and Ray Ralph who also dropped a goal, they were in the lead with barely minutes to go. Then came a sensational 90 yards run by Sean Waide of London-Irish and Ireland were winners by 12-10. Once before, back in 1906, Ireland had also deprived Wales of the Triple Crown.

A BLESSING . . . . AND A BOON

There were 65,000 people at Twickenham on Saturday, 21st January, 1933—and all the Welsh spectators in that crowd were praying hard. After all Wales had never won at Twickenham and the 23 years since 1910 when they first met there had been a long time. And their prayers were answered by one man—wing-threequarter Ronnie Boon from Cardiff. This was to be an historic afternoon for Wales and even more so for Boon. Bill Elliott of United Services had given England the lead by half-time with a try but minutes after the re-start, Boon appeared from nowhere, whipped up a stray ball that had come shooting back from a loose maul and dropped the neatest of goals. Then he capped it all by scoring a try to make it 7-3 for Wales and that was how it ended. A first for Wales at Twickenham . . . and all of their points from Boon in what was to be his second last game for Wales.

A FIRST FOR VIVIAN

At a time when international sides fielded two full-backs, W. J. Penny of England against Ireland in 1878 and T. W. Fray of England against Scotland in 1880 had scored tries from the full-back position. But up to Saturday, 10th March, 1934 no full-back in modern international rugby had succeeded in doing so. Then Wales took on Ireland at St Helen's, Swansea and up to five minutes from time, there was no score. Vivian Jenkins, the Welsh full-back and nowadays one of the game's most distinguished commentators, decided it was time to get Wales off the ground and, coming into a threequarter movement, he finished it off by diving over for a try which he converted. In those last fateful five minutes Wales were to take their total to 13 points and Jenkins wound up with seven points from his try and two conversions. More important, he had become the first full-back in modern rugby and in the history of the International Championship to score a try in an international game.

THE SCHOOLBOY WIZARD

At the beginning of the 1934-1935 season in Wales, the main topic of rugby conversation was the seventeen-year old Haydn Tanner, then a schoolboy at Gowerton Grammar School. He had already won his place at scrum-half on the Swansea first team and it was well known that more than one or two of the Welsh selectors wanted him for the international side. Others felt he was too young to be thrown into international rugby and then, too, there was the matter of his studies. However at the beginning of the 1935-1936 season, Swansea took on the touring All-Blacks at St Helen's and there, with a masterly display from Tanner and his cousin Willie Davies, another schoolboy, at out-half, Jack Manchester's men went down to their first defeat of the tour. After that there could be no question but that young Tanner had to go on to the Welsh side for their first international of that season, against New Zealand, on Saturday, 21st December, 1935. That, of course, was just the beginning of the glorious international career of one of the finest scrum-halves Wales have ever produced. But for the Second World War years, he would almost certainly have set a world record of international caps. On 26th March, 1949 in a 5-3 win over France at Colombes Stadium, Paris, Haydn Tanner played his 25th and last time for Wales. His 15 seasons of international rugby is still a Welsh record in 1974.

THEY WERE NEVER CAPPED

The saddest feature of the 1936-1937 international rugby season was the match in Belfast that had to be postponed with the unhappy result that three men selected to play for Wales in that particular game against Ireland were never to be capped. The match was due to be played at Ravenhill on Saturday, 13th March, 1937 and because of injuries to key players, including full-back Vivian Jenkins, three new caps—Tom Stone, Harry Edwards and Charles Anderson—were picked on the Welsh side. Unfortunately that was the week of a heavy snowstorm in Ireland and when the Welsh team landed safely in Belfast, they found that Ravenhill was under six inches of snow and there was no possibility whatsoever that the game could be played. Subsequently the game was re-fixed for Saturday, 10th April, but by then all the injured players on the Welsh side had recovered and were chosen to play. And Messrs Stone, Edwards and Anderson, were never to be capped for their country.

THE OLYMPIC MAN

Prior to the outbreak of the Second World War, he had been a fair rugby player but during the war years, he began to establish himself as a first-class sprinter and when he returned home to Wales in 1946, he proved that there were few men faster in Britain. In 1948 he was to win an Olympic silver medal in the 4 x 100 metres relay at London and he also represented Britain in the European and Empire Games. But, like every other Welshman he had his passion for rugby and immediately on his return from the war, he joined up with Newport. And on 18th January, 1947, then twenty-six and perhaps a little old for international rugby, he made his debut for Wales against England at Cardiff Arms Park. It was a quiet debut but he did well enough to ensure retention for the next game and the one after that . . . and the one after that. In fact, he was to go on for a long, long time. He made the Lions tour to Australia and New Zealand in 1950 at the age of twenty-eight. And he was still around on Saturday, 2nd February, 1957 when Wales went to Murrayfield to take on Scotland. That was the last time Ken Jones was to wear the jersey of his country but no man before or since has worn it so often in international rugby. It was his 44th appearance for Wales, then a world record and nowadays, still a Welsh record.

LEWIS JONES APPEARS

Lewis Jones, still three months short of his nineteenth birthday, made his debut for Wales at Twickenham on Saturday, 21st January, 1950 and collected himself five points from a conversion and a penalty goal. England opened the scoring with a try from John Smith which the South African Murray Hofmeyer converted and that, sadly, was England's lot for the afternoon. Cliff Davies and Roy Cale got tries for Wales to make it an 11-5 win. Scotland were not impressive that season and Lewis Jones kept up the good work by kicking a penalty goal which with tries from Malcolm Thomas and Ken Jones and a drop goal by Billy Cleaver gave Wales an easy 12-0 win at Swansea. Ireland, of course, were to be the last barrier to the Triple Crown and it was more than a battle. It was a titanic struggle that locked itself into a 3-3 draw with only seconds to go and in those seconds Malcolm Thomas with a glorious run on the wing became the national hero of Wales—for that year at least. After a lapse of 39 years Wales were Triple Crown champions again—their eighth time and with their 21-0 win over France they were also Grand Slam champions for the fourth time.

AND HE DID IT TWICE

Lewis Jones, the Llanelli full-back, who was to win 10 caps for Wales and who was flown out as a replacement to join Karl Mullen's Lions of 1950 in New Zealand and Australia, had quite a field day against Australia in the Lions international game against Australia at the famous Wooloongabba Ground at Brisbane. Apart from becoming the first Lions full-back to score a try in an international game, he wound up his afternoon with 16 points, which smashed the record for an international game in which the Lions were involved. Jones collected his 16 points from a try, a drop goal, two penalty goals and two conversions. Four years later, Jones, by now one of the Rugby League's top players, came back to Australia with the Britain team . . . and set another scoring record. He kicked 10 goals against Australia, which broke the Rugby League record which had been set the previous season by the Australian league international, Noel Pidding.

A NEW STAR IS BORN

There were two memorable features about Wales's game with Ireland at Cardiff Arms Park on Saturday, 10th March, 1951. There were two new caps and one of them Ben Edwards of Newport kicked the vital penalty goal that gave Wales a 3-3 draw. That was to be his first and last international for Wales. The other new cap fared a little better. He was twenty-one, a native of Trebanog and had been showing quite an amount of promise with his club Cardiff. Unlike the other new cap on the Welsh team that day, he was to go on to establish himself as one of the world's greatest out-halves. He won 29 caps for Wales, played in four international games for the Lions during their tour of South Africa in 1955. He had a remarkable career in rugby . . . and nowadays, as one of television's and radio's finest commentators and also a first-class journalist, Cliff Morgan is still quite a remarkable man.

THOMAS AGAIN

Malcolm Thomas, possibly one of Wales's finest threequarters, was back in the news in January 1952 but not with the try that everyone expected. Wales down 0-6 at one stage came back with tries by Ken Jones and Thomas, in the temporary absence of Lewis Jones, kicked the vital conversion that made all the difference. Scotland then came down to Cardiff Arms Park and a record crowd poured in with the fervent hope that the Welsh side might retrieve some of the honour they had lost in the previous year's 0-19 defeat at Murrayfield. The Welsh duly paid them back and Thomas was again in the news. Ken Jones scored a try and Thomas converted it and then proceeded to kick two penalty goals for an 11-0 win. The vital battle, with the rugby programme as it was then, wound up with a Triple Crown confrontation with Ireland at Lansdowne Road and it was never in doubt. Ken Jones marked the occasion by scoring for the third time in the three Triple Crown games that season and Wales ran out well on top by 14-3. They finished off the season by beating France at St Helen's, Swansea on 22nd March, 1952 and once again they had captured the Triple Crown and the Grand Slam.

FROM LEIGH

Everyone at the Leigh Rugby League club was satisfied that young Glyn John who was playing on the wing for them, could be a really outstanding addition to the club. But, not so very long afterwards Glyn Jones of St Luke's College and Exeter and Aberavon was playing on the wing for Wales in an international rugy union game against England in 1954 at Twickenham and he went on to win a second cap that season against Wales at Cardiff Arms Park. John had been signed for £400 by Leigh but he was only seventeen at the time. Subsequently, he repaid the £400 to Leigh and was re-instated to rugby union.

BOTH WERE NEW

The two full-backs chosen for the Welsh panel for the international game against England at Cardiff Arms Park on Saturday, 22nd January, 1955, were both without caps. Garfield Owens, who was on the team, was due to make his debut in the Welsh jersey and Arthur Edwards, the reserve, had no idea at all at the time that when Wales took the field for that game, he, in fact, would be standing in the last line of defence. On the previous day, while the Welshmen were training Owen injured himself and Edwards was brought in and, like all of the good rugby fairy stories, he kicked the only score of the game—a penalty goal of Wales's 3-0 win. Edwards held his place for the next game against Scotland and ended his international career with those two caps. Owen came back for the game against Ireland that season and eventually won six caps for Wales.

A DECISIVE BEATING

The vital day for Welsh rugby in 1956 was Saturday, 10th March—and the place was Lansdowne Road. They had pipped England by 8-3, beaten Scotland by 9-3 and it was another Triple Crown day for the Welsh. And they got away to an excellent start when full-back Garfield Owen with a splendid 45 yards penalty goal put them into a 3-0 lead at the break. Then, perhaps, with the Irish a little aggrieved that on that afternoon the Welsh wing-threequarter, Ken Jones, was equalling the world record of caps by their own George Stephenson, decided it was time to show the visitors a trick or two. Marney Cunningham, who was later to enter the priesthood, got a try, Cecil Pedlow converted it and then for good measure Pedlow kicked a penalty goal and Wales's dreams of the Triple Crown were gone on the wind. All they left Dublin with was a share in the world record number of international caps by their Olympic sprinter Ken Jones.

HIS FIRST FAME

It was quite a shock for every Welsh supporter when Cliff Morgan told his selectors that he was injured and not available to take his place against the Australians at Cardiff Arms Park on Saturday, 4th January, 1958. Into his place, however, came a young man who was to partner his Llanelli clubmate, Wynne Evans that afternoon. And they made a happy partnership as Wales went on to record their third win since 1908 over the Wallabies by 9-3, a drop goal, a penalty goal and a try to a try. Subsequently the young man who replaced Cliff Morgan that day was to win a second international cap for Wales at centre three-quarter that season. But a far greater fame was to come to him in 1971 in far-off New Zealand. His name was . . . Carwyn James.

SOME COMPENSATION

On Saturday, 28th April, 1958, George Parsons on his second visit to Wembley Stadium for the Rugby League Cup final won his gold medal when St Helen's took the trophy for the first time by beating Halifax 13-2. And that must have been just a little consolation for the abrupt ending to his international rugby career with Wales. He had won his first rugby union cap for Wales against England in 1947 and was, in fact, due to gain his second against France at Colombes Stadium on Saturday, 22nd March, 1947. Parsons, who was then playing with Newport, turned up at the station in Cardiff to join the team on their way to France but before he had a chance to board the train, he was sent home. They had heard stories that he had been approached by rugby league clubs and, although he said there was no truth in these, the Welsh rugby union refused to let him travel. A year later, when it became obvious that his future was bleak as far as further caps were concerned, he went north to join St Helen's and made his first Cup final appearance with them at Wembley in 1953 when they were beaten by Huddersfield. A week later, they walloped Huddersfield in the semi-final of the League championship and went on to beat Halifax 24-14 in the final at Maine Road.

THE ENTERTAINER

One of rugby's most talented entertainers of the 1960s was the "darling boy" of Wales—little David Watkins, who right at the height of his international career switched over to Rugby League with Salford. One of the finest drop-kickers in the history of the game, he was also an excitingly brilliant out-half and in addition to his 21 appearances for Wales he also made six international appearances for the Lions during their tour of New Zealand and Australia in 1966. Down under he made the headlines for a much publicised "altercation" with the giant Colin Meads of New Zealand, which, however, did not affect his subsequent play. After switching codes, Watkins was capped in League football for Wales and Britain.

THE LITTLE MAN FROM WALES

Little Gwynne Walters of Wales established himself as one of the most courageous referees of all-time when he stepped in between the gigantic New Zealand and French forwards in their battle royal at Colombes Stadium in February 1961. Dwarfed by the two captains and lost in the giants all around he laid his terms strictly and firmly on the line. Unless both sides cut out this battle to the death, he would send the lot off—all 30 players. And they got the message. From there on the game proceeded in orderly fashion. Walters, who with Kevin Kelleher of Ireland, is one of the world's most honoured referees, blew his first whistle in a game at the tender age of sixteen and refereed his first international game in 1959 when he had charge of the France v Scotland game at Colombes Stadium in Paris. He and Kelleher are now the world leaders in the matter of refereeing international games . . . and, perhaps the most unusual feature of Walter's career in sport is that he never played rugby!

THE LUCKY FOURTEENTH

If Alun Pask had been a superstitious young man, he might have worried a little when he travelled to Paris to win his first cap against the French at Colombes Stadium on Saturday 25th March, 1961. Before he walked on to the pitch that afternoon, he had the record behind him of having been a reserve on the Welsh side on 13 occasions. But this 14th time passed without a hitch. He won his first cap and then went on to make 26 consecutive appearances for Wales, which included winning the Triple Crown in 1965. Pask, remembered as one of the towering figures of rugby during his best years made two Lions tours, to South Africa in 1962 and to Australia, New Zealand and Canada in 1966, during which he made eight further international appearances for the tourists against South Africa, New Zealand and Australia.

WALES'S 10TH

There could not have been a better climax to the 1964 season. Wales had beaten England by 14-3 and Scotland by 14-12; Ireland had beaten England by 5-0 and Scotland by 16-6. The Triple Crown was at stake for the two countries when they faced each other at Cardiff Arms Park on Saturday, 13th March, 1965. The dapper David Watkins, later to be a Lion and later still to be a star of Rugby League, got things off to a good start with a fine try that Terry Price converted and in the second half Dewi Bebb, now one of the game's best known commentators, added a second. But Tom Kiernan kicked a penalty goal, to make it 8-3 before Terry Price dropped a goal from 50 yards out to raise Wales's lead to 11-3. Kevin Flynn then collected one of his typically opportunist tries for Ireland and with Kiernan kicking the conversion the score was 11-8 and it was still anyone's game. But in the end Terry Price with a soaring penalty goal wrapped it all up for Wales. After 82 years of international rugby, they had joined England in double figures where the Triple Crown was concerned. France, however, took quite a hiding from France that year at Colombes where at one sad stage they trailed by 0-22 and eventually managed to pull back to 13-22. Terry Price had the satisfaction of scoring in all four games with a total of 22 points.

WALES IN SOUTH AFRICA

Clive Rowlands, who was to lead Wales to the Triple Crown just a year later, captained the first Welsh side to undertake a short overseas tour to South Africa in 1964. They played four matches, including one full international against the Springboks and wound up with a record of winning two games, losing two and scoring 40 points while conceding 34. The top points scorer of the tour was Keith Bradshaw, who collected 19 points with two conversions, four penalty goals and a drop goal. The top try scorer was Dewi Bebb with three. In the international game at King's Park, Durban, the sides were level at half-time with a South African penalty goal from Keith Oxlee and a Welsh penalty goal by Bradshaw. And there was still no change up to the 20th minute of the second half. Then Lionel Wilson dropped a goal from 55 yards out and from there on it was easy sailing for the Springboks. Hannes Marais, Doug Hopwood and Nelie Smith went over for tries. Oxlee converted all three and then added a second penalty goal to give himself exactly half of the South African's total. This 24-3 win for South Africa still endures as the widest margin in the history of international games between the two countries. It also maintained South Africa's undefeated run against Wales since the sides met for the first time at Swansea in 1906. In their last meeting in 1970, the Welsh drew with South Africa at 6-6 and the record between the two countries is South Africa with six victories to none with one drawn. In the seven games, South Africa have scored 60 points and Wales have scored 15.

ON HIS MOTHER'S SIDE

In most of the family traditions in international rugby, playing prowess usually comes down on the male side. But in the case of Terry Price, the Welsh full-back who won eight caps for Wales between 1965 and 1967, it came through his mother's side of the family. Her father, Terry's grandfather Dai Hiddlestone, was capped at wing-forward for Wales against England, Ireland, Scotland and France in 1924 and was recalled for his fifth and final cap against Cliff Porter's "Invincibles" from New Zealand in 1924.

NINETY POINTS

Barry John made his international debut for Wales against Australia at Cardiff on Saturday, 3rd December, 1966 and made his first appearance in the International Championship against Scotland on Saturday, 4th February, 1967. In both games he failed to register a score but on Saturday, 11th November, 1967 he broke his duck with a drop goal against the New Zealand touring side at Cardiff. On Saturday, 25th March, 1972, he made his 25th and final appearance in the red jersey of Wales against France at Cardiff Arms Park and he said his goodbye with four penalty goals in Wales's victory by 20-6.

168

Those final 12 points brought his international scoring to an exact 90 points and he had become the highest points scorer in Welsh rugby history. His highest individual total in an international game came against Scotland on Saturday, 5th February, 1972 with 15 points from three penalty goals and three conversions. In that year's International Championship, with the two penalty goals and a conversion, his total for the three international games he played that season—the game against Ireland was cancelled—his total was 35 points, which was then a Welsh individual record for an international series in the championship.

ENGLAND AT THE END

Wales went to Murrayfield on Saturday, 1st February, 1969 and gave the poor Scots a sound hammering by 17-3, with Keith Jarrett contributing eight points from two penalty goals and a conversion. Ireland came next on the list on Saturday, 8th March, 1969—and this was the day that the Prince of Wales, 50,000 odd spectators at Cardiff Arms Park and a couple of million TV viewers saw Brian Price deliver one of the most famous right upper-cuts in rugby history—and Wales romped up by 24-11 and Keith Jarrett added another nine points from a penalty goal and three conversions to his collection. Next came England at Cardiff Arms Park and that was a rout. Maurice Richards sailed over for four tries to equal the Welsh record for a game and Keith Jarrett added 12 points with three conversions and two penalty goals in a 30-9 victory. This was Wales's 11th Triple Crown but a draw in Paris robbed them of the Grand Slam. Keith Jarrett however converted a try at Colombes Stadium to bring his total for the four games to 31 points.

A LITTLE OVER-CONFIDENT

With wins over England at Twickenham by 11-6 and over Scotland by 8-3, Wales flew into Dublin to take on Ireland on Saturday, 12th March, 1966—and never were 15 men more confident of winning. Particularly Alan Pask, who told Irish TV and radio listeners on the eve of the game that Wales would have no trouble in beating Ireland. It turned out to be an afternoon that no Welshman cares to remember.

Mike Gibson dropped a goal and Ireland were three points up and minutes later he kicked a penalty goal and the great Welsh were trailing 0-6 and at sixes and sevens with themselves. Gary Prothero at wing forward managed to slip over for a Welsh try to leave it 6-3 at the interval. But Barry Bresnihan, whose grandfather had been a world record holder in the triple jump, showed his ability to bound along with a delightful try that put Ireland 9-3 ahead. It made no difference that Keith Bradshaw kicked a penalty goal in the closing minutes. Wales, with their tails between their legs, had gone down to a sensational defeat—and could hardly count on a hero's welcome on their return home.

ARGENTINA, 1968

Wales had lost to New Zealand by 6-13, drawn with England 11-11, beaten Scotland 5-0 and lost to Ireland 6-9 in the 1967-1968 season . . . and then they set off on a short tour of Argentina to salvage a little prestige. That, too, however, was not to be a happy memory for the Welsh. In their six match tour, they were shocked 5-9 in the first unofficial international against the Argentinians, then beat Belgrano by 24-11, the Provincial Union by 14-3, drew 8-8 with Argentina "B" and drew with a selected XV 9-9 and finally beat Argentina 9-6 in the final unofficial international. That sobering tour for Wales had its effect the following season. They won the Triple Crown and also the International championship and Welsh rugby was back in its ascendancy again.

WALES DOWN UNDER

Led by Brian Price of Newport, Wales made their first tour of New Zealand and Australia in 1969 and played a six-match programme, which included three international games, two against the All-Blacks and one against Australia. They played five games in New Zealand, won two, lost two and drew one and scored 62 points while conceding 76. They won their only game in Australia by 19-16. Keith Jarrett came home with the top points scoring record with 32 from four conversions, seven penalty goals and a try in New Zealand and 10 in Australia with two conversions and two penalty goals. Top try scorer was Maurice Richards with five. The Welshmen opened their tour with a 9-9 draw with Taranaki at New Plymouth on 27th May, 1969 and then four days later moved to Christchurch to take on New Zealand in the first international.

NINETEEN POINTS DOWN

Saturday, 31st May, 1969 could hardly have been a worse day. It began with rain, then there was a mild downfall of snow and by the time Wales lined up at Lancaster Park, Christchurch to face the All-Blacks in their first meeting outside Wales, the ground was soaked and muddy. And Wales's performance that afternoon was just as depressing as the weather. Malcolm Dick went in for an early try for the All-Blacks and hooker Bruce McLeod added a second which Fergie McCormick converted and Wales were 0-8 down. Brian Lochore added another try, McCormick was spot on with the conversion and it was 0-13 against Wales. In the second half Ken Gray went surging over for a try and just before the end McCormick kicked a penalty goal to leave the All-Blacks ahead by 19-0. And that equalled the worst beating they had ever given Wales. Back in 1924 Cliff Porter's All-Blacks had also beaten Wales by 19-0 at St Helen's, Swansea. It was the third time in seven meetings that Wales had failed to register a score against New Zealand. Unfortunately, there was worse to come for the Welshmen on this short tour.

McCORMICK'S DAY

After the rout of Christchurch, Wales got back to form rapidly with an impressively comfortable win by 27-9 over a strong Otago side at Dunedin on 4th June, 1969 and followed that up by beating Wellington 14-6. Now they had to face New Zealand at Eden Park, Auckland and a revenge for the first international was badly needed. There was, however, to be no revenge. Instead there was the blackest day in the history of Welsh international rugby. They took the lead with a penalty goal by Keith Jarrett, Maurice Richards had a try and then Jarrett with a try and another penalty goal gave them a final total of 12 points. In the meantime Fergie McCormick, the All-Blacks full-back had taken off on a scoring spree. Alan Skudder, Ian MacRae and Ian Kirkpatrick scored tries and McCormick had converted all three, added five penalty goals and for better measure had also dropped a magnificent goal. It was the worst beating Wales had ever taken from New Zealand and McCormick with 20 of New Zealand's 33 points had set a world record for an international rugby game.

CONSOLATION AT SYDNEY

Wales played their first international game on Australian soil at the Sydney Cricket Ground on Saturday, 21st June, 1969 and found the Australians in quite a hurry. The Wallabies were due to fly out to South Africa the following morning and their urgency became quite apparent shortly after the start of the game. Arthur McGill landed a penalty goal in the fifth minute, five minutes later Phil Smith galloped over for a try which McGill converted and not very long after that McGill kicked a second penalty goal and the Wallabies, playing with all the style of champions, were 11-0 up before 20 minutes had gone. Was this to be another debacle for Wales? Keith Jarrett decided it was not to be a repeat of what had happened in New Zealand. He kicked a tremendous goal and a few minutes later Dave Morris went charging over for a try and at half-time Wales were only five points down. Two minutes after half-time, full-back John Williams, always ready to have a go in a running movement, came into the threequarter line and spreadeagled the Australians, before putting Davies over for a try and Jarrett with another fine kick put over the conversion and the scores were level. But not for long. Jarrett stepped up to a 50 yards penalty goal attempt and put the ball straight between the posts and it was 14-11 to Wales. Then with all the Welsh joining in on an all-out attack, John Taylor finished off the movement with a try and Jarrett collected his 10 points from the game with the conversion. It did not matter that Arthur McGill topped that individual performance just before the end with a try which he converted to give him 13 points from the game. Wales held out to win a great game by 19-16 and to record their first international win down under. On their way home, Wales stopped off at Suva and took on the Fijians and gave 24,000 spectators quite a treat in winning by 31-11.

SOME SCORING!

When Wales took on Fiji on 25th June, 1969 on their way back home from the tour of New Zealand and Australia, they were, in fact, facing the champions of the Third South Pacific Games ... and never before nor since has a major rugby nation gone against a "minnow" that had such a staggering scoring record. Fiji had played five "international games" in this tournament and had knocked up 437 points while conceding only 14 ... and that was in five outings! They beat New Caledonia by 113-0, Solomon Islands by 113-3, the Wallis and Fortuna Islands by 44-8, Papua by 79-0 and New Guinea by 88-3. There can hardly be another team in rugby history that knocked up 113 points twice in successive games. Wales, however, were not over-awed. They beat Fiji by 31-11.

A QUICK INVITATION

One of the worst blows that Welsh rugby could have suffered was Keith Jarrett's decision to turn to Rugby League in September 1969, when he joined Barrow for a fee of £14,000. At the time Jarrett had been capped 10 times for Wales and was still only twenty. Picked for his first international for Wales against England in 1967, just a few months after he had left school, his debut was sensational. In Wales' 34-21 win over England at Cardiff Arms Park on Saturday, 15th April, 1967, he scored 19 points to equal the Welsh record which up to then had been held by Jack Bancroft for 57 years. Jarrett kicked two penalty goals, scored a try and converted five tries. In his 10 games for Wales Jarrett scored 73 points for Wales with 17 conversions, 11 penalty goals and two tries and in the unofficial international against Fiji at Suva in June 1969 he kicked another 10 points with five conversions. Had he continued his rugby career, he would, of course have set an all-time Welsh scoring record. When he turned over to Rugby League, he had the unique distinction of being capped for Wales in his new code without ever having played a game under League rules.

MAURICE RICHARDS'S DAY

Saturday, 12th April, 1969 at Cardiff Arms Park got off to a bad start for Wales when Bob Hiller kicked England into the lead with a penalty goal but the afternoon brightened up when Maurice Richards with a delightful try made it 3-3 at the break. Keith Jarrett then sent Wales on their way to a resounding win with two penalty goals which were followed by a try from Barry John and another from Richards. Barry John dropped a goal and then it was Richards's turn to jump back on the scene with two more fine tries. Jarrett converted the two tries and in the end it was 30-9 with Hiller kicking all of England's points from penalty goals. This win brought Wales the Triple Crown for the 11th time ... and it also brought a share in a long-established record for the Welsh wing-threequarter, Maurice Richards. With his four tries, he equalled the record for a Welsh international that had been set by Willie Llewellyn against England in 1899 and which had been equalled by Reggie Gibbs against France in 1908.

THEY FAILED TO SCORE

In only one of their five international games in 1969-1970 did Wales fail to score—and that was the game that really mattered. They drew 6-6 with Dawie de Villiers' South Africans at Cardiff, beat Scotland by double scores 18-9 at Cardiff, took on England at Twickenham and came away with a 17-13 victory and they beat France by 11-6. The other game came against Ireland at Lansdowne Road on Saturday, 14th March, 1970 and the Triple Crown was at stake for them. This is still remembered as one of the worst debacles in Welsh rugby history. They had all their great men on parade, John Williams, John Dawes, Barry John, Gareth Edwards, Denzil Williams, John Young, Barry Llewellyn, Delme Thomas and Mervyn Davies ... and Ireland, as some people claimed, were getting just a little long in the tooth. But the ancient warriors of Ireland humiliated the Welsh that afternoon. Alan Duggan and Ken Goodall scored tries, Tom Kiernan converted one and kicked a penalty goal and Barry McGann dropped a goal and that all added up to a 14-0 win for Ireland. It was the fifth time that Ireland had halted the Welsh on the way to a Triple Crown.

ONLY THERE FOR THE CAP

Wales's Phil Bennett, who emerged in the 1970s as one of the world's great out-halves had a somewhat quiet and unspectacular start to his international career. It lasted just a few minutes but it was long enough to bring him his first international cap. In the dying moments of the France v Wales game at Colombes Stadium in March, 1969, with the score at 8-8, Gerald Davies, playing at centre that afternoon, dislocated his elbow and had to retire from the game. The twenty-year old Bennett duly warmed up, went in to the game as the first official Welsh substitute introduced during an international game and duly won his cap. It is on record however that he did not touch the ball before the final whistle!

THE 28 MINUTES INTERNATIONAL

Wales were trailing by 3-13 to England at Twickenham on Saturday, 28th February, 1971 and then came an even worse misfortune, Gareth Edwards injured himself and had to be carried off. In to replace him came the twenty-five-year old Raymond "Chico" Hopkins and from that moment on the game changed dramatically. David Duckham had opened the scoring for England with a try which Bob Hiller converted. Terry Davies crashed over for a try to make it 5-3 but England came surging back and M. J. Novak got a try which Hiller again converted to stretch the lead to 10-3. Worse was to follow for Wales. Hiller was spot on with a penalty goal and at half-time it was 13-3 and Wales seemed to be totally out of it. But with Hopkins' appearance on the field, everything changed suddenly. He set Barry John up for a try, then made one for John Williams and he dived over for one himself and with Williams making a successful conversion, Wales were in the lead by 14-13. And then to rub the final salt in England's wounds, Barry John dropped a goal and the final result was Wales 17; England 13. That game marked "Chico" Hopkins's first cap for Wales and as it transpired his international career was to have a duration of only 28 minutes. Sometime after his return from the 1971 Lions tour of Australia and New Zealand, during which he made 11 appearances, he turned professional. Ironically he made only the one international appearance for the Lions and that was in the first international against New Zealand at Dunedin on 26th June, 1971 and the duration of that was a little longer. Ten minutes after the start, Gareth Edwards was injured . . . and in came Hopkins as a reserve again. This time, however, he played for almost 70 minutes.

JOHN TAYLOR'S KICK

Wales won the Triple Crown for the 12th and last time in 1970-1971— and for that their thanks must always go to John Taylor. They beat

England by 22-6 and they won the Triple Crown at Cardiff Arms Park by beating Ireland by 23-9 but it was that match in between—against Scotland at Murrayfield—that really counted. This was an incredible game. Barry John kicked a penalty goal and Peter Brown levelled matters with another, then Brown kicked a second to put Scotland ahead 6-3. John Taylor raced over for a try which Barry John converted and it was 8-6 for Wales at half-time. Gareth Edwards with a try made it 11-6, then it was Brown again with a penalty goal and it was 11-9. Carmichael with a try made it 12-11 for Scotland but Barry John with a try switched the lead to Wales with 14-12. Chris Rea then went in for a Scottish try and Wales were down 14-15. Brown with a penalty goal left it at 18-14—and there was less than a minute to go. Then Gerald Davies went streaking through for a Welsh try and it was 17-18 to Scotland. There was time only for the conversion and the kick was entrusted to wing-forward John Taylor at the touch-line. He placed the ball carefully, went back and his left footed kick went soaring away towards the posts—and it was over for a dramatic 19-18 win for Wales. And that was really the victory that won them that season's Triple Crown.

THE 100 UP

Barry John kicked two penalty goals, a conversion and a drop goal for Wales against England at Cardiff Arms Park on Saturday, 17th March, 1971—and his goal marked quite a milestone in Wales's meetings with England at Cardiff Arms Park since 1965. In 1965, they had beaten England 14-3, in 1967 it was 34-21, in 1969 it was 30-9 and in 1971 it was 22-6. Just before John kicked his drop goal, Wales had totalled 97 points. As his kick went sailing over the bar to give Wales their 22-6 victory, it brought their total against England to an exact century of points in four games.

FIRST AS A SUB

The Lions selectors thought he was good enough to travel to New Zealand and Australia on the famous 1971 tour but it took the Welsh selectors just a little longer to be convinced that Derek Quinnell was a suitable candidate for international honours. After his return from

New Zealand, they named him as reserve only for their game against France at the start of the 1971-1972 international campaign and it is now a matter of record that Quinnell's first international appearance for Wales lasted barely a minute. When Mervyn Davies was injured in the last seconds of the game, Quinnell, who occupies the only place under the letter "Q" in the list of Welsh internationals, was brought in to collect h's first cap for his country.

THE CANADIAN ROMP

The Welsh took off for Canada in 1973 and in their five match tour won all five games and rattled up a total of 288 points while conceding only 41. They opened up in Vancouver with a 31-6 win over British Columbia, then beat Alberta by 76-6, Eastern Canada by 44-9 and Ontario by 79-0. In the unofficial international against Canada, Phil Bennett led the Welsh to a 58-20 victory and his contribution to the score was 24 points from a try, two penalty goals and seven conversions. In their 76-6 win over Alberta, forward A. J. Martin of Aberavon collected quite a record for himself by scoring 28 points from goal-kicks.

THE JAPANESE

The heartiest cheers that broke out at Cardiff Arms Park on Saturday, 6th October, 1973 were for a full-back by the name of Yamamoto who kicked two penalty goals and a tiny wing-threequarter named Itoh who scored two excellent tries. The cheers were a little more restrained for Wales who fielded close to their strongest international side to play Japan for the first time in Wales. The Japanese forwards were much too small to cope with the powerful Welsh pack and were eventually overwhelmed. The Welsh ran up 62 points to Japan's 14 and the top scorer was Phil Bennett, who kicked nine conversions and scored two tries for a personal total of 26 points.

KING EDWARDS

Wales's international game against England on Saturday, 16th March, 1974, marked a special milestone in the career of scrum-half Gareth Edwards. The only sad feature of it was that England, on that par-

" VICTORY OVER THE ALL BLACKS IS NO EXCUSE
— BESIDES, THAT WAS A MONTH AGO!"

ticular afternoon, chose to beat Wales at Twickenham for the first time since 1960. When Edwards took the field in this game, he was making his 36th appearance for his country. It also made him the most-capped scrum-half in the history of the game. Against France at Cardiff Arms Park on 16th February, 1974, he had equalled the world record of 35 which had been set up by his illustrious countryman, Dickie Owen of Swansea between 1901 and 1912.

BENNETT'S RECORD

England scored a sensational victory over Wales at Twickenham on Saturday, 16th March, 1974—and it was the first time for 11 years that the English had beaten the Welsh at Twickenham. But in Wales's defeat there was the consolation that out-half Phil Bennett with two penalty goals and a conversion had carried his total for the international championship to 36 points, one more than the record of 35 set by Barry John two seasons earlier.

THE ONLY BLOT

With the exception of South Africa, Wales have wins over all the major rugby countries. In their seven games against the Springboks since 1906 at Swansea, they have lost six and drawn one. Their biggest defeat was at Durban in 1964 when they crashed by 24-3. On three occasions, 1906, 1912 and 1960, they have failed to register a score against South Africa. The closest they came to victory was on a dark and muddy afternoon at Cardiff Arms Park on Saturday, 24th January, 1970, when scrum-half Gareth Edwards raced through the South African defence in the last seconds of the game to score a try in the corner to give Wales a dramatic draw. In the heavy mud, however, Edwards was not able to convert his own try.

AGAINST ENGLAND

Wales have played 79 international games against England, have won 35, lost 33, drawn 11 and, by present-day values, have scored 1,320 points. Under the values prevailing at the time, Wales's greatest margin of victory is 22 points. They defeated England 22-0 at Swansea in 1907 and in 1922 at Cardiff Arms Park won by 28-6. However, at Cardiff Arms Park in 1905, Wales won by two goals and five tries to nil, which by present day values would be 32-0. Their longest unbeaten run against England began with a win in Swansea in 1899 and ended with England's win at Twickenham in 1910. During that time, Wales had 10 wins and one draw.

AGAINST IRELAND

Using the present-day scoring values for the 76 matches they have played against Ireland, Wales need just one score at the beginning of the 1974-1975 season to pass the 800 points mark. In the 76 games since 1882 at Lansdowne Road, Dublin, Wales have won 45 games, lost 26, drawn 5 and have scored 799 points. Wales's greatest win over Ireland was at Cardiff Arms Park in 1920 when they scored three goals, a drop goal and three tries to a drop goal. The margin of victory under the values of the time was 24 points, under today's values it would be 30 points. Wales's longest run without defeat against Ireland began with the win at Swansea in 1913 and lasted until Ireland's victory at Lansdowne Road in 1923. This brought five wins in succession. Wales, however also have five wins in succession from 1907 to 1911 and, including a draw at Cardiff Arms Park in 1951, they also went without defeat against Ireland from 1950 in Belfast to their defeat at Lansdowne Road in 1956.

AGAINST SCOTLAND

Under the modern scoring values Wales defeated Scotland by 35-12 at Cardiff Arms Park in 1972, but if the same scoring values were applied to their 1911 game in Edinburgh, Wales's win that year by two goals, a drop goal and six tries to two tries and a drop goal would have to be regarded as the most decisive in their 78 games with the Scots. Wales have now won 43 of these games, lost 33 and drawn 2, and have scored, under present day values, a total of 828 points. The longest Welsh domination of these games began with the win at Swansea in 1908 and lasted until Scotland won at Edinburgh in 1920. This gave Wales seven successive wins.

THE FRENCH CHALLENGE

France's first three meetings with Wales were chastening experiences. Making their debut at Cardiff Arms Park in 1908, they were routed by three goals, a penalty goal and six tries to a drop goal. The following year in Paris, Wales scored their greatest victory over France winning by seven goals and four tries (47 points) to a goal (5), or, by present scoring values 58-6. At Swansea in 1910, Wales scored even higher with eight goals, a penalty goal and two tries but this time the French managed to do a little better with a goal, a penalty goal and a try. Wales have now played France on 46 occasions and have won 30, lost 13 and drawn three and, by present-day scoring values have scored 575 points. They had an unbeaten run from 1908 at Cardiff until they lost by a try to France's goal and a try at Colombes Stadium in 1928.

ON THE CREDIT SIDE

Wales have played 303 international games against England, Scotland, Ireland, France, South Africa, New Zealand, Australia, New South Wales and the New Zealand Native side. Of their 303 games, they have won 162, lost 119 and drawn 22.

THE WELSH TOTAL

From John Bevan, the Australian who captained Wales in their first international game against England at Mr Richardson's Field at Blackheath on 19th February, 1881, down to W. R. Blyth, who came in as a replacement for Wales's game against England on Saturday, 16th March, 1974, 755 players have worn the red jersey of Wales in international rugby.

KEEPING UP WITH THE JONES'S

Someone once said that if a Welshman had the name of Jones, the probability was that he had either played international rugby for Wales—or else one of his relations or distant cousins had. It could be close to the truth. Since Wales came into international rugby 54 players by the name of Jones have played for Wales. But they have not had it all their own way. Just to complicate matters for any historian trying to sort out the families of Welsh international rugby . . . there have also been 44 by the name of Davies, 37 called Evans, 35 Williamses, 32 Thomases, 19 Morgans, 17 by the name of Rees, 14 Lewises and 11 with the name of Jenkins. No other country in international rugby is ever likely to catch up with the Jones or indeed with any of the other famous Welsh families.

FRANCE

AND SO IT STARTED

The Federation Française de Rugby did not come into existence until 1920 but the game of rugby had been popular in the country from late in the nineteenth century. Introduced into France by young Englishmen working in the country who were mostly in the wine trade, the game caught on rapidly in the south of France, where it is still at its strongest, and gradually it spread out to become a thriving, healthy sport through-out the entire country. In 1893, Rosslyn Park became the first English club to play in France when they took on Stade Français and walloped them, but it is known that 10 years earlier a French side had gone to England to play three games against Civil Service, Hornsey Rise and Gravesend and had lost all three without scoring even a point. In January, 1906, the French played their first international game against Dave Gallaher's All-Blacks and were trounced 8-38. That year, too, they also played England and lost 8-35. Two years later they met Wales and were beaten 4-36, in 1909 they met Ireland for the first time and lost 8-19 and in 1910 they came together with Scotland for the first time and lost 0-27. In the meantime the South Africans had also played them during the tour of Paul Roos's 1906-1907 Springboks and that, too had been a defeat, by 6-55. The years before the First World War were embarrassing ones for France and the years between the two world wars were to bring banishment from international rugby. But after the Second World War, France were to become one of the major powers in world rugby.

THE FIRST OLYMPIC CHAMPIONS

According to the Olympic records, France became Olympic champions in rugby at the Paris Games of 1900 . . . but where they did so, how they did so and who, in fact, played for France, no one seems to know. The 1900 Olympic Games were a haphazard affair and brought some of the most hilarious and bizarre incidents in the entire history of the

Olympic movement and it is even on record that some of the gentlemen who won Olympic events were awarded prizes of umbrellas, shaving kits and walking canes! What the French rugby team received in recognition of their Olympic win will never be known. There is the suggestion that the Olympic final that year was a game between Racing Club de France and Stade Bordelais at the Bois du Bologne and that it was won by Racing Club. Unfortunately Racing Club have no records to show that their team of that year won the Olympic final. However the Olympic lists show that France were the Olympic champions of 1900—and that is a fact.

ALMOST A WIN!

The 1905 All-Blacks touring side had romped through Britain and Ireland, winning 32 of their 33 games, losing one and scoring a majestic total of 860 points, while conceding just eight. On the evidence of that, France were more than a little apprehensive about their possible fate when they met New Zealand at Parc des Princes, Paris on 1st January, 1906. It turned out to be a wet afternoon but over 3,000 hardy spectators turned up for the game—and that was not an inconsiderable crowd at the time. And as far as the All-Blacks were concerned, they provided full value for their audience. Putting on a tremendous show, they gave the Frenchmen a thoroughly decisive hammering and at the final whistle they had scored four goals and six tries to France's goal and a try. The reaction in France, however, was one of elation. Only one other side, Cardiff, in the All-Blacks tour had managed to score eight points against them. This as far as the French felt now put them on the same level as Cardiff. By the time they had finished assessing the French performance, the local critics were treating the game as little short of a win for France. This game now is a significant milestone in the history of French rugby. It was their first ever international game and to George Jerome, who was to win a second cap against England that year, fell the honour of scoring France's first try. France's second try in international rugby was scored by Cessieux—the French Federation has never been able to trace his Christian name—and the conversion was by Albert Branlat.

THE PRE-WAR YEARS

Between 1906 and 1914 when rugby was halted by the First World War, the French played 28 international games, lost 27 and won one.

They scored a total of 147 points and conceded the massive total of 707. Their one win was over Scotland at Colombes Stadium on 21st February, 1911, when they won by 16-15. Their scorers in that historic victory were Pierre Faillott, who became the first French international to score two tries in a game and George Latterade and George Peyroutou who added two more. Two of the tries were converted by Jean Combes.

YOU SHOULD NOT DO THAT!

Marcel Communeau was playing with Stade Français's second string when an injury to a player on the first team due to meet a Kent XV, gave him his chance of promotion to the first side. Communeau, a tearaway forward, had a sound game and capped it towards the end by suddenly popping up in a threequarter movement and scoring a wonderful try in the corner. On the strength of that he was selected on the first French international side to play Dave Gallaher's All-Blacks in 1906 and subsequently, he went on to win 20 caps for his country. But was the captain of Stade Français happy about it? Not on your life! He reprimanded Communeau for having the audacity to score a try against Kent. By his judgement forwards were not on the field to score tries! Following his appearance against the All-Blacks Marcel Communeau was demoted once again to the Stade Français's second team.

THE ENGLAND ROUT

The French made their first trip overseas for an international game when they took on England at Richmond, London in 1907 and what happened there was almost enough to drive them out of international football for ever. They were hammered by 41-13 and that was the afternoon that Danny Lambert ran in to score his record number of five tries for England. The only consolation to France was that A. H. Muhr scored their first try in the international championship and Pierre Maclos kicked their first penalty goal. Unfortunately, there was worse to come for poor France four years later when they made their first appearance at Twickenham. They did not even get a score as England ran up a total of 37 points and once again Lambert was on the mark for the English, this time with two tries, a feat he shared with Charles "Cherry" Pillman. To this day, it remains as England's greatest winning margin over France.

THE FIRST DROP

Charles Vareilles, who was to play five times for France between 1907 and 1910, became the first man to drop a goal for his country in their game against Wales at Cardiff Arms Park on Saturday, 2nd March, 1908. Unfortunately it did not matter very much in the final result which was a 36-4 win for Wales.

THE THREE WHO DID NOT

France did not play their first game of international rugby until they took on the All-Blacks led by Dave Gallaher at Parc des Princes, Paris on New Year's Day, 1906 and it woule be natural to expect that the list of French internationals should begin from that afternoon. However, in the list there are three men, who did not, in fact, ever represent France in international rugby—and they are Henri Armand, Franz Reichel and Louis Dedet. For the valuable part they played in the creation of French rugby, plus the fact that all three were the leading personalities of the first games played between French and English clubs in the 1890s, they were subsequently honoured by being named as French internationals and in the official list are numbered at 1, 2 and 3.

THE UNUSUAL 13th!

In the French official list of international players, he is shown as the 13th man to win a cap for the Tricolours. He had the honour of playing with France in their first-ever international against New Zealand at Parc des Princes in New Year's Day, 1906, when Dave Gallaher's men finished off their astonishing 1905-1906 tour of Britain, Ireland and France with 868 points in their 33 games, while conceding only 44. Furthermore that same man had the distinction of playing in France's first international against England at Richmond, London in 1906, when he scored France's first try against the English. Two years later at Leicester he won his third and last cap for France. Not an impressive tally of caps but at least it was historic. For France's great, bustling forward of that period, their 13th international, Allan Muhr was . . . an American!

THE FRENCH INTRUDER

Wales gave France a thorough trouncing at St Helen's, Swansea, on 1st January, 1910, winning by eight goals, a penalty goal and two tries to a goal, two penalty goals and a try—49-14. But the French, in a way, might have claimed extenuating circumstances. They had 14 recognised internationals on the field—and what one might term an "accidental" international. When the French team got together for this trip, the selectors discovered that one of their players was missing. Frantic 'phone calls revealed that he had been called up on military service and could not get leave to travel to Wales. Thereupon began a search for a man to fill the vacant spot. The handiest happened to be Joe Anduran who was working nearby. He, of course, thought it was all a huge joke and his wife thought it was an even bigger one still when she heard about it. The idea that Joe would be missing for family dinner on New Year's Day was unthinkable. She refused point-blank. But Joe was made of stern stuff. This was a chance to play for France and he intended to take it. He was off like a shot and as the records show Joe Anduran won his one and only international cap for France on New Year's Day, 1910. Alex Potter, that delightful historian of all things pertaining to French rugby wrote afterwards that from there on for many years, various Paris players turned up at the local railway station, with boots and kit at the ready in the hope that there might be another "Anduran" incident.

CHANCE OF A LIFETIME

With less than an hour to go to kick-off time at Colombes on 2nd January, 1911, France were almost ready to take the field against Scotland. Fourteen of the players were in the dressing room and stripping off for the game. But where was wing-threequarter Charles

Vareilles? He had won his first international cap for France against England in 1907, was now the proud owner of five caps for his country and he had been an automatic choice for this game. But there was no sign of him. He had arrived in at Colombes with the team but with the minutes now ticking away, it looked as though France might have to field with only 14 players. In desperation, French officials turned to the French sprinter Andre Frankquenelle, who had travelled with the party but only as a spectator. Would he play? After all he did play club rugby with the Sporting Club de Vaugirard. Frankquenelle was persuaded to turn out and even though Charles Vareilles eventually showed up just before 3 o'clock, Frankquenelle took the field. And as all good stories should end, Frankquenelle played a magnificent role in France's 16-15 victory—their first win in international rugby. He went on to win two further caps for France . . . and Vareilles never again played for his country.

IN THREE POSITIONS

Rene Lasserre, born at Bayonne in 1895, began his rugby career as a scrum-half but moved into the pack when he joined A. Bayonnais in 1912. The following season, however, he was tried at full-back—and it was as a full-back that he won his first international cap for France against Ireland at Paris in 1914. France went down 6-8 in that game but the nineteen-year old Lasserre was one of the striking successes of the game and he was an automatic selection for the next game against Wales in Swansea. Unfortunately, Lasserre did not make the trip to Wales. His parents decided he was much too young for such a long journey and, despite the passionate appeals of the French selectors, they refused to let him go. Then came the first World War and the disruption of the international series but Lasserre was back again in 1920 to play against Scotland. This time, however, he was named at centre. A year later, he was capped against Scotland, Ireland and Wales but not as a full-back or a centre. He had now become a wing-forward! In all, before he retired from international rugby at the end of the 1924 season, the versatile Lasserre won 13 caps for France, with the unusual distinction of having collected them in three different positions. In 1922, having lost every international game to England since 1906, Lasserre scored the try at Twickenham which brought France an 11-11 draw.

CHAMPAGNE LUNCHEON

When the French arrived in Cork to play Ireland at Cork Park on Easter Monday, 24th March, 1913, they were just a little surprised to discover that they were to be the guests of honour at a champagne luncheon at Cork on the same day. They were, however, relieved to find that the luncheon was planned for after the rugby international. To facilitate spectators who wanted to see the international and also the famous Cork Races, the match was played at 12.30 p.m. The Irish did not extend any hospitality in the rugby game and gave the French a sound hammering by 24-0. Then both teams headed off for Cork Park —and the champagne! Both teams duly watched the races, which incidentally, produced one epic event. In the Sea Steeplechase, Timothy II threw his rider Jack Murphy at a fence just in front of the stand and with that, Murphy's brother Tom, who had been watching the race, rushed down from the stand, mounted the horse and eventually carried on to win the race. It is on record that the French players were a little bewildered that Timothy II was declared the winner but they were also unhappy. Following the good French champagne, they had all plunged heavily on Charlemange, the only other finisher.

A DAY TO CRY

Adolphe Jaureguy, the French wing-threequarter who was to win 31 caps for his country between 1920 and 1930, was led weeping from the field at Lansdowne Road, Dublin on a March afternoon in 1920. But he was in the best of company for the reports of that France-Ireland game all agree that most of the other French players were also in tears. They were happy tears, however. France, after 15 years of international rugby, had scored their second win—and their first on foreign soil. Up against a powerful Irish side that included Ernie Crawford, Dickie Lloyd, P. J. Stokes, Sam Polden and Willie Roche, they had shocked every Irish spectator at Lansdowne Road by running in for five tries against Ireland's one try and a drop goal and had won by 15-7. France's only previous international victory had been against Scotland in 1911. Jaureguy's only comment when he had recovered sufficiently to celebrate the victory was "Fantastique. France will remember this day forever".

DID HE SCORE?

Wales scored their eighth successive win over France at Colombes Stadium on Saturday, 17th February, 1920 but it was a tight affair on the score of 6-5. But every Frenchman leaving that ground, including the fifteen players, were convinced that France had won—and had been "robbed" of victory. Wales scored two tries and Adolphe Jaurreguy had scored one for France which Struxiano had converted. Then Struxiano had taken a throw in, the ball was caught by his front row forward Constant and passed back to Struxiano who galloped over the line for what appeared to be a perfectly legitimate try. Unfortunately, the touch judge had his flag up. According to him it should have been a Welsh throw-in. The referee had already awarded the try but after consulting with the touch-judge he disallowed it. So France were out of luck again and indeed it was not until 1928 that France finally managed a win over Wales. This time, on Saturday, 9th April, 1928, they did it without any dispute. Roger Haudet scored two tries and Andre Behoteguy one of the two famous brothers to play for France added a conversion. Wales could only manage a try . . . and so for the first time since 1908 when they first met at Cardiff Arms Park, France had beaten the Welsh at last. But that 1928 win was at Colombes. There still had to be a day when they would beat Wales on Welsh soil.

ROBBERY BY DAY

On Saturday, 25th February, 1922, France seemed to have England beaten at Twickenham for the first time. There were just two minutes to go and the exuberant French were leading by 11-6. It had been quite an extraordinary game. H. L. V. Day had kicked two early penalty goals and with England over-running the French in every phase of play, that was still the score at the break. Then the French caught fire, their wing-threequarter Got picked up a pass and raced into the corner for a try. Two minutes later the giant Andre Cassayet took the ball at the back of a scrum and after clearing at least one English defender by jumping over him, he crashed over the line for a second try and it was 6-6. Now the French were rampant and Rene Lasserre, their towering utility player broke away and went streaking for the line for a third try which the captain Rene Crabos converted and it was 11-6

"BILL CAN SELL A LOVELY DUMMY
—HE'S A HOUSE AGENT!"

to France. And that was how it stood as full time loomed up. But within those two minutes Tom Voyce went over for an English try and with every Frenchman on the field in absolute dejection, H. L. V. Day kicked the vital conversion that drew the game. And, as Alex Potter, the great historian of French rugby recalls—Day did all the damage in borrowed boots! His kit had been mislaid at the English headquarters and when the English team set off for Twickenham, Day was left behind, still searching for his missing boots. He could not find them and finally in desperation he borrowed a pair of boots and they had to be sliced with a knife to fit him. But those boots were to do all the damage to France that afternoon. He kicked eight of England's 11 points.

THE OLYMPIC GAMES

Rugby disappeared from the Olympic Games after 1924 when the Americans hammered the French by 17-3 in the final at Colombes Stadium . . . and one can only wonder why? At the International Olympic Congress of 1921 at Lausanne, it was decreed that rugby should be removed from the sports in which competition might or might not be held at an Olympic Games and it should be placed on the definite programme so that "hereafter both association football and rugby would be a positive part of the Olympic games".

THE HIGHEST SCORE

France ran riot in their Olympic Games tie against Rumania in May 1924 and won by the record score of 72 points to 3 and this is the highest score ever put up by the Tricolours in a full international. Alas, and much to the astonishment of everyone in France who expected them to repeat the dose against the unfancied Americans in the final, the United States caused the sensation of the Games by winning 17-3.

THE BEHOTEGUYS

Two of the enduring names of French rugby during the 1920s are those of the brothers Andre and Henri Behoteguy, who between them wound up with 25 caps. Andre played against Ireland for the first time in 1924 and made his second four years later in Ravenhill in Belfast when he scored what was to be the try of that international season. With his beret clapped firmly on his balding head, he made a run on the left wing, then doubled back on his track when he found a wall of Irish defenders in front of him and then made straight across the field to the right, before switching again to the left to ground the ball between the posts. His immediate reaction was to race back and pick up the beret which he had lost in the process of an extraordinary run. His score, however, was not to win the game for France. They went down eventually by 8-12.

THE GREAT BREAK

On Saturday, 6th April, 1931, France beat England by 14-13 at Colombes Stadium, Paris . . . and that brought their international progress to a sad halt. For the next nine years, France were to languish under suspension by the International Board and, indeed, did not come back into the International championship until the 1946-1947 season. In February 1931, the representatives of the home unions had met in London and following a long discussion decided to sever connections with France. The letter announcing this unhappy decision pointed to the unsatisfactory state of the game in France—and there could be no question but that things were unsatisfactory in France at the time. Brutality had crept into the French game, particularly in their club championship, there was semi-professionalism, poaching of players by one club from another, cash bonuses for wins, and indeed, there were claims that several top players were living on their earnings from rugby. The message from the Home Union was simple—get your house in order and then we will reconsider. In time the French put their rugby house in order and on 27th March, 1939, Mr Harry Thrift, the old Irish international and then secretary of the International Board advised the French that relationship would be resumed. The war, however, made that impossible but in a gesture to show that everything was fine again, a British team travelled to Paris in February 1940 and beat France by 36-3. The French could not have cared less about the result—the main thing as far as they were concerned was that France were back in the international fold again.

THE WRONG PROPHECY

Many years earlier, having watched and played against the French, the immortal Welsh full-back Jack Bancroft had made the prediction that France would some day win on Irish, English and Scottish soil but that they would never do so on Welsh ground. But there had to be a first time and it came on Saturday, 21st February, 1948 at St Helen's, Swansea. France had not been impressive that season and had already lost to Ireland and Scotland and their hopes looked dim against Wales. But right from the start France led up front by those two great giants, Alban Moga and Roberto Soro and with Jean Prat, Guy Basquet and Jean Matheu to back them up, tore into the Welsh and the result was a battle royal that the French eventually won. No one was better than Roberto Soro, who to this day is immortalised in French Rugby as the "Lion of Swansea". He above everyone else was the hero of France's tremendous victory. Michel Pomathios, the delicate flyer of the French backline scored a try and their others came from Guy Basquet and Maurice Terreau. Andre Alvarez converted Pimathios's try and France went on to finish by 11-3 with Williams kicking a sole penalty goal for Wales. Now all that remained for France was to beat the English at Twickenham.

THE SUDDEN CHANGE

Just what did happen in the French dressing room at Twickenham on Saturday, 24th February, 1951? The real truth lies with the French selectors and they have to this day maintained an understandably discreet silence about the matter. The facts are that Jo Carabignac and Dacien Olive had been named on the French side to meet England and were just about to tog out in the dressing room. Then, for reasons best known to themselves, the selectors announced a sudden change. Andre Alvarez, at out-half and Alain Porthault at wing-threequarter, both of whom had travelled with the team as reserves, would replace Carabignac and Olive. The first indication the crowd had that there were changes was when the French team ran out on to the pitch. Fortunately for the selectors it was to be an historic afternoon for France. Brian Boobbyer opened the scoring with a try for England but France swept back with a fine try from Guy Basquet which Jean Prat converted and the score at half-time was 5-3 for France. France went well on top in the second half and with a try from Jean Prat, they stretched their lead. To complete his afternoon Prat then dropped a magnificent goal—and France, with the score at 11-3, had beaten England at Twickenham for the first time. One wonders whether or not that was consolation for Carabignac and Olive. Both had earlier been capped for France that season and were to be capped again the following year.

MORE TROUBLE

More trouble flared up again in the early 1950s between the French and the International Board. Once again, there were complaints that French rugby was returning to the unhappy state of affairs that had led to their suspension in 1931. A meeting was called for Dublin in February 1952 and once again the French were told to get their local affairs straightened out. Following a general assembly of all the clubs in the Federation Française de Rugby that year, an undertaking was given that there would be a close watch from there on for any hint of professionalism and that the strict code of amateurism would be adhered to at all times in the future. That satisfied the Home Unions—and to date, France have remained as a proud and nowadays extremely strong part of the International Championship.

THE BROTHERS PRAT

The name that everyone in rugby knew after the end of the Second World War was . . . Jean Prat. Born in 1923 he brought France from the mediocrity of the 1920s to the greatness of the 1950s. Beginning with his first cap in 1947, he set a record of 38 caps by the time he retired in 1955. In 1951, he was joined on the French team by his brother Maurice who was to win 25 caps for France, and to bring the family total to 63. During the 1953-1954 season Jean Prat captained France in their first ever share of the International Championship with England and France. And his greatest moment came against Bob Stuart's All-Blacks when he scored the only try of the game and brought France's first win over the New Zealanders.

THE FIRST FRENCH

At the invitation of the South African Rugby Board, the French took off on their first great overseas venture in 1958—and no one gave them the slightest chance of upsetting the Springboks. The French played 10 matches in South Africa, surprised most people by winning five of them, drawing two and losing two. In the process of a somewhat hilarious tour they scored 137 points and conceded 124. Pierre Lacaze, who went on the tour as the No. 2 full-back to Michael Vannier, wound up as the side's top points scorer with 34 points from 11 conversions, two penalty goals and two drop goals. Francois Moncla, one of France's great forwards was their top try-scorer with four.

ENTER A POLICEMAN!

Perhaps the most astonishing match played by France during their 1958 tour of South Africa was against the Junior Springboks at Port Elizabeth. After a tolerably peaceful first half, the game blew up into a free for all in the second and there was one unforgettable moment when a policeman marched on to the field to indicate to the referee that he had, in fact, made a wrong decision. The referee had awarded a try to the French winger Jean Dupuy but as the policeman pointed out, the touch judge had his flag up for a throw-in. This did not add to the happiness of the entire affair. Five minutes from time, when things had got completely out of hand and with the Junior Springboks leading by 9-5 the referee wisely called a halt to the proceedings. The French, of course, were highly indignant and this only added fuel to a fire that was already beginning to rage between the French and the South Africans.

AN UNEXPECTED DRAW

The Springboks brought in six new caps, including Hugo Van Zyl and the one-eyed Martin Pelser for the opening international game against France at Cape Town and no one in the vast crowd—and even the French officials were of the same mind—had the slightest doubt but that this would be a one-sided win for South Africa. And even when the French took the lead with an excellent drop goal from Pierre

Danos, there were still no worries. Sooner or later the Springokbs would find the measure of the temperamental Frenchmen and after that it would be easy going for the rest of the way. But time ticked on, half-time came and went and still the French stayed in front. Only towards the end of the game was South African honour salvaged when G. P. "Butch" Lochner went over in the corner for a face-saving try. Fifty two years after their first meeting in Paris, France at last had halted the Springboks' run of victories.

THE DROP ON THE SPRINGBOKS

France's elation after the historic draw at Newlands was sadly deflated a few days later when they ran into a Combined Western Provinces-Boland-South Western Districts side and took a sad 8-38 trouncing. Then it was into Ellis Park, Johannesburg for the second international against the Springboks and the French were somewhat subdued before the game. Pierre Lacaze was troubled with a shoulder injury plus a suspect ankle and he had to be given a strong shot of novocaine to get him into shape for the game. Wing-threequarter Jean Dupuy had a thigh injury and Lucien Mias had a sudden attack of sinus trouble. But all insisted on playing, particularly Mias, who was then the sole survivor of the French side that had been routed 3-25 by the South Africans at Colombes Stadium in 1952. France struck the first blow with a penalty goal from Lacaze, who at that stage was already limping badly Alan Skene came back with a try for South Africa and it was 5-3 at half-time with Mickey Gerber's conversion. In the second half Mias drove his pack along at an enormous pace and midway through the half, Pierre Danos took a ball from a line-out, fed it out to Lacaze, who mustered the strength from somewhere to drop a goal. Seven minutes from time Roger Martine found himself with an open gap—and the ball—and almost casually dropped the goal to give France a 9-5 victory. For the first time France had beaten South Africa and better still they had achieved it on Springbok soil on the sacred setting of Ellis Park.

TWICKENHAM AT LAST

England set the ball rolling against France on Saturday, 24th February, 1951 with a try from Brian Boobbyer and once again it seemed that France were doomed to another defeat. But shortly before half-time

Guy Basquet bounced over for a try and with a great kick Jean Prat sent the conversion between the posts and France were ahead at half-time by 5-3. Better things were to come in the second half when Jean Prat went sailing through the English defences for a try which he failed to convert but now it was 8-3 and the French tails were up. Time ran away and injury time was there when Prat, picking up a pass 30 yards out, picked his spot, steadied himself and dropped the neatest of goals. And that was how it ended with France ahead by 11-3. It was France's first win over England at Twickenham. The long wait of 39 years was over.

A RECORD CROWD

When France played Rumania at Bucharest on 19th May, 1957, they were watched by 95,000 people, who were in the Bucharest Stadium to see a soccer international which was part of the afternoon's programme. This figure matched the world record of 95,000 who had seen the Lions beat South Africa by a point at Ellis Park, Johannesburg on Saturday, 6th August, 1955. France's match against Rumania was one of the most dramatic in their history. After 47 minutes Rumania led by 12-6, then increased their lead to 15-6. Then gradually the score became 15-9, 15-12 and with five minutes to go it was 15-15. With the seconds running out Rumania were penalised and from 40 yards out Michel Vannier, the full-back elected to try for a drop at goal and it went dead straight between the posts to give France an 18-15 victory.

THE GREAT MIAS

He was just twenty when he won his first cap for France in 1951. Three years later, having given gallant service to his country, he decided it was time to call a halt. He was then a school teacher and had made up his mind to study medicine. He duly qualified as a doctor but, before doing his finals, he also provided some excellent medicine for France. Lucien Mias was persuaded to return to rugby to captain the French side which was to tour in South Africa and which was to beat the Springboks on their own soil for the first time since 1896. Mias led the tremendous revival in French rugby at the end of the 1950s, which was to bring the first sequence of outright wins in the International championship. In all he won 25 caps between 1951 and 1959, and nowadays is remembered as one of the giants of France's international rugby history.

YES, TEACHER

His school teacher liked soccer, so young Francois Moncla of Pau played soccer and had he continued with the game he might just have become a French international. But there was a change of teacher at his school and the new man did not fancy soccer. He was a rugby man, so young Francois Monclas switched to the new game and was, of course, destined to become one of the finest wing-forwards in the game. He won 30 caps for France and scored four tries in the short tour of South Africa is 1958 and collected another three in the following International championship. Moncla took over the captaincy of France after Lucien Mias had decided to retire for the second time in his career.

MICHEL VANNIER

When Michel Vannier returned home from the French tour of South Africa in 1958, he was a sorry sight. He hobbled from the plane in Paris on crutches and there could be no question then but that his outstanding career as France's full-back had come to an end. Both of his legs had been badly injured in the third game of the tour and he had spent most of his time in South Africa in hospital. But the extraordinary Vannier fought back to full fitness, made his way back on to the French side and when he finally called a halt to his international career against Wales in 1961, he had become his country's most capped full-back with 30 appearances against the major countries and a further 13 against the minor nations.

A GENTLEMAN

He was known as "The Rock"—and probably never was a nickname more apt for Alfred Roques, who was born on 17th February, 1925. As one of his ardent admirers once said of this bustling, powerfully-built forward whose feats of strength are remembered in every rugby country in the world—"A gentleman when playing against gentlemen". Which was possibly a nice way of getting over the fact that the massive Roques was one of the most feared men in the history of French rugby. He was one of the latecomers to rugby. Up to the age of twenty-six he was one of the local soccer stars in Cahors and was then persuaded to change over to rugby. He was eventually given a trial by the French selectors and at the age of thirty-three made his first appearance on the French international side. He was a tower of strength through France's golden era of the late 1950s and eventually went on to win 23 caps against the recognised countries before calling it a day at the age of thirty-nine—and he qualifies as one of the oldest men to play in international rugby.

THE FINAL GOAL

The French had beaten Ireland, England, Scotland and Wales on foreign soil, they had beaten the touring Australians and the All-Blacks and in that year of 1958 they were also to beat South Africa. But there was still one mountain to be scaled, one last goal to be reached—and that was to beat Wales on the sacred sod of Cardiff Arms Park. In 50 years of international rugby they had never managed to beat the Welsh when their games were held in Cardiff. Saturday, 29th March, 1958, therefore, must be a major milestone in the history of France. Led by Michel Celaya, they ran out on to a wet and sodden ground that cut up badly later in the afternoon. But the French made light of the conditions and won convincingly. Terry Davies opened the scoring for Wales with a splendid penalty goal from far out but France's full-back, Michael Vannier, brought the scores level with an elegant drop goal. Then the tiny scrum-half Pierre Danos slipped over for a try and Antione Labazuy converted. John Collins got a try for Wales but once again the French surged back and Pierre Tarricq ran in for a try which Labazuy converted. Then came the final clincher. Michael Vannier with all the time in the world and from 40 yards out dropped a goal and that was that. France had won by 16-6 . . . and the great citadel of Cardiff Arms Park had fallen at long last. The poor relations of international rugby in the pre First World War years were now a mature power in the world of the game.

MONSIEUR DROP!

France needed a win over Ireland at Colombes Stadium, Paris on Saturday, 9th April, 1960 to share the International Championship with England and they duly got it with a sparkling display of football that sent the Irish down to a 6-23 defeat. But when it was all over France, in addition to sharing the Championship, had also provided rugby history with another international "first". Pierre Albaladejo opened the scoring with a drop goal, followed it with another and after Niall Brophy had gone over for an Irish try, Michel Celaya and Amadee Domenech put the French into a half-time lead of 12-3. Right after the start of the second half Albaladejo dropped another goal for France and then Henri Rancoule had a try, Niall Brophy had his second for Ireland and finally Francois Moncla ended the proceedings with a try which was converted by Jacques Bouquet. A great victory but perhaps of even greater significance was the fact that Albaladejo had dropped three goals. It was the first time it had ever been done in international rugby. Albaladejo, born in 1933 and at 6' and 12 st 8 lbs a somewhat striking outhalf, had quite an extraordinary career with France. He was twenty-one when he won his first cap against England in 1954— and that was at full-back! For the next six years he became one of the forgotten men of French rugby and was not capped again until the game against Wales in 1960—and by now he was an outhalf! Before his international career ended in 1964 he was to win 22 caps for France. Following his record against Ireland in 1960, there could only be the one nickname for him in French rugby and he is still remembered as "Monsieur Drop".

A 500th MILESTONE

Jean Gachassin of Lourdes, one of the most entertaining players to represent France in international rugby—at various times he appeared at full-back, wing-threequarter, centre and outhalf and even deputised at scrum-half—played his first international game against Scotland in 1961 and then after scoring a try against Ireland, he disappeared from the scene for three years before returning to tour in South Africa with the Tricolours. In all he was to win 25 caps against the major countries and just missed an unique honour in the history of his country's rugby. The French, in listing all their internationals who have played against any country, name them from one onwards and Gachassin was, in fact, the 499th player to be selected for France. The historic 500th place went to George Bouguyon of Grenoble, who made his debut in 1961 against the Springboks and then went on to win seven caps.

FRANCE DOWN UNDER

The French took off on their greatest rugby adventure of 1961 when, under the captaincy of Francois Moncla, then thirty-one, they set off for New Zealand and Australia to play a series of 15 games. They won 8, lost seven and scored 180 points and conceded 179. Beginning with seven matches in New Zealand, they won the first two, beating a Combined XV at Nelson by 29-11 and then Taranaki by 11-9. They lost, however to Waikato by 8-22 in their third game and in the final outing before the first international against New Zealand at Auckland they went down 6-8 to Whangarei.

DON CLARKE AGAIN

France, meeting the All-Blacks for the fourth time since 1906 in Paris, were totally out of luck against New Zealand in their first international on New Zealand soil at Eden Park, Auckland on Saturday, 22nd July, 1961. Within a minute they were five points down through an unfortunate mistake by full-back Michel Vannier. His drop out went astray and Don McKay whipped up a gift chance and ran in for a try at the corner, Don Clarke converted with an enormous kick from the touch-line and from there on the French were struggling and, of course, they had to contend with Clarke. Pierre Albaladejo dropped a goal for France and within 10 minutes he did it again to give the French a brief lead. But Clarke stepped on to the scene again with one of his extra-special drop goals from far-out and in the second half Terence O'Sullivan went in for a try and Clarke wrapped up an 11-6 victory with another fine conversion.

THE NIGHTMARE GAME

France left Auckland to beat Bay of Plenty by 22-9 at Rotorua and then went down 3-5 to the New Zealand Maoris before beating Manawatu at Palmerston by 21-6. Then they moved to Wellington to play New Zealand and this turned out to be one of the most extraordinary in the history of international rugby. It was played in an absolute blizzard with a hurricane wind blowing snow and sleet across Athletic Park. The Irish international Andy Mulligan, who was covering the tour with the French party said subsequently that the game might just as well have been played on top of Mont Blanc. France won the toss and with the wind howling at their backs, the French failed to score in the first half. At the break the odds had lengthened to extraordinary depths on a New Zealand victory. Yet France, fighting into the gale were the first to score. Jean Dupuy picked up a pass almost 40 yards out and set off for the French line. By the time he reached it, he was too exhausted to run in around to the posts. He just collapsed over the line. Pierre Albaladejo went through the vain exercise of trying to make the conversion but the wind carried the ball away. In the absurd conditions it now seemed likely that this one score would decide the game. But it was not. Kel Tremain broke loose in the French "25" and went charging over for a try and the game was level. Now everything depended on Don Clarke's attempt to convert. Clarke placed the ball and instead of aiming at the posts, kicked dead straight for the corner flag at the far side of the field. Just as the ball reached its greatest height, the wind caught it, turned it at almost a right angle and it dropped between the posts. Clarke later described it as the most remarkable kick of his long career and added too that it was the greatest fluke of all the kicking he had done for the All-Blacks. It did however give New Zealand a 5-3 win and their fourth over France in the five games they had played since 1906.

A GRANDMOTHER AT THAT

France continued their 1961 tour by beating Southland 14-5 at Invercargill and got a satisfactory win by 15-6 over the famous Otago side at 15-6. Their next match, however, against South Canterbury at Timaru was to bring defeat—and the most hilarious incident of the tour. It was not a gentle game. The French, captained that afternoon by Michel Crauste, known variously as "The Mongol" and also "Attila", stood no nonsense in a game that was marked by a series of rugged exchanges. Crauste came in for his share of punishment on the field . . . but his most vehement attacker turned out to be a woman. After one particularly rough incident, Crauste took exception to the fact that he was being belaboured on the back and turned to retaliate. When he did, however, he discovered that it was a woman spectator who had rushed on to the field to add her little bit of fun to the proceedings. Eventually, having delivered a few well-chosen blows at the French captain, she was escorted from the field. Later, it was revealed that she was, in fact . . . a grandmother!

THE FINAL BLOW

After the blizzard of the second international, conditions were perfect for the third and final meeting between France and the All-Blacks at Lancaster Park, Christchurch and the French were more than confident that this time they could get the better of the home side. Unfortunately, it was to be a "Black Saturday" for French Rugby. The game began well with a try by All-Black John Graham but within two minutes Michel Crauste dived over for a try to level matters. That, sadly, was to be France's only score in the game. P. F. Little, Kel Tremain, V. M. Yates and even Colin Meads added further tries and then, of course, there was Don Clarke, who kicked 17 points. The final score was 3-32 against France, their worst defeat by New Zealand in an official international. Only once before had France taken such a hiding from New Zealand and that was by 8-38 in their unofficial game at Parc des Princes, Paris on New Year's Day, 1906. It was and still is the only time that France have lost all their international games in an overseas tour to one country.

IN AUSTRALIA

France played just the two games in Australia to end their 1961 tour and both were experiences. They went to Brisbane to play under floodlights for the first time and had a good win. Then they returned to Sydney to meet Australia—and ran into weather conditions that were almost as bad as the ones they had endured against New Zealand in the second international at Wellington. The Sydney Cricket Ground was an absolute morass when the sides ran out for the game and torrential rain lashed the stadium throughout the game. And the 10,000 spectators who had braved the elements to see this first France-Australia international game on Australian soil got quite good value for their money. Within fifteen minutes the French were six points up with two superb drop goals from Pierre Albaladejo and from there on it was plain but wet sailing for the Tricolours. Jean Pique, Pierre Lacroix and second row forward G. Bouguyon scored tries to give them a total of 15 points and all the Australians could muster against them was a try from Heinrich and a penalty goal from Ellwood. This marked a hat-trick of wins for France over Australia. France had beaten Trevor Allan's tourists in Colombes Stadium during the 1947-1948 trip and France had dished out quite a mauling to Bob Davidson's Wallabies with a 19-0 win also at Colombes during the Australian tour of 1957-1958.

SPANGHERO

Walter Spanghero was just twenty-one when he made his international debut for France against South Africa in 1964 and was the first of two famous brothers to play for his country. By the end of the 1973-1974 season he had brought his total of caps to 44, which leaves him second in the all-time record list behind his great rival Benoit Dauga with 50. His brother Claude joined him on the French side in 1972 and both of course, are still prominent in French club rugby.

THE FRENCH AGAIN

France returned to South Africa in 1964 under the captaincy of the legendary Michel Crauste and in a six-match programme they won five, lost one, scored 117 points and conceded 55. Their top points scorer was Pierre Albaladejo with 36 points from nine conversions, a penalty goal and three drop goals. Six of the touring party scored two tries each—Jean Gachassin, Jean Pique, Jean Dupuy, Christian Laborde, J-J Rupert and Michel Sitjar. In the opening game of the tour against Rhodesia, the French got off to a flying start with a 34-11 win and Pierre "Monsieur Drop" Albaladejo lived up to his nickname by dropping two magnificent goals. He also kicked five conversions to set a record of 16 points for a French touring player in a game in South Africa. In their provincial matches, the French beat Rhodesia, Griqualand West and Transvaal by comfortable margins but they were beaten by Western Province. A week after this defeat they faced the Springboks in the only international match of the tour at Pam Brink Stadium, Springs and this was to be another eye-opener for the South Africans.

A MEMORABLE WIN

Pierre Albaladejo provided a shock start to the international games at Springs. South Africa were penalised and within 50 seconds France were ahead with a magnificent penalty goal from almost 50 yards out. D. A. Stewart of Western Province levelled matters with a penalty goal and then right on half-time came the score that clinched a memorable win for the French. Benoit Dauga picked up a loose ball within his own half, made a few yards and sent Christian Darrouy off on a 60 yards run that ended with a glorious try in the corner. From the touch-line the accurate Albaladejo sent the conversion dead centre between the posts and France turned over with an 8-3 lead. Despite immense Springbok pressure the French held out gamely until a minute from time and then Dave Lawless broke through to score a try for South Africa. With the final kick of the game Stewart had his chance to bring the scores level but it sailed wide and the French had their 8-6 win. It was now 12 years since South Africa had beaten France and the score between them was two wins to France, two draws and one win to South Africa since their first official meeting in 1952. In those five games France had scored 23 points and conceded 47.

A HAT-TRICK OF TRIES

Christian Darrouy was under twenty when he scored his first international try for France and during the 1965-1966 season he smashed the French international try scoring record held then by Jean Dupuy at twenty-one but his total included scoring in a number of unofficial internationals against Italy and Rumania. In his 28 matches against International Board countries Darrouy totalled 14 tries and against Ireland at Lansdowne Road, Dublin in 1963, he equalled the French record of three tries in an international game with a genuine hat-trick. In his six matches against Ireland, Darrouy, regarded as one of the fastest wing threequarters in history, had the record of scoring six tries! His supreme moment was in the 1964 tour of South Africa when he intercepted a pass and ran 60 yards for the try that beat the Springboks by 8-6.

A RECORD RETURN

Guy Camberabero, then twenty-five, made his international out-half debut for France against New Zealand in 1961 and then disappeared into the wilderness as far as the French selectors were concerned. But six years later, after France had lost their first game of the season to Scotland, he was suddenly restored to favour and was named to partner his brother Lilian against the touring Australians at Colombes Stadium. And the little Camberabero brothers, known throughout French rugby as the "Two Fleas"—Guy was 5' 6" and Lilian 5' 4" and both weighed 10st 3lbs—really made their mark in this game. Between them they scored all of France's points in a 20-14 victory over the Australians. Guy kicked 17 points and then went on to score 10 against England, 14 against Wales and eight against Ireland. His total of 49 points is a record for a season in the International Championship. That season, however, he also scored 27 points against Italy at Toulon and his overall total for five international games in the one season is a French record. His 76 points were made up of eight penalty goals, seven drop goals, 14 conversions and a try.

A TRAGIC THREE DAYS

The saddest week in the history of French international rugby began on Sunday, 31st December, 1967. That evening on his way home to Lourdes after playing in a club game for Mont-de-Marson, Guy Boniface, the international centre-threequarter who had played in 23 games for France, was killed in a car accident. Boniface, one of the two famous brothers to play for France, and one of the most elegant centres the country had ever produced made his debut in the International championship in 1960 and was only thirty when he died. Only three days later another French international Jean Michel Capendeguy was also to lose his life in a road accident—10 days before he was due to win his second cap against Scotland. Just a month earlier he had been capped for the first time against New Zealand.

FRANCE STEP IN

Because of the Maori issue, the All-Blacks tour to South Africa in 1967 was called off and France were invited to step in for a 14-match tour, which was to include four international games—and three of these international games were to be played on successive Saturdays. Under the captaincy of Christian Darrouy, the French scored 209 points while conceding 161. Their top points scorer was Jean-Louis Dehez with 52 from eight penalty goals, five conversions and six drop goals and the top try scorer was Bernard Duprat with five.

ANNIHILATION

C. W. Dirksen, who had won his first cap against Australia in 1963, opened the scoring for South Africa in the first international game of France's 1967 tour and Henry de Villiers converted. Minutes later, Claude Dourthe lifted France's hopes with a sparkling try. But that, sadly, was to be France's lot on that unhappy afternoon. Piet Greyling and Jan Ellis went in for tries, de Villiers had converted both and then he kicked a penalty goal to leave France trailing by 3-18 at half-time. Dirksen, with a superb run of almost 60 yards added his second try to the total shortly after the start of the second half and de Villiers converted and then Piet Greyling finished it off with his second try for a 26-3 win for the Springboks. To this day, the result remains as France's worst defeat at the hands of South Africa in an official international game.

NO CHANGE

South Africa made no changes for their second international against France a week later—and as far as the result was concerned the game brought no change either for France. They were beaten badly and once again they could muster only three points and those came from a long-range penalty kick by Pierre Villepreux. South Africa took an early lead with a 60 yards penalty goal by Tiny Naude and coming up to half-time Eben Olivier went in for a try which Henry de Villiers converted. Dirksen added his third try in the two internationals and Jan Engelbrecht scored the final one which de Villiers converted for a 16-3 defeat of France. This was the first time in their years of official internationals that France had lost successive games to South Africa.

FORM AT LAST

South Africa with two international wins in the bag, decided to leave well enough alone and fielded an unchanged side for the third international game against France at Ellis Park, Johannesburg—and this, in itself was a record in the history of South African international rugby. However, this time they were to be out of luck. France suddenly re-discovered the form that had made them the top scorers of the Home International championship that year. Tiny Naude got the South Africans off to a promising opening with a penalty goal from 55 yards within three minutes but 10 minutes later with France surging into a concerted attack, their hooker Jean Cabanier was pushed over at the posts and Guy Camberabero duly added the conversion. Claude Lacaze put them further ahead with a mighty penalty goal from the halfway line but again within minutes South Africa went streaming through for a try by Eben Olivier. Naude then shot the Springboks into the lead but Camberabero dropped a goal. From there it was France all the way; Jean Trillo shot over for a try which Camberabero converted and within minutes the tiny out-half dropped his second goal to make it 19-9. In injury time the South Africans made the scoreboard look just a little healthier with a try from Jan Ellis which Piet Visagie converted. With this win France had maintained their unbeaten record at Ellis Park and the other significant feature of the game was that the final conversion marked Piet Visagie's first points for South Africa. By the time his international career ended, Visagie was to become South Africa's greatest scorer in international rugby with a total of 130 points.

ANOTHER DRAW

France's hopes of drawing the 1967 series with South Africa died in the fourth international at Newlands. The French started this game with a record by raising the total of players used by them in the four international matches to 25 and only Walter Spanghero, Benoit Dauga and Jean Fort returned home with the honour of playing in all four. France started well with a try from Spanghero and held it until half-time. Piet Visagie then dropped a goal for South Africa in the second half but Guy Camberabero restored the French lead with his drop goal. Henry de Villiers, however landed a penalty goal and it was all square at six points to the end. When the points were totted up at the end of the four internationals they showed that South Africa had scored exactly twice as many as France, 62 to 31. With nine games played since 1952, France had now won three, South Africa had won three and three had been drawn. It was level pegging.

THE GRAND SLAM

France had shared the International Championship with England and Wales in 1954 and with Wales in 1955 and had been outright winners in 1959, 1961, 1962 and 1967. But for the French there was still one vital hurdle to be overcome. Since the end of the Second World War, they had also beaten Australia, South Africa and New Zealand; all that was left to crown all their glory would be the Grand Slam. And that finally came in 1968. At Colombes Stadium, they beat Ireland well by 16-6 and then in a tight finish at Murrayfield, they pipped the Scots by 8-6. Next came Wales and this promised to be the toughest one. So it was with Wales leading by 9-3 at half-time. But Guy and Lilian Camberabero wrapped it all up handsomely in the second half and it finished with a great French victory on the score of 14-9. Between them that afternoon the Camberaberos collected 11 of the 14 points. And those two mighty atoms of French rugby were there again on a sunny April afternoon at Colombes to drive the French on to a 14-9 victory over England. It was the first time France had defeated all four countries in the one season and they had the Grand Slam for the first—and still the only—time since they had started in international Rugby over 60 years earlier.

THE SECOND DOWN UNDER

Led by Christian Carrere, France made their second tour down under to New Zealand and Australia in 1968 and came back home with the depressing record of having played four successive international games and losing all four. Their complete record was that they won nine of their 14 games, lost five and scored 197 points while conceding 142. The French were unimpressive in their opening games against provincial sides and with the programme arranged as it was, they found themselves up against the full might of the All-Blacks in the first international of the tour in only their fourth game in New Zealand. This was played at Lancaster Park on Saturday, 13th July, 1968, the eve of Bastile Day and it was not to be a happy afternoon for the French.

LAST MINUTE ARGUMENT

All the excitement, argument and controversy of France's first international of the 1968 tour of New Zealand came in the closing minutes of the game at Lancaster Park. With just five minutes to go New Zealand were ahead by 9-6. Fergie McCormick had kicked three penalty goals and Pierre Lacaze, a veteran of the previous tour in 1961 had dropped a goal and Pierre Villepreux had kicked a penalty for France. Then the New Zealanders were caught offside at a ruck just inside their own half and Villepreux, despite the clinging mud of a wet and sodden pitch, indicated that he would try for a penalty goal from just under 50 yards. The French full-back drove the heavy ball between the posts and the scores were level. Then came the final drama. The All-Blacks launched everything into one last final attack and stormed the French line. Villepreux fielded the ball and tried for touch but his kick went astray and within seconds had disappeared into a fierce maul between the two sets of forwards. For a moment or two no one seemed to know what was happening and then the referee blew his whistle and indicated that Earle Kirton was lying on the ball over the line. He awarded a try and a try it remained despite all the clamour of the Frenchmen who claimed that Kel Tremain had knocked the ball on and that Kirton also had been offside. But the referee was adamant. It was a try. It was several minutes before McCormick got around to taking the convert and he missed it and France had gone down 9-12. The French players trooped off in disgust, claiming loudly that they had been robbed of the draw they deserved.

THE SECOND DEFEAT

The bitterness of the closing minutes of the final moments of the first international game at Lancaster Park spilled over into the second meeting of France and the All-Blacks at Athletic Park, Wellington on 27th July, 1968. The busiest man on the field was referee John Pring of

Auckland who had to halt proceedings on several occasions to have words with the two captains, Marcel Puget of France and Kel Tremain of New Zealand. And Puget did not exactly make himself popular with Mr Pring by offering the ball to the New Zealanders every time the whistle went for an infringement. It was a bad-tempered game, fought out in every sense of the word by the two packs and in the end it was decided on penalty kicks. Fergie McCormick kicked three for New Zealand and Pierre Villepreux kicked one for France, quite a remarkable one from just on 65 yards out.

THE GOING TOUCH

For the first time on the 1968 tour, the French faced out-half Sid Going in the third and final international game against the New Zealanders at Eden Park, Auckland on Saturday, 10th August—and Going quickly showed his class. He raced in for two tries both of which were converted by Fergie McCormick, who landed a penalty goal as well and shortly before the first half closed Wayne Cottrell dropped a goal. At the break New Zealand led by 16-0. France, however, came back strongly in the second half and provided three magnificent tries from Jean Trillo, Christian Carrere and Jean-Pierre Lux and Claude Dourthe dropped a goal. McCormick, however landed another penalty goal to beat the Frenchmen by 19-12. The end marked the eighth time in succession that the French had been beaten by the All-Blacks.

A SAD FINISH

The 1968 French tourists flew out from New Zealand and into Australia —and into trouble. On 14th August, they took on Queensland at Ballymore Park, Brisbane and duly won without the slightest trouble by 31-11. But just a few minutes after he had galloped over for a fine try midway through the second half, the French international centre threequarter Claude Dourthe got himself involved in a mild fracas with the Australian international Jules Guerassimoff and for his sins, was sent to the line. It marked the first time in French rugby history that a member of the international side had been put off in a tour game. Dourthe was subsequently suspended for one game and that, unfortunately, happened to be the full international game against Australia three days later. France had never been beaten by Australia and at that particular time the Wallabies had gone seven games without a win. Everything pointed to a striking final flourish by the Tricolours and they gave promise of that by opening the scoring with a try from Walter Spanghero which was converted by Pierre Villepreux. Nine minutes before half-time Villepreux had to go off the field with an injury and he was replaced by C. Bouget, the Grenoble full-back, who later in the game became the second French full-back to score a try in an international game. Unfortunately for France it was not enough. Arthur McGill kicked a penalty goal in the second half for the Wallabies, Phil Smith had a try which McGill converted and then, after Bouget had scored his record-equalling try, John Ballesty dropped the goal that gave Australia an 11-10 win. It was the first time that France had lost to Australia.

THE SELECTORS PROBLEM

When the French selectors sat down to name their side to tour in South Africa in 1971, they had more than a slight problem on their hands. Roger Bourgarel of Toulouse was one of his country's finest threequarters at the time—he was eventually to win eight caps—but the problem was that he was coloured. They solved it by omitting him from the party and that, of course, brought close to a public outcry in France, so much so that after further discussion Bourgarel was included on the side and thus carved out his own special corner of rugby history by playing in South Africa and in the two international games. Bourgarel was one of the memorable successes of this 1971 tour in which the French played nine games, won seven, drew one and lost one. They scored 288 points and conceded only 92. Their widest margin of victory was 50-0 against Western Transvaal, and their only defeat was by 9-22 against South Africa in the first international game. Their top points scorer was out-half Jean-Louis Berot with 57 points from 15 conversions, six penalty goals and three drop goals. Roland Betranne took the try scoring honours with seven.

A RECORD HALF-CENTURY

The 1971 French tourists in South Africa opened up with a 22-13 win over Eastern Transvaal on 22nd May at Springs and full-back Pierre Villepreux headed the scoring with 10 points from two drop goals and two conversions. But it was to be an unfortunate game for Villepreux. He broke a bone in his back and that was the end of the tour for him. From Springs, the French moved to Potchefstroom on 26th May and set a record for themselves in South Africa by trouncing the Western Transvaal side by 50-0, scoring 12 tries and seven conversions. Roland Betranne with an exciting display became the first Frenchman to score four tries for a French touring side in South Africa and Jean-Louis Berot indicated what was to come from his foot during this tour by kicking a total of 14 points from seven conversions. Berot was again on the mark·in the third game against Transvaal at Johannesburg where the French chalked up their third successive win by 20-14. Berot kicked one conversion, two penalty goals and two drop goals for 14 points. But within two days, at East London on 31st May, as France beat Border by 30-6, Andre Marot topped Berot's best by kicking three conversions and three penalty goals for a personal total of 15 points. Prior to this, only four other French players had scored higher in South Africa. They were; Pierre Albaladejo with 16 points from five conversions, and two drop goals against Rhodesia during the 1964 tour, Pierre Dedieu with 17 points from four conversions, two penalty goals and a drop goal against Griqualand West during the same tour, Guy Camberabero with 18 points from six conversions, and two drop goals against Rhodesia during the 1967 tour and Jean-Louis Dehez, who set the all-time individual French record in South Africa with 19 points from two conversions three penalty goals and two drop goals in France's 25-6 win over South-West Africa Districts in 1967.

SIX IN A ROW

The French added a fifth successive victory at Cape Town on 5th June by beating Western Province by 21-6 and Berot collected another six points with three conversions. The tourists then moved on to Windhoek to beat South-West Africa by 35-6 and Berot was dead on form again. He kicked three conversions, two penalty goals and for extra measure, a drop goal. With six victories from six games behind them the French headed to Bloemfontein for the first international game against South Africa on 12th June. At that stage they had knocked up 178 points and had conceded only 45. However, there was now no hope that Pierre Villepreux would be able to take his place at full-back. He was in hospital with a plaster cast on his back. A further misfortune was that the side's captain Christian Carrere had picked up a mouth infection and had to drop out and Jean Trillo took over the leadership for the international. Scrum-half Max Barrau, too, was out of consideration with a knee injury. Still, on their astonishing record up to then the French hopes were high for victory in the 12th meeting between the two countries.

THE FIRST DEFEAT

The French were never even remotely in contention in the first international at Bloemfontein on Saturday, 12th June, 1971. While their strong pack was able to match the power of the Springboks up front, the vital difference between the two sides was in the back-play and here the South Africans scored heavily. Full-back Ian McCallum collected 13 points with two conversions and three penalty goals, Gerd Muller and Joggie Viljoen added tries and the inimitable Piet Visagie got himself into the scoring list with a spectacular drop goal. All the French could offer in return was a try by Jean Trillo and two penalty goals by Jean-Louis Berot. The only historic feature of the international was that South Africa's Frik du Preez was appearing for his country for the 34th time which gave him a new Springbok record ahead of Jan Engelbrecht and John Gainsford, both of whom had been joint record holders at 33 caps.

THE FINAL DRAW

The French returned to the scoring form against North East Cape at Cradock on 15th June with a 33-17 win and four days later, just a week after their first defeat by South Africa, they took on the Springboks again, this time at Durban and this was to close out their international meetings for the moment since 1952. It was the 13th meeting of the two countries in official internationals but the figure was not to bring luck nor for that matter bad luck to either side. In a game that bubbled with excitement from start to finish, they ended all square with identical scoring, a try, a conversion and a drop goal each. P. A. Cronje had South Africa's try, Ian McCallum kicked the conversion and Piet Visagie dropped his almost inevitable goal. Roland Bertranne scored

France's try, which was converted by Jean-Louis Berot who also dropped the goal. This was the fourth draw between South Africa and France in their 19 years of official internationals and France had three victories to South Africa's six with four drawn, with France having scored 91 points to South Africa's 159. Only the Lions, New Zealand and Australia have scored more victories over South Africa in international rugby.

IT TOOK A WHILE

Scrum half Jacques Fouroux of La Voulte was picked to play for France against Ireland at Stade Colombes in 1968 but four long years were to pass before he eventually collected his first international cap—and even then it was only by accident. He was fully fit for the 1968 game but was sensationally dropped a few days before the game when the out-half named for the match went down with an injury. As they are prone to do, the French selectors decided on a new half-back partnership and so, Fouroux instead of winning his first cap at Colombes wound up as a depressed and reluctant spectator. There was worse to come, however. Including that game, no fewer than nine scrumhalves played for France before the now thoroughly disillusioned Fouroux at last was given his chance against Ireland at Lansdowne Road on 29th April, 1972. He was fortunate that France played Ireland twice that season—the French agreed to a second fixture in Dublin when Scotland and Wales refused to travel to Ireland for their championship games—and even more fortunate that in the week before the game, France's top scrum-half Max Barrau, the original selection, had to cry off with an injury. Fouroux's first cap, however, was not won in auspicious circumstances. France crashed to a 14-24 defeat—the first and, of course, still the only time that they have been beaten twice in one season by Ireland.

UNDEFEATED

France took off to Australia in May 1972 and flew back home with their first undefeated record in a major overseas tour. Confined exclusively to Australia they went through a nine-match programme, with eight wins and a draw and scored 254 points while conceding

112. Their top points scorer was full-back Pierre Villepreux with 63 points from 17 conversions, seven penalty goals and two tries. Their highest score in the nine games was the 45 points they registered against Tasmania and their widest margin of victory was 34 points in their 37-3 defeat of Queensland. Their only draw at 14-14 came in the seventh game of the tour, an international against Australia.

VILLEPREUX'S START

Pierre Villepreux of Toulouse, who was to end his five year international career of 27 caps with the 1972 tour of Australia had a field day in France's opening game at Perth on 28th May, 1972. With France racing away to a 29-12 win, he kicked three penalty goals and two conversions and that put him well on the way to becoming the trip's top scorer. Bernard Duprat scored the first try in this game and Walter Spanghero and Oliver Saisset and Jack Cantoni had one each. There was even better to come in the second game at Adelaide where the French took off on their first real scoring spree of 44 points in beating South Australia by 44-19. Henri Cabrol, deputising for Villepreux in this game came up with 15 points from three conversions and three penalty goals. The top try scorer in this outing was wing threequarter Bernard Duprat with three. Tasmania were the next to go down with a 12-45 beating at Hobart and Sydney became the fourth victims by 9-15 on 6th June. The fifth game against the powerful New South Wales side at Sydney was a tight affair but the French survived with a 29-23 win and then for their final warm-up game before the first international at Sydney on 17th June, the French disposed of New South Wales Country by 25-15. At that stage the tourists had run up 187 points in six games and were warm favourites to beat Australia.

BARELY MADE IT

Walter Spanghero, followed by his brother Claude, led a confident French side out to meet Australia in their first international game at Sydney on 17th June, 1972 but 78 minutes after the start most of the confidence had been well and truly knocked out of the tourists. With just two minutes to go in a game that had been marked by brawling and fighting they were trailing 10-14 and Australia, despite having two men concussed, seemed to have matters well in hand. Then Jean-Paul Lux kicked ahead and followed up, grabbed the ball and tore over the Australian line, tackled hard at the last moment by full-back Russell Fairfax. In fact, Fairfax dragged Lux over the dead-ball line but the referee ruled that Lux had touched down before being hauled out of bounds. Villepreux missed the conversion and France had kept their unbeaten tour record—but only just.

THE LAST GASP

France disposed of Brisbane by 37-3 in their eighth game of the tour and four days later, they took on Australia again in the game that was to end the adventure down under. And again it was tight, much too tight for the French and in the end they almost threw it away by arguing with the referee, Mr Jim O'Sullivan of Sydney. It was not the most peaceful of internationals and O'Sullivan had to call a halt to the hostilities on more than one or two occasions. In the end it all came down to battle between the French and Australia's full-back Russell Fairfax. Jo Maso with two tries, Walter Spanghero with another and the conversions by Villepreux and Cabrol, left the French in a 16-12 lead with three minutes to go. Fairfax had kicked the Australians four penalty goals and now he kicked his fifth to make it 16-15. Time was just up when France were penalised again and this time they argued first with the referee and then lost 10 yards for not getting back from the penalty. Fairfax had the chance to win the game but a great kick went slicing inches wide of the posts and France had kept their unbeaten record of the 1972 tour. Those last 16 points had brought their total to 254—a record for a French touring side against a major country. If there was a regret, it was that Pierre Villepreux had played his final game for France. He had finished it on a high note, with a French record of 118 points in his 29 appearances aganst the major countries.

PIERRE VILLEPREUX

When Pierre Villepreux, regarded by many as France's greatest full-back said goodbye to international rugby at the end of the 1971-1972 season, he finished with 29 caps against the major countries—and also with the record of kicking France's longest penalty goal in international rugby. Against New Zealand in the Tricolours' tour down under in 1968, at Wellington, with 48,000 people watching him, he kicked France's only points of the game with a penalty goal from over 70 yards out.

62 APPEARANCES

Michel Crauste, born 1934, wore the jersey of France on 62 occasions but 19 of his international appearances were against the minor countries and his total of 43 against the International Board countries stood as a French record until it was surpassed by Benoit Dauga and Walter Spanghero. Crauste, who because of his sallow complexion and his famous moustache was nicknamed "The Mongol" retired at the age of thirty-two, at a time when most French people believed that he had years of international rugby still ahead of him. But, at least he left the scene with an unusual French record. From the wing-forward position, he scored a genuine hat-trick of three tries in France's 13-0 win over England at Colombes Stadium in 1962.

THE FINAL ROUND UP

Including the unofficial match at Parc des Princes in 1906, France and New Zealand met for the 12th time on Saturday, 10th February, 1973 at Parc des Princes and it brought France their second victory to New Zealand's 10. And it also brought a most unusual rugby record. France won the 12th meeting by 13-6 to bring their total of points to 84 since 1906 and New Zealand took their total to 197. France's tally is made up from 13 tries, eight penalty goals and five drop goals and two conversions. New Zealand's total comes from 35 tries, 19 conversions, 15 penalty goals and three drop goals. And the moment of history came just before the end of the first half at Paris on 10th February, 1973, just after Roland Bertranne had scored France's first try of the game. Little Jean-Pierre Romeu lined the ball up for the kick at goal and sent it between the posts. In the 67 years association between France and New Zealand, it was the first time that France had converted a try since New Year's Day 1906!

THE ONE HE MISSED

When France came to Lansdowne Road, Dublin on April 14th, 1973 for their final match of the season against Ireland, they needed only a draw to clinch the International Championship—and out-half Jean Pierre Romeu needed just one score to finish off his greatest season. Romeu had scored in every international game that season and in the process had knocked up a most impressive personal record of 42 points. He had scored 11 points against Rumania, 12 against Scotland, had followed that with five against New Zealand, two against England and just before the visit to Dublin had scored all of France's points in their 12-3 win over Wales in Paris. His 42 points had come from 10 penalty goals, two drop goals and three conversions. Lansdowne Road, however, was to become one of Romeu's most painful memories. He was given the easiest of chances to score, missed it in some extraordinary fashion and France went home without the draw they should have got had Romeu been in his normal form. Ireland led with penalty goals from Tony Ensor and Mike Gibson right up to 90 seconds from time. Then wing threequarter Jean Phliponneau went streaking over for a French try and everything hung on Romeu's attempt to convert. From the easiest of positions he sent the ball well wide of the posts and so France lost and the International championship that year ended in an unprecedented five-way split between Ireland, England, Scotland, Wales and France, with each side having won its two home games.

A SWARM OF BEES

With a 62-14 defeat by Wales and a 10-19 loss to an England under-23 side, the Japanese tourists of 1973 headed off to France and took another hiding from a French selection by 51-19 at Avignon but showed that they were learning fast by holding the French down to a 16-15 lead up to 55 minutes. A second French selection beat the Japanese by 29-18 at Perpignan but they eventually struck success with a 19-8 win over a further selection at Brive. In the unofficial international at Bordeaux, France beat Japan by 30-18 and led one famous French critic to describe them as "a swarm of bees on the field". The Japanese were highly delighted with their tour and their manager said later; "We have been preparing for this tour for eight years. At our present rate of progress it will take another eight to reach the standard of France but we will go back and start our further preparations now".

WELL IN THE RED

France, who began their international games far later than any of the other major countries, are well in the red in matter of international victories and defeats. They have played 221 games against England, Ireland, Scotland, Wales, South Africa, New Zealand, Australia and New South Wales and of these, they have won 78, lost 124 and drawn 19.

THE BREAKTHROUGH

After 15 successive defeats by Wales France finally broke this depressing record with their first victory in Paris in 1928 and by the end of the 1973-1974 season could boast of 13 victories. In all France have played Wales on 46 occasions, winning 13, losing 30 drawing three and at Cardiff in February 1974 brought their total of points against Wales to the nice round total of 400 points. On the present-day values, their top margin of victory over Wales was at Cardiff Arms Park in 1958 when they won by two goals and two drop goals to a penalty goal and a try (18-7). Their longest unbeaten run against the Welshmen began in Cardiff in 1958 and continued until they were beaten at Cardiff in 1962.

A LONG WAIT

France, who played the first of their 49 meetings with England at Paris in 1906, had to wait until 1972 to set their record win over England. At Colombes Stadium, they routed the English by five goals, a penalty goal and a try (37) to a goal, two penalty goals (12). In their 49 meetings, France have won 14, lost 29 and drawn six and have scored, under the present-day values, a total of 455 points. France have never scored more than three wins in-a-row over England and have achieved the hat-trick on two occasions, between 1954 and 1956 and 1966 and 1968.

FOUR REPLACEMENTS

To aid the Air Disaster Fund, set up after the appalling airliner crash near Paris following the France v England draw at Parc des Princes on Saturday, 2nd March, 1974, France and England met in an unofficial international game at Twickenham on Saturday, 21st April, 1974. No caps were awarded for this game which the French won by 26-7 but the meeting did provide a record. For the first time in an international rugby game, four replacements were used. Alan Morley of Bristol replaced Alan Old after 18 minutes and John Watkins of Gloucester came in for Roger Uttley after 40 minutes for England and on the French side Pecune came in for Vacher after 29 minutes and Benesis was replaced by Ugartemendia after 54 minutes. The game was watched by almost 50,000 spectators and the Air Disaster Fund benefitted by over £60,000.

AGAINST SCOTLAND

France's record margin over Scotland was in 1955 at Colombes Stadium, Paris where they won by a penalty goal and four tries to nil. In the 44 meetings between the two countries since 1910 at Edinburgh, France have won 19, lost 23 and drawn two and, on present day scoring values, have brought their total of points to 354. Their most successful run against the Scots began with the first of five successive victories at Paris in 1951 and ended with their defeat at Murrayfield in 1956.

AGAINST IRELAND

The French have scored more points against Ireland than they have against any of the other major countries. In their 47 matches against Ireland, they have won 21, lost 23 and drawn three and have scored, under present-day values, a total of 481 points. Their best performance against the Irish was at Colombes Stadium in 1964 when they scored three goals, a drop goal and three tries to a drop goal and a try, which under modern values would be a 33-7 win. Their longest unbeaten run against Ireland began with their win at Colombes Stadium in 1960 and lasted until their defeat at Lansdowne Road in 1969.

THE LONG SERVICE MEN

The French selectors are not noted for their consistency and have a well-known habit of changing their teams rapidly and regularly. However, eleven great players have managed to chalk up at least 10 seasons of international rugby with their country. They are Pierre Albaladejo (1954-1964), Andre Boniface (1954-1966), Elie Cester (1964-1974), Christian Darrouy (1957-1967), George Dufau (1948-1957), Adolphe Jaureguy (1920-1929), Rene Lasserre (1914-1924), Lubin Lebrere (1914-1925), Roger Martine (1950-1961), Jean Prat (1945-1955) and Walter Spanghero (1964-1973).

FRANCE'S TOTAL

From Henri Armand, the first man to be honoured with a French cap for rugby down to J. F. Gurdon who made his debut against Scotland at Murrayfield on Saturday, 16th March, 1974, 515 players have worn the French jersey in international games. Henri Armand, it is claimed, was the captain of the French team that won the Olympic Games championship of 1900 in Paris. This total, however, represents only those who have played against the recognised major countries in international rugby.

THE LIONS

HOW IT BEGAN

Two of England's most famous sportsmen of the time, Alfred Shaw and Arthur Shrewsbury, having enjoyed a most successful cricket tour of Australia in 1887, conceived the idea that a rugby tour on much the same lines might turn to be an equally successful and entertaining adventure. They went along to the Committee of the English Rugby Union and laid their plans before them. In its simplest form, their suggestion was that a representative rugby side should go on a pro-longed tour of both Australia and New Zealand. The Committee duly deliberated the matter and then declined to award their patronage to the project, which they felt was being organised for the benefit of individual promoters. They did add, however, that they would have no serious objection to the project provided that neither the promoters nor the players infringed in any way on the sacred matter of pure amateurism. From such a beginning, Messrs Shaw and Shrewsbury, with the able help of yet another famous cricketer A. E. Stoddart, who, in fact, was then in Australia on another cricket tour, got the entire matter under control. And so, on 8th March, 1888, the first Lions left England to begin their tour of Australia and New Zealand. They were not to return to England until 11th November, 1888.

SO THEY BECAME LIONS

Beginning with the ambitious adventure of A. E. Stoddart's side to New Zealand and Australia in 1888, there have been 19 overseas tours down under and to South Africa by combined teams from the four home countries of England, Scotland, Wales and Ireland. The original sides were not, however, wholly representative of the four countries. Stoddart's team, for instance, did not contain an Irish player, W. E. Maclagan's side in South Africa in 1891 was composed of English and Scottish players and the Reverend M. Mullineux's side of 1896 was, in the main, an England-Ireland selection. A. F.

Harding's touring side of 1908 was a Welsh-English selection but from there on the touring sides became truly representative of the four countries. During the 1924 tour in South Africa, the visiting side first became known as the Lions and as such they have been known ever since. It is generally accepted that the Lions nickname came from the use of the word by the newspapers and sports writers in South Africa at the time, who coined it from the lion symbol worn on the ties of the visiting players. It has now become customary to refer to all 19 tours to New Zealand, Australia and South Africa and indeed to Canada as Lions tours and the 468 selections who have participated in those 19 tours since 1888 are now all regarded as members of rugby's most exclusive band, the Lions—the team that never plays at home.

THE DEATH OF R. L. SEDDON

R. L. Seddon, who had won three international caps for England against Ireland, Scotland and Wales in 1887 was named to captain the first touring side to leave for Australia and New Zealand. But, alas, he was not to finish the tour. While sculling on the River Hunter at Maitland in Australia, his craft overturned and he was drowned. His place as captain was then taken by A. E. Stoddart, who before he ended his international rugby career was to win 11 caps for England. Stoddart, who was born in 1863 and died in 1915, is still remembered as one of the world's greatest cricketers. He represented England in Test cricket between 1887 and 1898 and in his career scored 17,062 runs. He captained England on seven occasions and against Australia at Melbourne during the 1894-1895 tour set his highest Test score of 173. In 1900, when he was persuaded to come out of retirement for J. T. Hearne's benefit match, he hit 221 runs in his last innings for Middlesex.

OTAGO FIRST AND LAST

The 1888 touring side opened their rugby mission to New Zealand with a game against Otago and won it by 8-3 and three days later they took on Otago again and this time won by 4-3. From there they moved on to Canterbury, whom they also played twice, winning the first by 14-6 and the second by 4-0. They were held to their first draw in New Zealand at 3-3 in the fifth game of the tour, lost to Taranaki Clubs in the seventh game and then having beaten Auckland 6-3 in a first game, lost the second one to Auckland by 0-4 three days later. Having played nine games, the tourists then headed off for Australia, where they remained for almost three months before returning to New Zealand to continue the tour. In their final 10 games in New Zealand they met Auckland again on two occasions and won the first by 3-0 and drew a second by a really extraordinary result in representative rugby 1-1. At the time a try was worth just one point. And that result was to be duplicated in the very last game of the tour against Wanganui when the score was again a try each. The top scorer of the 1888 touring side was the full-back A. E. Paul of Swinton with 24 points from nine conversions and two drop goals. The most prolific try scorer was the half-back James Nolan of Rochdale Hornets, who, in fact, had been born in Dublin and was thus the first Irishman to tour in Australia and New Zealand.

AN UNBEATEN RUN

R. L. Seddon's touring side of 1888 to New Zealand and Australia were beaten 0-4 in the ninth game of their trip. They went on to finish their tour unbeaten and that coupled with the unbeaten tour by W. E. Maclagan's side in South Africa in 1891 and the 20 successive victories by John Hammond's side in South Africa in 1896 until they went down 0-5 in the last game of that tour of South Africa, established an all-time record in the history of touring sides. In all, the three touring sides, the Lions of those days, went 65 matches without defeat.

THE PAPER CAP

Harry Eagles, a bustling forward, set an astonishing record during the 1888 tour of Australia and New Zealand and also has the unique distinction of having been awarded an international cap for England without ever having played for England. During the tour of Australia and New Zealand he played in all 35 official games and it is on record that he also took part in more than half of the games played under Victorian rules in Australia. On his return to England Eagles, who played with the Salford Club seemed certain to win his international cap for England, but as it happened England were in dispute with the other home countries at the time and did not play in any international games during the 1889 season. The English Union, however, picked an international side, which never played a game—and caps were awarded to 15 men. Among them was Harry Eagles, who, despite his "paper" cap, was never to play in an international game for England. His only consolation was that in the 1889 season he was a member of the Rest of England side which beat the champion county Yorkshire by three goals to nil at Halifax.

SOME EXTRA GAMES

The official record of the first Lions tour to New Zealand and Australia shows that they played 35 games, won 27, drew six, lost two and scored the round total of 300 points while conceding 101. In fact, however, the 1888 tourists played a further 18 games in Australia, of which six were won, 11 lost and one drawn. These extra games however were played under Australian Rules or Victorian Rules as they were known at the time . . . and it is on record that they did not please the august gentlemen of the English Rugby Union. In Marshall's famous book on rugby, there is the following opinion of those games. "One objectionable feature of the tour was the arrangement of the matches under Victorian Rules. This was done with a view to exhibiting the English players in those districts where the Victorian game was played and thus stamped the tour as an exhibition and as a means of making money for the promoters rather than as a visit of an English international side desirous of measuring its strength against fellow sportsmen in Australia and New Zealand. Had the tour been under the management of the Rugby Union, no matches under alien rules would have been arranged or permitted".

RULED OUT

J. P. Clowes, regarded as one of the top players in the North of England with his club Halifax and equally regarded as a certainty to make the England international team in time, was an automatic selection for the 1888 side to tour in Australia and New Zealand. And the said Mr Clowes duly travelled out with the team but as it turned out he spent a nine months holiday, without ever playing in a game. It seemed that prior to leaving, Clowes had been given £15 by the promoters of the tour and when Clowes was confronted with this he promptly admitted that it was true. The Yorkshire Rugby Committee immediately called for an investigation into the matter and their findings were that Clowes having received £15 for the express purpose of purchasing an outfit for his trip down under, had thereby received monetary consideration for playing football and, in their opinion was therefore a professional. Their decision was forwarded to the English Rugby Union, and they decided, on the evidence before them, that Clowes, in fact, had made himself a professional player. When this news was relayed to the promoters of the tour they refused to include Clowes in any of the games by reason of the fact that if they did, they might disqualify other members of the side. On the return home of the team to England every member of the side was asked to make an affidavit that he had received no monetary reward in any way throughout the tour. Mr Clowes, having had the benefit of a long holiday, disappeared off home and into the obscurity of rugby history.

THE PRIDE OF THE LIONS

There can be no doubt but that W. E. Maclagan's touring side of 1891 to South Africa were the greatest in the history of the Lions. They began their tour with a match against the Cape Town Colonies and won it by 15-1. And that solitary point, a try, by "Hasie" Versfeld was to be the only score registered against them in their 19 match tour. Their full record was that they won all 19 games and scored 223 points while conceding one. Their biggest win was over Natal by 25-0 and their tightest games were against Griqualand West and South Africa in the second international, both of which were won by 3-0. Their top try scorer was the 6' 3", 15st wing-threequarter R. L. Aston with 30 which still remains as a record for a Lions touring side. In addition to his tries, Aston also dropped a goal and kicked five conversions. The top points scorer, however was the England half-back Arthur Rotherham who finished with 81 points from 36 conversions, two penalty goals two tries and a goal from a mark. At this stage in rugby history a try was worth a point, a conversion two points and a drop goal or a goal from a mark was worth three points. Under modern scoring values, R. L. Aston's total for the tour would have been 133 points.

THE OLD STYLE

W. E. Maclagan, winner of 25 Scottish international caps over three decades and described by the Scottish historian C. J. N. Fleming as "a man of immense strength and physique, a superb tackler and a grand kick, although never a runner nor a tricky passer", led the second touring side from Britain and Ireland to South Africa in 1891. And, apart at all from the rugby played, it was quite an eventful trip. The tourists left Southampton on the S.S. *Dunottar Castle* on Saturday, 20th June, 1891 and 16 days later, weary, upset and just a little terrified, they eventually arrived in Cape Town. It had not been the most comfortable of trips and the fact that the captain, set on making a new record for the trip from England to South Africa which he eventually accomplished, had provided them with an experience that had left most of them in slightly bewildered uneasiness. Then midway through the tour, travelling by tug to catch the coaster Melrose, the pilot made a bad error and the tug just missed being run down and sunk by the coaster. All that, plus the fact that much of their travelling throughout South Africa had to be done on slow trains and quite often by horse-drawn coaches made the trip a thoroughly rough one from start to finish.

THE FIRST INTERNATIONAL

The Lions made their entry into international competition against South Africa at Port Elizabeth on Thursday, 30th July, 1891 and brought a crowd of 6,000 to the St George's Park stadium. W. E. Maclagan captained the touring side ane the first Springbok captain was H. H. Castens, who also created the unique double of captaining the first South African international cricket side. In 1894 Castens was to lead the first South African cricket side to tour in England. To R. L. Aston went the distinction of scoring the very first international try for a touring side. It came early in the first half and was followed by another from Scotland's international half-back W. Wotherspoon, whose try was converted by Arthur Rotherham. That put the score at 4-0 and that was how it ended.

TEN CHANGES

South Africa made no fewer than 10 changes for their second international against the Lions during the 1891 tour, but it made little difference. At Kimberley, the Lions took control of the game from the start and clinched the game early in the first half. The Lions full-back W. G. Mitchell made a mark just inside the South African half and with a magnificent kick, the ball struck the upright, rebounded on to the bar and fell over for the three points that began and ended the scoring. For the second time the Springboks had failed to score against the Lions. It was to happen to them again in the third and final international game of that tour. For this match at Newlands, the South Africans made eight changes but again they were outclassed. Maclagan got over for an early try which William Wotherspoon converted and just on time Aston went over for a try which was not converted. This third and final international of 1891 was unique in that the referee was H. H. Castens—the same man who had captained South Africa in their first international game against the Lions. Never before and never since has any man played in and refereed in the same international rugby series.

THE IRON MEN

Harry Eagles had set a record with the 1888 Lions of playing in every game. His record was to be equalled in 1891 in South Africa by four other tourists. R. L. Aston, J. Hammon, R. G. McMilland and W. G. Mitchell played in every game of the 1891 tour and they were just one ahead of W. E. MacLagan, R. Thompson, and W. E. Bromet, who played in 18. Only four members of the side, W. Wotherspoon, W. H. Thorman, B. G. Roscoe and W. Jackson, played in less than 10 games.

STILL ON TOP

The twenty-two-year old Randolph Aston (Blackheath and Cambridge University) who had been capped twice for England in 1890, went on a scoring spree with the Lions side which toured in South Africa in 1891 and came home with the magnificent total of 30 tries. This is still the top try-scoring feat by a member of a Lions touring party.

Aston gave early warning of what was going to happen by running in four tries against Kingswilliamstown and he repeated this against Transvaal Country. He also scored three tries in two games, against the combined Kingwilliamstown and East London side and against Pietermaritzburg. Aston was captivated by South Africa and talked so much about it on his return home to England that his brother, Freddie Aston, decided to settle down in the Transvaal. And he added to the family's rugby distinction by winning four South African international caps against the Lions touring side of 1896.

I'LL HAVE NONE OF THAT

W. E. Maclagan, the great Scottish forward who led the tourists to South Africa in 1891, was not a man to stand any nonsense and it is on record that he demonstrated this with some vehemence, at one stage of the tour. "Hasie" Versfeld had the audacity to cross the tourists line for a try in their opening game against the Cape Town Club and that did not please Mr Maclagan. This try, worth only a point in those days, was the sole score registered against his side and he decided that it would be the last. Later in the tour, in the game against the Transvaal, one of the local players managed to get over the tourists line with the ball but Maclagan who was close by, promptly picked up the struggling Transvaal player and carried him back out on to the field and dropped him well outside the "25". That taught the entire Transvaal team a valuable lesson and they went down tamely to their 0-22 defeat. Subsequently Maclagan's "gospel" spread throughout South Africa and very few later attempted to score against the tourists —at least not while the burly Scot was in the vicinity.

THE BROMETS

Edward Bromet, then a student at Cambridge University, was the second top try scorer to R. L. Aston during the 1891 tour of South Africa and played in 13 of the 19 matches, including two of the international games against South Africa. He was not, however, ever capped for England as was William Ernest Bromet who won 12 caps for his country between 1891 and 1896. But they played together against South Africa in 1891 and became the first brothers to play international football for a Lions touring side. Between them they made 31 appearances and played together on the touring side on nine occasions during the tour, including two of the international games against the Springboks.

SECOND TIME AROUND

With the arrival of the 1896 Lions, composed in the main of English and Irish players, in South Africa in 1896, John Hammond and P. F. "Baby" Hancock became the first two players to make a second tour overseas. Hammond, who captained the 1896 side, had been vice-captain to W. E. Maclagan in the 1891 side and Hancock, a 6′ 5″ giant, who weighed almost 18st, had first been capped for England in 1886-1887 and had been one of the great forward successes of the first side to visit South Africa. The 1896 side was also noteworthy in that it contained Louis and James Magee of Bective Rangers, the first Irish brothers to win selection on a touring side. In all there were 10 Irish players on the side and two of them Dr Tommy Crean and Robert Johnson were subsequently to be decorated with the Victoria Cross in the Boer War. Both Crean and Johnson remained on in South Africa for some time after the end of the tour and turned out regularly for the Wanderers Club in Johannesburg. Both had played in Ireland with the Wanderers Club in Dublin and another member of that famous club, F. M. Harvey, an Irish international in 1907 and 1911, was also to win the Victoria Cross. Three Victoria Crosses by three international players from the one club give Wanderers of Dublin an unique honour in the history of rugby.

BROKE THE DUCK

When Theo Samuels of Griqualand West came into the South African side in the second Test of the Lions 1896 tour of South Africa, he stepped right into the history books of Springbok Rugby. Although South Africa went down to an 8-17 defeat—their fifth successive defeat since they had entered international rugby in 1891—Samuels, a late substitute, got over to score a memorable try. It was South Africa's first ever try in international rugby. Subsequently Samuels played in the third Test, also lost 3-9 by South Africa, and he was there again for his third and last international appearance on Saturday, 5th September, 1896 at Newlands when South Africa faced the Lions. This marked an historic milestone in Springbok rugby. J. H. Anderson (Western Province) got over for a try and this was converted by his club-mate T. Hepburn, whose only appearance this was for his country. This was South Africa's first win in international rugby. They were not to be beaten again by a Lions touring side until the second Test of the 1910 tour.

THE OLD MAN OF THE LIONS

The oldest player and, indeed, the oldest captain to tour with a rugby side from these islands was John Hammond of Cambridge University, who led the tour to South Africa in 1896. He was then thirty-six and was still regarded as one of the finest forwards in the game. He was not, however, capped for England. Hammond made two tours to South Africa as a player and also went out for a third time in 1903 as manager of Mark Morrison's tourists.

JUST ONE DEFEAT

John Hammond's 1896 touring side began with a win by 14-9 over Cape Town Clubs, took their second game over Suburban Clubs by 8-0 and were then held to a scoreless draw by Western Province. From there on, however, they went undefeated right up to the final game of the tour when they were finally beaten 0-5 by South Africa at Cape Town. Their full record was; played 21, won 19, drew one and scored 320 points while conceding 45. Their full-back James F. Byrne of Moseley and England, who had the proud distinction of playing in all 21 games of the tour, was their top points scorer with 127 points from six tries, 29 conversions, nine penalty goals and six drop goals. The top try scorer was the Irish wing-threequarter Larry Bulger of Lansdowne with 20, a total which has been surpassed only by R. L. Aston of the 1891 touring side, in the history of tours to South Africa. James Byrne's outstanding performance was in the 25-0 win over Kingwilliamstown in the 10th match of the tour. He scored three tries, kicked three conversions and a goal from a mark which was then worth four points, for a total of 19 points which was to stand as an individual record for a Lions tourist for over 70 years.

A COINCIDENCE

By an extraordinary coincidence the first international match between the 1896 tourists and South Africa was played again at Port Elizabeth and on exactly the same day and date of the month, Thursday, 30th July, as the first meeting of the two sides had been in 1891. The only other coincidence was that South Africa again failed to score and this marked the fourth time in succession that they had failed to register a point against a touring side. W. G. Carey, later to become Bishop of Bloemfontein, scored the Lions first try and Larry Bulger became the first Irishman to score a try for the Lions in the second half and this with a conversion by James Byrne gave the Lions a comfortable eight points victory. The interesting feature of the South African side was that it was captained by an Englishman, Ferdie Aston, a brother of the famous R. L. Aston, who had scored a record number of 30 tries for the 1891 tourists in South Africa.

THE FIRST FOR THE SPRINGBOKS

The 1896 tourists duly won the second international game against South Africa at Johannesburg, the first time that an international game had been played in the city. But although the tourists ran up 17 points, it was a proud afternoon for the Springboks. They scored for the first time in an international match and the man who achieved that epic feat was wing-threequarter Theo Samuels, who had come into the side as a late substitute. He scored two tries and the second was converted by David Cope. Tommy Crean, now generally accepted as the personality of the 1896 tourists, scored the tourists first try, which was converted by James Byrne. P. P. Hancock added a second try to put the Lions into a 5-0 lead at half-time. Crean added a second try early in the second half and Byrne again converted and when P. F. Hancock launched himself through a battery of South African backs to score another try, the tourists with a 13-0 lead appeared to have it all neatly wrapped up. Then came Samuel's two tries and with the conversion by David Cope, the game became wide open again at 13-8. Crean, however, called for one final assault from his men and O. G. Mackie, the Cambridge University and England wing-threequarter dropped a neat goal to put the issue beyond all argument at 17-8.

ANOTHER VICTORY

The fact that the South Africans were learning fast from the tourists was evident in the third international game at Kimberley, where with 10 changes from the second international, the Springboks created quite a shock by taking the lead with a try from Percy Jones which put them into a 3-0 lead at half-time. Midway through the second half, however, O. G. Mackie got over for a try which James Byrne converted and shortly before the end, Byrne kicked a handsome drop goal for a 9-3 win. This result marked the sixth successive defeat for South Africa in their international history and in those six games they had scored only 11 points while conceding 45. In their next three games, the tourists beat Western Province by 32-0 and with just the one game of the tour left, the final South Africa international at Newlands, they looked certain to finish their tour without a defeat.

THAT FINAL WARM-UP

In their final game before the last international against South Africa of the 1896 tour, John Hammond's side took on Western Province at Newlands and had run riot for their most decisive win of the tour. Larry Bulger, who by then had become known as "Fat Cupid" scored four tries to bring his total for the tour to 20 and James Byrne had kicked four conversions to bring his points total for the tour to 127, which, as it transpired, was to be his final fling for the tour. His total was to stand as a record in South Africa by a tourist for 64 years until New Zealand's Don Clarke went ahead with 175 for the All-Blacks in 1960. It remained, however as a record by a member of a Lions touring side in South Africa until 1974. Despite his 20 tries in South Africa, Larry Bulger scored only two tries for Ireland during his eight international appearances between 1896 and 1898.

THE TWO FIRSTS

History was just around the corner when the 1896 tourists ran out on to the pitch at Newlands on Saturday afternoon, 5th September, 1896 to take on the Springboks in the final international game of the tour. It was a game that was to provide two famous "firsts" in the history of rugby football. South Africa made all the running from early on and midway through the first half after a tremendous drive forward by the Springboks forwards, Alf Larard went shooting in to ground the ball beside the posts. Tom Hepburn added the two points and, as it happened, despite a storming fight-back by the tourists in the second half, those five points were the only score of the game. For the Lions touring side, it was the first international defeat; more important it was the first international victory for South Africa. The pupils had finally overcome the masters. From that moment on South African rugby was in the ascendancy. The great days of the Lions in South Africa were over. Ironically, the try that had crushed the Lions came from an Englishman. Larard had emigrated from the North of England just two years earlier.

EVERY MATCH

James Frederick Byrne (Moseley), who won 13 caps as England's full-back between 1894 and 1898 and whose brother Francis also played for England in 1897, set a Lions touring record during the tour of South Africa in 1896. He played in all of the 21 games, which brought 19 victories, one draw and one defeat. The Lions only loss came in the last game of the tour at Cape Town where they went down 0-5 to South Africa. Byrne also set a scoring record of 127 points in his 21 appearances, which stood as the top mark for a tourist in South Africa until New Zealand's full-back Don Clarke scored 175 points from 20 games in 1960. Byrne's 127 points for the Lions stood as a record for three years until it was broken by half-back C. Y. Adamson, a member of the Durham Club, during the 1899 tour of Australia. Despite this Adamson was never capped for England. The present Lions scoring record is held by the Welsh out-half Barry John with 188 points during the 1971 tour of Australia and New Zealand. The most points ever scored by a member of any touring side is 246 which was achieved by Billy Wallace during New Zealand's tour of Britain, Ireland, France and Canada in 1905.

THE REV MULLINEUX STEPS IN

The Reverend M. Mullineux, who had toured with John Hammond's side in South Africa in 1896, was never to win an international cap for England, but he finished his career with international appearances for the Lions against both South Africa and Australia. His greatest claim to immortality in rugby, however, is that he led the 1899 Lions to Australia and at the time it was an unique tour. It was the first time that Australia had been given an entire tour and this was not to happen again until the South Africans made their long tour of Australia in 1971. The touring party consisted of 21 players, which included nine internationals from Ireland, England and Scotland and they accomplished a highly successful trip. They played 21 games, won 18, lost three and scored 333 points while conceding 90. After winning their first three games, they took on Australia in the first international game and their only score, a penalty goal by C. Y. Adamson was not enough to prevent the Australians from romping to a 13-3 victory. They finished the tour, however by beating the Australians 11-0, 13-0 and 11-10 in the remaining three international games. Top scorer of the tour was C. Y. Adamson, with 135 points from eight tries, 35 converts, 11 penalty goals and two drop goals and the top try scorer was the Welsh international Gwyn Nicholls with 12. The most surprising feature of this touring side was that not one of the uncapped players who travelled to Australia on this trip was ever subsequently capped by any of the home countries.

WHO WAS HE?

The Lions toured in Australia in 1899 and the records show that they won 18 of their 21 games, lost three and scored 333 points and conceded 90. And the records also show that E. Martelli (Dublin University) played full-back for the Lions in the first international match of the tour against Australia. What the records do not reveal is just exactly who the said Mr Martelli was? To this day, he remains as one of the mysterious figures of international rugby. There is no record that he ever played rugby at Dublin University, either on a first team or a second one and, in fact, there is no record that he was ever a student at the College. Efforts to identify him have failed totally and there is no evidence now available to show that he played rugby before or after the Lions tour to Australia. But obviously the Rev M. Mullineux of Blackheath, who captained the touring side of 1899 knew who he was and knew also that he had some claim to being a rugby player. And he was considered good enough to play against Australia. That is the only fact known that now guarantees him his place in rugby history.

THE 1903 TOURISTS

John Hammond had been vice-captain of the 1891 tourists to South Africa, captain of the 1896 side and he was to appear in South Africa for the third time in 1903 as manager of Mark Morrison's side which played a series of 22 games, including three international fixtures with South Africa. But Morrison, who won 23 caps for Scotland, was not to have the best of luck with his men. He wound up with the poorest record of a Lions touring side up to then. In their 22 games, they won exactly half, lost eight, drew three and scored 229 points while conceding 138. The top points scorer with 56 points from nine tries, a conversion, a penalty goal and six drop goals was R. T. Skrimshire, the Welsh international from Newport, who was also the top try scorer with nine. This is the only occasion in the history of the Lions touring side that the same man has been top points scorer and top try scorer. The 1903 opened their tour on a disastrous note by losing their first three games to Western Province Country, to Western Province Town and to Western Province. Their first win was 13-0 over Port Elizabeth, then after four successive victories they crashed twice in succession to Griqualand and then lost to Transvaal by 3-12. Morrison's men also made history in that they became the first tourists to lose an international series. Both R. T. Skrimshire and W. P. Scott, the Scottish international, played in all 22 games of the tour.

THE WALLACES

Ireland had five representatives on Mark Morrison's Lions of 1903 and provided the second set of Irish brothers to play on a touring side. They were James and Joseph Wallace, both of the Wanderers club in Dublin and both, of course, were to be capped for Ireland. P. S. Hancock, the England international, was also named for this tour and thus joined his brother P. F. "Baby" Hancock, who had toured in South Africa in 1891 and 1896, as another set of brothers to play for the Lions. By unanimous agreement at the end of the tour, A. D. Tedford of Malone and Ireland, was voted the outstanding forward of the 1903 tour. Tedford was to win 23 international caps for Ireland between 1902 and 1908.

A SCOTTISH CAPTAINCY

For the first international match of the 1903 tour in South Africa, both sides were captained by Scottish internationals. The Lions were led by Mark Morrison and the Springboks were skippered by Dr A. Frew, who had played for Scotland against England, Ireland and Wales in 1901. And just to make things a little more homely for Morrison, one of the South African forwards, W. M. C. Ewan, had already won 16 caps for Scotland before emigrating to South Africa. R. T. Skrimshire and the England international forward W. T. Cave scored tries for the Lions in the early stages of the game and J. L. Gillespie, the Scottish half-back converted both to give the Lions a 10-0 lead at half-time. South Africa, however, took control of the proceedings in the second half and tries from Fred Dobbin and Jimmy Sinclair, both converted by Barry "Fairy" Heatlie brought the first draw between the Lions and South Africa.

A PRESSING ENGAGEMENT

Barry "Fairy" Heatlie, who with J. M. Powell of Griqualand West, had played against all three Lions touring sides in 1891, 1896 and 1903, was invited to take over the captaincy of the Springboks for the second international game of the 1903 tour. But he declined on the grounds that he had a more pressing engagement. The game was to be played at Kimberley and he wanted to be in Cape Town where his wife was expecting a baby. Powell took over the captaincy and led South Africa to their second draw in international rugby. Both the Lions and the Springboks failed to score and their scoreless draw remains as the only one in the meetings between the two sides from 1891 to 1974.

THE FIRST SERIES WIN

The heavens opened for the third and final international game between Mark Morrison's tourists and South Africa at Newlands in 1903 and up to a few hours before kick-off there was the depressing possibility that the game might have to be called off. It went on, however, despite the fact that within a matter of minutes the pitch had disintegrated into a morass of clinging mud. There was no score in the first half but shortly after the break Joe Barry heaved his way over the line for a Springbok try and shortly before the end, Arthur Reid, playing in what was to be his only international for South Africa, ran in for a try which Barry Heatlie converted. With two draws and one win, South Africa had beaten the Lions in an international series. It was to be 53 years before South Africa lost another series in international rugby, and 71 years before they lost a series to the Lions.

THE 1904 TOUR

D. R. "Darky" Bedell-Sivright, who led the Lions on their 1904 tour of Australia and New Zealand was not the most popular of players. The famous Welsh historian, W. J. T. Collins, writing about him, said "I never liked him. He seemed to me to lack completely the chivalry which sets a crown on a great footballer". But even Collins agreed that while the Scot was relentless and some times even ruthless on the football pitch, he was still a superlative rugby player and deserved to be ranked with the greatest of his time. Bedell-Sivright, who played for Scotland on 22 occasions between 1901 and 1908 and who was to die in France during the First World War, always demanded a full and dedicated involvement from all the players under him and this was quite evident during the Lions tour of 1904 when he led them through an unbeaten run in Australia where they played 14 matches, winning all 14 with a total of 265 points while conceding 51. From Australia, the side moved on to New Zealand where they played five, lost two, won two and drew one and scored 22 points while conceding 33.

A PROBLEM OF LEAVE

D. R. Bedell-Sivright's Lions touring side of 1904 suffered from the problem that while there were some magnificent players in the four home countries at the time, very few of them were able to get leave of absence to make the long trip down under to Australia and New Zealand. In the end, when the team was finally formulated, there were only 12 international players in the party of 24. Among the 12 uncapped players there were five from Guy's Hospital and of these two, P. F. McEvedy and A. B. O'Brien, were, in fact New Zealanders, who were on their way back home. Neither, however, was ever to be capped for New Zealand although Dr McEvedy was subsequently to become President of the New Zealand Rugby Union in 1934. From an international point of view, all the four home countries were represented, but Bedell-Sivright was the only Scottish international in the party and the sole Irishman was R. W. Edwards of Malone who won his only cap against Wales that year. Wales had the strongest representation of internationals on the side with seven and they included the famous Tommy Vile, Percy Bush, R. T. Gabe and A. F. Harding.

FIRST AND LAST

The 1904 Lions opened their tour with a resounding win by 27-0 over New South Wales, then went on to beat the Combined Western Districts by 29-6 before going back to beat New South Wales again by 21-6. The Lions were, in fact to end their tour in Australia by meeting New South Wales for a third time and again they came out on top but only just by 5-0. Their most overwhelming victory of the tour was the 27-0 over New South Wales and in 13 of their matches they reached double figures. In the first international game against Australia at Sydney, they won by 17-0, scored 17 points again in the second which they won by 17-3 and in the third international they walloped the Wallabies by 16-0. This sequence of three successive wins over Australia with 50 points scored to three, has, of course, never since been duplicated by a Lions touring side.

FINAL DEFEAT

R. D. Bedell-Sivright's 1904 Lions landed in New Zealand with an unbeaten record behind them in Australia and they took their unbeaten streak to 16 games by beating the combined South Canterbury—Canterbury and West Coast side by 5-3 and the combined Otago—Southland side by 14-8. Then it was on to Wellington for the first ever international meeting between a touring side and the All-Blacks. And here on a sunny afternoon at Athletic Park their proud record came to an end. The scores were level at half-time at 3-3 with a penalty goal for New Zealand's Billy Wallace and a penalty goal from the Lions A. F. Harding. Then Duncan McGregor, the "Flying Scotsman" of

" IT'S ALWAYS DICEY TO WIN A
MATCH ON THESE OVERSEAS TOURS "

New Zealand rugby, strode on to the scene with two brilliant tries and it was 9-3 and the Lions had been beaten for the first time in New Zealand. It was not to be their last on that tour. Three days later they were held to a scoreless draw by the combined Taranaki-Wanganui-Manawatu side and just a week after their international defeat, they were well and truly trounced at Auckland by 0-13. Their final two games were the only times that Bedell-Sivright's Lions had failed to score in any of their 19 games. Their final tally of points in New Zealand, 22 scored and 33 against still remains as the only occasion in Lions history that a touring side has scored fewer points than their opponents.

McGREGOR'S TWO

There were 17 New Zealanders on the field at Athletic Park, Wellington in 1904 when the All-Blacks met the Lions for the first time in an international game. Included on the Lions side were the two threequarters, P. F. McEvedy and A. B. O'Brien, who were then medical students at Guy's Hospital in London. New Zealand finished on top by 9-3 and their hero of the afternoon was Duncan McGregor, known as "The Flying Scotsman", who scored two tries. This was New Zealand's first international victory on their own soil.

THE FIRST TO GO

Denys Douglas Dobson won his first cap for England at the age of twenty-two in 1902 and over the next two seasons he took his cap collection to six. As one of Oxford University's outstanding forwards of the time, he ws invited to join D. R. Bedell-Sivright's side to tour in Australia and New Zealand in 1904 and having some spare time at his disposal, he was delighted to accept. During the Australian portion of the tour, Mr Dobson took a dim view of a decision made by the referee, one Mr Henry Dolan in one of the games and, unfortunately, the exact game has not been recorded, and he had a few uncomplimentary remarks to make. Mr Dolan was gravely offended and on the grounds that Dobson had used unnecessary and obscene language he ordered him to the line. Subsequently Dobson apologised to the referee and following the investigation into the matter Dobson was exonerated from blame. But, at least Mr Dobson had got himself into history. He was, in fact, the first Lion or tourist, to be sent off, something that was not to happen again until 1968 during the tour of Tom Kiernan's Lions in South Africa when the Welsh international John O'Shea was given his marching orders.

THE 1908 TOUR DOWN UNDER

With Rugby League beginning to get a certain grip in New Zealand, and the fears that it might eventually become stronger than the Union game, the New Zealand Rugby Union appealed to the English Rugby Union to send another touring side down under as soon as possible to combat the increasing interest in the professional game. So A. F. Harding of Wales led his Lions to Australia and New Zealand in 1908. Unfortunately neither the Irish nor the Scottish Unions showed any particular relish for this tour and in the end the party of 28 was, in the main, an England-Wales selection. It did, however include the New Zealander Dr P. F. McEvedy, who was making his second tour with a Lions side. Harding, of course, too was making his second trip to Australia and New Zealand. The playing record of the 1908 Lions was that they won 16 of their 26 games, drew one, lost nine and scored 323 points while conceding 201. In their nine games in Australia, they were beaten 10-15 by Western, 3-6 by New South Wales but won the other seven in convincing fashion. Their points total in Australia was 139 for and 48 against. Then it was on to New Zealand to commence the major portion of the tour with 17 games, which included three international games against the All-Blacks.

THE HUMBLED LIONS

By the time they faced up to the All-Blacks at Dunedin for the opening international of the 1908 tour, the Lions had already won two and lost two games in New Zealand. They had kicked off with a 17-3 win over Wairarapa-Bush, but then had been beaten 13-19 by Wellington and 6-9 by Otago before beating Southland by 14-8. But the Dunedin international was to be a sore moment of truth for them. The All-Blacks, led by Billy Stead showed little respect for the Lions and with Jimmy Hunter in superb scoring form again, they raced away to an overwhelming 32-5 victory. And there was even worse to come. After drawing the second international, 3-3 at Wellington, the All-Blacks gave the Lions an even rougher going over in the final international and last game of the tour by hammering the Lions 29-0. With his final try in this game, which also marked his last appearance in the All-Black's jersey, Jimmy Hunter took his all-time total of tries for New Zealand to 49, which is still a national record.

THE POINTS

Top points scorer for the 1908 Lions in New Zealand was the Welsh international wing-threequarter Reggie Gibbs with 28 from five tries, two conversions and three penalty goals. The top try scorer was his countryman, John L. Williams with 9. Indeed, 24 of the 46 tries scored by A. F. Harding's Lions came from Welshmen.

AGAINST AND FOR

F. S. Jackson, the Leicester forward, was one of the uncapped players to tour in Australia and New Zealand with A. F. Harding's Lions of 1908 and no one on the side was more impressed with the New Zealand way of life than he was. He liked it so much that shortly after the tourists had returned home to Britain, Jackson packed his bags, returned to New Zealand and settled down there. Less than 30 years later, Jackson, who had never been capped for England, but had made one international appearance for the 1908 Lions against New Zealand at Dunedin, had the proud moment of seeing his son, Everard Jackson turn out for New Zealand. Everard Jackson made his debut in the All-Blacks jersey against Australia at Wellington in 1936 and in all made 11 appearances for New Zealand, including six international games against Australia and South Africa.

TOM SYMTH'S LIONS

Dr Tom Smyth, winner of 14 international caps for Ireland, led the 1910 Lions to South Africa for a programme of 24 games which were to include three international games against the Springboks. They won

13 of their games, lost eight, drew three and scored 290 points while conceding 236. Their most decisive victory of the tour was the 45-4 defeat of Transvaal Country and they lost two of their games by 19 points, 8-27 against Transvaal and 0-19 to Cape Colony. Top points scorer of the tour was Charles H. "Cherry" Pillman of Blackheath and England, a twenty-year old who captured the imagination of everyone on this tour. Operating mainly as a roving forward, although he also turned out more than once at scrum-half and out-half, he compiled 62 points from five tries, 17 conversions, three penalty goals and a drop goal. The top try scorer of the tour was M. E. Neale with 10 tries. One of the features of this 1910 touring side was that it included eight members of the Newport club which remains as an all-time Welsh club record for a Lions side.

THE FIRST INTERNATIONAL

With 10 wins in 16 games behind them, Tom Smyth's Lions went into their first international against South Africa at Johannesburg and it turned out to be a touch-and-go affair all the way. A. R. Foster, the Irish international, opened the scoring with a try but De Villiers brought the Springboks level just before half-time. South Africa then suffered a major blow when centre-threequarter Jack Hirsch, who had played against Ireland in the 1906-07 tour and was now winning only his second international cap, had his leg fractured in a tackle and was carried off. This unfortunate injury was to end Hirsch's international career. But even with 14 men, the Springboks raced away into what appeared to be an unassailable lead. Doug Morkel scored a try, Richard Luyt, one of two South African brothers on the side, scored a second which Morkel converted and with an 11-3 lead and less than 15 minutes to go, it seemed to be all over. But Jack "Ponty" Jones dropped a neat goal—his only one of the tour and J. A. Spoors, the Bristol winger went surging over for a try and the score was 11-10. Just before the end, however, having survived some fierce attacks by Tom Smyth and "Cherry" Pillman, "Hudie" Hahn went over for the Springbok try that clinched the game.

PILLMAN BACK

"Cherry" Pillman was out of action for over three weeks with a leg injury but came back to play in the second international against South

Africa at Port Elizabeth—and he lined out at fly half. And he turned out to be the Lions hero of the afternoon. Wally Mills had the opening score for South Africa with a try and they held this lead to half-time. Then Pillman with a superb break put J. A. Spoors in for a try and two minutes later, he outwitted the entire Springbok back-line with a dazzling run before sending M. E. Neale in for a try. Pillman added the conversion and the final score was 8-3 for the Lions. For the first time since Kimberley in 1896, they had, at last, beaten the South Africans again.

TWO SPRINGBOKS

One of the newcomers on to the South African side for the second international against the Lions at Johannesburg in 1910—and he was to hold his place for the third international—was Clive van Ryneveld of Western Province. Thirty-nine years later, his son, also Clive van Ryneveld, then at Oxford University, was to play international rugby for England against Scotland, Ireland, Wales and France. And, of course, Clive van Ryneveld was also to captain the 1960-1961 South African cricket side against the M.C.C.

AN UNHAPPY AFTERNOON

The versatile Charles "Cherry" Pillman was in the Lions side again for the third international match against South Africa which was played at Capetown exactly a week after the second meeting at Port Elizabeth and this time he appeared in the pack. But for Pillman, now acknowledged throughout South Africa as one of the finest players ever to visit the country and, indeed, for all the 1910 Lions party it was to be an unhappy afternoon. Shortly after the start, their full-back Stanley Williams damaged his back and they were down to 14 men. From there on, they were never in with a chance of salvaging the series. Gideon Roos had South Africa's first try which Doug Morkel converted and Fred Luyt, Piet Allport and H. J. Renecke added three more with Morkel converting two. The Lions only score came from a try by J. A. Spoors, which was converted by Pillman. Spoors who scored 24 points on the tour, wound up with the satisfaction of scoring in his three international appearances for the 1910 Lions against South Africa but seemingly that carried little weight with the England selectors back home. He never won an international cap for England.

THE LION CUBS

John Edward Raphael of Oxford and Old Merchant Taylors, one of England's finest centre-threequarters at the start of the century—he won nine caps between 1902 and 1906—led a "Mini-Lions" tour to Argentina in 1910. With players from England, Ireland and Scotland, they played six games, and won all six with a total of 211 points against 31. Raphael, also a gifted cricketer who scored a century for Oxford in the inter-Varsity match of 1903, had the distinction of scoring tries in three of his four colours appearances for Oxford. He died on 11th June, 1917 from wounds received at the Battle of Messines Ridge. He was then thirty-five.

LEVEL PEGGING

Dr Ronald Cove-Smith's Lions of 1924 will not go down in history as one of the more successful touring sides. They played 21 games, won nine, lost nine and drew three and in the process scored only 175 points, while conceding 155. They got off to a depressing start by losing their opening game 6-7 to Western Province Town and Country and barely scraped home in their second game by 9-8 against the Western Province Universities. They had their most convincing win in the third game with a 26-0 defeat of Griqualand West and then went undefeated for three games before losing two in succession to Orange Free State Country and to Orange Free State. This was followed by a draw and then they were into their first international game against South Africa at Durban.

SOS FOR CUNNINGHAM

The 1924 Lions were so crippled with injuries on the eve of the first international match against South Africa at Durban that a frantic SOS was sent out to Bill Cunningham, the former Irish international with eight caps who was then living in Johannesburg. That in itself was historic. Cunningham is unique in that he became a Lion without being selected or being sent out from one of the home countries as a replacement. The next item of history in this second international was the selection of the South African captain. P. K. Albertyn had been one of the most promising centre threequarters in South African rugby in

1919 but then damaged his knee so badly that he was advised never to play rugby again. He later went to England to study medicine and on his return to South Africa in 1924 got an invitation out of the blue to play in the Springbok trials. At the time he thought it a joke but he turned up and on the result of his performance was nominated to play against the Lions—and as captain in his first international. As it happened he was a total success and went on to win all of his four South African caps that year against the Lions. The final touch of history about this tour was provided by the famous Irish forward Jammie Clinch. When he arrived at Durban he was following in the footsteps of his father A. D. Clinch, who 28 years earlier had also been a Lions tourist in South Africa.

BENNIE OSLER'S DEBUT

Cove-Smith's Lions lost the first international at Durban by 3-7—and they also had their first look at a young man, a twenty-two year-old out-half, who was to become one of the immortal personalities of world rugby. His name was Bennie Osler and as he was to do on so many occasions subsequently, he left his indelible imprint on the proceedings. After J. Aucamp, also making his Springbok debut in this game, had opened the scoring with a well-taken try, the inimitable Osler, one of the game's greatest kickers, dropped a magnificent goal to put the Springboks into a lead of 7-0. H. Whitby had a try in the second half for the Lions but from there on Osler, with shrewd kicking that frustrated and indeed infuriated the Lions, kept South Africa in their slender lead.

OSLER AGAIN

The 1924 Lions second outing against the South Africans in the international game at Johannesburg was again dominated by Bennie Osler. He gave them the lead with a penalty goal in the first half and then, with a succession of sparkling moves in a one-sided second half, he sent the Springboks away to a great 17-0 victory. Kenny Starke, Phil Mostert, Van Druten and P. K. Albertyn scored tries and Osler had just the one conversion. On the evidence of this result, all the odds were heavily in favour of a third successive Springbok win when the two sides came together again at Port Elizabeth. This was the one the Lions had to win if they were to have any ambitions of squaring the series. And they came close to winning. In a game that was marred by a gale-force wind, and the Lions played against it in the first half, Bill Cunningham gave them a shock lead with a well-engineered try. Unfortunately, just on half time the giant Van Druten battered his way across the line to level the scores. The second half brought further frustration from Osler. With the tourists playing with the strong wind at their backs, he retaliated with the only weapon open to him—the constant kick to touch. It was a tactic that paid off. The Lions never got a real chance of scoring and had to be satisfied with their draw. The series, however, was then lost. The fourth and final international —and this was the first time that four international games had been played in a tour by the Lions in South Africa—was now of little more than academic interest.

TEN FOR STARKE

Kenny Starke of Western Province, who was to win his four inter-national caps for South Africa during the Lions tour of 1924, joined the exclusive club of those who have scored 10 points for the Springboks in an international game, in the fourth and final game against Cove-Smith's men at Newlands. The score was 16-9 for South Africa. He went over for two tries and dropped a goal. Johnny Bester and Jack Slater added two further tries and the Lions nine points came from tries by A. T. Voyce and S. W. Harris with Voyce also kicking a penalty goal. This was the second last game of the tour and in the final one the Lions beat Western Province by 8-6. In the total summing up, they had come out on level terms with nine wins, nine losses and three draws in the 21 games. Their top points scorer was the England international A. T. Voyce with 37 points from six tries, five conversions and three penalty goals. The top try scorer was the uncapped William Wallace of the Percy Park Club with nine. Five of Wallace's tries came in the third game of the tour against Griqualand West and to 1974 his feat stood as a record for a member of an international touring side in South Africa. Wallace, who played at wing-threequarter, made one international appearance for the Lions during the tour.

D. J. MACMYNE'S TOURISTS

The Scottish international forward, D. J. MacMyn of Cambridge University, who was to win 11 caps for his country, led the "Mini-Lions" to Argentina in 1927 and his side which included England, Ireland and Scotland international players ran riot against the unfortunate Argentinians. They played nine games, won all nine, had just three penalty goals kicked against them and scored a total of 295 points. They played four unofficial international games with Argentina and beat them successively by 37-0, 46-0, 34-3 and 43-0.

F. D. PRENTICE'S MEN

The 1930 Lions to New Zealand and Australia were led by the Leicester and England forward, Frank Douglas Prentice, who in 1947 was subsequently to become secretary of the English Rugby Union. Prentice, who won three international caps for England in 1928, was then thirty-three and was one of 13 England internationals in the Lions side. Scotland had just the one representative on the 1930 Lions, W. B. Welsh of Hawick, Wales had six and Ireland had five. In all they played 28 matches in New Zealand and Australia and won 20, lost eight and piled up 624 points while conceding 318. The top points scorer of the side was surprisingly a forward, the twenty-three year old Brian Black, with 63 points from five tries, 18 conversions and four penalty goals. The top try scorer was the England centre threequarter Anthony Novis with 13. The 1930 Lions most decisive win of the 28-match programme was their 41-3 defeat of the Combined Waikato-Thames Valley-King County side, although in an unofficial game against Western Australia in the final outing of the tour they won by 71-3. Surprisingly this unofficial game did not provide the highest aggregate score of a Lions game during this tour. Against Victoria in the final official game of the tour, they won by 41-36 for a total of 77 points. Their worst defeat of the tour was against New South Wales when they were beaten 28-3.

CONTROVERSIAL START

The 1930 Lions began their 28-match programme with a game against Wanganui and the result was never in any doubt. Unfortunately, however, this particular fixture was to spark off a minor controversy, which was subsequently to lead to an even greater one and, indeed, in the end, it left a sad taste of bitterness all around. At half-time, as was the custom in New Zealand, the Wanganui side left the field and proceeded to their dressing room and that brought an immediate, sharp and reprimanding reaction from the Lions manager, Mr James "Bim" Baxter. Under no circumstances would he tolerate this, which was in direct breach of the laws of rugby union. At a later stage the same Mr Baxter, who had won three international caps for England in 1900 and who was later to become the 28th President of the English Rugby Union, sparked off more bitterness with his criticism of the New Zealander's use of the seven man scrum with an eighth forward used as a rover. It was following this tour that changes were made in the scrummaging laws by the International Board and the All-Blacks were forced to conform to the three-man front row. Ted McKenzie, then the New Zealand selector and also a member of the Management Committee of the New Zealand Rugby Union took exception to Mr Baxter's attitude and from there to the end of the New Zealand portion of the tour there was a distinct and marked coolness between the officials of both sides.

SOBEY INJURED

The great backbone of the 1930 Lions was expected to be the out-standing partnership of scrum-half Wilfred Sobey and Roger Spong, who had already come to an excellent understanding in the England side. Unfortunately, in the opening game against Wanganui, Sobey was injured and was out for the rest of the tour. Despite the loss of his partner, Spong created a tremendously strong and new partnership with Ireland's Paul Murray and they were to be two of the outstanding successes of the tour. Murray, of course, was one of the most versatile players on the tour and appeared on the wing, in the centre, at out-half and also at scrum-half. Under their prompting the Lions won their opening four games by wide margins, then lost two in succession to Wellington and Canterbury but resumed their winning streak right up to the first international game against New Zealand at Dunedin.

THE WHITE ALL-BLACKS

To avoid a clash of colours with the 1930 Lions who wore blue jerseys with white shorts, the All-Blacks appeared in unusual garb for the opening international game against the Lions at Dunedin on 21st June, 1930. They wore their traditional black shorts and black stockings but their jerseys were . . . white! The change of colours did not bring them luck. Within a matter of five minutes they were three points down when Paul Murray shot a smart pass out to Roger Spong who cross-kicked neatly to James Reeve who crossed for an easy try in the corner. That was still the score at half-time and the All-Blacks, under the intimidating gaze of Lions manager Mr Baxter, did not retire to their dressing room. They took to the sideline instead for a chat on tactics and those same tactics paid off right at the start of the second half. The All-Blacks took a quick heel near the Lions "25" and with a smart passing movement G. F. Hart, in his New Zealand debut, went tearing over for a try. George Nepia attempted the conversion but the ball struck the upright high up and dropped just wide. Time was almost up and the score was still 3-3 when Ivor Jones and John Morley had their moment of sheer glory. Jones whipped up a ball in his own "25", broke through the New Zealand cover and set off on an 85 yards run with only George Nepia to stop him. He ran on, committed Nepia to the tackle and just as he did, he sent a pass to Morley who was backing up and the Welsh international went streaking away for a glorious try. And that was the final score 6-3 for the Lions—and a first victory over New Zealand. It was to be 29 years before the second came.

NICHOLLS BACK

Mark Nicholls, one of the great Invincibles of 1924-1925 was brought back to play for New Zealand in the second international game of the Lions 1930 tour at Christchurch and as it happened he made all the difference. He marked a ball within five minutes of the start, dropped a goal but this was quickly wiped out by Carl Aarvold who went in for a try which Prentice converted. Shortly after this the Lions lost Paul Murray through injury and he was out for the remainder of the game. Ivor Jones moved in to take over at scrum-half and after Oliver had given the All-Blacks the lead with a try which Nicholls converted, Jones sparked off an excellent move which was to bring Aarvold his second try of the game. Prentice again converted but the All-Blacks, aided by a try from G. F. Hart which had been master-minded by Mark Nicholls, hung on to win by 13-10. And the third international at Eden Park, Auckland went in much the same pattern. H. M. Bowcott had a first half try for the Lions which Prentice converted and the All-Blacks came level with a try from F. W. Lucas which Mark Nicholls converted. Hugh McLean ran in two tries for New Zealand in the second half, and Mark Nicholls dropped a goal and that was that. The Lions came back with a late try from Carl Aarvold and Brian Black made the conversion to leave the final score at 15-10. New Zealand were back to their winning ways and they intended to keep things just that way.

A RECORD CROWD

For the final international of the Lions 1930 tour in New Zealand, a record crowd of almost 45,000 saw the All-Blacks administer a sound beating to the tourists. Porter and Cooke each had two tries for New Zealand, Strang and Batty had one each and Strang converted two. Novis had a try for the Lions which Black converted and David Parker, the Welsh international, kicked a penalty goal. With the international series lost, the Lions exacted a small compensation by walloping the combined Marlborough-Nelson-Golden Bay side by 41-3 before setting sail for Australia for the last seven games of the tour. But there was still the bitterness before they left New Zealand. Ted McKenzie, still smarting from the lash of Mr Baxter's earlier remarks and actions, made it clear that New Zealand would play rugby in the way they had been playing it. As long as he had a say in the matter their rules would remain unaltered. If others did not want to play them as they were, then they could play somewhere else but New Zealand.

THE END OF A TRIP

Within a week of landing in Australia, the 1930 Lions went down to their fourth successive international defeat of the tour and that was a surprise. They had opened the Australian portion of the trip by whipping the New South Wales side by 29-10 and that Waratahs side still had most of the men who had made such a successful tour to Britain and Ireland just three years earlier. Seeing that the full Australian international side was made up of most of the same New South Wales players, the outcome of the international game at Sydney looked to be a foregone conclusion. But the Lions were caught napping and in a

"THERE GOES ALEC MAKING ANOTHER FORWARD PASS!"

grim battle were nosed out in a dramatic finish by 6-5. Subsequently they beat Queensland by 26-16, an Australian XV by 29-14, lost then to New South Wales in their return match by 3-28 and wound up the official tour with a 41-36 win over Victoria. Then came the final romp of the tour, a light-hearted affair against a makeshift Western Australian XV. The purpose of this game was to popularise the game in Western Australia. The result, however, a 71-3 win for the Lions, could hardly have done much for the morale of the Western Australian players.

ARGENTINA AGAIN

Under the captaincy of Bernard Gadney, a second "Mini-Lions" side toured in Argentina in 1936 and the party of 23 was made up of 19 English players, two Scots and the two Ireland internationals, C. V. Boyle and Charlie Beamish. They played 10 games, won all 10, and finished with 399 points while having only 12 scored against them. Their biggest win was over Argentina Pacific XV by 62-0 and they also defeated Buenos Aires by 55-0. Only in three games did the Argentinians manage to score against the tourists. Olivos XV managed a penalty goal, Old Georgians XV kicked two penalty goals and Belgrano XV got the only try scored by any of the Argentinian sides during the tour. In the unofficial international game against the full Argentina side at Buenos Aires, the tourists won by 23-0, which, in fact, was their lowest winning margin of the 10 games! One of the top scorers of the tour—and, sadly, his record was never properly tabulated—was the Russian prince Serge Obolensky, who had made his four appearances for England that year against Scotland, Ireland, Wales and the New Zealanders.

SAMMY WALKER'S LIONS

In the last of the pre Second World War rugby tours, Ireland's Sammy Walker, one of the great forwards of his time, led the 1938 Lions to South Africa to play 23 matches, including three international games. His men, however, played 24 games. An unofficial fixture was arranged against the Western Province Country Districts and the shock of that particular game was that the Lions were beaten 7-12. In the official 23 match programme, the 1938 Lions won 17 of their 23 games, lost six and scored 371 points while conceding 211. Their top points scorer was the Welsh international forward A. R. Taylor of Cross Keys with 53 points from four tries, seven conversions and nine penalty goals. The top try scorers were England's E. J. Unwin and Wales's E. Jones with 10 each. The 1938 Lions most decisive win was 42-3 over North-East Districts and their worst beating was 8-26 by Northern Province. The break-down of the 1938 Lions was nine English, eight Irish, eight Welsh and four Scottish players.

THE FIRST INTERNATIONAL

On the Springboks way home from their memorable tour of New Zealand in 1937, their captain, the great Philip Nel had announced his retirement in spectacular fashion by tossing his football boots into the sea. And so for the first international against the Lions at Ellis Park, Danie Craven, then in his final season of international football, was named as captain. To back him he had most of the side that had beaten New Zealand in the previous year's series down under. Going into this first international Sammy Walker's men had already completed 14 games of the tour of which they had lost three and they were given little hope of matching the Springboks. And they did not. They were well and truly trounced by 26-12 on 6th August, 1938. D. O. Williams ran in two tries for the Springboks, Tony Harris and Fanie Louw added another two and full-back Gerry Brand, with four conversions and two goals added the extra 14 points, which equalled Bennie Osler's all-time record for an international game. The Lions four scores came from three penalty goals by Vivian Jenkins and one from A. R. Taylor. But the game was memorable for two particular kicks. From close to the touch-line and within his own half Brand dropped one of the greatest goals ever seen in South Africa but even that was upstaged by Jenkins's effort. After the Springboks had been penalised in the Lions half, the Welsh full-back indicated that he wanted to try for a penalty goal and that brought hoots of derision from most of the 36,000 spectators. But Jenkins lined up the ball carefully and sent it spinning dead centre between the posts. Subsequently, it was officially measured and the distance was 63 yards.

THE END OF BRAND

Before the start of the second international at Port Elizabeth, both South Africa and the Lions were in trouble with their full-backs. The Springbok star Gerry Brand injured his thigh in training for this game and had to drop out. As it happened, this injury was to end his international career with South Africa after 16 caps. In these 16 appearances he had scored 55 points for South Africa and in the 46 games in which he had worn the Springbok jersey his total was 293 points, which is still a South African record. The Lions full-back Vivian Jenkins, who was plagued with injury during this tour, was also forced to drop out of the second international and, in fact, wound up the tour by playing in just the one international game. This second meeting at Port Elizabeth was never in any doubt as far as the South Africans were concerned. They raced into a half-time lead of 10-0 and eventually romped home by 19-3. Ben du Toit, Flappie Lochner and Johnny Bester scored tries, Freddie Turner kicked two conversions and also added two penalty goals. With his 10 points Turner joined the exclusive club of those who have scored double figures for South Africa in an international game. The Lions only score came late in the game from a try by the Scottish forward Laurie Duff. With this win, the Springboks had been unbeaten by the Lions since the second international game at Port Elizabeth in 1910.

AN IRISH AFTERNOON

A. F. Markotter, then the Grand Old Man of South African rugby, provided a sound piece of advice for the Lions manager Jock Hartley before the selection of the Lions side to face South Africa in the final international game of the 1938 tour. "Put all your Irishmen into the side"—he said—"and you might just win this game". Hartley took the advice and so for the last meeting at Capetown, the Lions took the field with an unprecedented number of Irish internationals in the side—C. V. Boyle, Harry McKibbin, George Cromey, George Morgan, Sammy Walker, Bob Graves, Blair Mayne and Bob Alexander. And that breath of the shamrock on the Lions side brought an historic victory at Cape Town on Saturday, 10th September, 1938. Playing with a strong wind behind them in the first half, the Springboks overcame the shock of an early try by the Welsh winger E. Jones, and streaked ahead with tries from Turner, Bester and Lotz and Turner converted two to put the South Africans 13-3 ahead at the break. Then came a dramatic fight back by the Lions. G. T. Dancer lived up to his name by waltzing over for a smart try which Harry McKibbin converted and then Bob Alexander smashed his way over the Springbok line for a try and with McKibbin putting over a 40 yards penalty, the Lions were in front by 14-13. A penalty goal by Freddie Turner put the Springboks back in front again but almost immediately the Scotland full-back Charlie Grieve dropped a goal and again it was the Lions in front by 18-16. Just before time George Cromey sent Laurie Duff away for a try and that final score of 21-16 marked the Lions first win over the Springboks for 28 years.

HE FAILED TO SCORE

Blair Mayne, one of the most remarkable and most colourful characters to play rugby for Ireland, travelled to South Africa with the 1938 Lions, was one of the towering successes of the tour . . . but yet he came home with a most unusual distinction. Those 1938 Lions set an astonishing record in that 28 of the 29 players on tour scored in one way or another. The only member of the party who failed to get into the scoring list was Mayne! Capped six times for Ireland just before the outbreak of the Second World War, Blair Mayne won the D.S.O. and two bars during his army career and was to die tragically in a motor accident after he had settled down in his native Belfast.

DOWN UNDER IN 1950

Ireland had won the Triple Crown in 1947-1948 and again in 1948-1949 and it was inevitable that their representation on the 1950 Lions to tour in New Zealand and Australia would be strong. And it was. Nine Irish internationals were selected and the captaincy went to the twenty-three-year old Karl Mullen, who thus became the third Irishman to captain a touring side after Tom Smyth in 1910 and Sammy Walker in 1938. Wales, however took the major representation on the 1950 side with 13 and this became 14 when Ireland's George Norton was injured and Lewis Jones was flown out to replace him. Scotland had five players on the side and England had just the three. The 1950

Lions played 29 official matches in New Zealand and Australia and won 22, lost six and drew one. They scored 570 points and conceded 174. Their top points scorer was the Welsh international Malcolm Lewis with 96 points from nine tries, 18 conversions and 11 penalty goals. But he just barely made it ahead of the replacement Lewis Jones who compiled 92 points from two tries, 22 conversions, 13 penalty goals and a drop goal. The top try scorer was Wales's Olympic sprinter Ken Jones with 16. The top win by the Lions in New Zealand was their 30-0 defeat of the combined Waikato-Thames Valley and King Country side and their highest margin of victory in Australia was the 47-3 rout of New South Wales Country. In an unofficial match on their way home the Lions took on Ceylon and won by 44-6.

THE REPLACEMENT

For Ireland's full-back George Norton, the 1950 Lions tour of New Zealand and Australia was a sad and short one. One of the finest kickers in the game at the time, he had already knocked up nine points in New Zealand when he turned out in the fifth game of the tour against Southland. And that was to bring his tour to an end. He fractured his arm and, subsequently, at the suggestion of the New Zealand Rugby Union a replacement was flown out to join the party. The newcomer was the nineteen-year old Lewis Jones of Wales, who was destined not only to become one of the major personalities of the tour but later one of the memorable figures of international rugby both in the union and league codes.

THE FIRST INTERNATIONAL

Karl Mullen's Lions began their tour of New Zealand with a 24-win over the combined Nelson-Marlborough-Golden Bay-Motueka side and followed that with a 24-9 win over Buller and a 32-3 win over West Coast. Then came defeat 9-23 by Otago and another by 0-11 at the hands of Southland before they went into the first international game against New Zealand at Dunedin. The Lions made all the early running in this game and John Robins with a penalty goal, Jack Kyle with a dazzling try and Ken Jones with another memorable try put them into a 9-3 lead at half-time with New Zealand's only score, a try coming from centre-threequarter R. A. Roper, who was winning his second All-Blacks cap. Bob Scott reduced the leeway to 9-6 with a fine penalty goal in the second half and then, with barely minutes to go, the New Zealand captain Ron Elvidge shot over for the try that levelled the scores.

A BRIGHT START

No one could have made a brighter start to a rugby tour than the twenty-year old Welsh international Malcolm Thomas. In the opening game against the combined Nelson-Marlborough-Golden Bay-Motueka side at Nelson, the Lions won by 24-3 and Thomas contributed a record 21 from six penalty goals and a try. Unfortunately, because of injuries, Thomas, who wound up as the tour's highest scorer with 96 points, was able to play in only 12 games, which included two internationals against New Zealand and one against Australia.

THE SERIES WON

The All-Blacks duly wrapped up their series against the Lions of 1950 by winning the second international match at Christchurch by 8-0 and the third at Wellington by 6-3. Pat Crowley opened the scoring in the second international with a try and before half-time Roper went over for a second try which L. S. Haig of Otago converted and that, despite a remarkable display by Ireland's Jack Kyle in the second half but which brought no scores for the Lions, was how it ended. The third international was one that should never have been lost by the Lions. Robins gave them an early lead with a penalty goal and for most of the game the All-Blacks were down to 13 players, one of them being their captain who had been carried off with chest and face injuries and also with concussion. But Elvidge made a most unexpected and dramatic return to the game in the second half and it was quite obvious that he knew little about what was really going on. But in one glorious moment of inspiration, he raced into the threequarter line to make the extra man and dived over for a try which he, subsequently, had to have explained and described to him. With the score at 3-3, Bob Scott kicked the penalty goal that gave the All-Blacks their third series win over the Lions since 1908.

THE LIONS ROAR

With 58,000 spectators at Eden Park, Auckland on Saturday, July 29, 1950 in their second last game of the tour in New Zealand, the Lions took on the All-Blacks for the fourth time and this meeting over-shadowed all that had gone before. It all revolved around just one try, unquestionably the greatest of the 1950 tour. Hector Wilson started the proceedings off with a try for New Zealand which Bob Scott converted, but Lewis Jones closed the gap to two points with an excellent penalty goal. However, right on half-time Bob Scott, with one of his special efforts, dropped a magnificent goal from over the halfway line to leave the All-Blacks in an 8-3 lead at the break. Fifteen minutes from time Peter Henderson added another try for New Zealand and it was 11-3. Then shortly before the end came the try that is still a regular topic of rugby conversation in New Zealand. With the Lions pinned on their own line and the All-Blacks attacking strongly the ball went back to Lewis Jones well behind his own line. He took the pass from Jack Kyle and then, instead of the expected relieving kick to touch, he decided to run the ball. And so he did, right up to the "25" and then beyond it up to the halfway mark. Only Bob Scott was in his way but Peter Henderson was also converging to cut him off. Lewis Jones moved straight at Scott, committed the New Zealander to the tackle and then with a lob more than a pass, he sent the ball over Henderson's head right into the hands of Ken Jones. And the Olympic sprinter was gone in a flash with the entire New Zealand side in vain pursuit. He made the final 50 yards to ground the ball for a try and Lewis Jones, his co-partner in one of the finest tries in rugby history, duly kicked the conversion. It did not win the game for the Lions but it added a final accolade to the esteem that every New Zealander had for Karl Mullen's 1950 Lions.

TO AUSTRALIA

The 1950 Lions left New Zealand with a win by 14-9 over the New Zealand Maoris and then headed for Australia where they opened up their six match programme with a 47-3 win over New South Wales Country. They followed this by beating New South Wales 22-6 and then in the first international game at Sydney against Australia, they won by 19-6. A week later they took on Australia again at Sydney and this time their victory was even more pronounced by 24-3. They beat Metropolitan Union by 26-17 and then came the shock of the tour, a defeat in the final game 12-17 by a New South Wales XV.

IN PLASTER

Dr Douglas Smith, the Scottish international threequarter, arrived in New Zealand for the 1950 Lions tour with his arm in plaster—and did not make his first appearance in the Lions jersey until the 18th game of the tour against the Combined Manawatu and Horowhenua side. In his remaining matches, however, and he played in one of the international games against Australia, he managed to get into the scoring lists with 11 points from three tries and a conversion. The same Douglas Smith, however, was to come back again to New Zealand with a later Lions side and was to be rewarded with a little more success. He was manager of the 1971 Lions, the first to beat New Zealand in a series.

ROBIN THOMPSON'S LIONS

Under the captaincy of Robin Thompson, one of Ireland's great international forwards of the 1950s, the 1955 Lions to South Africa wound up with the record of winning 18 of their 24 matches, losing five and drawing one. In the process they scored 369 points and conceded 196. Their top points scorer and also the top try scorer of the tour was the nineteen-year old Irish wing-threequarter Tony O'Reilly with 48 points from 16 tries. Thompson's Lions started the tour on a low note by losing their opening game to Western Transvaal by 6-9 but after a 24-14 win over Griqualand West in the second, stayed unbeaten for six games before going down to Eastern Province by 0-20. This, in fact, was their worst defeat of the tour and the only game in which they failed to register a score. Their highest margin of victory was 28 points, which they achieved twice in beating North-Eastern Districts by 34-6 and Orange Free State by 31-3. Their one draw was a high scoring one, 17-17 against Eastern Transvaal.

A WORLD RECORD

Before a world record crowd for a rugby game of 95,000 at Ellis Park, Johannesburg on Saturday, 6th August, 1955—and it is estimated that more than 5,000 more got in to see the game—Robin Thompson's Lions began their international series against the Springboks. This was the 13th match of the tour but for all those who played in it and watched it, it was not an unlucky one. By general agreement it was one of the finest international games ever played, and there could hardly have been a more dramatic finish. Cecil Pedlow opened the scoring for the Lions with a try but Van der Schyff with two penalty goals and a try by Theunis Briers, converted by Van der Schyff sent the Springboks into an 11-3 lead. The Lions struck back with a try from Jeff Butterfield and Angus Cameron put over the conversion to leave the score at the break with South Africa two points ahead. Shortly after the start of the second half, when the Lions had lost Reg Higgins with injury, Cliff Morgan, the Welsh wizard of the time, went over at the posts and Cameron converted to put the Lions ahead by 13-11. Then came a flashing try from Jim Greenwood, followed by another from Tony O'Reilly and with Cameron converting both, the Lions were 23-11 up. Sias Swart, playing in his first and only game for South Africa, broke through for a try and then on the stroke of normal time Chris Koch battered his way over for a try which Van der Schyff converted. Now the score was 23-19 for the Lions and with seconds to go Theunis Briers got over for a try to narrow the gap to a point 23-22. Everything now depended on Jack Van der Schyff's attempt at conversion. It had to be the last kick of the game and it was not a difficult one. But the kick shaved the posts and it was all over. For the first time since 1896, South Africa had been beaten in the opening game of an international series and those 23 Lions points represented the highest number that had ever been recorded against a Springbok side in the 64 years of their international involvement.

A HAT-TRICK OF TRIES

For the second international game against the Lions in 1955, South Africa made five changes and one significant switch. Tom Van Vollenhoven, who had played at centre in the first game was moved to wing-threequarter for the game at Newlands. It turned out to be a profitable switch. The Lions opened the scoring after 20 minutes with a penalty goal from Angus Cameron but Van Vollenhoven brought the Springboks level with a try and at half-time it was 3-3. That was the end of the game as a battle. Within minutes after half-time Van Vollenhoven went streaking away for his second try and two minutes later collected his hat-trick. Wilf Rosenburg added yet another, full-back Roy Dryburgh also had a try, Theunis Briers scored the sixth and Dawie Ackermann added the seventh. Dryburgh converted two of the tries and all the Lions could offer in return was a try from Jeff Butterfield and another from Bryn Meredith. With their seven tries, the Springboks had created a record for an international game in South Africa, Roy Dryburgh had become the second South African full-back to score a try in international rugby—the first was Percy Allport in 1910—and Tom Van Vollenhoven had joined "Boetie" McHardy, Johan Stegmann and Hennie Van Zyl as the only four South Africans to score a hat-trick of tries in an international game. McHardy and Stegmann had both accomplished their three tries in the same match—against Ireland at Lansdowne Road back in 1912, and Van Zyl got his hat-trick against Australia in 1961.

ROBIN THOMPSON OUT

An injury against Northern Transvaal put the Lions captain Robin Thompson out of the third international game against South Africa at Pretoria—and so he missed the second international win of the tour. With Cliff Morgan as captain, the Lions took the lead with a drop goal from Jeff Butterfield and England's scrum-half D. G. S. Baker sent them into a 6-0 lead with a penalty goal. Roy Dryburgh then dropped a goal from 55 yards out but Butterfield promptly raced over for a try to restore the six points margin. Dryburgh closed the scoring with a penalty goal for South Africa. It was the Lions second victory over South Africa since the final international game at Newlands in 1938.

THE 16th FOR O'REILLY

Robin Thompson's Lions were never really in the hunt in the fourth and final international game of the 1955 tour at Port Elizabeth. With Thompson back after injury, they went into a 5-3 lead in the first half with a try from J. T. Greenwood which Cecil Pedlow converted to a try by Theunis Briers. But the second half was one-way traffic. Briers scored almost immediately, Ulyate added a second then came another from Van Vollenhoven and Ulyate then dropped a goal to put the score at 17-5. Retief then went in for a try which was converted by Dryburgh who had also converted Ulygate's try and it was 22-5. Just on time, however, Tony O'Reilly dived over for his 16th and last try of the tour. Unfortunately, in doing so, the Irishman dislocated his shoulder and that ruled out any possibility of being able to increase his try tally in the final game against East African XV which the Lions won by 39-12.

THIRD ON THE LIST

With his 16 tries in South Africa in 1955, Tony O'Reilly moved to third place in the list of individual Lions try-scorers on tours of South Africa. The record of 30 was set by R. L. Aston (England) on the 1911 tour and Larry Bulger (Ireland) scored 20 on the 1896 tour. O'Reilly had the distinction of scoring three tries in two games during the tour, against North-Eastern Districts and also against Transvaal.

RONNIE DAWSON'S LIONS

Under the leadership of Ireland's twenty-six-year old captain and hooker, Ronnie Dawson, the 1959 Lions which toured in Australia, New Zealand and Canada, set an all-time record for a touring side from these islands by amassing a total of 842 points. In the process they also scored 165 tries, another record for a Lions side. Their full record was: played 33, won 27, lost six, scored 842 points and conceded 353. Their biggest win in Australia was in their opening game against Victoria by 53-18, their most convincing win in New Zealand was 64-5 over the Combined Marlborough-Nelson-Golden Bay-Motueka side and they wound up the tour with their final game in Canada where they trounced Eastern Canada by 70-6.

TWO OVER THE TON

David Hewitt, then nineteen and a student at Queen's University, Belfast, was the top points scorer of the 1959 Lions with 112 points from 13 tries, 20 conversions, 10 penalty goals and a drop goal. And he was joined over the century mark by the Welsh full-back Terry Davies who reached 104 from 28 conversions and 16 penalty goals. Top try scorer was Ireland's Tony O'Reilly with 22 and that added to his 16 from the previous Lions tour in South Africa gave him an all-time Lions record of 38. England's wing-threequarter Peter Jackson was second in the try-scoring table to O'Reilly with 19. O'Reilly's 17 tries in New Zealand was also a record in that country by a member of the Lions touring sides.

THE FIRST DEFEAT

Ronnie Dawson's men kicked off the 1959 tour down under with a 53-18 win over Victoria but in their second game in Australia went down 14-18 to New South Wales. They recovered smartly to beat Queensland by 39-11 and then in the first international game against Australia they scored a decisive win by 17-6. Their next game brought a 27-14 win over New South Wales Country Districts and they finished off the Australian portion of the tour by winning the second international at Sydney by 24-3. Their full record in Australia was that they won five of their six games, lost one and scored 174 points while conceding 70. But this portion of the tour also brought a minor disaster. In the second game against New South Wales, Niall Brophy, the Irish wing-threequarter turned sharply and fractured a bone in his ankle, and that was the end of the tour for him. He was subsequently replaced by W. M. Patterson of the Sale club in England.

UNDER FLOODLIGHTS

The 1959 Lions game against Queensland at the Brisbane Exhibition Ground brought the only tour fixture that was played under floodlights and it was a personal triumph for Ireland's David Hewitt. Dawson's men took a little time to get accustomed to playing under the lights and led by only 8-6 at half-time. But in the second half they ran delightfully riot. Hewitt wound up with a personal tally of 21 points in the Lions total of 39 points with a glorious try, two penalty goals and six conversions. Hewitt had already scored 10 points against Victoria and so after two games he had a total of 31 points and was obviously heading towards becoming the top scorer of the tour. He added a further six points with two penalty goals against Australia in the first international and added a further two penalty goals in the final international against the Wallabies. Leaving Australia, he already had 43 points in his bag.

FOLLOWING DAD

For the twenty-one-year old Beverley Risman, an England international who had the distinction of scoring tries in both of his Lions appearances against Australia, his visit down under had a very significant and sentimental association. His father, the legendary Gus Risman, had previously toured on three occasions in Australia and New Zealand in 1932, 1936 and 1946, with the Britain Rugby League side and had played in 12 internationals against Australia and three against New Zealand. His son, of course, was also to add two appearances against New Zealand to the two he made against Australia with the 1959 Lions. Subsequently, of course, Beverley Risman was to follow his father into rugby league and in the World Cup of 1968 had the added distinction of playing against both Australia and New Zealand under the League code. In his 1959 tour with the Lions Risman wound up with a total of 62 points from six tries, 16 conversions and four penalty goals.

INTO ALL-BLACK COUNTRY

The 1959 Lions got the New Zealand portion of the tour off to quite a remarkable start by hammering Hawkes Bay 52-12 in their first match and followed this by beating East Coast-Poverty Bay by 23-14. They disposed of Auckland by 15-10 and overwhelmed the New Zealand Universities by 25-13. With this record, they went in as strong favourites to beat Otago in the fifth game of the tour. This was to be an eye-opener for them. They were never allowed to settle down to their smooth play by a tremendous Otago back and in the end took a humiliating drubbing by 8-26. From there on, however, they stepped back to form and won their next two games before moving to Dunedin to take on New Zealand in the first international match of the tour.

THE LIONS V. DON CLARKE

Even the most fervent supporters of New Zealand rugby regarded the All-Blacks victory in the first international as a calamity. This turned out to be one of the most extraordinary games in the history of the international rugby and one newspaper on the following morning even gave the result as Don Clarke 18 points; Lions 17 points. There were almost 45,000 spectators present at Dunedin on Saturday, 18th July, 1959 to watch a game that was marred by penalties. The referee, Mr A. L. Fleury, awarded at least 35—and some accounts say the figure was as high as 40—during the game and in the end no one was either happy or satisfied with the outcome. Tony O'Reilly opened the scoring for the Lions with a try, Malcolm Price had added a second and David Hewitt had landed a penalty goal to put their half-time score at nine points. In the second half Peter Jackson had a try and Terry Price added a second which Bev Risman converted and the Lions total for the game was a more than respectable 17 points. But it did not do them any good. Don Clarke, the All-Blacks full-back, had been given 10 kickable penalty attempts and he put six of them between the posts, two from over 50 yards out. Clarke's performance still remains as a world record for the most penalty goals by a player in an international game. The only consolation for the New Zealanders was that his performance had broken the record of five penalty goals which South Africa's Aaron Geffin had kicked to beat them in their international at Newlands in 1949.

CLARKE AGAIN

Having lost only one game since the first international—a 14-20 upset against Canterbury—the Lions went on to Wellington for their second meeting with New Zealand. And once again they ran into Don Clarke. This time, however, he was away off form with his kicking. For this game the All-Blacks selectors brought back a young man, by name Colin Meads, who had been dropped for the first international and also introduced another young man, Ralph Caulton. And Caulton celebrated his first international jersey by scoring two tries, but a try from the English sprint champion John Young and a conversion by Terry Davies who also kicked a penalty goal left the Lions in an 8-6 lead with time running out. Then Clarke, who had been well off the mark with his licking that afternoon, popped up in a new role as far as the Lions were concerned. With the All-Blacks threequarters running the ball, the giant full-back came racing into the line and, proceeding to throw the neatest of dummies, he crashed over for a try. And the final straw for the Lions was that he converted his own try to win the game by 11-8.

THREE DOWN

In the third international against New Zealand at Christchurch, the Lions were never in the hunt and went tumbling down to an 8-22 defeat. Needless to remark they had to contend again with Don Clarke, who knocked up 10 of the All-Blacks 22 points. David Hewitt scored a try for the Lions which J. Faull, the Welsh international converted, and then kicked a penalty goal. In his second international for New Zealand Ralph Caulton collected another two tries, Colin Meads also had one and R. J. Urbahn added a fourth. Clarke kicked two conversions, a penalty goal and for good measure also dropped a goal. In his three internationals up to then against the Lions he had collected 33 of New Zealand's 51 points!

VICTORY AT LAST

From their defeat in the third international, the Lions made an impressive build up for the fourth and final international by beating the New Zealand Juniors by 29-9, the Maoris by 12-6, the combined Bay of Plenty-Thames Valley side by 26-24 and North Auckland by 36-13. Then it was in to Eden Park, Auckland for their last hope of beating the All-Blacks. And although Don Clarke was again in kicking form, this time they managed it. With a glorious try from Peter Jackson, another sensational try from Tony O'Reilly and an equally memorable one from Bev Risman, they put nine points on the scoreboard. Clarke had his chances to win the game but he managed to kick only two penalty goals to bring his total for the four international games to 39 points, which, of course, is still an all-time record for an All-Black. For the Lions it was an afternoon to remember. It was the first time since the first international match of the 1930 series at Dunedin that the Lions had beaten New Zealand and it was only the second time since 1904 that the tourists had beaten the All-Blacks.

A. R. SMITH'S LIONS

Arthur Smith of Oxford University and Scotland captained the 1962 Lions to South Africa and they wound up their 24 match programme by winning 15 games, losing five and drawing three. They scored 331 points while conceding 160 and their top points scorer was the England full-back John Willcox with 67 points from 17 conversions and 11 penalty goals. Captain Arthur Smith just pipped Niall Brophy for the top try scoring with eight to the Irishman's seven. Their most decisive margin of victory came in the very last game of the tour with a 50-0 result against East Africa and their worst defeat was by 14-34 at the hands of South Africa in the last international game of the series.

BACK IN SOUTH AFRICA

Gordon Waddell of Scotland, who wound up as the great utility player of the 1962 Lions in South Africa had also been a member of Ronnie Dawson's Lions in New Zealand and Australia in 1959. But the trip to South Africa and his selection to play in two of the international games against the Springboks completed a special family record for him. Thirty-eight years earlier, his father Herbert Waddell, also a Scottish international, had been a member of Cove-Smith's Lions in South Africa and had played in three of the international games against the Springboks. Between them the two Waddells won 33 caps for Scotland and made five appearances for the Lions.

TWO LOSSES

The 1962 Lions went unbeaten for six games before coming up against Northern Transvaal and this was to bring two losses. They lost the game and they lost Richard Sharp. Sharp had his jaw fractured in this game which the Lions lost 6-14 and he was out of the tour for almost six weeks: on his return he never showed anything of the form with which he had begun the tour. This, unfortunately came on the eve of the first international game against South Africa at Ellis Park, Johannesburg and his place on the Lions side went to Gordon Waddell. This was to be a disappointing international game but it did provide two excellent tries which brought a 3-3 draw. John Gainsford, taking a ball close to the halfway line, streaked along the touch line to go over for a great try in the corner. In the second half and into the same corner, Ken Jones ended a 60 yards run to get the equaliser. This was the fourth draw between the Lions and South Africa since 1891.

A CONTROVERSIAL FINISH

All the excitement of the second international between the 1962 Lions and the Springboks came in the last 10 minutes. The two sides had been deadlocked up to then but when the Welsh international Keith Rowlands was caught offside just outside his own "25" Keith Oxlee kicked South Africa into the lead with the easy penalty goal. The Lions, however, came storming back and right on the dot of time forced a scrum on the South African line. As Dickie Jeeps put in the ball, Ireland's international second row forward Bill Mulcahy made a call to hold the ball and push. The scrum moved forward and collapsed on the South African line, Keith Rowlands fell on it and it seemed to everyone that the Lions had scored a pushover try. The referee, however, Mr K. Carlson of East London, ruled it out. He had been unsighted and he ordered a five yards scrum. In a wealth of argument and controversy the match ended but as far as the records were concerned it was a win for South Africa and that was that.

OXLEE'S EIGHT

Keith Oxlee, who was to set an South African record of 88 points in his 19 appearances for the Springbok international side between 1960 and 1965, had the afternoon that every young player dreams about at Newlands in the third international game against the 1962 Lions. South Africa won the game by 8-3 and Oxlee had the satisfaction of scoring all eight points, with a try, a conversion and a penalty goal. Richard Sharp, with a drop goal, had the Lions only score. The most interesting feature of this international game was that when Oxlee scored his try close to time he brought South Africa's total of points in international rugby from 1891 to 999 points. With his conversion, he took them over the 1,000 points.

A RECORD WIN

With the series won, the South Africans opened up in a big way against the Lions in the final international game at Bloemfontein, which was also the second last game of the 1962 tour. They won it by 34-14 and it brought two significant records. Mannetjies Roux scored two tries, M. R. K. Wyness, John Gainsford, Johann Classen and Hugo van Zyl scored tries and Keith Oxlee converted five and also kicked two penalty goals. John Willcox kicked a penalty goal and one conversion for the Lions whose tries came from Mike Campbell-Lamerton, Keith Rowlands and R. C. Cowan. The final margin of victory, 34-14 remains as South Africa's greatest win over the Lions in all the tours since 1891 and up to 1974. Oxlee with his 16 points set an individual scoring record for a South African in an international game which also endures to the present day.

A RECORD FOR JEEPS

With his appearance in the fourth and final international match of the 1962 Lions tour in South Africa, England's international Dickie Jeeps set a record of 13 international appearances for the Lions. He had begun with four during the 1955 tour of South Africa, added two more against Australia and three against New Zealand during the 1959 tour and had played in all four international games of the 1962 tour. Jeeps made his England scrum-half debut in 1956, a year after his first Lions international appearance and eventually went on to win 24 caps for England. Apart from his Lions appearances against Australia and South Africa, he also played for England against both of these countries and had the distinction, too, of touring in South Africa with the Barbarians in 1958.

THE 1966 LIONS

With Des O'Brien, the former Irish international as manager and Mike Campbell-Lamerton of Scotland as captain the 1966 Lions which toured in Australia, New Zealand and Canada wound up with the record of winning 23 of their 35 games. They lost nine, drew three and in the process ran up 524 points while conceding 345. Their top points scorer was Stewart Wilson, the Scottish full-back with 90 points from a try, 18 conversions, 17 penalty goals and the top try scorer was the Welsh international Dewi Bebb with 14. In the Australian portion of the tour, their greatest victory was the 60-3 defeat of Western Australia and their best performance in New Zealand was beating West Coast-Buller by 25-6. The 1966 Lions worst defeat was 3-20 to New Zealand in the first international game at Dunedin.

A CLEAN SHEET

The 1966 Lions opened their tour of Australia with a resounding 60-3 win over Western Australia and went through their eight match-programme without defeat, although they were held to a 6-6 draw by New South Wales, in the fifth game. In their eight games, they scored 202 points and conceded 48. In the first international against Australia at Sydney they had to struggle hard for an 11-8 victory but in the second international they totally overwhelmed the Wallabies and scored 31 points without a score from the Australians. This is the greatest ever win recorded over the full Australian international side by a Lions touring side. But this portion of the tour was also to bring tragedy. Ireland's centre threequarter Jerry Walsh, who had already scored three tries for the Lions in Australia got the sad news that his father had died and he had to return home immediately. He was replaced by another Irish centre, Barry Bresnihan, who wound up the tour with a total of 15 points from five tries.

BEATEN FIRST TIME

In contrast with Australia where they had begun the tour on the highest of notes, the 1966 Lions came a sad cropper in their first game in New Zealand and were defeated 8-14 by Southland. They won their second game but in the third they tasted defeat again, this time by 9-17 to Otago. Wellington beat them 20-6 in the fifth game of the tour and although they went undefeated through the next four games, their performances indicated that they were not likely to trouble the All-Blacks in the opening international at Dunedin. And they did not. In front of a record crowd for a Dunedin international game of over 44,000 spectators, they were given a merciless hiding. New Zealand's

20 points came from a try, a conversion and two penalty goals from full-back Mick Williment, a drop goal from Mac Herewini and a try each from Bruce McLeod and Brian Lochore. And they could have had much more but for the fact that Williment, normally the best of kickers, missed some easy penalty goal attempts. The Lions only score came from a penalty goal by Stewart Wilson.

DOWN AGAIN

The 1966 Lions began to pick up more than a little after their shattering defeat by the All-Blacks in the opening international and with five impressive wins in succession, they arrived at Wellington for the second international fixture. David Watkins captained the Lions for this game and after Stewart Wilson had kicked two penalty goals, Watkins dropped a neat goal to put nine points on the scoreboard at half-time. But they were only a point ahead of the All-Blacks who had a try from Kel Tremain which was converted by Mick Williment who also kicked a long range penalty goal. Early in the second half Mike Gibson scored what appeared to be a perfectly legitimate try but the referee ruled that he had taken a forward pass and disallowed it. New Zealand had tries in the second half from Colin Meads and A. G. Steel and Williment had converted Meads's try for a total of 16 points. Wilson added another penalty goal to leave the Lions four points down at the final whistle, by 12-16.

A WHITEWASH

Mike Campbell-Lamerton's 1966 Lions ended their tour in New Zealand without an international win. In the third international at Christchurch on Saturday, 27th August, 1966, David Watkins and Ronnie Lamont scored two magnificent tries for the tourists but the final result was 19-6 for the All-Blacks, whose scores came from two penalty goals from Mick Williment, who also converted two tries by Waka Nathan and Tony Steel added the other try. The final international at Eden Park, Auckland brought in a crowd of over 60,000 and they had the pleasure of seeing the All-Blacks chalk up their fourth successive win over the Lions by the comfortable margin of 24-11. Waka Nathan, Ian MacRae, Tony Steel and Malcolm Dick had tries for New Zealand and Mick Williment kicked three conversions and a penalty goal. Mac Herewini completed their 24 points with a drop goal. Sandy Hinshelwood and Colin MacFadyean had tries for the Lions and Stewart Wilson converted one and also kicked a penalty goal. With this defeat of the Lions, the All-Blacks for the first time in their rugby history had completed a 4-0 record in a series. Mick Williment, by scoring in all four international games, had come up with a total of 37 points, just two short of the record set by Don Clarke against the Lions in 1959.

NOT SO EASY

In their sole international game against Canada, which also happened to be Canada's first rugby international fixture, the Lions won 19-8 at Toronto on 17th September, 1966. And this win, which was not achieved without effort, removed just a little of the embarrassment which the Lions had undergone just three days previously. Heading back home from New Zealand, they had taken on British Columbia in a warm-up game at Vancouver and had crashed 3-8, which had to be the shock of the rugby year. The Lions paraded their full strength for the international game against Canada and after a difficult first half which brought them only eight points, they finally gained control of the proceedings in the second and eventually ran out winners by 19-8.

TOM KIERNAN'S LIONS

Ireland's full-back Tom Kiernan, making his second Lions tour, was named to captain the 1968 side which played a 20-match programme in South Africa. They came home with the record of having won 15 games, lost four, drawn one and scoring 377 points while conceding 181. Their top points scorer was England's full-back Bob Hiller with 104 which came from two tries, 19 conversions, 18 penalty goals and two drop goals. The top try scorers were Scotland's Sandy Hinshelwood and Gareth Edwards of Wales, both with six. The highest margin of victory in any of the 20 games was 28 points which they achieved in beating Eastern Transvaal on Saturday, 29th June, 1968 and North East Cape by 40-12 on Monday, 22nd July, 1968. Their worst defeat was in the final international game against South Africa at Ellis Park, Johannesburg, on Saturday, 27th July, 1968 when they went down by 6-19. The only defeat at the hands of a provincial side was also at Ellis Park on Tuesday, 18th June, 1968 against Transvaal who won by 14-6.

TWO SURPRISE OMISSIONS

When the 30 names were announced for the 1968 Lions tour of South Africa, there were two shock omissions—the Welsh back Keith Jarrett and Ireland's No 8 forward Ken Goodall. Both had played magnificently in the international championship and seemed cast-iron certainties to make the trip. In Goodall's case, there were extenuating circumstances as far as the selectors were concerned. He was due to sit for university examinations in June and had asked the Lions selectors to excuse him for the opening stages of the tour, provided, of course, they decided to select him. They refused and that was that. Jarrett, however, was not even listed as a reserve . . . but, in the end, he did travel but even that was not without its complications. Two days before the Lions party got together for the trip, Bob Lloyd, the Harlequins and England centre threequarter, realised that, like Goodall, he too was caught up in university examinations and he asked the selectors to be excused for the early games of the tour. The selectors could do nothing else but refuse and Jarrett was then elected to the side. Unfortunately, when the team flew out to South Africa, Jarrett was not in the party. He was in hospital in London with acute tonsillitis and it was several days before he could follow the Lions to South Africa.

WEST GOES OUT

During the final training sessions at Eastbourne before the Lions took off, wing-forward Bryan West of Northampton and England realised that his fitness was suspect and when he realised that he was finding it increasingly difficult to train without pain in his legs, he went to the selectors and told them of his situation. With less than 48 hours to go to take-off time, the selectors had no option but to take him out of the side. He was immediately replaced by the Scottish international Rodger Arneil. At a later stage, however, a fully recovered West was

277

to make it to South Africa. Like Ken Goodall, he eventually went out as a replacement. But like Goodall, too, he was not to have any conspicuous success on the tour. He played only two games, both against provincial sides and Goodall, injured shortly after his arrival, was to play in only one game, also against a provincial side.

THE OPENING GAMES

Tom Kiernan's Lions opened the 1968 tour at Potchefstroom on Saturday, 18th May, 1968 with a 20-8 win over Western Transvaal and the Irish full-back had the distinction of kicking the first penalty goal of the tour. Scotland's Jim Telfer had the first score of the tour with a try but just after half-time Kiernan kicked his first penalty goal which at the time brought the scores level at 6-6. Just over two months later, at Ellis Park, Johannesburg on Saturday, 27th July, Kiernan was to kick the last points of the 1968 tour, again with a penalty goal. In all, he was to score 84 points on the tour, from nine conversions, and 22 penalty goals—and of these 84 points, 35 were to take him into a special place in rugby history.

UNBEATEN RUN

Following their defeat of Western Transvaal, the 1968 Lions went off on an unbeaten run, which brought wins over Western Provinces by 10-6, South-Western Districts by 24-6, Eastern Province by 23-14, Natal by 17-5, Rhodesia by 32-6 and then it was into Pretoria for the first international game against South Africa. And this, in fact, marked a milestone in South African rugby. For the first time, the new International Rugby Board law, permitting four reserves to be nominated for injured players, came into effect. And Ireland's Mike Gibson became the first reserve to go into an international game between the Lions and South Africa. In the 30th minute of the first half the Welsh out-half Barry John was carried off with a fractured collar-bone and the Irishman went in to take his place. This was doubly unusual in that in the opening game of the tour against Western Transvaal, Gibson had been carried off with an injured ankle and had been replaced by his countryman Barry Bresnihan, who became the first replacement to play in a game for a Lions touring side. Tiny Naude with a penalty goal from 55 yards out and Piet Visagie with another from close in put the Springboks into a 6-0 lead after 20 minutes but Bill McBride then tore over for a try which Tom Kiernan converted. Naude added a Springbok try which Visagie converted and then Kiernan kicked a penalty goal. Dawie de Villers had a try for South Africa, which Visagie converted but again Kiernan was on the mark with a penalty goal. Visagie with a penalty goal and then Frik du Preez with a try stretched the Springbok lead to 22-11 before Kiernan with two penalty goals made it 22-17 Tiny Naude then kicked a penalty goal and Kiernan kicked one to leave the final score at South Africa 25; Lions 20.

KIERNAN'S RECORD

With his conversion and his five penalty goals for the Lions in the first international at Loftus Versfeld, Pretoria, Tom Kiernan set his first record in South Africa during the 1968 tour. His 17 points established an individual scoring record for an international game against South Africa. The previous record of 12 points had been set by the Australian, B. J. Ellwood, in the Wallabies defeat of the Springboks at Sydney in 1965. Ellwood had kicked four penalty goals. Kiernan's five penalty goals also equalled the record set by Aaron Geffin, who had kicked his five against the New Zealanders at Newlands in 1949. Only one man in rugby history, Don Clarke of New Zealand, has kicked six penalty goals in an international game—and he did it against the Lions at Dunedin in 1959—and Kiernan's five goals is now shared in second place with A. Geffin (South Africa), A. N. McGill (Australia), R. Fairfax (Australia), and F. McCormick (New Zealand).

NO WELSH FORWARD!

Perhaps the most surprising feature of the Lions second international game against South Africa at Port Elizabeth on Saturday, 22nd June, 1968 was that there was not a Welsh forward in the pack! And, indeed, the only Welsh player in the 15 was scrum-half Gareth Edwards. As it happened this was the only occasion on the tour when the Lions were not to be defeated by South Africa. It was not a memorable game and all 12 points came from penalty goals. Piet Visagie and Tiny Naude kicked one each for the Springboks and Tom Kiernan kicked two for the Lions. The only worthwhile feature of a dull game was that by kicking two penalty goals, Kiernan had now scored 23 successive points in the two international games.

THE CASE OF JOHN O'SHEA

The Lions beat Eastern Transvaal by 37-9 at Springs on Saturday, 29th June, 1968 but by the time it was all over, the result was of minor consequence. The case of John O'Shea had taken over as the major outcome of the game. Shortly after Ireland's wing forward Mick Doyle had put the Lions into a 23-6 lead, scrum-half Roger Young was deliberately obstructed as he went for a ball. O'Shea, a Welsh international held off the Eastern Transvaal forward who had impeded Young and was struck. O'Shea retaliated and within seconds there was a melee. O'Shea was then caught in the act of trying to catch up with the Eastern Transvaal forward Johann Britz and was ordered off the field by the referee H. Wooley of Eastern Transvaal. On his way to the dressing room O'Shea was attacked by a spectator and in the end, when police had removed his assailant, the Welshman was escorted to safety. Subsequently a committee accepted O'Shea's apology for what had happened and he was reprimanded but he was not suspended for any games, and, in fact, turned out in the next game against Northern Transvaal. O'Shea, however, had taken his place in Lions history as only the second player to be dismissed from the field of play since the first tour was made to South Africa in 1891.

KIERNAN AGAIN

Tom Kiernan came back to Loftus Versfeld, Pretoria on Wednesday, 3rd July, 1968 to lead the Lions against Northern Transvaal, just a month after he had kicked his 17 points against South Africa in the first international of the tour on the same ground. And he was again in sparkling form. After two minutes Richards gave the Lions the lead with a try which Kiernan converted but Fourie de Preez reduced the lead with a snap try just a few minutes later. Gerard Pitzer then put the Northern Transvaal side ahead with a try which was converted by full back D. Pretorious and this was followed by another try from de

Preez which Pretorious converted and the Lions were 5-13 down. Kiernan kicked a penalty goal but just on half-time Piet Steyn dropped a goal to leave the Lions trailing 8-16 at the break. Mike Coulman had an early try for the Lions in the second half and Kiernan kicked the conversion and then followed that with a penalty to level the scores. Ireland's full-back then added yet another penalty goal and three minutes later landed a fourth to put the Lions ahead by 22-16. Pretorious kicked a penalty just before time to leave the final score at 22-19 for the Lions. Kiernan had contributed 16 points with his two conversions and four penalty goals which brought his total for his two visits to Loftus Versfeld to 33 points. His performance sent all the local historians chasing through their record books and it was unanimously agreed later that the Irishman had set yet another record for two consecutive games at the Pretoria ground.

YET AGAIN!

Piet Visagie got South Africa to a flying start in the third international game against the Lions at Capetown on Saturday, 13th July, 1968 with an early penalty goal but Tom Kiernan with a penalty goal brought the sides to 3-3 at half-time. Three minutes after the start of the second half, South Africa's great forward Lourens went thundering over for a try and Visagie with a kick from the touchline added the extra two points to make it 8-3. South Africa added the finishing touch with a gigantic kick from over 50 yards by Naude which left the score at 11-3 with time up. Kiernan, however, added a penalty goal in injury time and for the second time in an international game on the tour had kicked all of his side's points. With his six in this game, he had now kicked 29 successive international points against South Africa.

THE FINAL FLOURISH

The intriguing prospects for the final international game of the 1968 tour between the Lions and South Africa at Ellis Park, Johannesburg on Saturday, 27th July, 1968 were whether South Africa could go through the series without defeat, whether they could maintain their unbeaten record against the Lions since the international at Pretoria in 1955 . . . and, of course, whether Ireland's Tom Kiernan could establish a world record of points for an international series. All the prospects were fulfilled. South Africa, with tries from Mannetjies Roux, Jan Ellis, Eben Oliver and Syd Nomis and two conversions by Piet Visagie put up a total of 19 points and won comfortably to the Lions six points. And those six points from the tourists came once again from the boot of Tom Kiernan, who for the third international game in succession had scored all his side's points against South Africa. Those six points had brought his total to 35 and they still remain as the most number of consecutive points kicked by a player in international rugby.

AN IRISH OUTING

With the completion of the 1968 tour at Ellis Park, Johannesburg, where South Africa completed the international series with a total of 61 points to the Lions 38, it marked another extraordinary milestone in the Lions history. For the first time since the touring sides had been representative of all four home countries, the entire Lions total in the series had come from the players of one country—Ireland. Bill McBride, also destined to become one of the record-makers of rugby, had scored the opening and only try of the Lions four international appearances and the remaining 35 points had been kicked by Tom Kiernan, with one conversion and 11 penalty goals.

BOB HILLER'S CENTURY

For England's full-back Bob Hiller, who had played in only eight matches of the 1968 Lions tour—and all were against provincial sides —the 19th game against North East Cape at Cradock on Monday, 22nd July, was to be a significant outing. The Lions won as they pleased with seven tries from Mick Doyle, Billy Raybould, Keith Jarrett, John Taylor, Sandy Hinshelwood, Delme Thomas and Barry Bresnihan, and Keith Jarrett also kicked a penalty goal. Hiller, going into this game had scored a total of 88 points in his seven outings and with his 16 points in this game from two penalty goals and five conversions, he took his total to 104 to become the only century-maker of the 1968 tour. His outstanding game had been against Border. In the 26-6 win, he had scored 23 points from a conversion, five penalty goals and two drop goals. His sequence in his eight matches was 12, 14, 10, 11, 13, 5, 23, 16. With his 104 points he had become joint fourth in the top scorers for Lions touring sides since 1891. The leader then was C. Y. Adamson of the 1899 tourists in Australia with 135, John Byrne scored 127 in the 1896 tour of South Africa and David Hewitt with 112 and Terry Davies with 104 had both topped the century during the 1959 tour of Australia, New Zealand and Canada. Hiller, however was to come back into the news must three years later, when he was selected for the 1971 Lions side to tour in Australia and New Zealand.

JOHN DAWES'S LIONS

In what was to become the finest tour in the long history of the Lions, John Dawes of Wales led his men to Australia and New Zealand in 1971 and they came home with the proud record of playing 26 games, winning 23, losing two, drawing one and scoring 580 points while conceding 231. In the New Zealand portion of the tour they played 24, won 22, drew one, lost one and scored 555 points and gave away 204. Most important of all, however, was the fact that in New Zealand, they beat the All-Blacks twice, drew once in their four games and became the first Lions to win a series against the New Zealanders. To add to that they went through their campaign of provincial matches without losing one. Their top points scorer was Barry John of Wales with 188 points from 28 penalty goals, eight drop goals, 31 conversions and six tries. This, of course, made him the most prolific Lions scorer of all time since the first touring side travelled to South Africa in 1891. The previous record had been held by C. Y. Adamson of the 1899 side which had toured in Australia. Some authorities credit John with having scored seven tries on this tour for a total of 191 points but in his own book, published in 1974, he gives his total as 188. The top try-scorer was also a Welsh international, John Bevan with 18. This made Bevan the fourth top try scorer for a tour behind R. L. Aston (England) who had 30 in the tour of South Africa in 1891, Tony O'Reilly who had 22 in 1959, and Larry Bulger (Ireland), who had 20 in the 1896 tour to South Africa. Ireland's O'Reilly, of course, remains as the top Lions try scorer with his 22 in New Zealand and Australia in 1959 and the 16 he scored four years earlier in the 1955 tour of South Africa.

38 POINTS AHEAD

The 1971 Lions greatest margin of victory was their 38 points in the defeat of Wellington at Wellington on 5th June, 1971 by 47-9. In this game, their fifth successive victory in New Zealand, John Bevan scored four tries, Mike Gibson had two and John Taylor, Barry John and Sandy Carmichael had one each. Barry John also kicked five conversions and two penalty goals for a personal total of 19 points and John Williams and Mike Gibson had a conversion each. The Lions worst defeat was 12-22 in the second international game against New Zealand on 10th July at Christchurch.

JOHN'S FIRST RECORD

When Barry John ran on to the field at Wellington on 6th July, 1971 to turn out for the Lions against the New Zealand Universities, he was just six points away from equalling a 34-year old record. During the South Africans tour of New Zealand in 1937, full-back Gerry Brand had scored an exact century of points, the most ever put up by a tourist down under. It took John no time at all to equal the record. He started off with two penalty goals to bring his total to 100 and then just before half-time he scampered through a bewildered Universities defence for a fine try which he then converted. In those 40 minutes he had taken the record to 105 points. But he was far from finished. He landed another penalty goal, dropped a goal and kicked two further conversions for a total of 21 points from the game and he walked off the field with the new tourist record of 115 points. Eventually, of course, he was to take that record to 188 points in New Zealand. In all, Barry John was to make 17 appearances during the 1971 tour and he finished by scoring in all 17. His lowest contribution was his one conversion in the game against the North Auckland side on 7th August.

A RECORD FOR HILLER

England's full-back Bob Hiller wound up his international career with the sad distinction of playing in two Lions tours without ever playing in an international game for the touring side. But, with his scoring feats in Australia and New Zealand he set one of the Lions finest records. During the 1968 tour in South Africa he had topped the century mark of points with 104 and in 1971 he did even better with 110 points from 25 conversions, 16 penalty goals, two tries and two drop goals. Between the 1968 and 1971 tours he made just 19 appearances, all against provincial sides and is the only Lion to score successive centuries of points. With his full total of 214 points from 19 appearances for the Lions he averaged better than 11 points per game.

A RUDE START

In the light of what was to follow, the 1971 Lions could hardly have got away to a worse start to their tour of Australia and New Zealand. After a training session under floodlights, they took on Queensland at Ballymore Park, Brisbane on 12th May and with a record crowd present to watch the tourists, the Lions got off to a rude and somewhat shattering awakening. They started with an impressive flourish with a penalty goal from Bob Hiller in the second minute and the general feeling among the crowd at that stage was that they were about to see the annihilation of poor old Queensland. But Jeff McLean, the Australian international, kicked two penalty goals and full-back Lloyd Graham dropped a goal and the scoreboard had a surprise look about it at half-time with the Lions trailing by 3-9. Graham dropped a second goal in the second half to stretch the lead to 12-3 and although John Spencer went in for a try which Hiller converted, Bob Miller put a further three points on the board with a penalty goal. The game was in injury time when Hiller landed a great penalty goal but by then it was too late to save the Lions from going down to defeat by 11-15.

NEW SOUTH WALES BEATEN

After their initial defeat by Queensland, it was confidently expected that the Lions would wind up with a second defeat in Australia when they met the powerful New South Wales side, led by Australian international Greg Davis, at Sydney Oval on 15th May. But, by now the Lions had recovered from the fatigues and time lag of their flight from England and they were quite a different proposition. Barry John kicked his first points of the tour with a penalty goal, John Dawes went over for a try which John converted and the Lions were eight points up in 12 minutes. Arthur McGill, the Australian international full-back, kicked a penalty but John Bevan went over for his first try of the tour and the half-time score was 11-3. The rest of the game was a matter of penalty kicks. Barry John kicked one and Arthur McGill kicked three and the final score was 14-12 for the Lions. It was the Lions first win on that afternoon of 12th May. They were not to taste defeat again until 10th July.

TWELVE ON THE TROT

The 1971 Lions played their first game in New Zealand at Pukekohe on 22nd May and won it easing up by 25-3, and from there on it was an unbeaten record all the way for 12 successive games, leading up to the first international meeting with New Zealand at Dunedin on 26th June. At that stage they had run up 307 points and conceded 110. Under the captaincy of Colin Meads, the All-Blacks attacked strongly in the opening minutes, which were to bring tragedy for the Lions. Gareth Edwards was injured and taken off the field and his replacement was "Chico" Hopkins. The All-Blacks maintained their powerful pressure, but all against the run of the play, the first score of the game came from the Lions and from their prop-forward Ian "Mighty Mouse" McLauchlan. It was to be McLauchlan's only score of the tour but it was a vital one which turned the first international game. Although Fergie McCormick kicked a penalty goal to level the scores before half-time, Barry John restored the lead with a penalty goal after 16 minutes of the second half and wrapped it all up for the Lions with a second penalty goal just on time. It was the first time since 1930 that the Lions had beaten the All-Blacks in the opening game of an international series.

THE ALL-BLACKS STRIKE BACK

Fergie McCormick of Canterbury, who had worn the All-Blacks jersey on 43 occasions since 1965, had to shoulder most of the blame for New Zealand's defeat in the first international at Dunedin. He had missed several easy penalty attempts and the selectors duly punished him by dropping him for the second international against the Lions at Christchurch on 10th July. L. W. Mains was given his first international cap at full-back and he marked the occasion by scoring seven points in his debut. New Zealand opened the scoring with a try from Ron Burgess and their next try came from Sid Going and was converted by Mains which put the All-Blacks ahead 8-3 to the Lions try scored by Gerald Davies. Barry John kicked a goal just before half-time to leave it 8-6 at the break. The referee, J. P. Pring of Auckland, awarded a penalty try to New Zealand in the second half after Gerald Davies had tackled Bryan Williams from behind just when it looked as though the All-Blacks wing-threequarter was about to fall on the ball over the Lions line. Mains converted to put the All-Blacks ahead by 13-6. Burgess then added another try and after Davies had scored a second try, Mains put over a penalty to make it 19-9. Ian Kirkpatrick had the final try for the All-Blacks and Barry John dropped a goal to leave the scoreboard at 22-12. The series was square and New Zealand were confident again.

LOCHORE'S RETURN

In a desperate bid to give deeper strength to their pack, the New Zealand selectors brought the great Brian Lochore out of his retirement to play in the third international match against the Lions at Athletic Park, Wellington on 31st July, 1971. But well though Lochore played, it was not enough to halt the Lions from scoring their second international win. Within the space of 18 fateful minutes the Lions scored 13 points and as a game it was all over. After three minutes a quick pass from Mike Gibson to Barry John saw the Welshman drop a goal. Gerald Davies went surging in for a try and John was on the mark with the conversion and then John went in for a try on his own and he converted that, too. New Zealand's only score came in the second half from full-back L. A. Mains with a try. With this win, the Lions had ensured a share of the series. Everything now depended on the final international at Eden Park, Auckland a fortnight later.

HISTORY AT LAST

The New Zealanders made five changes for the final international game at Eden Park, Auckland on Saturday, 14th August, 1971. The Lions decided to field the same side that had won the third international game. And this, of course, was the game that was to be the Lions finest hour—even though it ended in an honourable draw. The All-Blacks took the lead after five minutes with a try from W. D. Cottrell and L. W. Mains kicked the conversion. Eight minutes later Mains kicked a penalty goal and the All-Blacks were into an 8-0 lead. Barry John kicked a penalty goal to narrow the gap and then Peter Dixon went over for a try which John converted and it was 8-8 at half-time. Two minutes after the start of the second half John kicked a penalty goal but T. N. Lister again brought the scores level with a try. Within five minutes the Lions were in the lead again with a magnificent drop goal by John Williams but just before full-time Dixon was caught offside and Mains kicked the vital penalty goal that drew the game. A great finish to a great tour and it brought the Lions their first win in a series over New Zealand and, indeed, their first series win in any tour of the century.

JOHN AND MAINS

With the completion of the international series between the Lions and the All-Blacks, the aggregate scoring was 90 points of which the Lions had scored 48 to New Zealand's 42. Barry John wound up with the honour of having scored in all four internationals and he contributed 30 of the 48 points. L. W. Mains, the New Zealand full-back, who had made his debut in the second international game also had the distinction of scoring in each of the three internationals in which he played and he collected 18 of the All-Blacks 42 points. And perhaps the other significant personality of the series was Mr John Pring of Auckland. He was the referee in all four international games.

THE CANTERBURY AFFAIR

There were over 50,000 spectators at Lancaster Park, Christchurch on 19th June, 1971 to see the Lions take on Canterbury in the 11th match of the 1971 tour of Australia and New Zealand and what they saw made them eventually leave the stadium in silence. For this was to be one of the sad days of modern rugby football, a confrontation that was subsequently to be headlined as "The Game of Shame". The Lions won the game by 14-3 but their losses were heavy. Scotland's international Sandy Carmichael was brutally attacked and struck so often that he was partially blinded. Fergus Slattery, the Irish international had two of his front teeth badly damaged, both Mike Gibson and Gareth Edwards were kicked while lying on the ground, John Pullin was stretched by a punch, John Dawes was felled by a blow when he was not even close to the play and Ray McLoughlin had a bone smashed in his hand when he was eventually goaded into retaliation. In all, nine of the Lions players needed medical attention and, indeed, as a result of that afternoon at Lancaster Park both Sandy Carmichael and Ray McLoughlin were finished with the tour and subsequently returned home. It was a day that even the most fervent of Canterbury supporters wanted to forget in a hurry.

THE GOINGS

Sid Going, who at the start of the 1974-1975 season had made 62 appearances in the All-Blacks jersey since his debut against Australia in 1967, played six times against the 1971 Lions in New Zealand. He appeared in all four international games and also played for the New Zealand Maoris and for North Auckland against the Lions. In the North Auckland game, played at Whangerei on 7th August, he was joined by his two brothers, Ken T. Going and B. L. Going, which marked the only occasion during the 1971 tour that three brothers had played in the one game against the Lions. Going's first appearance against the Lions in 1971—and he was joined by his brother Ken in this game—was for the New Zealand Maoris at Auckland on 2nd June and they went down to a 12-23 defeat. This was another of the more unsavoury games of the tour and Sean Lynch, the Irish prop-forward, picked up a most unwanted record shortly after the start. Coming away from a line-out Lynch, who was to become one of the great successes of the tour, was clobbered savagely and dropped in his tracks by one of the Maori forwards. Lynch had to retire from the game after 14 minutes and that injury cost him a stitch in the face for every minute he had been on the field. His 14 stitches on the face was one of the unhappy individual records of the tour.

THE LIONS SHARE

Cardiff Rugby Football Club, founded in 1876, and which in 1948 had the supreme honour of providing 10 members of the Welsh international side that met Scotland, also has the proud record of having supplied a record number of players to the Lions touring sides up to the end of the 1973-1974 season. In the tours that began with the trip to South Africa in 1891 and up to and including the Lions tour of South Africa in 1974, Cardiff hold the club record of having provided 30 Lions players.

THE BALLYMENA GIANT

Bill McBride, the genial 6' 3", 16st 8lb second row forward from Ballymena, Co. Antrim, led the 1974 Lions to South Africa and brought them back home with an unbeaten record in 22 games. They won 21 drew one and scored 729 points while conceding 207. In between the 1974 Lions set up a constant stream of records and the giant McBride collected a few to add to his own magnificent collection. This was a record fifth Lions tour for him—at the time it was two more than any other had made—and by playing in all four games against South Africa he took his number of international appearances to the all-time record of 17. Prior to leaving for South Africa, McBride had set a world record of 57 international caps with Ireland and that with his 17 caps for the Lions, plus an additional one for Ireland when he led the Irish XV against the President's XV on Saturday, 7th September, 1974, took his grand total of international rugby appearances to a majestic 75 at the start of the 1974-1975 season.

A FLYING START

Back in 1955, Robin Thompson's Lions had opened their tour of South Africa at Potchefstroom and had got off to a depressing start by losing their first game. Bill McBride's 1974 Lions also began their tour of South Africa at Potchefstroom but they did it in style by walloping Western Transvaal to the tune of 59-13. That was the highest score ever registered by a Lions side in South Africa up to that time. There was, however, better to come. McBride's men followed this by beating South West Africa 23-16, Boland 33-6, Eastern Province 28-14 . . . and then they took on South-Western Districts at Mossel Bay on 29th May. This was to be a most significant milestone in the history of the Lions. They won by 97-0 to set an all-time record for Lions scoring in any tour. This was also the highest number of points scored by a touring side in South Africa—12 more than the previous mark held by the All-Blacks with their 85-0 win over North-East Cape in 1970. The 16 tries scored in this game—they came from J. J. Williams (6), G. Evans (3), J. P. R. Williams (2), F. Slattery, M. Davies, J. Moloney, A. Old and T. Grace (one each), was also a record for the Lions. England's Alan Old collected 37 points in this match from a try, a penalty goal and 15 conversions and this gave him the record of the highest score by a touring player in any one game, the highest by a Lion in South Africa and, of course, also the highest by a Lion in any tour since 1891. J. J. Williams's six tries in this fixture was also a record for a Lion in South Africa and equalled the performance of David Duckham who got his six against West-Coast Buller on the 1971 Lions tour of Australia and New Zealand.

A PRESENT FOR BILL

Bill McBride was thirty-four on Thursday, 6th June, 1974 and two days later the Lions came up with a very special birthday present for him at Newlands. They beat South Africa by 12-3 and that was the Lions first win over the Springboks for 19 years and their first victory at Newlands since 1938. Snyman gave South Africa the lead with a drop goal after 22 minutes but Bennett brought the Lions level before half-time with a penalty goal. Bennett added two further penalty goals in the second half and Edwards dropped a goal to wrap it all up The Lions continued on their winning way and had 11 impressive wins behind them when they faced up to South Africa for the second international game at Pretoria on Saturday, 22nd June, 1974—and this turned out to be quite an afternoon for the tourists. Prior to this game, only two sides had ever scored five tries against South Africa in an international game—the Lions of 1955 and the All-Blacks in 1965. Bill McBride's men went one better—they scored six as the Lions went on to humiliate the Springboks by 28-9. This was the worst defeat South Africa had ever suffered in international rugby, the previous worst being the 3-20 beating they took from the All-Blacks in 1965. J. J. Williams scored two tries in this second international game of the tour and it marked the first time that a player had got two tries against the Springboks in South Africa.

THE SERIES WON

Following the victory in the second international, the Lions swept on to another five wins before the third international against South Africa at Port Elizabeth on Saturday, 13th July, 1974. And this was a game to bring more history. Before 55,000 spectators at the Erasmus Stadium, it was never a contest as the Lions romped to a 26-9 victory. J. J. Williams duplicated his record of the second international game by scoring two tries, Gordon Brown had another, Phil Bennett dropped two goals and Andy Irvine kicked two penalty goals and a conversion. And Brown's try had a depressing significance for the South Africans. It brought the total of points scored against South Africa in international rugby to exactly 1,000.

FIRST THIS CENTURY

By winning the third international, the Lions had beaten South Africa in a series for the first time in this century and after that all that really remained was whether or not the tourists could achieve the Grand Slam by winning all four international games. But it was not to be. With 21 wins behind them, a record for a touring side in South Africa, McBride's men played the last game of the tour, against South Africa, at Ellis Park, Johannesburg on Saturday, 27th July, 1974—and at the end the scoreboard showed 13-13. Snyman put the Springboks into an early lead with a penalty goal, then Uttley had a try for the Lions which Bennett converted but Snyman with a second penalty goal levelled the scores, before Irvine put the Lions into a 10-6 lead at half-time with a try. In the second half South Africa came level with a try from Cronje and then moved ahead with a third penalty goal from Snyman. Before the end, however, Irvine, with a penalty goal brought the scores to 13-13 and that was that, although in the very last minute Ireland's Fergus Slattery appeared to have got over for a try which referee Mr Max Baise ruled out.

THE LAST ANALYSIS

The 729 points scored by Bill McBride's 1974 Lions now stands as the highest number of points by a touring side in South Africa and is made up of 107 tries, 59 conversions, 56 penalty goals and five drop goals

Scotland's Andy Irvine was top scorer with 156 points from five tries, 26 conversions, 27 penalty goals and one drop goal in 15 appearances and shattered the previous Lions record in South Africa held by James Byrne with 127 since 1896. Phil Bennett also topped the century mark with 103 points from a try, 15 conversions, 21 penalty goals and two drop goals in his 11 appearances. Gordon Brown also came home with a record. He scored eight tries, two of them in the international games—the highest ever registered by a forward in a tour of South Africa. The 79 points scored by the Lions over South Africa in the four-match international series is also a record against the Springboks in a series and the Lions 107 tries in their 22 games is also a record for a tour of South Africa. In the four international games the Lions used only 17 players . . . and South Africa made use of a record 32, including 20 new caps!

ALL THE LIONS

Beginning with the trip to South Africa in 1891 and up to the end of the 1973-1974 season 468 players have been honoured with selection on touring sides from these islands. England have contributed the top number with 182, Wales comes next with 122, Ireland are third with 90 and Scotland have provided 74. It was not until the tour to South Africa in 1924 that the touring sides became truly representative of England, Scotland, Ireland and Wales and since then the number of Lions has been 222, with 76 from Wales, 56 from England, 48 from Ireland and 42 from Scotland.

THE INTERNATIONALS

The first international game ever played by the Lions was by W. E. Maclagan's side against South Africa at Port Elizabeth on Thursday, 30th July, 1891 and they played their 75th and last at Ellis Park, Johannesburg on Saturday, 27th July, 1974, when Bill McBride's men met South Africa. In the 75 international games they have played the Lions have won 30, lost 36, drawn nine and have scored 748 points and conceded 795.

AGAINST THE ALL-BLACKS

With the completion of the 1971 tour in New Zealand, the Lions had met the All-Blacks on 24 occasions and their record is very much on the debit side. Of the 24 games, the All-Blacks have won 17 and the Lions have won 4 with three drawn. The All-Blacks have scored 337 points to the Lions 187. The highest score registered by the All-Blacks was their 32 points in the first international of 1908 in which they defeated the Lions by 32-5. The highest number of points scored against the All-Blacks in an international meeting was the 17 in going down to a 17-18 defeat at Dunedin on 18th July, 1959.

JOHN WILLIAMS'S DROP GOAL

When John Williams, the Welsh full-back, sent a superb drop kick sailing straight and true between the posts at Eden Park, Auckland on Saturday, 14th August, 1971, he scored the last three points that have been registered against the All-Blacks by the Lions. And it took the Lions total in their 159 matches in New Zealand since 1904 to 2,565. L. W. Mains scored New Zealand's final penalty in that drawn game at Auckland in 1971 and his three points brought the All-Blacks total against the Lions since 1904 to 1,337. The Lions full record in New Zealand, including international games is that they have played 159, won 113, lost 36 and drawn 10, scoring 2,565 points and conceding 1,337.

AGAINST THE AUSSIES

The Lions have a most impressive record against the Australians. They lost the first international in 1899 and then went on an unbeaten run until the Wallabies defeated them by 6-5 in 1930. In all the Lions have played Australia 14 times, have won 12 and lost two and have scored 219 points while conceding 58. Their highest aggregate of points in a series against Australia was in 1899 when they scored 50 points while giving away only three in three games.

THE AUSTRALIANS TO DATE

At Sydney on 15th May, 1971, the Lions led by John Dawes beat New South Wales by 14-12 and their scorers were Dawes himself with a try, John Bevan with a try and Barry John with two penalty goals and a conversion. Those 14 points brought the Lions all-time total for games in Australia to 1,710 points. Their overall record in Australia since 1888 is that they have played 89 games, including internationals, and have won 76, lost only 10 and drawn three. Against the 1,710 points they have scored, they have conceded 567.

THE SPRINGBOK CONFRONTATION

The Lions began their long series of international games against the Springboks by winning the first six games against South Africa. The South Africans, however, took over after that and with 36 matches now played, the score stands in South Africa's favour with 17 victories to the Lions 13 with six games drawn. In the 36 matches played the Lions have scored 223 points and the Springboks have scored 314. The highest aggregate of points reached by the Springboks in a series with the Lions came in 1955 when they totalled 75 points in four games. The Lions reached their highest aggregate in the 1974 series with 79 points from the four games, three of which they won.

THE LAST FROM IRVINE

Scotland's Andy Irvine kicked the last penalty goal for the Lions in their 22nd and final match of the 1974 tour of South Africa and those three points against South Africa at Ellis Park, Johannesburg on Saturday, 27th July, 1974 brought the Lions total of points in South Africa since 1891 to 3,512. Their full record is that the Lions have played 220 games in South Africa, of which they have won 157, lost 46, drawn 17 and have conceded 1,714 points.

THE GRAND TOTAL

Starting with the first match played by A. E. Stoddart's side against Otago in New Zealand in 1888 and ending with the final game by Bill McBride's men at Ellis Park, Johannesburg on Saturday, 27th July, 1974, the Lions have played 474 games, including international matches. Of these they have won 351, lost 93, drawn 30 and in the process of the 474 games have scored 8,181 points and conceded 3,655 points.

NEW ZEALAND

THE PIONEERS

Although they are now designated the "Maoris", the first tourists to play in Britain and Ireland were, in fact, the New Zealand Native Side. The party of 26, which was led by Joe Warbrick, included 22 Maoris but four others, Patrick Keogh, William Elliott, Christopher Madigan and George Williams, were brought in to strengthen the side. All 26 players, however, were natives of New Zealand. The tourists played their first game in England on 3rd October, 1888 and celebrated it with a good win over Surrey and they finished 25 weeks later against the Southern Counties on 27th March, 1889. In those 25 weeks they played an astonishing number of 74 games, including three official international games and the final tally was that they won 49, drew five and lost 20. They scored 394 points and conceded 188. Their most outstanding wins were over Ireland, Swansea, Newport, Yorkshire, Gloucestershire, Somersetshire, Blackheath, Halifax and Manchester and their worst defeats came from Middlesex and Halifax. On leaving England, they travelled to Australia to continue the tour and finally ended it off in New Zealand with another 17 games before they disbanded. In all, between Britain, Ireland, Australia and New Zealand, the New Zealand Native side played 107 successive games, of which they won 78, drew six and lost 23. Their points tally at the end was 772 for and 305 against.

THE FIRST CAPTAIN

Joe Warbrick of Hawke's Bay, one of the first memorable personalities of New Zealand rugby, not only captained the New Zealand Native Side of 1888-1889, he was also the prime mover behind the adventure to Britain and Ireland. With the help of James Scott, who was to become the tour manager, and Thomas Eyton, who acted as treasurer during the tour, he organised the entire affair and finally got it under way. The Warbricks were well represented in the playing party of 26—

his brothers, Arthur, Albert, William and Frederick also travelled. James Scott, however, was probably the vital man on this tour. Right from the start he realised that to keep the tour going, money would be essential and to ensure a constant flow, he arranged the staggering programme of 74 games in Britain and Ireland. Prior to the tour, there were more than suggestions and hints that the members of the New Zealand Native side were not strictly amateurs but it is on record that the entire tour in Britain and Ireland was conducted on the most stringent amateur lines. The English Rugby Union insisted that all accounts should be submitted to them for scrutiny.

A LITTLE ON THE BUSY SIDE

One can only wonder how a playing member of a modern touring side would look at the incredible programme which the New Zealand Native Side of 1888-1889 faced during their tour of Britain and Ireland. The month of November, 1888, was a particularly busy one. They played in Northumberland on 3rd November, Stockton on 5th November, Tynemouth on 7th November, Halifax on 10th November, Newcastle on 12th November, Hartlepool on 14th November, Cumberland on 17th November, Carlisle on 20th November, Hawick on 22nd November, Cumberland again on 23rd November, Westmoreland on 24th November, Swinton on 25th November and Liverpool on 28th November. To cap all that, they crossed to Dublin on 29th November and on 1st December, they took on Ireland in a full international at Lansdowne Road and won it by 13-4!

QUITE AN ARGUMENT

The New Zealand Native Side of 1888-1889 had their views about certain interpretations of the laws of rugby. So too had the English and Welsh sides they met. Unfortunately, the views clashed strongly and were a much-publicised bone of contention from beginning to end of the tour. The climax, an unhappy one, was reached in England's international game with the tourists at Blackheath on 16th February, 1899. This was England's only international game of that season and they duly won it—but not without fierce argument. It seems that at half-time, Mr Rowland Hill, the referee announced he had awarded a try to England towards the end of the first half, even though at the time it appeared that Harry Lee had grounded the ball before any Englishman had touched it. This angered the tourists—but there was worse to follow. Right after the start of the second half, R. T. Ellison made a tackle on England's Andrew Stoddart and in the process, ripped the Englishman's knicks from him. Play stopped while the New Zealanders made a ring around Stoddart. But while this was going on, one of the English forwards, Frank Evershed picked up the ball and raced off to the corner flag where he touched down for a try. The remaining New Zealanders promptly disputed the legality of the try and while the argument was going on with Mr Hill, the same Evershed picked up the ball again, walked with it to the posts and claimed the try there. The referee awarded the try, the goal was kicked—and with that five of the New Zealanders walked off the field. Play was held up for a considerable period. Joe Warbrick eventually managed to get his men back on the field but, by all accounts, the New Zealanders lost a great deal of interest in the proceedings after that. Fortunately, the same accounts also add that full harmony was restored between everyone at the pleasant function which followed the game.

PLAY UP NEW ZEALAND!

The New Zealand Native Side of 1888-1889 brought at least two sets of kit with them, but both were definitely all-black. One set carried a breast badge, which depicted a set of goalposts, a rugby ball, the New Zealand silver fern and carried underneath the words—"Play Up, New Zealand". In the official team photograph for the game against England at Blackheath, the team members wore an all-black strip and the only emblem on the jersey was the silver fern on a badge which was in the shape of a rugby ball. The black jerseys had white collars and all the players wore short black-and-white ties.

THE INTERNATIONALS

The 1888-1889 New Zealand Native Side played three international games during the tour and all the members of the three sides which faced them—Ireland, England, Wales—were awarded caps. The New Zealanders, however, collected nothing but the honour of playing.

They were never recognised as New Zealand international players. The New Zealanders beat Ireland on 1st December, 1888 by four goals and a try to a goal and a try. At Swansea, they were beaten by Wales, by a goal and two tries to nil and lost to England by a goal and four tries to nil. At the time a goal counted three points and a try just one point.

THE TOP SCORER

Pat Keogh, who claimed after the defeat of Ireland that his father living back in New Zealand would never forgive him for scoring a try against the "old sod", was one of the four non-Maoris in the 1888-1889 touring side and was their most prolific scorer with 34 tries, which has since been surpassed on a tour only by Jimmy Hunter of New Zealand in 1905-1906. Keogh was one of the great personalities of the side and his unorthodox play at half-back completely upset some of the sides he opposed during the tour. There is even a story that on one occasion, he picked up the ball after a scrum, tucked it neatly under his jersey and raced 30 yards to score a try before anyone realised that the ball had disappeared! Two years later Keogh was declared a professional by the New Zealand rugby authorities.

A NEW ZEALAND NATIVE

Colonel Wynward, with his 57th Regiment, was despatched from England to New Zealand to put an end to the Waikato War and having accomplished his mission, he liked New Zealand so much that he remained there for several years. His son W. T. Wynward was one of the first to take an interest in the new game of rugby in New Zealand and became quite a proficient player and, in fact, although an Englishman by birth, he was a member of the first touring side to visit Britain and Ireland. He was one of the top performers in the backline for Joe Warbrick's New Zealand Native Side which in 1888-1889 performed the prodigious feat of playing 74 games in 25 weeks. Although W. T. Wynward was never to be named as an All-Black, his grandson J. G. Wynward toured in Britain and Ireland and France with Jack Manchester's New Zealand side of 1935-1936 and before his retirement in 1938 had worn the All-Blacks jersey in 13 matches, although he never played in an international game for New Zealand.

OPAI'S TRY

New Zealand, with a backbone of the men who were to form the all-conquering All-Blacks side which toured in Britain, Ireland and France in 1905-1906, played their first official international game on 15th August, 1903 and duly won it by the impressive margin of 22-3. Billy Wallace, later to become one of the immortals of rugby football had the honour of scoring New Zealand's first points in international football with a penalty goal and he wound up this particular game with a total of 13 points. New Zealand's first try in international rugby came from "Opai" Asher shortly after the start of the second half. Albert Asher, who stood little over 5' was one of the game's great personalities in New Zealand at the time but this match in Australia was, in fact, his only international appearance in the All-Blacks jersey. Subsequently he turned to the new rugby league game and later toured in Australia with the Maori league side.

A TOUGH PREPARATION

The New Zealand side to tour in Britain, Ireland and France in 1905-1906 went through a tough preparation before leaving for England. Part of the touring side travelled to Australia to play two games against New South Wales in July, 1905 and then the full Australian side came to New Zealand to play the All-Blacks. All the games were won and the New Zealanders set sail with an undefeated record. During the 1905-1906 tour, which also embraced games on the way back home against British Columbia, Canada, the New Zealanders played 35 games, won 33, lost one and scored an all-time record of 976 points and conceded only 59. Their top scorer was Billy Wallace with 246 points from the 26 games in which he played.

A RETURN VISIT

When he arrived in Britain with the All-Blacks touring side of 1905-1906, wing-threequarter G. W. Smith was making a return visit to England. Three years earlier, he had made the trip to win the British A.A.A. 220 yards hurdles championship with a time of 16.0 seconds. Smith, regarded as the fastest back in international rugby at the beginning of the century was New Zealand 100 yards champion in 1898, 1899, 1900, 250 yards champion in 1900, 120 yards hurdles champion in 1899, 1901, 1903 and 440 yards hurdles champion in 1897, 1898, 1899, 1901 and 1902. Smith wound up as second top try scorer of the 1905-1906 tour with 20 tries in Britain and Ireland. He collected four tries in the first game against Devon but following an injury in the match against the West of Scotland, he was forced to miss six games before returning to score his 20th try against Glamorgan.

A CASUAL AFFAIR

The 6,000 spectators, who turned up at Exeter on 16th September, 1905 to see the All-Blacks open their tour of Britain, Ireland and France with a game against Devon, got quite a surprise when the tourists romped away to a 55-4 victory. But, it is on record, that they were even more surprised at the turn out of New Zealand's full-back, George Gillett. He played throughout the game, wearing . . . a soft hat! But then as England international Leonard Tosswill, who had won three caps in 1902, pointed out: "Gillett had little to do. He touched the ball only twice during the game". Not to be outdone, the great Billy Wallace turned out in the next game against Cornwall, wearing a floppy sun hat. He, too, had little to do at full-back in the way of defensive work, but managed to get himself among the scorers with a try and four conversions. By the end of the tour and including the final stages in Canada, Wallace had become the top tour scorer of all time in rugby history with the massive total of 246 points from 26 games.

THE TOP WIN

The New Zealander tourists of 1905-1906 recorded their most decisive victory at West Hartlepool, on 11th October, 1905. Before 20,000 spectators, they hammered the Hartlepools by 63-0. G. Smith scored their first try after five minutes and this was converted by Billy Wallace. At the end when the tally was counted up Jimmy Hunter had scored four tries, Henry Abbot, three, Smith and Frank Roberts two each and Wallace, Bob Deans, John Stead and John O'Sullivan had scored one each. Wallace converted nine of the tries to bring his personal total for the romp to 21.

With 831 points against 22 from 27 overwhelming victories, the All-Blacks of 1905-1906 moved into Wales on Thursday, 14th December, 1905 to face Wales, Glamorgan, Newport, Cardiff and Swansea. All five games, the hardest of the tour, were to be completed on 30th December. On 13th December, the All-Blacks had routed Yorkshire at Leeds by 40-0 and spent most of the following day on the long and tiring journey to Cardiff. Two days later, a record crowd saw the referee Mr J. D. Dallas of Scotland, call the teams together for the kick-off—and it was easy to see the said Mr Dallas. He wore ordinary clothes, even to an orthodox wing collar and wore ordinary walking shoes. Wales eventually won the game—but the controversy over the try that New Zealand's threequarter R. G. Deans did or did not score can still provoke bitter and long argument in New Zealand and Wales. Wales went ahead after 23 minutes with a try from the flying Teddy Morgan and that was still the position five minutes from time. Then Deans, in a breakaway by the All-Blacks took a pass close to the touchline inside the Welsh "25" and as he claimed afterwards, he grounded the ball over the Welsh line and was then pulled back by a Welsh player. The referee, all of 30 yards behind the play, decided, however, that Deans had been "held up" and ordered a scrum back. The New Zealanders were sore and, indeed, on the following day, Deans sent the following telegram to the Daily Mail in London; "Grounded ball six inches over line. Some of Welsh players admit try. Hunter and Glasgow can confirm was pulled back by Welshmen before referee arrived—Deans". The Welsh, of course, denied emphatically that it was a try and so the immortal "Deans Controversy" began. To his dying day, which, unfortunately, was in 1908, Deans always insisted that his try was genuine and as late as 1924, one or two Welshmen agreed that it was. But the score of Teddy Morgan remained and New Zealand had lost their first game of the tour and their first international. They then went on to finish off their tour in Britain by beating Glamorgan 9-0 on 21st December, Newport 6-3 on 23rd December, Cardiff 10-8 on 26th December and Swansea 4-3 on 30th December. Their last score, a drop goal was, fittingly, kicked by their top scorer, Billy Wallace.

SOME HUNTER!

The twenty-six-year old Jimmy Hunter, a five-eight from Taranaki, began the New Zealand 1905-1906 tour of Britain, Ireland and France with two tries in the All-Blacks rout of Devon by 55-4 at Exeter on 16th September, 1905. He eventually wound up the tour with a total of 42 tries which is still the all-time record for any player on an international touring side. The 5' 6" Hunter scored in 16 games and on three occasions, against Northumberland, Oxford University and Bedford, he went over for five tries. His sequence in his 16 scoring games was: 2, 3, 2, 2, 2, 1, 4, 5, 1, 2, 5, 1, 5, 2, 2, 3.

FIVE ON THE TROT

Duncan McGregor of Canterbury became the first New Zealand player and still the only one to score five consecutive tries in international games when he ran in the first three for the All-Blacks against England at the Crystal Palace, London, on 2nd December, 1905. And he is still the only All-Black to score four tries in an international game. McGregor, a wing-threequarter, had played for New Zealand in the last international against the Lions in 1904 and had scored the second and third tries in the All-Blacks 9-3 win. His next cap came against England in 1905 and he scored the first three tries before half-time. Subsequently he scored a fourth try in this game but his sequence was interrupted by the forward F. Newton, who scored New Zealand's fourth try in their win by five tries to nil.

A ROUGH EDUCATION

One of the most unusual overseas trips made by a New Zealand touring side was in 1913 when they took off for the United States and Canada. This was to be an "educational" affair for the Canadians and the Americans—and it certainly was. The New Zealanders engaged in 16 games, scored the massive total of 610 points and managed to concede six! The New Zealand side was led by Alex McDonald, who had been a member of the famous 1905-1906 side which had toured in Britain, Ireland and France. Their visit, however, was to have a profound effect on rugby at the San Francisco Olympic Club, Stanford University, the University of California and the Los Angeles club, all of whom were beaten by wide margins. Just seven years later, an American team, composed in the main from members of these sides, was to win the Olympic rugby final at Antwerp in 1920 and in 1924, quite a few of the 1920 team were back again to lead America to a second successive Olympic victory. Four American rugby players, Charles Doe, John O'Neill, John Patrick and Rudy Scholz won two Olympic gold medals each and are, of course, unique in the history of rugby.

THE WORST EVER?

When the final whistle blew at Eden Park on Wednesday, 23rd July, 1924, over 25,000 spectators poured on to the pitch to chair off their local heroes. There could be no question but that Auckland, winners by 14-3, had proved a significant point. As far as the spectators and the Auckland players were concerned, this victory demonstrated conclusively that Auckland had been treated with a biased disapproval by the New Zealand selectors. The following morning's newspapers in Auckland echoed the feelings of everyone in Auckland. Their honest and much publicised opinions were that Auckland's opponents the day previously were downright bad and, unquestionably, the worst ever to wear the New Zealand jerseys. The opponents? Cliff Porter's All-Blacks, who, less than a week later, were to sail to Plymouth, England, to begin the 1924-1925 tour of Britain, Ireland and France!

THE INVINCIBLES

Nineteen years after the first All-Blacks had made their first appearance in England against Devon—and almost to the day—the second All-Blacks opened their 1924 tour of Britain, Ireland, France and Canada at Devonport on 13th September, 1924 and their game, too, was against Devon. This time, however, the opening victory was not quite so spectacular. The New Zealanders, led by Cliff Porter, won 11-0. They took 30 minutes to get their first score and to K. S. "Snowy" Svenson went the honour of their first try on the tour. A. E. Cooke added a second, which was converted by George Nepia and H. W. Browne got a third try just after half-time. But after this uneasy start, the 1924-1925 All-Blacks went on to set one of rugby's greatest records. They played 30 games in Britain, Ireland and France, won all 30 and scored 721 points and conceded 112. They finished off the tour in Canada with a win by 49-0 over Vancouver and a win over Victoria by 68-4. Ever since, the 1924-1925 New Zealanders have been known as "The Invincibles".

PARKER'S THREE

The 1924-1925 New Zealanders moved in to Wales for the first time on 27th September, 1924 to take on Swansea and they confessed to being just a little apprehensive about the game. There was still the bitter memory of the All-Blacks controversial defeat by Wales in 1905, plus the fact that in the very last game of that tour 19 years earlier, they had just scraped home by 4-3 against Swansea in the last game of the tour in Britain and Ireland. And, by all the pre-match promises this time, Swansea planned to do much better. It was not to be, however. The All-Blacks struck their first really impressive form of the 1924-1925 tour and surged away to an astonishing 39-3 victory. Indeed, the only little comfort for Swansea after this totally unexpected annihilation was that they had scored the first points of the tour against the All-Blacks. Dai Parker, winner of 10 caps for Wales, kicked a penalty goal—and even that was a mite fortunate. The ball bounced on the cross bar before dropping over.

A SUCCESSFUL PLEA

The first major and unpleasant incident of the 1924-1925 tour of Britain, Ireland and France by Cliff Porter's All-Blacks came against Newport at Newport on 2nd October, 1924. Midway through the second half, at a stage where the proceedings had become more than a little rough, the New Zealand threequarter Gus Harte was knocked unconscious in a late tackle by one of the Newport forwards. The referee, one Mr Albert Freethy of Neath, who was destined to play a more publicised role in the story of the 1924-1925 tour, promptly ordered the Newport forward Tom Jones to the line. And Jones would certainly have gone off but for the intervention of Cliff Porter and his men. They pleaded for leniency and after a short discussion, Mr Freethy allowed Jones to remain on the field. The same Mr Freethy, however, was not to be so lenient, three months later, when New Zealand met England at Twickenham.

" HERE, FRED, YOU TAKE IT OVER THE LINE
—I'M NOT IN A MOOD FOR ADULATION ... "

A MINUTE TO SPARE

With 81 points in their bag from their opening five games in which they had conceded only three points, the 1924 All-Blacks took the field against Newport and, as it transpired, this turned out to be their closest game of the tour. They came within just a minute of defeat. Billy Friend scored for Newport in the first half and Jack Wetter, then the captain of Wales, converted the try to put the local club up by 5-0 at half-time. Twenty minutes of the second half were to go by before the New Zealanders scored. From a scrum in front of the Welsh posts, their scrum-half J. J. Mill got over for a try and Mark Nicholls converted to level matters. Nicholls then kicked a goal but within minutes Newport struck back with a try by G. E. Andrews, who was to be capped for Wales two years later. Fred Barker, the Newport full-back converted with a magnificent kick from the touch-line and Newport led by 10-8. Time was almost up when "Snowy" Svenson took a pass from Maurice Brownlie and with a tremendous run, scored far out. With the last kick of the game Nicholls got the convert and the New Zealander's unbeaten record remained intact.

DECISIVE BUT ROUGH

The New Zealanders most decisive victory in Britain and Ireland during their 1924-1925 tour was the 41-0 rout of Cumberland on 25th October, 1924 and, surprisingly, it was also one of their toughest and roughest games. The saddest feature of it was that at the final whistle, the All-Blacks threequarter Gus Hart, who had scored four tries, was struck by a Cumberland player and the All-Blacks did not take kindly to that. In the end the two teams were escorted to their dressing rooms by a police escort.

THE FIRST INTERNATIONAL

Ireland, captained by wing-threequarter Harry Stephenson, provided the first international opposition for Cliff Porter's 1924-1925 All-Blacks at Lansdowne Road, Dublin on 1st November, 1924 and it was quite stern and unexpected opposition. On an appallingly bad afternoon, the Irish held New Zealand scoreless for 60 minutes and then the All-Black

wing-threequarter "Snowy" Svenson went over for a try whic
George Nepia failed to convert. Five minutes later Mark Nicholl
kicked a penalty goal and that was that. Porter's comment after th
game was that it had been hard, "a little harder than we had anticipated
—he added.

REVENGE!

Revenge for 1905! That was the war-cry given to the All-Blacks o
1924-1925 before they set out for Britain, Ireland and France. This wa
the international game that counted—the one against Wales at S
Helen's, Swansea, on 29th November, 1924. Other games could b
lost and it would not matter, but let this one be lost and there would b
little welcome for the All-Blacks on their return home. But the Welsl
too, had their fierce pride in winning this game. They had been th
only country to lower the All-Blacks colours in 1905; another wi
now would put another glittering gem in their crown. Unfortunately
it was never really a battle. Mark Nicholls kicked a penalty goal fo
New Zealand after five minutes, Maurice Brownlie crashed over for
try a few minutes later and Nicholls added the extra two point:
Just on half-time W. E. Irvine came tearing out of the pack to launc
himself over for a try and the All-Blacks were 11-0 ahead. New Zealan
kept up the pressure in the second half. "Snowy" Svenson went ove
for a try and then Irvine added a second and with Nicholls again con
verting, the All-Blacks strode away to a record 19-0—a margin o
victory that was to stand as Wales's worst beating by a New Zealan
side until 1969 when they were beaten by 33-12 at Eden Park.

A SAD IMMORTALITY

Cyril Brownlie of Hawke's Bay played just eight minutes of Ne
Zealand's game against England at Twickenham on Saturday, 3r
January, 1925—and those eight minutes were to give him a sa
immortality in the history of rugby. In front of 60,000 spectator:
including the Prince of Wales, who had been introduced to both team
before the kick-off, the New Zealand forward was sent to the line—
the first man to be dismissed from an international game. Many version
of the "Brownlie Incident" have since been given, most of them to th

ffect that Brownlie, described as one of the most good-natured men of he 1924-1925 All-Blacks, was harshly and perhaps unfairly treated and punished. In a statement issued after the game by the referee, Mr Albert Freethy of Wales, he said: "In some loose play, the ball had been ent away and two or three English forwards were lying on the ground. C. Brownlie was a few feet away from them and as he came back he deliberately kicked the leg of an English forward who was lying ace downward on the ground. I had taken my eye off the ball for the moment and, therefore, I saw exactly what happened. Previous to this I had warned each side generally three times and, therefore, I had no option but to send Brownlie off the field. I much regretted having to do this but in the circumstances I had no alternative but to take this drastic action". This international, the fifth game that Mr Freethy had refereed in which the All-Blacks had played, was the last appearance of the 1924-1925 All-Blacks in Britain and Ireland and, despite playing with only 14 men, they won by 17-11 and thus wound up this part of he tour with an unbeaten record. In their indignation over the sending off of Cyril Brownlie, most of the New Zealand players refused to attend the official dinner following the international game and between hen and the time the party left for France, they also remained totally aloof from all the English officials and players.

THE TOP MEN

Mark Nicholls, who made 51 appearances in the All-Blacks jersey and who is still remembered as one of the country's finest half-backs, was New Zealand's top scorer of the 1924-1925 tour in Britain, Ireland and France. His total was 103 points and the twenty-two-year old Nicholls compiled it with a try, six penalty goals, three drop goals and 35 conversions. Behind him came full-back George Nepia with 70 points from 29 conversions and four penalty goals. The All-Blacks top try scorer was Gus Hart of Canterbury with 20.

SCOTLAND OUT

Cliff Porter's All-Blacks of 1924-1925 went through their international campaign without a defeat and the only regret was that they did not get the chance of beating Scotland. The Scots, for reasons best known to themselves and which were never revealed, declined to meet New Zealand during that tour and, indeed, no matches at all were played in Scotland during the tour. One reason offered was that the Scotland Union took a dim view of the English Union's refusal to give control of the tour to the newly-formed Four Home Unions Tours Committee. Another was that the Scottish noses were still a little out of joint because the New Zealanders had made a handsome profit out of the 1905 game. On that occasion, the Scots had refused to give the New Zealanders a guarantee of £200 and decided instead that the All-Blacks should play for the gate, which, as it happened, came to quite a considerable figure. Whatever the reason was, the Scots refused to meet the New Zealanders in 1924 and that was a pity. It might have been one of the great games of the tour. Scotland were to win the Triple Crown for the sixth time that season.

WHERE ARE THE ALL-BLACKS?

Everyone in Toulouse, it seemed, wanted to see the All-Blacks of 1924-1925. They had gone through Britain and Ireland without defeat, had taken on a French XV at Colombes Stadium in Paris on 11th January, 1925 and had won easing up by 37-8 and, now on 18th January, they were to meet France in a full international at Toulouse. But, with the minutes ticking away towards the 3 o'clock kick-off, the All-Blacks dressing room was empty. The local French officials were in desperation and searchers were despatched in all directions to locate the missing New Zealanders. Eventually they were found, outside the Toulouse Stadium. With the thousands pouring in to see the game, they could not get near the official entrance for the officials and players. Eventually, local officials solved the problem. They broke down a wall, pushed the New Zealanders through and then, after a fierce fight through the crowds, they eventually managed to get them to the dressing room. The All-Blacks finally got on to the pitch, which, by then, was ringed with French soldiers and within 10 minutes went ahead with a try by Cliff Porter, who was playing in his first international game of the tour. The All-Blacks went on to win by 30-6 and their final points in Europe were fittingly kicked by Mark Nicholls who had also scored in the first game of the tour. His conversion of the last try brought the New Zealanders total for 32 games to 721 points. Against that, they had conceded only 116 points.

NEPIA'S ABSENCE

The one man certain for the Maoris tour of 1926-1927 had to be the legendary Maori full-back George Nepia, then the best-known personality of rugby football. He had been the only New Zealander to play in every game of Cliff Porter's All-Blacks tour of Britain, Ireland and France in 1924-1925—the tour that brought the title of "Invincibles". But when the Maoris set sail from Wellington to begin their tour with the opening games in Australia, Nepia was not with them. He had, in fact, been on his way to Wellington to join the party when he heard the news that they had gone without him. It was many years later before Nepia discovered what had happened. It seems that on the eve of the Maoris departure, at one of the final receptions for the team, a telegram signed "George Nepia" was read out. It said that he was not available for the tour. The extraordinary feature of this unusual case was that Nepia had not sent the telegram. In the magnificent rugby book, *I, George Nepia*, written by George Nepia and New Zealand's great writer, Terry McLean, Nepia says: "If Sherlock Holmes were still alive, I would willingly employ him to elucidate for me the mysteries of 1926 . . . the trails are cold but surely not too cold for such a man as he. Even now, forty years later, I would like to have the mystery explained".

THE MAORIS

Under the captaincy of W. P. Barclay—and somewhat surprisingly under the wing of the French Rugby Federation—a 27-strong team of Maoris left New Zealand on a tour which was to take them to six countries—Australia, Ceylon, France, England, Wales and Canada. Including the first games they played in New Zealand before setting out, they played, in all, 40 games between 17th July, 1926 and 9th February, 1927 and won 30, drew two, lost eight and scored 741 points while conceding 255. In the tour of France and England and Wales, their record was: played 31, won 22, lost seven and drew two, scoring 459 points and conceding 194. This touring side played only the one international game, against France at Colombes Stadium and won by 12-3. Their most impressive win was against a Selection Français which they took by 25-12 and their worst defeat was 0-20 to Devonshire. In Wales, they had the satisfaction of beating Cardiff twice by 18-8 and 5-3 and Swansea by 11-6.

FIRST TOUR TO SOUTH AFRICA

Described somewhat over optimistically as the finest rugby side ever to leave New Zealand, Maurice Brownlie's All-Blacks, containing nine of the famous 1924-1925 Invincibles, landed in Capetown in 1928 to begin their first tour of South Africa. Sadly, they were to be in for a rude and salutary awakening. In their 22-match tour, they were beaten by Cape Town Clubs in their second game, beaten in their fourth game by Transvaal and failed to score, took a humiliating hammering in their opening international game with the Springboks and eventually wound up their tour by losing five games, drawing one and winning 16. They played one extra unofficial game against Western Province Universities and won by 14-9. In their 22-game record, they scored 339 points and conceded 144. In the international series of four games they drew 2-2 and scored 26 points while conceding 39. Their top points scorer was D. F. Lindsay of Otago with 60 points from 22 conversions, four penalty goals and a drop goal. Top try scorer was C. A. Rushbrook with 10. The 1928 All-Blacks greatest winning margin was their 44-8 defeat of Rhodesia in the 11th game of the tour and their worst defeat was 0-17 against South Africa in the first international game. Their only draw against the Northern Provinces brought a record of 18-18.

A POPULAR MAN

Eighteen men had the distinction of appearing in all four international games between South Africa and New Zealand during the All-Blacks tour of 1928—and, of these, seventeen were players. Ten New Zealanders and seven South Africans played in the four internationals. The 18th was the referee . . . Mr V. H. "Boet" Neser. At the request of the New Zealanders, he was the unanimous choice as referee for all four games.

OSLER'S DAY

The first international meeting of South Africa and New Zealand on South African soil, at Kingsmead, Durban on 30th June, 1928, was a personal triumph for the Springboks out-half Bennie Osler—and a chastening 80 minutes for the All-Blacks. South Africa lost their centre threequarter Bernard Duffy after five minutes—he was accidentally kicked on the head—and the Springboks played the remainder of the game with only 14 men. That, however, did not make any difference to the All-Blacks chances. Osler dropped a goal in the first half, dropped a second shortly after the start of the second half and then kicked two penalty goals in succession before wing-threequarter Jack Slater raced over for a try to make the final score 17-0. To this day, this remains as the worst defeat ever inflicted on New Zealand by South Africa and Osler's 14 points set a record for an international game which stood until Aaron Geffin kicked 15 points against the All-Blacks at Newlands in 1949.

DIFFERENT VALUES

The second international game of the 1928 tour between the All-Blacks and South Africa at Ellis Park, Johannesburg was featured by two drop goals—each of different value. Shortly after the start, the South African hooker marked a clearance just outside the All-Blacks "25" and elected to try for a drop at goal. He put the ball straight between the posts to give South Africa a 3-0 lead but several minutes later H. F. Lindsay brought New Zealand level with a penalty goal. Bennie Osler then brought his total for the two internationals to 17 points with a penalty goal and the South Africans held their lead until 10 minutes from time. From a scrum on the "25", the ball came back to R. T. Stewart, who passed it out to his out-half Bill Strang, who steadied himself and dropped his goal. This one, however, was worth four points and New Zealand had levelled the international series by 7-6. Strang's reward was that he was dropped for the third international against South Africa.

A FITTING RETURN

One of the enduring mysteries of the 1928 tour of South Africa by New Zealand is why the All-Blacks refused to call on the legendary Mark Nicholls for the first three international games against the Springboks. No satisfactory answer has ever been put forward. However, more because of injuries to several players than anything else, Nicholls was called in for the vital fourth international game

313

against South Africa on Saturday, 1st September, 1928 at the Newlands Ground, Capetown. No one could have made a more fitting return to international football than Nicholls who had been touch judge for the previous three international games. Within three minutes he put New Zealand ahead with a penalty goal and after Van der Westhuizen had scored a try for South Africa which Osler converted, Nicholls was again on the mark with a penalty goal before half-time to put New Zealand into a 6-5 lead at the break. J. P. Swain sent the All-Blacks further ahead with a try. Then, with just five minutes to go Nicholls put the crowning seal on New Zealand's victory. Taking a pass from scrum-half W. C. Dalley, midway between the halfway mark and the "25", he drop-kicked the wet, muddy and heavy ball dead centre between the posts. The universal feeling in South Africa after this game was the Springboks would more than likely have lost the series of four international games had Nicholls been called on to play in all four. Why he was not? . . . is still an intriguing question in New Zealand.

DOWN TO SWANSEA

Jack Manchester of Canterbury led his 1935-1936 All-Blacks off to a fine flourish with a 35-6 win over Devon and Cornwall in their opening game of the tour. And they continued on their merry way, until, like the All-Blacks of 1905, they crossed into Welsh territory. They crashed 3-11 to Swansea and this was the only occasion on the tour that they went down to a club side. In all, Manchester's All-Blacks played 28 games, won 24, drew one and lost three, while scoring 431 points and conceding 180. Their 431 points came from 88 tries, 36 conversions, 16 penalty goals, one goal from a mark and 11 drop goals. They lost their international games against Wales and England and this was the first time that New Zealand had lost more than one international game in their tours to Britain, Ireland and France. Top scorer was full-back G. D. M. Gilbert, with 118 points from 29 conversions, 16 penalty goals and three drop goals. Their leading try scorer was threequarter T. H. C. Caughey with 14. The most decisive victory recorded by the 1935-1936 All-Blacks was their 35-6 win over Devon and Cornwall. Their only draw, 3-3 was against Ulster at Ravenhill. Following their tour of Britain and Ireland—France was not included—they played two games in Canada, won both and scored a further 59 points and conceded three.

A NAME IS A NAME

He liked to be known as "Tori" Reid and he was one of the striking successes of Jack Manchester's All-Blacks side which toured in Britain, and Ireland in 1935-1936. Reid, who was then twenty-two, stood 6' 2", weighed 14st 13lbs, and was, perhaps surprisingly, the only Maori in the touring party. His first appearance in the All-Blacks jersey was against Devonshire and Cornwall in 1935 and between then and 1937 when his international career ended, he made 27 appearances for the All-Blacks, including Test games against England, Scotland, Wales, Ireland, Australia and South Africa. As for his liking to be known as "Tori", perhaps it was understandable. He had possibly the most unusual Christian name in the history of rugby . . . Sanatorium!

THREE FOR CAUGHEY

After a lapse of 30 years, New Zealand faced Scotland at Murrayfield, Edinburgh on Saturday, 23rd November, 1935 in the opening international game of the 1935-1936 tour. Playing in an all-white strip, the Scots got away to a magnificent start with a try from F. C. Fyfe in the corner, but within a matter of minutes the All-Blacks came surging back for a try from T. H. C. Caughey right under the posts. Full-back G. D. M. Gilbert converted and that was the beginning of the end for Scotland. W. E. Hadley went over for a try which Gilbert converted, then Caughey went in for his second and the All-Blacks led at half-time by 13-3. Scotland's captain R. W. Shaw reduced the lead with a try which W. C. Murdoch converted but Caughey then went in for his third try of the game and Gilbert added the two points to give the All-Blacks an 18-8 win. The significant feature of this game, however, was that it marked the first time the New Zealanders had used three front-row men in an international game in Britain and Ireland.

OBLENSKY'S DAY!

A twenty-year old Prince, the only Russian to play international rugby, shattered Jack Manchester's 1935-1936 All-Blacks in their 28th and final game of the tour. Saturday, 4th January, 1936 was Prince Alexander Oblensky's day and his incredible performance sent the All-Blacks tumbling to their worst defeat in Britain and Ireland. Oblensky, nick-named "Obo", made his debut for England in this international and began it well with a splendid try early on. Then, just before half-time, in a memorable move from halfway Oblensky took a pass from Peter Candler and instead of going for the right corner, he raced obliquely across the field to the left, spreadeagled the entire New Zealand defence and swerved in for one of the great tries of international football. Hal Sever added a further try for England and their three tries with a drop goal from Peter Cranmer, took England to a 13-0 win. It was the only time the New Zealanders had failed to score on this tour and only the second time they had failed to register a score in a tour of Britain and Ireland.

WALES AGAIN!

The All-Blacks of 1935-1936 went back home with the impressive record of having won 24 and drawn one of their 28 games in Britain and Ireland but they were never really forgiven for Saturday, 21st December, 1935. On that afternoon, with wins behind them over Scotland and Ireland, they turned out at Cardiff Arms Park to take on Wales—and lost the one match they really wanted to win. They scored first with a try from Nelson Ball and led by 3-0 at half-time. Then in five sensational minutes Wales stormed into a 10-3 lead. Cliff Jones got over for their first try and then the wing-threequarter C. Rees-Jones had a second. Vivian Jenkins converted both. But the All-Blacks were not done. Full-back Gilbert dropped a goal to make in 7-10 and Ball had his second try to level the scores. Gilbert took the convert, looked to have missed it and the score of 10-10 went on the board. The referee, Cyril Gadney, however, halted play and ordered the scoreboard to be changed to 12-10 for the New Zealanders. He was satisfied that the convert had been successful. So it remained until four minutes from time. Wilf Wooller then began the move that won the game. He kicked ahead and Rees-Jones was up to dive on the ball for the winning try for Wales. It did not matter that Jenkins missed the convert Wales had won and the score over New Zealand was now two games to one.

THE FORTY-NINERS

Fred Allen of Auckland, who had won his first international cap against Australia in 1946, led the All-Blacks in their second tour to

South Africa in 1949—and it turned out to be the worst tour in the history of All-Black rugby. Their full record was that they played 24 games, won 14, lost seven, drew three, scored 230 points and conceded 146. They also played an unofficial game against the Western Province Town clubs and drew 11-11. Their highest margin of victory was 25 points in their 28-3 win over North Eastern Districts and their worst defeat was 0-9 to Border. Top points scorer was the famous full-back Bob Scott with 60 points from a try, nine conversions, 11 penalty goals and two drop goals and the top try scorer was Peter Henderson with seven. But the most depressing feature of the tour from a New Zealand point of view is that they were beaten in all four international games—a disaster that had never been their portion in any previous tour by the All-Blacks.

THE BOOT STEPS IN

With decisive wins, 20-0 over Orange Free State, 5-0 over Transvaal, 19-8 over Western Transvaal and 31-3 over Natal, in their four warm-up games leading to the first international game against South Africa at Newlands in 1949, the All-Blacks were the strong favourites to beat a somewhat makeshift Springbok side. But a bulky prop-forward, by name Aaron Geffin, to be known ever after as "The Boot", stepped into the picture and sent the New Zealanders tumbling down to defeat. Bob Scott gave the All-Blacks the lead with an early penalty goal, Peter Henderson added a try which Scott converted and Jim Kearney dropped a goal to put the All-Blacks into an 11-3 lead at half-time. South Africa's goal had come from a penalty by Geffin who had been delegated to take the kick after their recognised kicker Jack van der Schyff had failed with two early and easy attempts. The second half belonged to Geffin. He got four penalty attempts and he kicked all four to win the game for the Springboks by 15-11. Geffin's performance, which was to stand as a South African international record for 13 years, broke the previous record of 14 points in an international game which had been set by Bennie Osler against New Zealand at Durban in 1928 and which, subsequently, had been equalled by Gerry Brand against the Lions at Johannesburg in 1938.

A SECOND DEFEAT

New Zealand went down to their second international defeat of the 1949 tour at Ellis Park and once again "Okey" Geffin was on the mark, although this time without the extraordinary accuracy he had shown in the opening international. Bob Scott had New Zealand's first penalty goal but Geffin cancelled that out almost immediately with one for South Africa and Hannes Brewis with a try put the Springboks into a 6-3 lead at half-time. Tjol Lategan added another try for South Africa in the second half and after Jim Kearney had dropped a goal for the All-Blacks, Brewis tidied it all up with a drop goal to give South Africa a 12-6 win. This was the first time that South Africa had ever beaten New Zealand in the first two games of a series between the two countries.

ANOTHER GEFFIN AFFAIR

After a certain lapse in his kicking in the second international Aaron Geffin came right back to form for the third international of the 1949 tour at Durban and within 10 minutes had the New Zealanders in dire trouble. They were penalised twice and Geffin with two magnificent kicks put the Springboks into a 6-0 lead. J. W. Goddard got over for a New Zealand try after 15 minutes but immediately after half-time Geffin knocked all the fight out of the New Zealanders by kicking his third penalty goal and that ended the scoring.

THE FINAL STRAW

The final international game between South Africa and New Zealand at Port Elizabeth in 1949 was to be the last bitter straw for the All-Blacks. Never before had they needed a win so badly. Defeat now would mean their first "whitewash" on an international tour in South Africa. Only once previously on a tour, in Australia in 1929, had they lost all their international fixtures. That, however, had been a three-match tour and they had already equalled that dismal record in South Africa in 1949. New Zealand got off to a heartening start at Port Elizabeth with a try by Paul Johnstone and held their lead until half-time. Then Geffin moved into the picture again. With a penalty from far out and

" IT'S ALRIGHT FOR THEM —THEY "
CAN SHELTER IN THE SCRUMS

close to the touchline, he put the ball between the posts and scores were
level. Fonnie du Toit followed that up with a try and Geffin was on
the mark again to convert it. Hannes Brewis dropped a goal and
although Ron Elvidge came back with a try which Bob Scott converted
it was South Africa's game and the Grand Slam of four victories in
succession. That, coupled with South Africa's two wins in succession
in New Zealand in 1937 gave the Springboks six wins in a row over
New Zealand, which is still a record for meetings between the two
countries. Of the 47 points scored by South Africa in the four 1949
international games, 32 came from the boot of Aaron Geffin, which
was to stand as a record until 1968 when Ireland's Tom Kiernan
scored 35 points for the Lions against the Springboks.

A HAPPY DEBUT

The twenty-five year old Ron Jarden, from Lower Hutt, Wellington
made his debut for New Zealand during the tour of Australia in 1951
and in his third appearance in the All-Black jersey he set a record which
still remains unbroken. Picked to play at wing-threequarter against
Central West at Parkes, Jarden finished off the game with a personal
total of 38 points, made up of six tries and 10 conversions. Up to 1974
this was the record for the most points scored by a player in an inter
national touring side. Between 1951 and 1956, Jarden won 16 caps for
New Zealand against Australia, England, Scotland, France, Wales
Ireland and South Africa.

THE FOURTH ALL-BLACKS

The Fourth All-Blacks, led by Bob Stuart of Canterbury, toured in
Britain, Ireland, France, Canada and the United States in 1953-54 and
went back home with the record of playing 36 games, winning 30
losing four, drawing two and scoring 598 points while conceding 152
However, if one removed the Canadian and American portion of the
tour, their record did not look quite so impressive. In Britain, Ireland
and France and excluding the match against the South-Eastern Counties
of England which was classified as unofficial and which they won by
21-13, their record was: played 31, won 25, lost four, drew two and
scored 446 points and conceded 129. They began in Britain with a 24-

win over Southern Counties and went seven games unbeaten until they met Cardiff at Cardiff Arms Park, where they lost 3-8. Their top scorer of the tour was Ron Jarden with 73 points in Britain, Ireland and France, from 10 tries, 11 conversions and seven penalty goals. Their total of 446 points in this part of the tour came from 89 tries, 48 conversions, 18 penalty goals and eight drop goals. The top margin of victory achieved by the Fourth All-Blacks was 32 points, against the South of Scotland (32-0) and Combined Services (40-8). Their two draws were against Swansea (6-6) and Ulster (5-5). Ulster, of course, had also drawn 3-3 with the 1935-1936 All-Blacks.

THREE FOR WALES

Saturday, 19th December, 1953 was to be another sad day for New Zealand. Wales had beaten the All-Blacks of 1905-1906 and the All-Blacks of 1935-1936 and now they were to stretch their lead in the series to 3-1 when Bob Stuart led his New Zealanders to Cardiff Arms Park. Wales scored first with a try from their prop forward S. Judd of Cardiff, which was converted by wing-threequarter G. Rowlands, but the New Zealanders struck back with a fine try by Ian Clarke, which was converted by Ron Jarden who also kicked a penalty goal to leave the All-Blacks in front by 8-5 at half-time. Rowlands kicked a penalty goal early in the second half to level the scores and then in a dramatic finish, Olympic sprinter Ken Jones took a pass at full tilt and raced away for the winning try. For the third time in almost 50 years, New Zealand had been beaten at Cardiff Arms Park.

A TIGHT SHAVE

New Zealand recovered from their defeat by Wales to beat Ireland by 14-3 at Lansdowne Road, Dublin on 9th January, 1954 and England by 5-0 at Twickenham on 30th January, 1954. Then they moved to Murrayfield on Saturday, 13th February, to meet Scotland in their fourth international of the tour. And that provided them with the tightest of shaves. Scotland, with 13 defeats in succession behind them prior to this meeting, were hardly expected to provide any anxious moments for Bob Stuart's men but when it was all over the margin between the two sides was just a penalty goal which Bob Scott had kicked eight minutes after half-time. The general verdict was that the New Zealanders had been fortunate. This win, however, close though it may have been, at least gave the New Zealanders a better international record than their predecessors of 1935-36, who had lost two of their international games in Britain and Ireland.

"MONSIEUR RUGBY"

Bob Stuart's Fourth All-Blacks had their most chastening moments of the 1953-1954 tour when they travelled to France. On 24th, February 1954, they took on South-West France at Bordeaux, a side which included only two internationals, and went down 8-11. This was the first time an All-Blacks side had been defeated in France and there was a further shock in store for them just three days later at Colombes Stadium when they met the full force of the French international side. Five minutes before half-time Henri Domec began a passing move just inside the French half and this was carried forward by Robert Baulon and Paul Labadie. With the New Zealanders retreating desperately Labadie finally got a pass to Jean Prat and "Monsieur Rugby", with three All-Blacks hanging on to him, crashed over the line for a try—the only score of the game. This defeat, the second in succession for the All-Blacks—this had never happened on any previous New Zealand tour—was the only game in Britain, Ireland and France in which the All-Blacks had failed to score. It was, of course, also France's first victory over New Zealand in international rugby.

IN NORTH AMERICA

Bob Stuart's All-Blacks of 1953-1954 played five games in North America and won all five. They beat Victoria by 39-3, the University of British Columbia by 42-3, British Columbia Mainland by 37-11 the University of Southern California by 14-6 and the California All Stars by 20-0.

WHINERAY IN SOUTH AFRICA

Although they finished by losing the international series 2-1 with one game drawn, Wilson Whineray's third All-Blacks to tour in South Africa in 1960 wound up with a highly impressive record, the best by any touring side in the country since the Lions of 1896. They played 26 games, won 20, lost four, drew two and scored 441 points while conceding 164. Their top margin of victory was 39 points which they achieved in their opening game of the tour against Northern Universities and they went unbeaten for seven games before going down 0-13 to South Africa in the first international, which was their worst defeat of the tour and the only game in which they failed to score. Don Clarke was their top points scorer with 175 points from a try, 32 conversions, 32 penalty goals and four drop goals. Clarke played in 20 games of the tour and his 175 points still stand as the all-time record for a touring player of any country in South Africa. The New Zealanders' top try scorer was Terry Lineen with 10.

ALL SQUARE AFTER TWO

In the 19th international game between New Zealand and South Africa—the opening international fixture of the 1960 tour at Johannesburg on Saturday, 25th June, 1960—the All-Blacks went down to their second worst defeat in history by the Springboks. Hennie van Zyl raced in to plant the ball between the posts for their first try and Roy Dryburgh kicked the conversion to put South Africa ahead by 5-0 at half-time. Midway through the second half Van Zyl went over for a second try and this time Dick Lockyear added the points. Shortly afterwards Lockyear kicked a penalty and the final score of 13-0 was the highest by the Springboks since they beat the All-Blacks by the record margin of 17-0 back in 1928. Don Clarke, however, led the way to revenge in the second international game at Newlands. He gave New Zealand an early lead with a 35-yards penalty goal, later converted a try by Colin Meads and finished off his afternoon with a superb drop goal from far out. South Africa's only reply was a try by Keith Oxlee.

A STORMING FIGHT BACK

With five minutes to go and a lead of 11-3, South Africa looked to have the third international against New Zealand at Bloemfontein all sewn up—and in the end they were fortunate to survive to an 11-11 draw. Dick Lockyear put the South Africans ahead with a penalty goal in the first half but a minute after the re-start Don Clarke, with one of his special efforts from 50 yards out levelled matters. Keith Oxlee, however, slipped in for a smart try, which Lockyear converted and that with a penalty goal from Lockyear left the Springboks with a comfortable lead of eight points as the game went into its closing minutes. Then South Africa were penalised and from five yards inside his own half Clarke sent a tremendous kick soaring between the posts to cut the lead to five points. With less than a minute to go Frank McMullan whipped up a kick ahead and dived over in the corner to make it 11-9. Now everything depended on the final kick of the game—the conversion attempt by Clarke from right on the touch line. The full-back took his time and then in a deathly silence he ran up and the ball went flying high and straight between the posts. It was a dramatic draw—the first since their scoreless game at Wellington 39 years earlier.

ALL-BLACKS DOWN AGAIN

Five minutes after the start of the fourth and final international match of the 1960 All-Blacks tour of South Africa, New Zealand's wing-threequarter Frank McMullan broke through a gap and went streaking towards the Springboks line. He seemed to have a try at his mercy but Keith Oxlee, with a despairing run managed to strike the back of McMullan's foot. The New Zealander stumbled and fell but retained possession of the ball and crawled over the line. The referee Ralph Burmeister, however, disallowed the try. McMullan had been tackled and therefore could not play the ball again. He promptly gave a penalty against McMullan. And that was probably the decisive moment of that international game. Although New Zealand took the lead fifteen minutes later with a penalty goal from Don Clarke, the South Africans gradually took over the proceedings and with a penalty goal by Dick Lockyear and a try by the one-eyed Martin Pelser which was converted by Lockyear, they won 8-3 and left New Zealand still without a series win in South Africa. The reward for the South Africans was that all 15 who had beaten New Zealand in this final international were automatically chosen to go on to the tour to Britain, Ireland and France. This tour would be led by the twenty-three-year old Avril Malan who in leading the Springboks against the All-Blacks in the two final internationals had become his country's youngest rugby captain.

WITHIN A MINUTE

Could there be a finer start to an international debut in rugby than to handle the ball within a minute and score a try with 60 seconds? It happened to New Zealand's Don McKay on Saturday, 22nd July, 1961 against France at Eden Park, Auckland. This was the first time that the local boy McKay had ever worn the All-Blacks jersey. Full-back Don Clarke kicked off for New Zealand and his mighty kick put the ball over the French goal-line. France's full back Michel Vannier took the drop out, the ball went loose and McKay was on to it in a flash and went shooting over in the corner for a try. It is possible that it may be the fastest try ever scored in international rugby. Some accounts of the game claim that it all happened in 50 seconds, but most agree that McKay's try certainly came in the first minute.

THE ODD MEN OUT

Lock forward Stan Meads and out-half Tom Wolfe were really the odd men out after New Zealand's game against Northern New South Wales at Quirindi on 30th May, 1962. Of the All-Blacks side which cantered to the remarkable win of 103-0, they were the only two who failed to score. The slight consolation for Northern New South Wales was that they had helped to set several rugby records. This was the greatest margin of victory ever achieved in a game by an international touring side and the number of tries scored, 22, was also a record for an international touring side. With his contribution of eight, New Zealand's wing-threequarter, Ron Heeps, also scored the most tries by a player in a tour game. New Zealand's total was made up of 22 tries, 17 conversions and a penalty goal.

WILSON WHINERAY AND CO

The Fifth All-Blacks, led by the twenty-eight-year old Wilson Whineray of Auckland, played 36 matches in Britain, Ireland, France and Canada in 1963-1964, winning 34, losing one and drawing one. Their points total was 613 points for and 159 against. In the Britain, Ireland and France portion of the tour, they played 34 games, won 32, lost one, drew one and scored 568 points while conceding 153. Their 568 points came from 111 tries, 47 conversions, 30 penalty goals and 17 drop goals. Their top scorer was full-back Don Clarke with 136 points from 25 games and his total came from 32 conversions, 18 penalty goals, five drop goals and one try. Their top try scorer was Malcolm Dick with 19 from 23 appearances. The All-Blacks greatest margin of victory was 33 points in their 36-3 rout of the Barbarians at Cardiff Arms Park in the last game of the tour in Britain. Their only defeat came in the third game against Newport and the only draw was against Scotland in the 26th game of the tour. In their two games in Canada, the All-Blacks beat British Columbia under-25 XV and also British Columbia, both at Vancouver.

THE ONLY DEFEAT

With 51 points from their first two victories, Whineray's All-Blacks went in to Wales for their third game to play Newport at Rodney Parade and this brought them their only defeat of the tour. The All-Blacks were completely contained by this remarkable Newport side and the final blow came when the Welsh out-half David Watkins whipped the ball to Stuart Watkins who crosskicked in the New Zealand "25". From the tremendous loose maul that followed, the ball came back to Newport's centre, J. R. Uzzell, who steadied himself and dropped a goal. In all during this tour only four drop goals were scored against the All-Blacks but this was the vital one they never forgot. Only twice more on the tour were the All-Blacks to be held scoreless in a game but in the second, against Scotland, they also prevented the opposition from scoring. The third against South-West France was also a scoreless draw.

A LITTLE HISTORY REPEATED

When the New Zealanders ran out at Iffley Road to begin their 1963-1964 tour of Britain, Ireland and France, Malcolm Dick of Auckland was wearing the All-Blacks jersey for the first time. And the twenty-two-year old wing-threequarter, who also doubled as an out-half, put his mark on the game with a glorious run of almost 40 yards which brought a try just beside the posts. That news, when it reached back home in New Zealand, was greeted with a special delight in the Dick household.

Exactly 26 years earlier, his father John Dick had made his debut in the All-Blacks jersey in the international game against South Africa at Wellington and he, too, had celebrated the occasion with a try. Malcolm Dick, who played in 23 matches for the All-Blacks, during this 1963-1964 tour, finished as the side's top try scorer with 19 and his 57 points made him the third top points scorer of the tour behind Don Clarke with 136 and Mac Herewini with 74. His first international try, however, did not come until the final international game of the tour against France. Dick, who went on to make 15 international appearances for New Zealand, made 55 appearances in the All-Blacks jersey and scored 126 points from 42 tries. Only Jimmy Hunter of the 1905-1906 All-Blacks touring side, with 49 tries has scored more tries for New Zealand than Malcolm Dick.

FORTUNE'S TRY

The All-Blacks opened their international campaign of the 1963-1964 tour with the game against Ireland at Lansdowne Road, Dublin on Saturday, 7th December, 1963, and it looked to be a foregone conclusion. But the Irish, captained by Jimmy Kelly, got away to a sensational lead when Alan Duggan pushed the ball to Gerry Walsh, who in turn flung out a long pass to Johnny Fortune on the wing. Fortune, making his international debut, took the ball in his stride and with the New Zealand backs anticipating a whistle for a knock-on, he galloped over the line for a try which Tom Kiernan converted. Coming up to half-time Kel Tremain got over for an All-Blacks try but Don Clarke failed with his attempt to convert. Ireland held out until 15 minutes from time. Then Clarke, with a magnificent penalty goal from 40 yards out put the All-Blacks ahead by 6-5 and that was how it ended. New Zealand still had their unbeaten record against Ireland.

NOT THIS TIME

Wales were looking for a hat-trick of victories over the All-Blacks at Cardiff Arms Park when the two countries met on Saturday, 21st December, 1963 but there was to be little joy for the 58,000 Welsh supporters who watched the proceedings. In less than four minutes Don Clarke booted the All-Blacks into the lead with an easy penalty goal and fifteen minutes into the second half, B. A. Watts dropped a goal to clinch matters. After 58 years, New Zealand had at last won an international game over Wales at Cardiff Arms Park. The Welsh, however, were still 3-2 ahead in the series.

ENGLAND GO DOWN

When the New Zealanders met England at Twickenham on Saturday, 4th January, 1964, it was the third meeting between the two countries in eight months. England had toured in New Zealand during the previous summer and had lost the first international at Eden Park by 11-21. The second at Lancaster Park, however, was a much closer battle with England failing by 6-9. On the strength of that second game, England were expected to give the All-Blacks more than a good run for their money at Twickenham. But this was a game that started disastrously for the English. Twice Simon Clarke was penalised for lying on the ball and twice Don Clarke punished him for it with penalty goals. Then R. W. Caulton went in for a try at the corner and the All-Blacks led by 9-0 at half-time. The second half was little more than a formality. Colin Meads got his second try of the tour and Clarke duly converted to leave the final score, 14-0. This marked the All-Blacks seventh defeat of England in their eight games since 1905, and the third time that England had failed to score against them.

NO CLEAN SWEEP

The scoreboard at Murrayfield, Edinburgh on Saturday, 18th January, 1964, told the story; Scotland o; New Zealand o. Once again the All-Blacks had failed in their bid to return home with victories over the four home countries. They had lost to Wales in 1905, Scotland had refused to meet the 1924 tourists, Wales and England had beaten the 1934-1935 side and Wales had won again in 1953-1954. But, at least they were still unbeaten in the international campaign and now all that remained was the game against France on 8th February, 1964. And this was a game that demanded revenge for the shock defeat of Bob Stuart's All-Blacks at Colombes Stadium in 1954.

HEREWINI TAKES OVER

The first shock of New Zealand's international game against France at Colombes Stadium, Paris on Saturday, 8th February, 1964 was that Don Clarke missed two reasonably easy penalty goal attempts in the opening minute. The second shock was when captain Wilson Whineray pointed to out-half Mac Herewini when a third penalty goal chance came up in the 10th minute. Herewini duly kicked the goal and did all the kicking for the rest of the game. It was the first indication that the legendary career of Clarke, the greatest kicker the game of rugby has known, was coming towards its end. Herewini's successful kick levelled the score—Pierre Albaladejo had earlier kicked a penalty for France—and, from there on, in a rough-and-tumble game, the New Zealanders were well on top. Ralph Caulton added a try for New Zealand before the end of the first half and in the second Chris Laidlaw with a drop goal and Ken Gray with a try wrapped it all up neatly for New Zealand. In their three other games in France, the All-Blacks beat France "B" by 17-8, a South-East France XV by 8-5 and played a scoreless draw with a South-West France XV.

THE FINAL FLOURISH

For their final game in Britain, Ireland and France, Wilson Whineray's All-Blacks of 1963-1964 exploded with all the power and magic within them and put on one of the most memorable displays in rugby history. Against the Barbarians, they ran the ball from end to end of the field and finished off the afternoon with a win by 36-3—their finest victory of the tour. And how fitting it was that the final try should come from the man who led them. A sparkling move by Allan Stewart and Colin Meads brought the ball to Whineray, who threw a superb dummy and then went tearing for the line and his only score of the tour. Don Clarke kicked the conversion and it was all over. The All-Blacks total was compiled by Waka Nathan with two tries, Kel Tremain, Colin Meads, Stewart Graham, Malcolm Dick, Ralph Caulton and Wilson Whineray with a try each and Don Clarke kicked six conversions. And just to make it an all-round day for New Zealand, it was an All-Blacks who got the Barbarians only score. Ian Clarke, the only member of the party surviving from Bob Stuart's All-Blacks of 1953-1954, was a guest Barbarian for the day and he dropped a goal for the first score of this wonderful game.

THE SIXTH ALL-BLACKS

Brian Lochore's Sixth All-Blacks opened their 1967 tour of Britain, Ireland and France with a 33-3 win over the North of England at White City, Manchester on Wednesday, 25th October, 1967 and finished it off with a win by 11-6 over the Barbarians at Twickenham on Saturday, 16th December. This was a short tour and, in all, the All-Blacks played 15 games, won 14, drew one, lost none, and scored 294 points while conceding 129. They had, in fact, been due to play 17 games but, because of the foot-and-mouth disease in Ireland that season, the fixture against an Irish Combined XV and the international meeting with Ireland were cancelled. So the All-Blacks had to return home once again without the satisfaction of beating the four home countries in international rugby. Top scorer of the 1967 All-Blacks was full-back Fergie McCormick with 100 points from the 11 games he played in Britain, Ireland and France. His total came from a try, 23 conversions and 17 penalty goals. He also scored a further 18 points in his 12th appearance against British Columbia at the Empire Stadium, Vancouver. Top try scorer was Bill Birtwistle with eight. The 1967 All-Blacks most decisive margin of victory in Britain, Ireland and France was 30 points in their 33-3 win over North of England. Their only draw, 3-3, was against an East Wales XV at Cardiff Arms Park in the 16th game of the tour. In their two games in Canada, they won by 36-3 against British Columbia and 40-3 against Eastern Canada at Montreal. Their overall record was: played 17, won 16, drew one, scored 370 points, conceded 135 points.

A TRIFLE EARLY

It seemed that everyone was in a hurry at Twickenham on Saturday, 4th November, 1967. Mr D. C. J. McMahon, the Scottish referee, for reasons best known to himself, started the game six minutes before the advertised kick-off. The New Zealanders, too, wasted no time and in fact, scored their first try within those six minutes and by half-time, with tries from Earle Kirton, Bill Birtwistle, Chris Laidlaw and Kirton again, three converted by Fergie McCormick, they led by 18 points to England's try by Bob Lloyd which was converted by Don Rutherford. Malcolm Dick added another try for the All-Blacks early in the second half and McCormick converted to put them 23-5 ahead. After that it did not really matter but Peter Larter kicked a penalty goal for England and Lloyd, whose first game for his country this was, eventually got over for a second try to leave the final score 23-11. New Zealand had now met England on eight occasions since 1905 and had won seven.

ALL SQUARE

The sixth meeting of New Zealand and Wales since 1905 turned out to be a mildly depressing affair at Cardiff Arms Park on Saturday, 11th November, 1967 and perhaps its most memorable feature was that after 62 years, the series was square again with three victories each. Wales's captain, Norman Gale, won the toss and, to the astonishment of his own countrymen, elected to play into the fierce wind and driving rain. The All-Blacks made good use of both and after 12 minutes when Billy Raybould was caught offside, Fergie McCormick kicked a sound penalty goal. Five minutes later, Bill Birtwistle went over for a try in the corner and McCormick used the wind beautifully to kick the conversion from the sideline. New Zealand led 8-0 at half-time and then Barry John dropped a goal for Wales and for a few moments there was the possibility of an exciting finish. But Bill Davis added a second try for New Zealand and again McCormick was dead on target with the conversion. Shortly before the end Norman Gale kicked a penalty goal to leave the All-Blacks 13-6 in front at the final whistle.

IT WAS NOT GENTLE

France won the fighting and New Zealand won the game. So said one newspaper report of the 1967 All-Blacks game against France at Colombes Stadium on Saturday, 25th November, 1967. Certainly it was not a drawing room affair and the injury countdown after the proceedings showed that Ian Kirkpatrick had a definite broken nose, Earle Kirton had a suspected broken nose, Colin Meads had a bad gash in the head and Graham Williams had to have several stitches for a cut on the forehead. And on the French side, Claude Dourthe had a badly bruised face and Pierre Villepreux had two broken ribs. The New Zealanders won but only after a desperate and bitterly fought battle with the French, who came back to lead at one stage in the second half. McCormick opened the game with a penalty goal for the All-Blacks but Jean Gachassin levelled matters with a splendid drop goal from 40 yards out. Sid Going put the All-Blacks back into the lead with a try and again France came level with a penalty goal from Villepreux. Tony Steel added a try for New Zealand which McCormick converted but in the seventh minute of injury time in the first half Villepreux put over a penalty goal to leave the half-time score 11-9 in favour of the All-Blacks. Ten minutes after the start of the second half, Villepreux was again spot on with a penalty goal to put France ahead and they stayed there for 20 minutes. Then a try by Kirkpatrick converted by McCormick, followed smartly by another try from Malcolm Dick and again converted by the full-back sent the All-Blacks into a 21-12 lead. Andre Campaes had a try for France in the closing minutes and that was that. After eight meetings between the countries the margin was now 7-1 for the New Zealanders.

MEADS SENT TO THE LINE

No one had any trouble in picking out Colin Meads at the start of the international game between New Zealand and Scotland at Murrayfield, Edinburgh on Saturday, 2nd December, 1967. To protect his head and the gash which he had collected from the boot of a Frenchman in the international game at Colombes Stadium, he was wearing a heavy white bandage and this, in turn, was covered by a special and distinctive yellow headgear. Sadly, there was no problem, either, in picking out Meads just two minutes from the final whistle. He was on his way to the dressing room—the second New Zealand international to be sent to the line in the 62 years of tours to Britain, Ireland and France. Seconds earlier, Meads had broken from a ruck and as Scotland's out-half David Chisholm bent down to pick up the ball, the New Zealander lunged forward with his right foot. The referee Kevin Kelleher of Ireland blew his whistle and went to Meads. He then raised his arm, pointed to the players' entrance and after a slight hesitation Meads left the field. Subsequently, an adjudicating committee convened by the International Rugby Board, considered the referee's report and issued a statement; "The referee, Mr K. D. Kelleher of Ireland, having formally warned C. E. Meads of New Zealand for foul play and misconduct earlier in the game, making clear any repetition would mean dismissal from the playing enclosure, is supported in the action he took. Meads has been severely admonished,

nd warned as to his future conduct, and is suspended for the next
wo games on the tour". Apart from the dismissal of Meads, the New
Zealand victory was not overly memorable. Ian MacRae opened the
coring with New Zealand's first try against Scotland for 32 years
nd McCormick kicked two penalty goals in the first half. Bill Davis
ad New Zealand's second try five minutes from time and McCormick
dded the two points. David Chisholm dropped a goal for Scotland
n their 3-14 defeat. This was the fifth meeting of the two countries
since 1905 and the Scots were still without a win.

THE LAST FLING

As Wilson Whineray's All-Blacks had done four years earlier, Brian
Lochore's 1967 All-Blacks kept their special wine to the last final fling
against the Barbarians at Twickenham on Saturday, 16th December,
1967—and it was the best of vintage champagne. Stewart Wilson,
Scotland's captain, put the Barbarians into the lead with a magnificent
50 yards drop goal but Earle Kirton also dropped a goal to leave the
half-time score 3-3. The Barbarians took back the lead in the second
half with a try by Bob Lloyd and held grimly on to their 6-3 margin
all the way to the end of the 40 minutes. The clock said the game was
over, all that remained was injury time—and in those fateful four
minutes came all the drama. Tony Steel broke away on a blistering
run and when he was pulled down he got his pass to Ian MacRea who
went over for the try that levelled the scores. McCormick missed the
conversion but there was still a treat in store. In the fourth and final
minute of injury time, Brian Lochore fielded a long kick from the
Barbarians full-back, Wilson, and set off on a run for the line. Earle
Kirton and Tony Steel were there with him and a superb passing
movement ended with Steel over the line for a glorious try. McCormick
kicked the conversion and the All-Blacks had finished their tour
unbeaten with an 11-6 victory.

AN ALL-BLACK DAY

Wales, with three wins from their nine meetings with New Zealand,
had their worst outing against the All-Blacks at Eden Park, Auckland
in 1969. In their first international of the tour at Lancaster Park, Wales

had been beaten by 19-0, which equalled the previous record margin that the New Zealanders had set up during their 1924 tour at St Helen's, Swansea, and by an unusual coincidence the scoring had come in the same way—four tries, two conversions and a penalty goal. Unfortunately for Wales, there was worse in store for them at Eden Park. Here the All-Blacks margin of victory was 21 points with a 33-12 result. The major difference between the two sides was the kicking. New Zealand's full-back Fergie McCormick kicked five penalty goals, three conversions and also dropped a goal. His total of 24 points is still the individual points scoring record in an international game.

BRIAN LOCHORE'S MEN

Brian Lochore's All-Blacks of 1970—the fourth to tour in South Africa—returned home to New Zealand with a vast collection of records. But, like their predecessors in 1928, 1949 and 1960, they came back without the achievement they really wanted. They failed to beat South Africa in a series in South Africa. In all they played 24 matches, ran up the astonishing total of 687 points which exceeded the previous best total by a touring side in South Africa by over 200 points and conceded 228. They won 21 of their 24 games and lost the other three, all to South Africa. Their highest winning margin, a record for a touring side in South Africa was the 85-0 win over North East Cape and their record of 17 tries in this particular game was also an all-time record. They scored in every game and their lowest was the three points in their 3-14 defeat by South Africa in the third international game. Their top scorer was Fergie McCormick with 132 points from four tries, 33 conversions and 18 penalty goals in 14 matches. The top try scorer was Graham Thorne with 17, the most by any touring player in South Africa in this century. Prior to Thorne's achievement, R. L. Aston had scored 30 tries with the Lions in 1891 and Larry Bulger had scored 20 in 1896. In all the New Zealanders scored 135 tries, an improvement on the previous record of 94 by the Lions of 1955. The All-Blacks also won all of their matches against provincial sides, a feat which had never previously been achieved by a visiting All-Blacks side.

TEN ON THE TROT

In their first 10 games of the 1970 tour, New Zealand beat Border 28-3, Paul Roos XV 43-9, Griqualand West 27-3, North West Cape 26-3, South West Africa 16-0, Eastern Transvaal 24-3, Transvaal 34-17, Western Transvaal 21-17, Orange Free State 30-12 and Rhodesia 27-14. With that glorious record behind them, they went into the first international match against South Africa at Pretoria and all the odds seemed to be in their favour. But at Loftus Versfeld, they went down to their first defeat and it was decisive. Dawie de Villiers put South Africa three up after three minutes with a try, then they went six up after eight minutes and were nine up after 12 minutes and as a battle it was all over. Syd Nomis had a try, Ian McCallum kicked a conversion and two penalty goals and Piet Visagie dropped the neatest of goals. All New Zealand could offer in return was a try from Bryan Williams and a penalty goal from Fergie McCormick.

A SWIFT RECOVERY

The New Zealanders made a rapid recovery from their defeat at Pretoria and in their very next game administered a severe trouncing to Eastern Province by 49-8 and followed this by beating Boland 35-9. Then came South Africa again, this time at Newlands on 8th August. And all the dramatic excitement in this titanic struggle came in the closing seconds with South Africa hanging on grimly to an 8-6 lead. Joggie Jansen had scored a try for South Africa which had been converted by Ian McCallum who had also kicked a penalty goal and the two All-Blacks tries had come from Chris Laidlaw and Ian Kirkpatrick. Time was just up when the All-Blacks surged into one last desperate attack and the ball was in Bill Davis's hands close to the line when he was brought down by Mannetijies Roux coming at him from a far offside position. He was penalised straightaway and with 50,000 South African supporters hushed into a fearful silence, Fergie McCormick stepped up to take the kick. And he made absolutely no mistake with it. In the 28 matches between the two countries since 1921, New Zealand had won for the 12th time. It had been a hard game. The injury countdown afterwards showed that at least six players needed stitches when the final whistle went.

BACK ON TOP AGAIN

With their victory over South Africa, the All-Blacks went off again on a scoring spree. South Western Districts went down by 6-36, Western Province were beaten by 29-6, South African Country got hammered by 45-8, Natal were beaten 29-8 and South Universities were crushed by 20-3. But as had happened earlier, the New Zealand scoring machine ground almost to a halt when they faced up for the third time to South Africa at Port Elizabeth on 29th August. For this game South Africa called back J. A. "Lofty" Nel, who had last played in the Springbok pack five years earlier and at 36 years, he was to become the oldest man ever to play for South Africa. And he turned out to be one of their great trump cards as the New Zealanders went down by 3-14. His tremendous work with J. L. "Moff" Myburgh, who at just under 20st was probably the heaviest man ever to play in international rugby, had a thoroughly upsetting effect on the New Zealand pack, who played a subdued second fiddle all through. Bryan Williams kicked a penalty goal for New Zealand and that was their lot. Gert Muller had two tries for South Africa and McCallum kept up his international scoring record by kicking the conversion and two penalty goals.

THE LAST INTERNATIONAL

Gerald Kember, making his international debut for New Zealand in the final game of the 1970 tour of South Africa made it a memorable occasion for himself but it was not enough to save the All-Blacks from defeat at Ellis Park on Saturday, 12th September, 1970. He set a record of 14 points for New Zealand in an international game against South Africa with four penalty goals and a conversion of Bryan Williams' try. But his performance was duplicated by Ian McCallum who also kicked four penalty goals for South Africa and a conversion. The difference between the two sides was that South Africa scored two tries, from Piet Visagie and Gerd Muller. With his 35 points from the four international games Ian McCallum set an all-time record for South Africa in a series of international games against New Zealand. With this final game between New Zealand and South Africa, the two countries had met on 30 occasions since 1921 with South Africa winning 16 to New Zealand's 14, with two drawn. Fittingly the last series had provided 59 points, the greatest number scored in the eight series between the two countries.

AND ALL-BLACKS TOO!

Young Jamie Hendry, as first year student at Perth University, thought it was all a big joke. A nineteen-year old Scot, born in Edinburgh, he had come to Australia in 1969 and was playing rugby with the university side. To suggest that he might play for the All-Blacks, well, that could not be serious. But it was. The New Zealanders were on their way to South Africa for the tour of 1970 and had stopped over in Perth for two games, one against a President's XV and the other against Western Australia. The game against the President's XV was on a Sunday and that ruled out New Zealand's scrum-half Sid Going. Because of his religion, he never played on Sundays. In the circumstances, young Hendry was being invited to take over Going's place and to appear as a guest player for New Zealand. So he did and after their victory, he was duly presented with the All-Blacks kit he had worn during the game. There was a similar occurrence in Australia in 1960 when, due to injuries, the All-Blacks were unable to field a full fifteen against Queensland and on that occasion, E. T. Stapleton of New South Wales wound up with a most unexpected honour. He

SOME COMPENSATION

The New Zealanders worked out their disappointment of the international defeat by South Africa by running riot against North-East Cape at Burgersdorp on 2nd September, 1970. They led 36-0 at half-time, took that to 59-0 after 10 minutes of the second half and when the referee finally called a halt to the proceedings, the score had reached 85-0. In all the All-Blacks scored 17 tries, four from Graham Thorne, three from Ian Kirkpatrick, two from Sid Going, Keith Murdoch, Malcolm Dick and Buff Milner and one each from Bill Davis and Bruce McLeod. The star of the afternoon however was Gerald Kember who kicked 14 conversions and two penalty goals for a total of 34 points—the most ever scored by a tourist in South Africa up to then. On the strength of that display, Kember who had toured with the 1967 New Zealanders in Britain, Ireland, France and Canada, was to win his first international cap for New Zealand in the final international game at Johannesburg.

turned up to watch the game and instead found himself playing, and in an All-Blacks jersey at that. Stapleton had been an outstanding Australian international and had won the first of 16 caps against New Zealand in 1951 and the last, also against New Zealand in 1958. He was invited to become a guest player on the New Zealand side and he duly helped them to an easy win. The interesting feature of these two cases is that E. T. Stapleton and Jamie Hendry are now included in the list of the 700 men who have played in official games for New Zealand up to the start of the 1974-75 season.

THE SEVENTH ALL-BLACKS

The All-Blacks preparations for their 1972-1973 tour of Britain, Ireland and France began with an internal tour of New Zealand in May 1972. They went through a quick programme of nine games and won all nine convincingly, scoring 355 points in the process and conceding 88. Their highest margin of victory was against Marlborough (59-10) and their lowest was 16 points in beating the New Zealand Junior XV by 25-9. This tour was followed by three official international games against Australia, all of which were won with surprising ease as the All-Blacks knocked up 97 points while conceding 26. On their way to England, the All-Blacks beat British Columbia by 31-7 at Vancouver and defeated New York All-Stars at New York by 41-9.

A BRIGHT START

The All-Blacks full-back Joe Karam of Wellington, a twenty-year old of Lebanese parentage, scored the first points of the 1972-1973 tour in Britain, Ireland and France with a penalty goal against the Western Counties at Kingsholm, Gloucester on Saturday, 28th October 1972. He also had the distinction of scoring their last points, again with a penalty goal, against France at Parc des Princes, Paris on Saturday, 10th February, 1973. To add to that feat, he wound up as the All-Blacks top scorer with 138 points from 19 appearances—and he scored in each of the 19 games. His 138 points came from two tries, 24 penalty goals and 29 conversions. Making his international debut against Wales, he became the first player to kick five penalty goals in an international game in Britain, Ireland and France and also the third New Zealander to do so in any international game. Subsequently he went on to play in all five international games of the 1972-1973 tour—quite a remarkable achievement for a youngster who began the trip as the No 2 full-back in the New Zealand party. The first choice was Trevor Morris but he, unfortunately, was injured in the game against the New York All-Stars and, by the time, he had recovered, young Karam had established himself without argument as the automatic selection for the international games. With his 138 points, Karam became New Zealand's second highest scorer on a tour in Britain, Ireland and France behind Billy Wallace's 214 points for the All-Blacks of 1905-1906.

THEY LOST FIVE!

Ian Kirkpatrick's Seventh All-Blacks played 30 games in Britain, Ireland and France and won 23, scoring 568 points and conceding 254. On the debit side, however, was the depressing fact that they lost five games and drew two—and that makes them the most unsuccessful of the All-Blacks sides since the tours began with Dave Gallaher's party of 1905-1906. The previous worst had been Jack Manchester's side of 1935-1936 which had gone back home with three defeats and two draws. Kirkpatrick's men went down to Llanelli, North-West Counties, Midland Counties West, the Barbarians and France. Their highest margin of victory during the tour was 40 points in their 43-3 defeat of Neath and Aberavon on 24th January, 1973 and their worst defeat was 11-23 against the Barbarians at Cardiff Arms Park on 27th January, 1973. Their two draws in succession were in Ireland—against Ireland at Lansdowne Road, Dublin on Saturday, 20th January, 1973, which came four days after their 3-3 game with Munster at Musgrave Park, Cork.

SURPRISINGLY EARLY!

After a sparkling opening to their tour at Kingsholm, Gloucester on Saturday, 28th October, 1972 when they trounced Western Counties by 39 points to 12, the Seventh All-Blacks created their first little history at Stradey Park, Llanelli on Tuesday, 31st October. They crashed 3-9 to Llanelli. No previous All-Blacks side to Britain, Ireland

and France had lost a game at such an early stage of a tour. E. T. E. Bergiers scored a try for Llanelli in the first half and this was converted by Phil Bennett. Ten minutes from time the Llanelli wing-threequarter, Andy Hill, kicked a penalty goal. The All-Blacks only contribution to the scoring was Joe Karam's first half penalty goal from 40 yards.

THE FIRST IN ENGLAND

Before 12,000 spectators at Workington, Cumberland, on Wednesday afternoon, 22nd November, 1972, the North-West Counties of England scored an historic win over the Seventh All-Blacks. This marked the second defeat for Ian Kirkpatrick's men in just eight games. Trevor Morris had a penalty goal to put the All-Blacks into the lead but the North-West came level within two minutes with a fine drop goal from their centre, C. S. Wardlow. Grant Batty struck back with a try and then the North-West moved ahead with a try from wing-threequarter P. S. Maxwell, which was converted by outhalf A. R. Cowman. Just on half-time, however Trevor Morris sent the All-Blacks into the lead again with a penalty goal. They stretched their lead with a try from George Skudder—and then came disaster for the All-Blacks. Grant Batty was penalised for delaying a throw-in and Cowman kicked a penalty for the North-West to narrow the gap to two points. Then, just before the end, Maxwell went streaking away for his second try of the afternoon. The final score was 16-14 for the North-West Counties and with it they marched in to rugby history. They had become the first team in England, apart from the international side, to beat the All-Blacks and it had taken 67 years to achieve this feat.

A KICKING DUEL

Within two minutes of their opening international game of the 1972-1973 tour, against Wales at Cardiff Arms Park on Saturday, and December, 1972, the All-Blacks were in front. Full-back Joe Karam kicked a simple penalty goal—and that began an intriguing kicking duel between himself and the Welsh out-half Phil Bennett. Between them they decided this game. Young Karam got six penalty goal chances and kicked five of them. Bennett got seven and kicked four. Keith Murdoch added a try to Karam's three penalty goals in the first half and that put the All-Blacks into a lead of 10 points at half-time. Edwards had kicked a penalty for Wales in the 24th minute. John Bevan had a try for Wales at the start of the second half and then Bennett kicked his second penalty goal to bring the score to 13-10. Karam stepped back into the picture with a fourth penalty goal to make it 16-10 and then Bennett put over another penalty to leave it 16-13. A fifth penalty goal from Karam lifted the scoreline to 19-13 and Bennett just as quickly changed it to 19-16. With just a few minutes to go Bennett got the chance to make it level but his soaring penalty kick from 40 yards out swerved inches wide of the posts—and it was all over. It was the ninth meeting between the two countries and New Zealand had now stretched their supremacy to 6-3 since 1905-1906.

THE MURDOCH INCIDENT

No one, apart, of course, from those directly involved in it, will ever know what really happened at the Angel Hotel, Cardiff on the night of Saturday, 2nd December, 1972—and in the early hours of the morning of Sunday, 3rd December, 1972. Certainly there was trouble after the official banquet for the All-Blacks and Welsh teams—and one 29-year old Keith Murdoch of Otago, described variously as a cattle-drover, farm labourer, lorry-driver, bar bouncer and strong man, became the central figure of what has since become known as the "Murdoch Affair". Reports of incidents had been following the All-Blacks around on their tour and it was alleged that the giant 17st, 6' 0" second row forward had been involved in most of them. Following the dinner at the Angel Hotel, there had definitely been a fracas involving the New Zealander and some of the security guards. The upshot was that on the Sunday evening, the All-Blacks manager Ernie Todd released a statement to the effect that Murdoch would be disciplined. Surprisingly, however, Murdoch was listed for the next game against West Midlands at Moseley on the following Wednesday. On the Monday morning, however, Murdoch was taken out of the official coach and within a matter of an hour it was announced that he was being sent back home to New Zealand. By that night Murdoch was on the aeroplane for home. However, he disappeared from the aircraft when it landed at Darwin in Australia and the next report from him was that he intended to stay on in Australia. There have been many, many versions of the "Murdoch Affair" and there is probably truth in most of them. But until Keith Murdoch breaks his silence, no one will ever know really just what did happen at the Angel Hotel.

GOING'S TRY

The All-Blacks kept their unbeaten international record against Scotland with a 14-9 win at Murrayfield on Saturday, 16th December, 1972. But, like all their games against the Scots since 1905, it was a hard battle and it was not until shortly before the end that Sid Going, with a glorious 50 yards run, wrapped it up with probably his best try of the tour. The All-Blacks took the lead in the first half with a try by Alex Wyllie which Joe Karam converted but shortly after the re-start Andy Irvine kicked a penalty goal for Scotland. Grant Batty had a try for New Zealand but this was followed by a Scottish drop goal from Ian McGeechan and Irvine then closed the gap to a point with a penalty goal from the halfway mark. The game was in injury time when Going snapped up a bad pass by Alisdair McHarg and tore away for the try that sealed the issue.

THREE UP!

With wins over Wales and Scotland, Ian Kirkpatrick's All-Blacks notched up their third international victory at Twickenham on Saturday, 6th January, 1973 with a 9-0 win over England. All they needed now was to beat Ireland and they would be the first All-Blacks touring side to go home with victories over the four home countries. Ian Kirkpatrick got New Zealand off to a heartening start at Twickenham with a try after eight minutes and Joe Karam kept up his record of having scored in every game in which he had played, by kicking the conversion. The only score of the second half came after 15 minutes with a drop goal from Bryan Williams.

JUST MADE IT

With just five minutes to go at Lansdowne Road, Dublin, on Saturday afternoon, 20th January, 1973, Tom Grace shattered the All-Blacks dreams and ambitions of becoming the first New Zealand side to beat

England, Scotland, Wales and Ireland during a tour. At that moment, the score was 10-6 for the All-Blacks. Barry McGann had opened the proceedings with a penalty goal but a try by Sid Going, converted by Joe Karam had put the All-Blacks ahead by 10-3 at half-time. Then late in the game McGann had kicked a second penalty to make it 10-6. From the kick-off after this penalty goal, the ball went straight into touch. Ireland won the scrum-back, John Moloney kicked ahead and from the ruck Moloney got possession again and sent the ball to Grace on the wing. Grace, with only Joe Karam facing him, kicked over the full-back's head and then, in a desperate sprint he got the touchdown just inches away from the dead-ball line. McGann's attempt to convert was made in dead silence—and there were none more silent than the All-Blacks—but a fine kick which appeared to be going straight for the posts, was caught by the breeze and it swirled inches wide. The All-Blacks unbeaten record in the internationals was safe but once again they had failed to win those vital four international games on a tour of Britain and Ireland. This, incidentally, was the All-Blacks second draw against an Irish side in four days—they had been held to 3-3 by Munster at Musgrave Park on 16th January—and it marked the first time in any of their tours to Britain, Ireland and France, that they had been held to level pegging in two successive games. Ireland's out-half Barry McGann had the distinction of scoring in both games.

UP AND DOWN

The finest victory of the 1972-1973 All-Blacks was followed by their worst defeat. On 24th January, 1973 they walloped Neath and Aberavon at Neath by the resounding margin of 40 points (43-3) and three days later at Cardiff Arms Park, they went down by 12 points (11-23) to the Barbarians. Like their previous games the New-Zealand - Barbarians match was an epic and brought two of the finest tries of modern rugby. It opened on the highest of notes with a try by the Barbarians. Phil Bennett went back to collect a kick ahead which had landed 10 yards from the Barbarians line and elected to run. With a baffling sequence of delightful sidesteps, he dodged a succession of New Zealanders and then whipped the ball to John Williams, who passed to John Pullin. John Dawes was the next to receive the ball and he took play over the halfway line before handing on to Tom David who, in turn, delivered the ball to Derek Quinnell. Gareth Edwards then moved into the picture, intercepted Quinnell's pass to John Bevan and went streaking 30 yards to score. Bennett then kicked a penalty goal, converted Fergus Slattery's try and before half-time John Bevan put the Barbarians into a 17-0 lead. This was the greatest first half score ever put up against an All-Blacks side in their long history. Joe Karam kicked a penalty goal, Grant Batty scored a try—and this was followed by the second great try of the game. Batty snapped up the ball close to the touch-line and faced with full-back John Williams, he kicked to the right of Williams and then raced around him on the left. He collected the ball again and sped off for a brilliant try to make the score 11-17. John Williams, however, scored a final try for the Barbarians and then converted it for a 23-11 win.

THE LAST DEFEAT

The 1972-1973 All-Blacks left England with a defeat in their tour of Britain and Ireland and they finished the tour in France with another. On 31st January, 1973, at Tarbes they beat a French Selection by 12-3, three days later at Lyons they beat a second French Selection by 23-8 and on 7th February, they beat a third French Selection at Clermont-Ferrand by 6-3. Then they moved to Parc des Princes in Paris on Saturday, 10th February for their final game of the tour—the full international against France. And they were well and thoroughly beaten. Claude Dourthe gave France a four points lead early with a try and Joe Karam, in his 19th game, scored again with a penalty goal. But just before the end of the first half, the French wing-threequarter Robert Bertranne shot over for a try which Max Barrau converted. Karam kicked a second penalty goal for the All-Blacks but Jean Pierre Romeu stretched France's lead with his penalty goal and that was the last score of the Seventh All-Blacks tour of Britain, Ireland and France. The most significant feature of it was that, with his two penalty goals, Joe Karam had created an all-time New Zealand record of scoring in every game he had played on the tour.

THE FINAL BOW

When referee Mr J. P. G. Pring of Auckland sounded the final whistle at Eden Park on 14th August, 1971 to bring the New Zealand v Lions game to a close in a 14-14 draw, it marked the end of a glorious chapter in the history of New Zealand rugby. Colin Meads had worn the All-Blacks jersey for the last time and there were 56,000 spectators there to say an honourable goodbye to him. Meads, surely the greatest forward of his time and perhaps of all time in the history of rugby football had worn his first All-Blacks jersey against New South Wales in 1957 and finished his long and proud career that afternoon in Auckland, 1971, by wearing it for the 132nd time—a record for a New Zealander. During that time he had played in 55 full internationals, which was to be a world record until it was surpassed by Willie John McBride of Ireland in 1974.

SEVEN SONS AND DADS

In over 100 years of New Zealand rugby, seven father-and-son combinations have worn the All-Blacks jersey. They are E. F. Barry (1932-1934) and Kevin Barry (1962-1963) but Kevin, although he wore the All-Blacks jersey on 23 occasions never played in an international game, Handly Brown (1924-1926) and Henry Browne (1935-1936), both of whom toured with New Zealand but did not play in an international game, John Dick (1937-1938) and Malcolm Dick (1963-1970), W. R. Irvine (1923-1930) and I. B. Irvine (1952), Charles Purdue (1901-1905) and G. B. Purdue (1931-1932) and Henry Roberts (1884 and E. J. Roberts (1913-1921).

THE BROTHERS

Twenty-six sets of brothers have worn the All-Blacks jersey and the most famous are probably the Brownlies, the Clarkes and the Meads. There were the three Brownlies, Cyril, Lawrence and Maurice, but Lawrence did not, however, play in an international game. Between them, the two Meads brothers, Colin and Stan, made 162 appearances in the New Zealand jersey. but this has been surpassed by the Clarkes, Don and Ian, who wore the All-Blacks jersey on a record 172 occasions.

ENDED AS IT BEGAN

New Zealand's legendary full-back Don Clarke of Waikato, pulled on his first All-Blacks jersey in an international game and he took off his last All-Blacks jersey in an international game. He made his debut for

New Zealand in the international against South Africa at Christchurch in 1956 and opened the scoring with a penalty goal. He ended his 89 appearances in the New Zealand jersey with his international appearance against Australia at Wellington in 1964 and fittingly he had the final score of the game—a conversion of P. H. Murdoch's try. Clarke set the staggering record of 781 points in his 89 appearances for New Zealand. His total came from eight tries, 173 conversions, 120 penalty goals and 15 drop goals.

ONLY 40 GAMES LOST

In over 100 years of rugby, the All-Blacks have played only 161 international games and of these, 64 have been against Australia. Their record, however, is strikingly impressive. They have won 110, lost only 40 and 11 have been drawn. The 160 international games have been against Australia, South Africa, the Lions, England, Scotland, Wales, France and Ireland. They have yet to be beaten by either Scotland or Ireland. In their 64 games against Australia, they have won 47, lost 13 and drawn four. This was their record at the start of the 1974/75 season.

THE 1974 TOUR

Under the captaincy of A. R. Leslie, New Zealand toured in Australia in 1974 and returned home unbeaten with 11 victories and one draw in their 12 games. They scored 432 points, from 73 tries, 40 conversions, 16 penalty goals and four drop goals, and conceded 60 points. The All-Blacks won the first international game at Sydney by 11-6, drew the second at Brisbane, 16-16 and won the third at Sydney by 16-6. Ian Kirkpatrick, the former All-Blacks captain brought his total of tries in international rugby to 12 during this tour and this is a record for New Zealand in international games.

KARAM'S RECORD

New Zealand full-back Joe Karam, who had scored in all of his appearances during the 1972-1973 tour of Britain, Ireland and France, again had the distinction of scoring in all of his appearances during the

1974 All-Blacks tour of Australia. And he had his most remarkable hour in the All-Blacks annihilation of Southern Australia in the first match of the tour at Adelaide. The tourists, playing under floodlights set the towering record of 117 points against Southern Australia's six points and in a game which brought the tourists an almost incredible total of 21 tries, Karam scored two. To those two tries, he added 15 conversions and a penalty goal for 41 points, which broke the record of 38 points set by All-Black Ron Jarden against Central West during the 1951 tour in Australia.

THE LEGENDARY MEADS

Since they entered international rugby 700 New Zealand players have worn the famous All-Blacks jersey in international and tour games. Of these 478 have been capped for New Zealand against the Lions, Australia, South Africa, England, Ireland, France, Wales and Scotland. The country's most-capped international is the legendary Colin Meads (King Country) with 55 from 1957 to 1971. During that time Meads made 132 appearances in the All-Blacks jersey and is the only New Zealand player to date to reach the century mark.

SOUTH AFRICA

SOUTH AFRICA'S GREEN

B. H. "Fairy" Heatlie (Western Province), who won his six caps against Lion touring sides, is South Africa's most enduring international. He made his first international appearance for his country in the second Test against the Lions in 1891 and also played in the third Test that year. Against the Lions touring side of 1896, he made two further appearances and was again picked to play for South Africa in the first and third Tests of the Lions tour in 1903. His international career spanned 13 seasons. Heatlie, however, has a greater claim to fame in South African history. He was responsible for introducing the green jerseys which the Springboks now wear. For the Test at Cape Town against the 1896 Lions, Heatlie, who was captain of the Old Diocesan Club, whose colours were green, captained South Africa in this Test and decided to use his club's jerseys. In green, the South Africans recorded their first international win and seven years later when Heatlie again captained South Africa in a Test game against the Lions at Capetown, he insisted on using the Old Diocesan jerseys again. South Africa won and also took the series—and from that day on, green became the international colour of South Africa's rugby teams.

SECOND HONOURS

W. M. C. McEwan (Edinburgh Academicals) and A. Frew (Edinburgh University) had the unique distinction of playing for both Scotland and South Africa. McEwan, who won 16 caps for Scotland between 1894 and 1900 and Frew who won his three Scottish caps in 1901, later settled down in South Africa. McEwan won two caps for South Africa against the Lions touring side of 1903 and Frew was also honoured by the Springbok selectors for the first Test that year.

THREE DADS AND SONS

Despite the extraordinary tradition of rugby in South Africa, only three fathers have been followed into the Springbok jersey by their sons. They are Alf Walker (1921-1924) and Harry Walker (1953-1956),

348

Cecil Jennings (1937) and Mike Jennings (1969-1970) and Felix du Plessis (1949) and Morne du Plessis (1971). There have been 22 sets of brothers in international games for South Africa since 1891 but only twice have three brothers played for the Springboks. They are the Luyts, Freddie, Dick and John, who were contemporary between 1910 and 1913. They have the all-time record of having appeared together in three international games against Scotland, Wales and England during the 1912-1913 tour of Britain and Ireland. The other three brothers were Jaap, Dolf and Martiens Bekker, between 1952 and 1960. The most remarkable family in South African rugby are, of course the Morkels. In all 10 Morkels played for South Africa and all were related but they were only two sets of brothers in the ten—Harry and Royal (1921) and Gerry Morkel (1912-1921) and Jackie (1912-1913).

ON HIS OWN

His mother wanted to call him Gerald and his father, one of the stalwarts of the local rugby club, Hamilton, wanted to call him . . . Hamilton! They compromised and so the youngster, born in 1906 was duly christened Gerald Hamilton Brand. His father introduced him to rugby at an early stage and eventually Gerry Brand went on to be chosen for Western Province, with whom he became an outstanding full-back. In 1928 he won his first international cap against the touring New Zealanders and between then and 1938 he was to collect 16 caps for the Springboks. Brand, who wore the Springbok jersey on 46 occasions, wound up his career with a record number of points by a South African in official tour games including international matches. His record, which still endures, of 293 points, was made up of 100 conversions, 25 penalty goals, three drop goals and the remaining six points came from the only two tries he scored in his 46 games. His most famous kick was his drop goal for South Africa against England during the 1931-1932 tour of Britain, Ireland and France. He took the ball 55 yards out and his successful kick carried over the dead-ball line into the crowd. This kick was estimated at 90 yards and is recognised as the longest drop goal in the history of rugby.

THE FIRST SPRINGBOKS

The first South Africans, led by Paul Roos, opened their tour of Britain, Ireland and France, with a resounding win by 37-0 over East Midlands and followed this by beating Midlands, 29-0, and Kent, 21-0.

They won 15 games in succession before going down to their first defeat against Scotland on Saturday, 17th November, 1906 at the famous Glasgow soccer stadium, Hampden Park, before a crowd of 32,000. Including the game against France, which ended the tour, the South Africans played 29 games, won 26, lost two, drew one and scored 608 points while conceding 87. Their highest margin of victory in Britain and Ireland was 44 points in their 44-0 defeat of Northumberland and in France they had a margin of 49 points in beating the French national side by 55-6. Their only draw, 3-3 was against England at the Crystal Palace on Saturday, 8th December, 1906 and their worst defeat was 0-17 against Cardiff in their final game in Britain. Their top scorer in Britain and Ireland was half-back H. W. "Paddy" Carolin, with 75 points from six tries, 16 conversions, three penalty goals and four drop goals. Bob Loubser was the side's top try scorer with 22 in Britain and Ireland and he also added two more in the defeat of France, which was not classified as an official game. Loubser, who was then twenty-two, played in 23 of the 29 games, and, indeed, was the only back to appear in all four of the official international games plus the fifth against France.

DEFEAT AT HAMPDEN

With 15 successive victories behind them—the latest a 32-5 win over the South of Scotland four days earlier—the first South Africans took on Scotland at Hampden Park, Glasgow on Saturday, 17th November, 1906 and went down to a totally unexpected defeat. In fairness, however, this game, played on a sodden and muddy pitch, provided more injury problems for the Springboks than the whole of the tour up to then had brought. Their great forward D. J. "Koei" Brink damaged his leg early on in the first half and was off the field for almost 20 minutes. Dietloff Mare, also one of the big men of the pack, had two of his fingers broken and had to be taken out of the scrum to play as an extra wing-threequarter. Early in the second half, full-back A. W. F. Marsburg was kicked accidentally on the head and had to be carried off on a stretcher. Somerset Morkel was then taken out of the pack to play at full-back and the South Africans were down to six forwards for most of the second half. Wing-threequarter Grant McLeod had Scotland's first score with a try and five minutes from time, their other wing-threequarter A. L. Purves went over for the second to leave the final score 6-0. This was South Africa's first international game outside their own country and their first against an international side other than the Lions.

NOT THIS TIME

Wales had been the only side to beat the All-Blacks of 1905-1906 and 45,000 supporters turned up at Swansea on Saturday, 1st December, 1906 with the firm belief that the first South Africans were to be given the same treatment. But it was not to be and, in fact, it was a sad and depressing afternoon for all the Welsh at Swansea. Steve Joubert had an early try for South Africa and Japie Krige raced over for a second to put the Springboks into a 6-0 lead at half-time. Midway through the second half, J. W. E. Raaff, a 6' 3" and 16st forward, went straight through the Welsh defences for a try and Joubert converted for an 11-0 win. This still remains as the greatest margin by which South Africa have beaten Wales in an international game in Wales.

THE ONLY DRAW

South Africa were again caught up in trouble when they met England at the Crystal Palace, London on Saturday, 8th December—their fourth international game on four successive Saturdays. Wing-threequarter Japie Krige had been rushed to hospital during the previous week with appendicitis and their other outstanding back Anton Stegmann had injured a leg against Ireland and was also out of the side. Shortly after the start Somerset Morkel was injured, had to be carried off and the Springboks finished with 14 men. They took the lead in the first half with a try from forward W. A. Millar but England came level in the second half with a try from Freddie Brooks and a dour game eventually petered out into a 3-3 draw. It was the South African's only draw of the tour and they were not to be held to level pegging again in a tour of Britain, Ireland and France until 1931-1932.

TWO FOR GIBBS

New Year's Day, 1906 did not go down in the history of South African rugby as a happy one. It brought them to Cardiff Arms Park to face Cardiff and on the evidence of all previous form that season, they looked to be all set to end their tour of Britain and Ireland with a comfortable win. Already on the tour, they had beaten Newport 8-0, Glamorganshire 6-3, Wales 11-0, Monmouthshire 17-0 and just three days earlier they had cruised to an easy win over Llanelli by 16-3. Seing that Llanelli had already beaten Cardiff, the odds were firmly on the South Africans to finish out in Wales on a top note. As it came out, they went down to a shattering defeat. For the first time on the tour they failed to score against a club or county side and the Cardiff winning margin of 17 points still remains to this day as the South Africans worst defeat in a tour of Britain, Ireland and France. Not until 1965 were the Springboks to be beaten again by 17 points and that was in New Zealand when they crashed 6-23 to Wellington. Cardiff's scorers on that historic afternoon were Reggie Gibbs (two tries), Gwynn Nicholls (a try), J. L. Williams (a try), H. B. Winfield (a penalty goal and a conversion).

THE YOUNGEST

Steve Joubert, selected to tour with the South Africans in 1906-1907, played in the three international games against England, Wales and Ireland. When he made his international debut against Ireland at Balmoral, Belfast on Saturday, 24th November, 1960, he was just under nineteen and a half years old and remains as the youngest player ever to be capped for South Africa.

THE SECOND SPRINGBOKS

Billy Millar's second Springboks left for home with the record of having played 27 matches with 24 victories in their 1912-1913 tour of Britain, Ireland and France. They lost three games and scored 441 points while conceding 101. Their top scorer was full-back Douglas Morkel with 68 points which came from two tries, 16 conversions and 10 penalty goals. The top try scorer was E. E. "Boetie" McHardy with 20. Their highest margin of victory was the 38-0 win over Ireland at Lansdowne Road, Dublin on Saturday, 30th November, 1912 and their worst defeat by 3-9 came at Newport.

SURPRISE CHOICE

Billy Millar of Western Province, who had toured in Britain, Ireland and France with the first Springboks, was a somewhat controversial captain of the second South African touring side of 1912-13. He was the last player to be named to the touring panel and the selectors had another player in mind to captain the side. But the South African Board, by a large majority, decided that the twenty-eight -year old Millar should lead the side. He was one of three survivors of the first Springboks. The others were the thirty-three-year old F. J. Dobbin, who was named as vice-captain and full-back Douglas Morkel who was then twenty-six. One of the features of this second Springbok side was that the wing-threequarter and centre-threequarter positions filled by Anton Stegmann and Japie Krige on the 1906-1907 side were filled in 1912-1913 by their younger brothers Jan Stegmann and Willie Krige.

A BROTHERLY AFFAIR

For their tour of 1912-1913, South Africa bought two sets of brothers— the Morkels and the Luyts—to Britain, Ireland and France and they had the proud distinction of being represented in the four official international games against Scotland, Ireland, Wales and England. Gerhard Morkel at full-back and his brother Jackie Morkel in the centre played in all four games and for extra family measure they were joined in all four by their cousins, D. F. T. Morkel and W. H. Morkel. The Luyt brothers, however, were to set an unique record on this tour. Three of them, Dick at centre, Freddie at scrum-half and John in the pack, played together against Scotland, Wales and England—and this is the only instance in rugby history of three brothers playing together on an international side. But for the fact that John Luyt was injured in the match against Scotland, he would have joined his brothers for the game against Ireland. The Morkels and the Luyts also played against France in the last major game of this tour but while France awarded caps for this game, the South Africans did not and it is not included in their list of official internationals.

THE SPRINGBOK HEAD

With 106 points scored and only 19 conceded in their first six games, Billy Millar's 1912-1913 Springboks arrived in Newport on 24th October, 1912 and ran into one Fred Birt right at the top of his form. Birt, who played at full-back for Newport, had won his first international cap for Wales the previous season and was regarded as one of the best kickers in the game at that time. This game against the South Africans, however, was to be the high point of his career. Shortly after the start, with a splendidly-taken drop goal, he put Newport into a shock lead and, although Douglas Morkel struck back with a try, the local club were still ahead 4-3 at half-time. Despite tremendous Springbok pressure in the second half, Newport held on grimly to their lead and then Birt stepped back into the picture again. The South African threequarter Van der Hoff fumbled a kick ahead by the Welsh international Jack Wetter and Birt, following up at a smart pace, whipped up the ball and scampered over the line for a try. To complete his afternoon, he converted his own try and it was all over. The Springboks had been beaten by 9-3—and for Newport, there was a special trophy. This was the first time a South African side had brought the now traditional Springbok head to be presented to the first side to beat them on the tour. The head was duly presented to Newport's captain Walter Martin and it is still on proud display to this day at the Newport clubhouse at Rodney Parade.

A SECOND DEFEAT

Following their defeat by Newport, the 1912-13 South Africans resumed their winning ways and chalked up another seven victories before facing London at Twickenham. This brought their second defeat of the tour and also the first penalty try of the Springbok tours in Britain, Ireland and France. In the first half "Cherry" Pillman broke away with the ball at his feet and dribbled right up to the South African threequarter-line. He kicked diagonally ahead and W. S. D. Craven, the London wing-forward raced ahead to dribble the ball on. But when he looked certain to score, South Africa's Gerhard Morkel obstructed Craven and the referee, A. O. Jones, a former England cricket captain, promptly awarded a penalty try, which was converted. London moved into a 10-0 lead with a try from Pillman which was also converted. Eventually London survived to win by 10-8. This, as it later transpired, was to be a historic victory. Nearly 40 years later and almost to the day, the 1951-1952 Springboks were to lose their only game of that tour—and again the margin was 10-8 and again the side was London Counties.

THE INTERNATIONALS

The 1912-1913 South Africans met Scotland in their 16th game of the tour at Inverleith, Edinburgh on Saturday, 23rd November, 1912 and thoroughly avenged their 1906 defeat. "Boetie" McHardy gave them a first half lead of three points with a try and the Scots were never in with any sort of a chance in the second. Jan Stegmann scored two tries, "Boy" Morkel had one and Gerhard Morkel and Douglas Morkel each converted a try and the Springboks romped home to win by 16-0. Exactly a week later, at Lansdowne Road Dublin on Saturday, 30th November, they gave Ireland their worst beating in international rugby by 38-0, which was to remain as an international record defeat until Scotland were beaten 44-0 by South Africa at Murrayfield during the 1951-1952 tour. South Africa's 10 tries came from Jan Stegmann (3), McHardy (3), Jack Morkel (two) and Joe Francis and Billy Millar (one each). Gerhard Morkel kicked three conversions and Fred Luyt had one. The third international was against Wales at Cardiff Arms Park on Saturday, 14th December, 1912 and this was to be the toughest of the international campaign. In the end South Africa survived with a penalty goal, kicked in the 15th minute by Douglas Morkel. With the one game left against England, South Africa had scored 57 points and conceded none.

A RECORD SPOILED

The 1912-1913 Springboks duly beat England at Twickenham on Saturday, 4th January, 1913 and for the first time a touring side had won all their four international games to Britain and Ireland. But what would have been a remarkable record was spoiled 10 minutes after the start when the English wing-threequarter Ronnie Poulton-Palmer made a glorious run along the touch-line to cross for a magnificent try. His try represented the only points scored against the South Africans in their four international games. Jack Morkel levelled the scores with a try and Douglas Morkel added a further six points in the second half with two penalty goals. Douglas Morkel had the distinction of scoring in all four internationals and his two penalty goals in the second half also brought the English their first defeat at the famous Twickenham ground which had been opened in 1909.

JUST THE ONCE

Only once during their 1912-1913 tour did the South African tourists fail to score and that was against Swansea in their third last game of the tour in Britain and Ireland on Saturday, 28th December, 1912. In the game before this they had taken a slim revenge for their 1906 defeat by beating Cardiff 7-6 but it was obvious at this stage that the Springboks were beginning to feel the wearying effects of a long tour. D. J. Thomas scored a try for Swansea 19 minutes after the start and that was sufficient to decide the game.

THE FINAL FLOURISH

Billy Millar's second Springboks played their 27th and final match of the 1921-1913 tour at Bordeaux and won easing up by 38-5. This was regarded as an "unofficial" game but at least it gave the South Africans the satisfaction of completing the Grand Slam against Scotland, Ireland, Wales, England and France. Their top scorer against France was Douglas Morkel with three conversions a penalty goal and a drop goal, which it is claimed, travelled well over 90 yards.

DOWN UNDER

The first South African side to tour in Australia and New Zealand in 1921 was captained by Theo Pienaar of Western Province, who was destined to wind up his rugby career without an international cap. The Springboks opened their tour with four games against provincial sides in Australia, all of which were won and they scored 83 points while conceding 38. During this portion of the tour, they also had an unofficial outing against a Victoria side and won by 51-0. In the major portion of the tour in New Zealand, they played 16 games, including three internationals, won 14, lost one and drew one and scored 230 points while conceding 63. Their top scorer was Gerhard Morkel, the full-back, with 57 points from 22 conversions, three penalty goals and one drop goal. The top try scorer was Bill Zeller with 14. In New Zealand their top margin of victory was 31 points in their 34-3 defeat of South Canterbury. Their worst defeat was in the first international game against New Zealand in which they went down 5-13. Only in two games did they fail to score and both were scoreless draws, against Taranaki in the second game of the tour and against New Zealand in the final game.

JUST LIKE DAD!

Alf Walker of Natal won his first South African cap during the tour of Australia and New Zealand in 1921. He played in the first Test against the All-Blacks in which South Africa went down to a 5-13 defeat and again in the Third Test which ended in a scoreless draw. During 1924, he represented South Africa in all four games against the British and Irish Lions touring side and finished his international career with six caps. Twenty-nine years later, in 1953, Harry Walker of the Orange Free State won the first of his four South African caps against the touring Australians. His other three came against Australia and New Zealand during the Springboks tour of 1956. The Walkers were the first father and son to represent South Africa in international rugby. The only other family to achieve this distinction in South Africa are Felix du Plessis and his son Morne du Plessis. Felix, representing Transvaal, was capped three times against New Zealand in 1949 and Morne, representing Western Provinces, won his first cap against Australia in 1971. Cecil and Mike Jennings also wore the Springbok jersey but while Cecil made one international appearance against New Zealand in 1937, his son Mike, who toured in Britain, Ireland and France in 1970-1971, did not make any international appearances.

THE FIRST TRY

With nine games behind them, including a 4-6 defeat by Canterbury, the South Africans headed for Carisbrook, Dunedin on 13th August, 1921 for the first international game against New Zealand. And wing-threequarter Attie van Heerden, later to become a South African Olympic sprinter, took the honour of getting their first score down under. He broke away and as the New Zealand full-back C. N. Kingstone of Taranaki dived to tackle him, Van Heerden sailed over his head and raced on to score a try which Gerhard Morkel converted. The second half, however, belonged to New Zealand. "Moke"

Belliss went over for a try and this was converted by the nineteen-year old Mark Nicholls. This was Nicholls's debut in an All-Blacks jersey and he was, of course, to become one of the legendary heroes of New Zealand rugby. Percy Storey added a second try for New Zealand and Nicholls was again on the mark with the conversion. Shortly before the end, New Zealand's wing-threequarter Jack Steel took a pass on his own "25" and ran 85 yards to score. The pass to Steel had been an awkward one and it is recorded that for most of the run, he had the ball behind his back and only close to the line did he eventually manage to pull it around to the front and to safety. His try made it 13-5 for New Zealand. As had happened to them in their first tour of Britain, Ireland and France in 1906, South Africa had again lost the opening international.

A FLYWEIGHT

There was quite a gasp of astonishment from the capacity crowd at Eden Park, Auckland on Saturday, 27th August, 1921 when Billy Sendin ran out on to the field with the South African side to face the All-Blacks in their second meeting on New Zealand soil. Among the gigantic Springbok forwards—Royal Morkel was the heaviest at 17st 6lbs—there was no problem at all in picking out the tiny Sendin. Always conscious of his real weight—and he was worried that the selectors might be influenced against him if they knew his correct poundage—Sendin claimed to be over 9st. But, on this particular afternoon, the scales beforehand had shown him to be 115 pounds or 8st 3lbs. That leaves him as the lightest man to play for South Africa and possibly the lightest ever to play in international rugby. Despite his weight, Sendin, in this his one and only appearance for South Africa, got the first score of the game with a try and his outstanding display at scrum-half sent the Springboks on their way to their first win against the All-Blacks in New Zealand. In all, South Africa have now played 30 international games against New Zealand since 1921 and have 16 wins to New Zealand's 14 with two drawn. Their greatest win against the All-Blacks was at Durban on 30th June, 1928 when the score was 17-0 and their worst defeat by New Zealand was the 3-20 at Auckland on 18th September, 1965.

AN UNIQUE RECORD

By playing in the South African pack in their international game against New Zealand on 13th August, 1921, Frank Mellish (Blackheath and Western Province) collected one of rugby's most extraordinary records, that of playing for two countries in the same year. Capped first for England in 1920 with four caps against Scotland, Wales, Ireland and France, he had won a further two against Ireland and Wales in 1921 before returning home to his native South Africa. Mellish played in the first international against New Zealand, was dropped for the second but was restored to the side for the third. Later he was to play for South Africa against the Lions of 1924 and he finished his international career with six caps for South Africa . . . and six for England.

THE FINAL DROP

With 40,000 spectators, then a record for New Zealand, and with many of them encroaching on the sidelines at Eden Park, Auckland on 27th August, 1921, the Springboks had their first international victory outside of their own country and Europe. The tiny Billy Sendin had their first score, a try, which was converted by Gerhard Morkel, but A. L. McLean, in his first appearance for New Zealand, brought the All-Blacks level with a snap try which Mark Nicholls converted. An intriguing deadlock throughout most of the second half was finally broken by Gerhard Morkel. A long clearance by the All-Blacks wing threequarter Jack Steel was fielded by the Springbok full-back just on the halfway mark and without hesitation, he dropped a magnificent goal to leave the final score 9-5.

NOT A SCORE

With a win each, the final international game between South Africa and New Zealand at Athletic Park, Wellington on Saturday, 17th September, 1921, was a crucial one. It ended, however, with honour to both sides in a scoreless draw. In the history of South Africa v New Zealand games from 1921 to 1970, this is still the only occasion when both sides have failed to score. One of the features of this first series in New Zealand was that South Africa had made use of the five Morkels, Harry, Royal, Gerhard, Boy and Henry over the three international games. Only Harry and Royal were brothers but all were related.

THE THIRD SPRINGBOKS

Benny Osler led the third Springboks to Britain and Ireland in 1931-1932 and while there were widespread criticisms of the match-winning tactics he employed, there could be no argument but that he got the successful results that he wanted for his men. Osler put most of his faith and reliance in his forwards and with their ability to get a steady possession, he brought his side up the field by kicking monotonously and steadily for touch. Only when South Africa were close to their opponent's goal-line, did Osler bring his threequarters into action. His methods were not well received—the general opinion was that he overdid the kicking—but they paid off with a record of; played 26, won 23, lost one, drew two and 407 points scored for 124 against. The only defeat of the third Springboks came in the 13th game, against Midland Counties, and the two draws were against South of Scotland and Devon and Cornwall. Only in one game did they fail to score and that was in the 0-0 draw with South of Scotland. Their highest margin of victory was the 41-0 win over Durham and Northumberland and in their only defeat by Midland Counties, they went down by 21-30. The top scorer of the tour was Gerhard Brand, their full-back with 72 points from two tries, 25 conversions, four penalty goals and a drop goal. The top try scorer was Morris Zimmerman, a wing-threequarter, with 14.

NOT SO SLOW

Charles Slow, who had to wait until 1934 to win his only cap for England, had the afternoon of his short rugby career against the touring South Africans at Leicester in the 13th match of the tour. Playing for Midland Counties, he struck sensational form and with his drop goal just after the start he paved the way to the only defeat of South Africa on this tour. This was an afternoon when Benny Osler dropped himself and his place at out-half went to Michael Francis. Without the influence of Osler, the South Africans opened up their game more than normally and paid the penalty for it. They were led 19-6 at half-time and although they pulled the lead back to three points, 24-21, towards the end, the Midland Counties with Ireland's international George Beamish leading a tremendously strong pack, came back to win the game by 30-21. Those 30 points still endure as the most ever scored against the Springboks either overseas or at home. Slow, who was killed in 1939, added two tries to his drop goal and his 10 points made him the top scorer against South Africa in that tour. No player in England, Ireland, Scotland or Wales, has scored double figures in any one game against the Springbok touring sides since 1906.

WALES THE FIRST

With 17 games behind them, the 1931-1932 Springboks played their first international game of the tour against Wales at St Helen's, Swansea on Saturday, 5th December, 1931 and it marked the international debut of a 21-year old, who was to become one of the remarkable personalities of South African and world rugby—Danie Craven. And he was one of the great successes of a bitterly fought game, under appalling weather conditions. Wales took the lead in the first half with a try by Will Davies and they held it to half-time. George Daneel of Transvaal brought the scores level with a try midway through the second half and in a towering finish, the South Africans went ahead with a try by Ferdie Bergh and Benny Osler converted it to leave the final score 8-3.

AGAINST IRELAND

On the evidence of their comfortable win by 30-3 over Ulster at Ravenhill on Saturday, 12th December, 1931, the South Africans were expected to have little trouble in dealing with Ireland at Lansdowne Road on the following Saturday. But this was a game that followed closely on the pattern of the Springboks first international win of the tour over Wales a fortnight earlier. Larry McMahon kicked a penalty goal for Ireland and with Jammie Clinch, Jack Siggins and George Beamish leading the Irish pack in a glorious battle, the Irish were still in front at half-time. Early in the second half, however, Morris Zimmerman followed up a long kick ahead by Osler and he got by Ireland's full back Jim Egan for a try to level the scoring. Ireland held out until eight minutes from time. Then Frank Waring broke through for a try and this time Osler converted with a good kick. The final score of 8-3 was the same as that of the game against Wales and it marked South Africa's third win over Ireland since 1906 and the Springboks had scored 61 points to Ireland's 15.

BRAND'S AFTERNOON

The international meeting of South Africa and England at Twickenham on Saturday afternoon, 2nd January, 1932 was in its dying minutes and with South Africa three points ahead and in total command of the proceedings, quite a few of the crowd had already left the stadium. It had not been a particularly exciting game and the Springboks had gone into the lead in the first half with a try from Benny Osler. Thereafter the only feature of the game had been the various attempts by out-half Osler and full-back Gerry Brand to drop goals. Osler had tried four and all had failed. Brand had missed three but one from just on the halfway line had gone just inches wide of the posts. Then, just two minutes from time, Brand fielded a kick ahead by England's full-back Robert Barr and ran diagonally from his own "25" into the centre of the field. With an open space he steadied himself and then dropped for goal. It was a tremendous kick, soaring high into the air and dead straight between the posts. It dropped far behind the dead-ball line. Brand had taken the kick seven yards inside his own half and when a measurement was put on the length of the kick after the game, the distance was over 90 yards—the longest successful drop goal in the history of rugby. With this 7-0 win over England, the Springboks now needed only a win over Scotland to complete their second Grand Slam of the home countries.

DOWN AGAIN

For the third time in an international game of 1931-1932, the South Africans were led by three points at half-time, when they met Scotland at Murrayfield on Saturday, 16th January, 1932. In dreadful weather conditions—heavy rain, a gale-force wind and occasional snow—the Scots got off to a sensational start. Within two minutes out-half H.

Lind of Dunfermline intercepted the ball and streaked over for a try, and the Scots stayed in front until midway through the second half when Benny Osler levelled the scores with a try. Shortly before the end, at a time when a draw seemed inevitable, Danie Craven slipped away from a scrum on the Scottish "25" and got the winning try. The Springboks had won the four internationals scoring 29 points and conceding only nine.

NEVER AGAIN

The very first international game between South Africa and Australia at Newlands in 1933 was to have been a red-letter day for the young Leon Barnard of South Western Districts. Regarded as one of the up-and-coming wing-threequarters of the time, he had been selected to make his international debut for the Springboks in this game. Unfortunately, because of illness in the week preceding the game, he had to cry off at the last minute. He was replaced by Freddie Turner of Eastern Province, who had to be flown from Port Elizabeth for the game and it is almost certain that Turner was the first player to be flown to an international rugby game. It was Turner's debut for South Africa and he made the most of it. He was retained for the next two games against Australia and subsequently went on to win 11 caps for his country. As for Leon Barnard, he wound up his rugby career without ever winning a cap for South Africa.

THE BRAND NAME

With the score between the two countries at three wins each and one match drawn, South Africa headed down under in 1937 for their second visit to New Zealand. On the way, they played nine matches, including two internationals, in Australia and their overall record was; played 26 games, won 24, lost two, drew none and they scored 753 points while conceding 169. Their record in New Zealand was 17 played with 16 wins, one defeat and 411 points for and 104 against. Their top points scorer was full back Gerry Brand with 190 points from 16 games, which came from 69 conversions, 16 penalty goals and a drop goal. Brand also scored a further 19 points during that tour in an unofficial game against South Australia. In the New Zealand portion of the tour, Brand scored an exact 100 points in 13 games. The Springboks highest win was their 47-7 win over Otago and their only defeat was the 7-13 in the first international against New Zealand. The touring side's top try scorer was F. G. Turner with 16.

DOWN FIRST TIME

Philip Nel, who captained the 1937 touring side to Australia, was a spectator when South Africa took on New Zealand in their first international at Athletic Park, Wellington and he saw the Springboks down to their first defeat. Dave Trevathan put New Zealand into the lead with a penalty goal and after D. O. Williams had scored a try for South Africa, Trevathan restored the lead with a second penalty goal. New Zealand stretched their lead with a try from John Dick and shortly before full-time Dave Trevathan sealed the issue with a fine drop goal. Just on the whistle John White dropped a goal for South Africa. With this win, New Zealand moved into a series lead of 4-3 with one game drawn.

LEVEL AGAIN

Following their defeat by New Zealand, South Africa went on the rampage in their next four games against provincial sides and knocked up 119 points, while conceding only 20—and then they faced the All-Blacks again, this time at Lancaster Park, Christchurch. Jack Sullivan put the All-Blacks ahead with two early tries and they were 6 points up at half-time. Fred Turner had a second half-try for South Africa which was converted by Brand, who then proceeded to kick a 55-yards penalty goal and from there on it was South Africa all the way. Ebbo Bastard added another try, Brand kicked the conversion and once again the series was level between the Springboks and the All-Blacks.

THE THIRD INTERNATIONAL

Philip Nel, destined to become one of his country's most famous rugby captains, gave South Africa the lead with an early try in their third international game against the All-Blacks in 1928, at the Crusader

Ground, Port Elizabeth. This was converted by Bennie Osler and a further try by Manus de Jongh gave South Africa an 8-6 lead at half-time against the New Zealand tries scored by Bert Grenside and Ron Stewart. George Daneel scored a try for South Africa in the second half. With his conversion in this game Osler had taken his international total to a record 19 points for the series.

SPRINGBOKS LEAD

There was a record crowd of 55,000 at Eden Park Auckland in 1937 to see the Springboks in their final international game of the tour against New Zealand and, for most of them, it was a depressing afternoon. The South Africans won by 17-6, which still stands to the present time as their most decisive victory over the All-Blacks in New Zealand. Wing-threequarter, E. Babrow, playing in what was to be his last international, opened the South African scoring with a try and within minutes the Springboks struck again with a try from Ferdie Bergh, which was converted by Gerry Brand. Dave Trevathan kicked a penalty goal for New Zealand but Babrow went in for a second try and the half-time score was 11-3 for South Africa. D. O. Williams with a try made it 14-3 and Fred Turner added another to make it 17-3. Trevathan landed a second penalty goal six minutes from time but by then the All-Blacks were a well-beaten, even demoralised side. This was South Africa's first series win against New Zealand and the overall record was now 5-4 in their favour with one game drawn.

A BRAVE FORWARD

One of the outstanding forwards in the famous South African side which toured in New Zealand and Australia in 1937 was Mauritz van den Berg, who made three international appearances against the All-Blacks. And he must also be noted in rugby history as one of the most courageous men to play at international level. He had been a victim of polio as a youngster and this had left him with one leg shorter than the other!

ALL ON HIS OWN

Prop-forward Aaron "Okey" Geffin, now remembered in rugby history as "The Boot" Geffin, had the supreme satisfaction of winning two Tests for South Africa all on his own. When New Zealand went down to an 11-15 defeat at Newlands during their tour of 1949, all of South Africa's points came from Geffin, who kicked five penalty goals. Then, in the Third Test at Durban, when South Africa won by 9-3, he did his solo act again with three penalty goals. And so began the legend of "The Boot" Geffin. The popular story was that after being taken prisoner-of-war at Tobruk, he smuggled a rugby ball into the camp and spent all his leisure time practising his place-kicking—and in his bare feet at that! The truth was that while Geffin did play in the rough-and-tumble rugby games of the prison camp, no one ever asked him to do any place kicking. In fact, prior to his first international game against New Zealand in 1949, Geffin had not been recognised as a kicker. On the eve of that game, after his team-mates, J. H. Van der Schyff, Hannes Brewis and F. P. Duvenage, the designated kickers of the side, had been off form with their penalty attempts, Geffin was given a try and everything went right for him. Even that did not convince the selectors. Van der Schyff failed with two penalty attempts against New Zealand before Geffin was called to take over the job and, of course, he kicked South Africa to victory. In his seven Test appearances for his country, Geffin scored 48 points and in his 17 appearances in the Springbok jersey, he scored 121 points.

JUST ONE DEFEAT

Under the captaincy of the thirty-three-year old Basil Kenyon, the South African party set sail from Capetown on 14th September, 1951 to tour in Britain, Ireland and France. Over four weeks later they played their first game against the South-Eastern Counties at Dean Court, Bournemouth on Wednesday, 10th October, and won it by 31-6. By the time they ended their tour in mid-February, 1952, they had played 31 games, won 30, lost one and scored 562 points while conceding 167. Their top points scorer was prop-forward Aaron Geffin with 89 points from a try, 25 conversions and 12 penalty goals. Johannes Karl Ochse was their top try-scorer with 15. The Springboks highest margin of victory was their 44-0 rout of Scotland and their only defeat was at the hands of London Counties by 9-11 in the 10th game of the tour. The South Africans scored in every game and reached double figures in 25 of the 31 games.

JUST ONE TEST

The tragic figure of the 1951-1952 Springbok touring side in Britain, Ireland and France was their captain, the thirty-three-year old Basil Kenyon. He had toured with South Africa in New Zealand in 1949 and had made his international debut in the fourth game of the series. He was expected to be one of the dominating personalities of the 1951-1952 tour but as it transpired he was unable to play in any of the international games and before the tour ended he had announced his retirement from rugby. His playing career came to an end with an unfortunate accident in the third game of the tour against Pontypool and Newbridge at Pontypool Park on Thursday, 18th October, 1951. In a loose maul a finger was stuck in his right eye. Kenyon played in three further games but just before the game against Cambridge University on Thursday, 8th November, it became known that he was suffering from a displaced retina and that he would have to go to London for observation and a possible operation. Kenyon, in fact, had two operations and when he was discharged from hospital on New Year's Eve, he re-joined the Springboks at Eastbourne and announced that his rugby days were over.

SO NEAR

There could not have been better news for the two Fry brothers, Stephen Perry and Denis James, when the 1951-1952 South African party was named for the tour of Britain, Ireland and France. Both were chosen, Stephen as a forward and Denis as a centre or out-half. Neither had been capped for South Africa and this tour, as it transpired, was to bring elation to one brother and a sad frustration to the other. Stephen played remarkably well in the early games of the tour and went on to win his first Springbok cap against Scotland on 24th November, 1951. Subsequently he was capped in all the internationals on this tour and went on to win 13 caps in all before his international career ended in 1955 against the Lions touring side. But for Denis the tour brought more than a mild heart-break. He was named as the first "alternative" selection for the four international games against Scotland, Ireland, England and France—and four times he was not needed. He played in 17 of the tour games but he wound up his career in rugby without a cap.

THE KICK OF A LIFETIME

With just five minutes to go at Twickenham on Saturday, 10th November, 1951, the South Africans looked to be heading steadily towards their 10th successive win of the 1951-1952 tour. Then Arthur Grimsdell stepped up to take the kick of his rugby career—the one that was to bring the Springboks their only defeat of the tour. At the time, the tourists were leading 9-8, had a solid grip on the game and had the London Counties side well contained. Basie Viviers had given them an early lead in the first half with a penalty goal but Nim Hall had cancelled this out with a drop goal. Jack Matthews, with a try converted by Grimsdell, then sent the London side into an 8-3 lead but in two fateful minutes before half-time the Springboks had come surging back with tries from Chris Koch and Martinus "Tjol" Lategan for a 9-8 lead at the break. The South Africans made all the strong pace in the second half but a strong and at times almost desperate London Counties defence managed to prevent them from adding to their lead. Then, five minutes from time the Springboks were penalised at a line-out just inside their own half and Grimsdell, the No 8 forward, was delegated to try for a shot at goal. And he duly obliged with a kick that went dead centre between the posts. As soon as the teams reached their dressing rooms, Hennie Muller made the formal and traditional presentation of the Springbok head to the London Counties captain, Jack Matthews.

A MEASURE OF REVENGE

Back in 1906, South Africa had played their first international game outside their own country—against Scotland at Edinburgh. And they had been well beaten by 0-6. Six years later they had exacted a fair measure of revenge by beating Scotland 16-0 at Murrayfield. Now, 45 years after that first defeat, on Saturday, 24th November, 1951, they

were to meet Scotland for the third time—and this time, their revenge
was to be really sweet. For 17 minutes at Murrayfield that afternoon,
there was no score and then the deluge began. And 70,000 spectators
were shocked into a bewildered silence. "Salty" Du Rand scored the
first try for South Africa and this was followed a minute later by a try
from Ryk van Schoor which was converted by "Okey" Geffin. Chris
Koch added another try, Geffin converted, Hannes Brewis dropped a
goal and before half-time Koch went over for a second try to leave the
Springboks 19-0 ahead at the break. Willem Delport had an early try
in the second half, Geffin converted, Basie van Wyk then added a try
and again Geffin converted. Hennie Muller scored between the posts
and Geffin added the points to leave the South Africans in a 34 points
lead to nil after 17 minutes of the second half. Martinus Lategan then
ran 50 yards for a try and Geffin was again on the mark to make it
39-0. Ernst Dinkelmann scored the last try and Geffin ended the
agony for Scotland with a great conversion from far out. This win
still stands as South Africa's greatest victory in an international game
against the home countries, their highest margin of victory in any
recognised international game. It also equalled their previous tour
record, also 44-0, which the 1906-1907 side had put up against
Northumberland. For Scotland, of course, it endures as their worst
defeat in an international game.

HE DID NOT REMEMBER!

Within six minutes, South Africa were down to 14 men in their second
international of the 1951-1952 tour, against Ireland at Lansdowne
Road on Saturday, 8th December, 1951. Their centre threequarter
Ryk van Schoor took a kick on the head and was carried unconscious
to the dressing room. He was, however, to make a dramatic comeback
and score a vital try. A. W. Browne of Dublin University put Ireland
ahead with a try which G. W. Murphy converted in the 17th minute
but just on the point of half-time "Basie" Van Wyk had a try to leave
the Springboks trailing by two points at the interval. "Chum" Ochse
ran in for a try early in the second half to put South Africa into a 6-5
lead and that was how things stood with just 13 minutes to go. In the
meantime, however, Van Schoor, totally against the doctor's orders,
had come back on to the field and he was to play a vital role in the
decisive closing minutes. First Brewis dropped a goal, then Van Wyk

had a try and finally Van Schoor wrapped it all up. With a magnificent solo effort, he went shooting through the Irish defences for a memorable try which Aaron Geffin converted to give South Africa a 17-5 victory. Van Schoor had to be told afterwards about his try. He did not even remember returning to the field and he had to have his try explained to him later that evening.

THREE IN SUCCESSION

With their wins over Wales and England, the 1951-52 South Africans wound up with a Grand Slam of wins over the four home countries for the third time in their tours of Britain and Ireland. Both games, however, were hard earned wins. They beat Wales with a try from Ochese and a drop goal by Brewis to a late try by Bleddyn Williams and against England, a try by Pieter "Fonnie" Du Toit, converted by Hennie Muller and then a penalty goal from Muller gave them a five points margin over the English who had a try from Chris Winn.

THE FINAL SWEEP

The Springboks 31st and final game of the 1951-1952 tour, at Colombes Stadium, Paris on Saturday, 16th February, 1952, was also a "first". Although South African and French sides had previously met during the 1906 and 1912 tours, this was the first official international game between the two countries. And the first "official" score between South Africa and France came from the French out-half Jo Carabignac of Agen with a drop goal after 14 minutes. That, however, was to be France's only score. Paul Johnstone opened South Africa's account with a penalty goal, followed this with a try and then a second try at the start of the second half. Dinklemann, Muller, Delport and Van Wyk added further tries and Muller and Johnstone each had a conversion. This 25-3 win was to remain as a South African record over France until 15th July, 1967 when France went down 3-26 in their international game at Durban.

SOUTH AFRICA'S FIRST

After South Africa's shock defeat by Australia in the second international game of the Wallabies 1953 tour in South Africa, the Springbok selectors made drastic changes for the third international game to be played at Durban a fortnight later. And among the new caps announced for the Durban game was Harry Newton Walker of Orange Free State. His selection was to bring a notable "first" in South African rugby. Thirty two years earlier, Alfred P. Walker of Natal had won the first of six South African international caps by playing against New Zealand in the Springboks first tour down under. With Harry Newton Walker's selection to play against Australia in 1953, they became the first father-and-son combination to play for South Africa. For added measure Alf Walker's brother and Harry Newton Walker's uncle, Henry Walker, had won three international caps against the Lions of 1910 in South Africa.

A CAPTAIN'S PART

For their third tour to Australia and New Zealand in 1956, South Africa were captained by Basie Viviers, who also wound up as the top points scorer of their 29 match programme. He scored 107 points, from two tries, 34 conversions, nine penalty goals and two drop goals. The South Africans overall record was: 29 played, 22 won, six lost, one drawn and they scored 520 points while conceding 203. In New Zealand, they played 23, won 16, lost six, drew one and scored 470 points for 177 against. Their top try scorer was Tom van Vollenhoven with 16 tries. He, of course, later became one of the greatest players in English Rugby League with St Helen's and in his 381 appearances for the club scored the sensational number of 393 tries. The Springboks greatest margin of victory during the 1937 tour of New Zealand was 38 points in their 41-3 defeat of the combined Nelson-Marlborough-Golden Bay-Motueka side. Their worst defeats were by New Zealand (10-17) and New Zealand University (15-22). They did, however, score in all of their games.

DOWN AGAIN

For the third time in a tour of New Zealand, the Springboks lost their opening international game when they went down 6-10 to the All-Blacks at Carisbrook, Dunedin. On a bitterly cold afternoon, in a bruising battle which at various stages had no fewer than seven players taking treatment, Ron Jarden opened the scoring with a try which he converted and later he was to convert Tiny White's try. B. F. Howe had a try for South Africa and R. G. Dryburgh kicked a penalty goal. The South Africans, however, exacted a fair measure of revenge in the second international at Wellington. R. H. Brown with a try gave the All-Blacks a 3-0 lead at half-time, but it was all South Africa in the second half and tries from D. F. Retief and J. A. Du Rand and a conversion by Basie Viviers took them to a decisive 8-3 win. It was, however, to be their only international win against the All-Blacks on this tour.

THE NEW BOY

For the third international game against the 1956 Springboks at Christchurch, the New Zealand selectors decided to gamble on a youngster who had already shown impressive form for Waikato in their win over South Africa in the opening game of the tour. He was brought in to wear his first All-Blacks jersey at full-back . . . and his name was Don Clarke. And he duly marked the occasion with two penalty goals and a conversion. New Zealand's other scores came from tries by Ron Jarden, Maurice Dixon and Tiny White. Butch Lochner and W. Rosenberg had tries for South Africa, both of which were converted by Basie Viviers. Don Clarke was to put on a repeat performance in the fourth and final international at Eden Park, Auckland. He converted Peter Jones's try and also put over two long-range penalty goals. In the closing stages Dryburgh had a try for South Africa which Viviers converted to leave the score at 11-5. This defeat was a significant one for South African rugby. For the first time in 60 years they had lost an international series and it was also the first time they had lost one to New Zealand in the history of their meetings since 1921.

DIDN'T PLAY A GAME

The unluckiest member of the 1956 South African side which toured in Australia and New Zealand was C. J. "Basie" Van Wyk who had won the first of his 10 caps for South Africa during the 1951-1952 tour of Britain, Ireland and France. Shortly after landing in Australia and in a practice session before the South Africans first match in Australia, he fractured his leg and was out of contention before the tour had even started.

NEVER A CAP

A combined Western Province-Boland-South Western Districts took on the French touring side of 1958 and walloped them by the handsome margin of 38-8. And out-half Giepie Wentzel kicked 21 of those 38 points. On the strength of his kicking he was named to play for South Africa in the full international game against France at Ellis Park, Johannesburg on the following Saturday. Unfortunately, Wentzel had injured his shoulder in that rout of the French and was forced to call out of the international side. It was an injury that was to lose him the one prize he wanted in rugby. Although he was picked to travel with the South African tourists to Britain, Ireland and France in 1960-1961 and made 11 appearances, he was to finish his career without an international cap. Ironically, he was named on the side to play against France in the final international of the tour, but for the second time in his short career, he was forced to withdraw with a re-occurrence of the same injury that had prevented him from playing against France in 1958.

THE FIFTH SPRINGBOKS

Avril Malan's Fifth Springboks set a record for a touring side in Britain and Ireland in 1960-1961 by going 29 successive matches without defeat. In the 30th game at Cardiff Arms Park, they went down 0-6 to the Barbarians—their only loss in a tour which embraced 34 games in Britain, Ireland and France. Their overall record was: played 34, lost one, drew two and they scored 567 points while conceding 132. Their top scorer was Richard John Lockyear with 79 points from 29 conversions and seven penalty goals. Their top try-scorer was John Gainsford with 17. The Springboks greatest margin of victory was their 42-0 win over Western Counties at Kingsholm, Gloucester on Saturday, 10th December, 1960. In 24 of their games, they reached double figures and in only two did they fail to score. The tour began with a 29-9 win over Southern Counties at Brighton on Saturday, 22nd October, 1960 and ended with the scoreless draw against France at Colombes Stadium, Paris on Saturday, 18th February, 1961.

BATTLE AT CARDIFF

With 53 points from their first two victories, the 1960-61 Springboks moved to Wales to take on Cardiff at the Arms Park on Saturday, 29th October, 1960. They won comfortably enough but the manner

"ONE MORE TACKLE AND THIS SHIRT'S HAD IT"

in which they achieved it did not please the Welsh. The Springboks put on a vigorous display of hard, unrelenting forward power that brought a succession of "incidents" and the subsequent public criticism of these was to remain with the touring side for the remainder of the trip. Martin Pelser opened the scoring with a try after 32 minutes and Richard Lockyear kicked the conversion. In the second half Lockyear kicked a penalty goal and before the end, after Fanny Roux had been obstructed, the referee awarded a penalty try and Lockyear kicked the goal.

ALMOST ABANDONED

After 25 minutes in the second half of South Africa's first international game of the 1960-1961 tour, against Wales at Cardiff Arms Park on Saturday, 3rd December, 1960, the referee, Mr J. A. S. Taylor of Scotland, halted the proceedings and called both teams together. He pointed out that, in the appalling weather conditions, he was now unable to make out the touch-lines or the goal-lines and, also because of the mud, it was becoming increasingly difficult to distinguish between the two sides. Both captains, however, agreed to carry on. South Africa were then three points up with a penalty goal by Keith Oxlee and felt they could win. The Welsh, only three points down, were equally confident that they could still pull the game around to their way. But Oxlee's goal was to be the only score of the game and, as far as the South Africans were concerned, they had crossed their most difficult international hurdle. Exactly 48 years earlier in their first international game against Wales, to be played at Cardiff Arms Park, South Africa had beaten Wales by . . . a penalty goal to nil. The conditions however in 1960 were just a little worse. Twenty four hours later, the Cardiff Arms Park pitch was swamped in three feet of flood water.

THE PUSH-OVER!

In the most controversial ending to an international rugby game at Lansdowne Road, South Africa beat Ireland by 8-3 and maintained their record of having beaten the Irish in their five meetings since 1906. To this day the Irish maintain that the Springboks should never have been awarded the try that won the game. Full time was up and the proceedings had gone into injury time when South Africa were awarded a scrum close to the Irish line. There were only 90 seconds left and the score was 3-3. Tom Kiernan had kicked a penalty goal for Ireland in the first half and John Gainsford had levelled the scores with a try shortly after the start of the second half. With this scrum, the South Africans had their last chance of victory. They got down smartly and with a tremendous push drove the Irish back six or seven yards. Astonishingly the referee, Mr Gwilym Treharne of Wales, did not call the South Africans back. Richard Lockyear put in the ball and with another shove the South Africans forced the Irish over their own line. As the ball came back, several South Africans fell on it and eventually Hugo van Zyl was credited with the try. Lockyear kicked the conversion and that ended the game.

FOUR UP AGAIN

England followed the fate of Wales and Ireland at Twickenham on Saturday, 7th January, 1961. With a try by Doug Hopwood, converted by Frik du Preez just on the stroke of half-time, South Africa collected their third international win of the tour and now needed to beat only Scotland for their fourth grand slam of the home countries. And they did that with seven points to spare at Murrayfield, Edinburgh on Saturday, 21st January, 1961. Doug Hopwood went over for a try after 20 minutes and just before half-time, Johann Claassen, their huge second row forward, playing in his 20th international for South Africa, scored his first try—and only one—of the tour. Arthur Smith had a try for Scotland early in the second half which was converted by full-back Ken Scotland but Frik du Preez put the issue beyond all doubt by kicking two penalty goals. Arthur Smith's try was the only one scored against the South Africans in the four international games.

THE SPRINGBOK HEAD

For 29 games, the South Africans had carried the Springbok head around with them. Finally, at Cardiff Arms Park on Saturday, 4th February, 1961, they parted company with it and handed it over to Ireland's Ronnie Dawson, who captained the Barbarians on that fateful afternoon. During the previous week, with his playing strength now reduced to 19 fit players, South Africa's manager Ferdie Bergh had suggested that this final game should be a "gala exhibition" with mixed sides being fielded. But the Barbarians committee politely declined the suggestion. As they pointed out the real attraction of this final fixture would be fifteen Springboks playing against fifteen Barbarians. And that was how it was and the Barbarians with tries from their two Welsh forwards, W. D. G. Morgan and H. J. Morgan, both scored in the first half, were the first and only side to lower the colours of the 1960-1961 South African touring side.

ALLEZ FRANCE

The 1960-1961 South Africans began the French portion of the tour with a resounding win over South-West France at Bordeaux on 8th February, 1961 and followed this with another impressive win over France "B" by 26-10 at Toulouse. In their final warm-up game before the full international against France at Colombes Stadium on Saturday, 18th February, they took on a Pyrenees-Basque Coast XV at Bayonne and won easing up by 36-9. In three games in France they had scored 91 points and conceded 22—and that was to be their final tally in France. Neither South Africa nor France could score in the full international at Colombes. The most memorable feature of it was that after 10 minutes, the Welsh referee, the diminutive Gwynne Walters of Wales, halted the game, took both captains to one side and gravely warned both Avril Malan and Francois Moncla that if there was one more outbreak of fighting, he would abandon the game. From there on, things continued in a more orderly and civilised fashion but a tremendously exciting battle eventually ended in a scoreless stalemate. It marked the first time in 54 years that South Africa had failed to win a test in Britain, Ireland and France. Their previous defeat, their first on foreign soil, had been against Scotland during the 1906-1907 tour.

SHORT AND BITTER

On Saturday, 10th April, 1965 at Lansdowne Road, Dublin, South Africa's proud record of never having been defeated in an international game during a tour of Britain, Ireland and France, since they had been beaten by Scotland at Hampden Park, Glasgow on Saturday, 17th November, 1906, finally came to an end. They were beaten 6-9 by Ireland and the man who kicked the vital penalty goal to give the Irish their first win over the Springboks was full-back Tom Kiernan. Ireland took the lead in the seventh minute with a try from wing-threequarter Pat McGrath but D. A. Stewart brought the scores level with a penalty goal and the deadlock remained until the 17th minute of the second half when W. J. Mans put the Springboks ahead with a try. Kiernan promptly cancelled that out with a penalty goal and then five minutes from time he kicked his second penalty goal and the Springboks record was gone. This was the second game of South Africa's short tour of Ireland and France and for them it was a disastrous tour. They played five matches, won none, lost four and drew one. They scored 37 points and conceded 53. Prior to the match against Ireland, they had drawn with the Combined Provinces in Belfast and lost to the Irish Universities. In their trip to Scotland, they lost first to Scottish Districts and then went down 5-8 to Scotland at Murrayfield. Top scorer and also the leading try-scorer on this Springbok side which was captained by Avril Malan, was J. Schoeman with nine points from three tries.

THE 1965 TOUR DOWN UNDER

Dawie de Villiers led the fourth Springboks to tour down under in 1965 and in their 30 match tour of Australia and New Zealand they played 30 games and won 22. They drew none, lost eight and knocked up 669 points while conceding 285. Their top points scorer was centre-threequarter W. J. Mans with 116 points which came from 13 tries, 28 conversions, six penalty goals and one drop goal. The top try scorer was centre threequarter Jan Engelbrecht with 20. The side's top win in New Zealand was their rout of New Zealand Universities by 55-11 and their worst defeats were by Wellington (6-23) and New Zealand (3-20). Only in one game did they fail to score and that was in the second international against New Zealand which they lost 0-13.

A SAD YEAR

When the Springboks lined out against New Zealand in the first inter-national game of the 1965 tour, they had the sad record behind them that year of having lost four successive international games. They had

" GENTLEMEN, GENTLEMEN ! THIS IS NEITHER
THE PLACE NOR THE TIME TO DISCUSS POLITICS "

been beaten by Ireland, Scotland and twice by Australia. In this first international at Athletic Park, Wellington, the All-Blacks were to hand South Africa their fifth defeat on the trot. Dawie de Villiers won the toss and elected to play into the 50 miles-an-hour gale in the first half and they were only six points down at half-time. Bill Birtwistle scored a try after five minutes and just on the stroke of half-time Kel Tremain had added a controversial second. It was generally accepted that Tremain had taken the ball in an offside position before going over the line. Keith Oxlee dropped a goal for South Africa in the second half but the All-Blacks held out grimly to win by 6-3. The second international, however, at Carisbrook, Dunedin, was never a close affair. Kel Tremain got an early try for New Zealand, which Mick Williment converted and in the 33rd minute Bruce McLeod added a second. In the second half Ron Rangi had a try and Williment completed the scoring with a splendid conversion. The South Africans had now lost six international games in succession and for the second time in 44 years had lost two in succession to the All-Blacks.

THE COMEBACK

With New Zealand ahead at half-time by 16-5 in the third international game at Lancaster Park, Christchurch on 4th September, 1965, the odds on a South African victory were remote. Yet, with one of the greatest fight-backs in rugby history, they eventually ran out winners of a remarkable game by 19-16. With the wind behind them. Tremain, Rangi and Moreton scored tries for the All-Blacks in the first half and Mick Williment had converted two and also landed a superb penalty goal from almost 50 yards out. South Africa's reply in a one-sided first half had been a try by John Gainsford, converted by Tiny Naude. It did not seem possible then that South Africa could break their losing sequence. But they did. Within four minutes G. S. Brynard shot over for a try and eight minutes later he went through again and this time his try was converted by Naude to narrow the gap to three points. In the 23rd minute John Gainsford raced in for a try and the scores, were level. With just three minutes to go South Africa were awarded a penalty close to the touch-line and about 35 yards out. Naude, all 6′ 5″ of him, was entrusted with the kick and from out of the mud, he duly planted the ball between the posts. There was now the possibility that they might yet square the series. This game which set an aggregate record of 35 points for a game between South Africa and New Zealand up to that time, also marked two other significant records in rugby. On the South African side that afternoon was John Gainsford making his 29th international appearance which was a new record for a Springbok and on the New Zealand side, Colin Meads with 31 appearances had edged out Don Clarke as his country's most capped player.

A CHANGE OF OFFICIALS

The only casualty of the third international match between South Africa and New Zealand at Lancaster Park in 1965 was Pat Murphy—and he was the referee. After 21 minutes he called the two captains together and explained to Dawie de Villiers and Wilson Whineray that he had pulled a hamstring muscle and could not carry on. They agreed that Alan Taylor, one of the touch judges, should take his place. There had never been anything quite like it in the history of New Zealand rugby but, by all accounts, Mr Taylor of Canterbury did an excellent job.

THE FINAL CURTAIN

The South Africans went on a scoring spree after their 19-16 international win at Christchurch. They walloped the New Zealand Universities by 55-6, hammered Hawke's Bay by 30-12 and routed the combined Bay of Plenty-Thames Valley side by 33-17. With 118 points from three games, they went into the final international at Eden Park, Auckland with their confidence high and their tails up. And, indeed, things still looked reasonably bright at half-time with New Zealand ahead by only three points from a try by "Red" Conway. They looked even brighter when Tiny Naude kicked a huge penalty goal to level matters after 11 minutes of the second half. Then, unfortunately, came the deluge. Birtwistle whipped up a loose ball and ran 40 yards for a try. Ian Smith added two more, Mac Herewini dropped a goal and Ken Gray finished off the afternoon with a try which Fergie McCormick converted. The final score of 20-3 on 18th September, 1965 at Eden Park is still South Africa's worst defeat in international rugby by another country. For the moment, it also marked their last time to play on New Zealand soil.

UYS THE FIRST

At half-time at Ellis Park, Johannesburg on 2nd August, 1969 in the opening match of the Australians international series against South Africa, the Springboks captain Dawie de Villiers had to drop out of the game with an injured shoulder. Into his place for the second half came Piet Uys, who at that stage in his career had made 10 international appearances for South Africa since he toured with the Springboks in Britain, Ireland and France in 1960-1961. But this particular appearance for his country gave him his own special niche in South African rugby history. He was the first substitute to be used by South Africa in an international match.

THE RECORD BREAKER

With the very last kick of the fourth and final international between South Africa and Australia at Bloemfontein during the Wallabies tour of 1969, Piet Visagie converted Eben Oliver's try and took his total of points for 14 international games to an all-time South African individual scoring record in international football. But in that particular series of four games against Australia, he had also scored a total of 43 points and this brought him further records. It broke the record of 35 points for a series in South Africa which had been set the previous year by Ireland's Tom Kiernan in his international games for the Lions. It also surpassed the world record of 39 points for a series which New Zealand's Don Clarke had set against the Lions in 1959. With his conversion of Eben Oliver's try in 1969, Visagie took his total of points to 88, one ahead of the former holder Keith Oxlee. Since then he has gone on to play in 25 international games in all for South Africa and his total at the end of the 1973-1974 season stood at 130 points. He compiled these from six tries, 20 conversions, 19 penalty goals and five drop goals. In six of his international appearances Visagie had the distinction of scoring 10 or more points for his country. He scored 10 against the Lions in 1968, did it twice against Australia in 1969 and scored 12 points twice, against France in 1968 and against Australia in 1971. His top performance was against Australia at Johannesburg in 1969, when he collected 15 points from three penalty goals and three conversions. On the South African domestic front, Visagie set a Currie

Cup record by scoring 33 points for Griqualand West against Rhodesia on August 3, 1968. Griqualand West won by 57-3 and Visagie amassed his scoring with nine conversions, two tries, two penalty goals and a drop goal.

VISAGIE ON THE MARK

Led by scrum-half Dawie de Villiers, South Africa made a short tour of France in October-November, 1968 and wound up with a record of playing six games, winning five, losing one and scoring 84 points while conceding 43. Out-half Piet Visagie accounted for exactly half of the Springboks total and his 42 points came from a try, three conversions, one drop goal and 10 penalty goals. The South Africans top winning margin was 21 points when they beat Provence-Coast in Toulon by 24-3 and their only defeat was by 3-11 to a South-West France XV at Toulouse. In the first of their two international games with France, at Bordeaux, Visagie, with four penalty goals, kicked the Springboks to a 12-9 win, with France's scores coming from two tries by Benoit Dauga and a third from Jean-Marie Bonal. Their second meeting, at Colombes Stadium, Paris turned out to be a magnificent battle and was touch-and-go right up to the final whistle. Marcel Puget and Lucien Paries put France into a 6-0 lead with drop goals and just on half-time Visagie narrowed the gap to three points with a close-in penalty goal. It took the Springboks until the 21st minute of the second half to draw level with a try from Jan Engelbrecht. Six minutes later, Dawie de Villiers got over for a try and Visagie converted for an 11-6 lead. Sid Nomis added another try which Visagie converted to make it 16-6 but then the French came storming back with a try by Eli Cester, which Paries converted. In a tremendous finish, the South Africans held out to maintain their unbeaten international record in France. However, in that beating by a South-West France XV at Toulouse, they had lost another record. This was the first time a Springbok side had ever been beaten in France.

THE SIXTH SPRINGBOKS

No group of young men in sporting history took as much punishment off the field as the Sixth Springboks. From the moment they arrived in England to begin their 1969-1970 tour of Britain and Ireland, Dawie de

Villiers men were subjected to unceasing demonstrations and protests and incidents that all too often made the front pages of the newspapers rather than the sports pages. As the prime targets of the anti-Apartheid groups, they were harried relentlessly and remorselessly and spent most of their two months of the tour under constant police protection. There were hundreds of ugly incidents, including an effort to hijack the team coach and also an attempt to set fire to their hotel at Bristol. Yet, despite all the demonstrations, despite the sad fact that all of their games involved the protection of large squads of police, the Springboks completed their tour. In the circumstances, their poor playing record is understandable.

THEY LOST FIVE

When the Sixth Springboks wound up their 1969-1970 tour with a 21-12 victory over the Barbarians at Twickenham on Saturday, 31st January, 1970, their record was: played 24, won 15, lost five, drew four, points for—323, points against—157. In relation to previous long tours to Britain and Ireland, their record was dismal. No previous South African touring side had lost as many games or drawn as many. No South African side had ever conceded so many points. For the first time, too, on a long tour of Britain and Ireland, South Africa failed to win an international game. Their greatest margin of victory was 34 points in their 37-3 defeat of the North and Midlands of Scotland at Aberdeen. Their five defeats were to Oxford University (3-6), Newport (6-11), Gwent (8-14), Scotland (3-6), England (8-11) and their four draws were against Western Counties (3-3), Ireland (8-8), Scottish Districts (3-3) and Wales (6-6). Top scorer on the tour was Piet Visagie with 61 points from one try, 11 conversions, 11 penalty goals and a drop goal. Their top try scorer was Andy Van der Watt with seven. Because of the troubles in Northern Ireland, the game against Ulster on Saturday, 29th November, 1969, was cancelled. Instead the Springboks played an unofficial game at Leashore, Cheshire against a combined New Brighton and N.I.F.C. side. The South Africans won by 22-6.

A FIRST DEFEAT

Because of the demonstrations, the venue for the Springboks first game against Oxford University on Wednesday, 5th November, 1969 was kept a closely guarded secret until late on the night before the game. Then it was announced that the Springboks would make their debut at Twickenham and, as it transpired, it was an unhappy debut. The demonstrators were there in full force and to a background of incessant jeering, abuse and whistling, Dawie de Villiers' side went down to a 3-6 defeat. The New Zealander Chris Laidlaw, at scrum-half for Oxford, was the master-mind of this shock win and his tactics, based on his great experience with the All-Blacks, completely upset the Springboks. Piet Visagie kicked the first points of the tour with a penalty goal in the first minute of the game but three minutes later, the Oxford full-back N. G. Heal levelled the scores with his penalty goal. Shortly before half-time Heal kicked a second penalty goal and that ended the scoring in the game. It marked the first time that South Africa had been beaten in the opening game of a long tour in Britain and Ireland.

MULLER'S DAY

The 1969-1970 tour of Britain and Ireland was not a happy one for wing-threequarter Gert Muller. Shortly after the side had arrived in England, he got the sad news that his father had died and he had to return home to South Africa. Subsequently, having rejoined the tour, he was injured and, in all, he played only in five games. He did, however, have one afternoon to remember—against the North and Midlands of Scotland at Linksfield Stadium Aberdeen on Tuesday, 2nd December, 1969. With the South Africans winning by 37-3, he scored four tries and became the first Springbok to achieve this since Morrie Zimmerman had scored his four against Midland Counties during the 1931-1932 tour. Surprisingly, Muller was not South Africa's top scorer in this game. Henry de Villiers kicked a penalty goal and also had five conversions.

THE FIRST INTERNATIONAL

With Murrayfield under the guard of over 800 policemen and the crowd limited to 30,000, South Africa went down 3-6 to Scotland in their first international game of the tour on Saturday, 6th December, 1969. Shortly before half-time Piet Visagie kicked a penalty goal for South

Africa but after eight minutes of the second half, Scotland's new cap, full-back Arthur Smith levelled matters with his penalty goal. Then, seven minutes from time, Smith made his international debut something worth remembering. He came into the Scottish line just outside the Springboks "25" and with a flying run, he went straight through the South African defences to score a try.

A LONG WAIT

England had drawn 3-3 with the first Springboks at the Crystal Palace, London on Saturday, 8th December, 1906. This was followed by four defeats at Twickenham in 1913, 1932, 1952 and 1961. Now, on Saturday, 20th December, 1969, after 63 years, England finally defeated South Africa in an international game. The afternoon got off to a good start for South Africa with a penalty goal by Piet Visagie in the sixth minute, followed by a try from Piet Greyling which Visagie converted and with half-time looming up, South Africa were in a comfortable 8-0 lead. Next came a glorious try from England. A move started by new cap Nigel Starmer-Smith was carried on by Alan Bucknall and a final bout of passing by Peter Larter and Keith Fairbrother eventually put Larter over for a try. Bob Hiller closed the gap to two points with a penalty goal from 35 yards in the 20th minute of the second half and two minutes later, hooker John Pullin crashed over for a try which Hiller converted.

A LATE SAVER

With 40 minutes of the second half gone, South Africa looked odds on to beat Ireland in their international of the tour at Lansdowne Road, Dublin on Saturday, 10th January, 1970. They were leading 8-5 and looked to have the game firmly under control. Ireland had taken the lead in the 12th minute with a magnificent try from Alan Duggan which was converted by Tom Kiernan. South Africa came back with a penalty goal by Henry de Villiers to leave the half-time score at 5-3. After 30 minutes of the second half Piet Greyling had a try for South Africa and Henry de Villiers converted. Full time came and went. The game dragged on into the eighth minute of injury time. Ireland's wing-threequarter Alan Duggan made a break but with his path closed he kicked into the centre, right in front of the South African posts. Jan Ellis fielded safely but was brought down by the Irish forwards. He failed to release the ball and Mr T. F. E. Grierson (Scotland) promptly blew his whistle. Tom Kiernan took the easy penalty and it was 8-8. South Africa had now lost two international games and drawn one. In just over a month, they had established the worst international record of the six South African touring sides since 1906.

THE LAST MINUTE AGAIN

Tom Kiernan's last minute penalty goal had robbed the South Africans of victory at Lansdowne Road. They were to experience the same frustration in their final international game of the tour against Wales at Cardiff Arms Park on 24th January, 1970. Again it came in the last minute and the man who brought it was Wales's scrum-half Gareth Edwards. Henry de Villiers put the Springboks in the lead with a penalty goal but Edwards came back with his penalty goal to leave the half-time score at 3-3. Early in the second half Sid Nomis went over for a try and South Africa held their lead into injury time. Then, in the final move of the game, the ball came back from a ruck and Edwards picked it up and he went streaking away to score at the corner flag. Edwards failed with the conversion attempt and with the score at 6-6, the Sixth Springboks had failed to win any of their four international games. The only consolation at Cardiff Arms Park was that they had maintained their unbeaten record against Wales since 1906. With this game South Africa completed 30 games against Scotland (8), Ireland (8), England (7) and Wales (7). They had won 21, lost six and drawn 3 and scored 338 points while conceding 139.

THE OTHER RECORDS

Apart from their playing record, Dawie de Villiers' Sixth Springboks were also responsible for some other sad records during their 1969-1970 tour of Britain and Ireland. In all, over 20,000 policemen were used at their games and for the South Africa v Ireland game at Lansdowne Road, Dublin, it was estimated that 2,500 policemen were on duty.

THE FIRST TO AUSTRALIA

The South Africans, still smarting from the demonstrations that had marred their 1969-1970 tour of Britain, Ireland and France, ran into another barrage of protests and incidents when, under the captaincy of Hannes Marais, they undertook their first full and exclusive tour of Australia in 1971. But they survived all the trouble and demonstrations and, in a tour that included three international fixtures, they became the first Springbok touring side to complete a tour without defeat. Their full record was that they played 13 games, won 13 and scored 396 points while conceding 102. Their greatest margin of victory was the 50-0 defeat of Victoria at Melbourne on 3rd July, 1971 and in four of their games they ran up more than 40 points. The closest any side came to them was the full Australian XV in the second international at Brisbane on 31st July, when the final score was 14-6 for the Springboks. Their top try scorer was Hannes Viljoen of Natal who scored 16 in his 10 games on the tour. Top points scorer was Ian McCallum with 87, which brought his all-time total in the Springbok jersey to 134 from 15 games.

VILJOEN'S FIVE

In the opening game of their 1971 tour in Australia Hannes Marais's Springboks routed Western Australia at Perth by 44-18 and the two star performers in this game were Hannes Viljoen of South Africa and Bob Thompson, the Western Australian forward who had yet to win an international cap for his country. South Africa ran in 10 tries in this game, four of which were converted and the remaining six points came from two penalty goals. Viljoen collected five of these tries which moved him into joint second place on the Springboks all-time record of try-scorers in a game. To his 15 points, Ian McCallum added 14 with four conversions and two penalty goals and their other tries came from Snyman with two, de Vos, Marais and du Plessis. But Thompson, who was to be brought into the Australian side for the final international game of this tour also had his afternoon of personal glory. With a try and five penalty goals which yielded his side's full 18 points, he established a record of scoring a record number of points against a South African touring side since they first moved outside their own country in 1906-1907. It is, of course, also an Australian record performance against any international touring side.

VISAGIE'S POINTS

In their second game of the 1971 tour in Australia, the Springboks took on South Australia at Adelaide on 30th June and again it was a runaway victory by 43-0. And this will be remembered as Piet Visagie's game. He kicked five penalty goals and kicked five conversions and his 25 points sent him to the top of South Africa's all-time list for the most points ever scored by a Springbok in a tour game. The previous record had been held by full-back Gerry Brand, who in fact achieved 24 points twice in tour games. In 1937 when South Africa beat Western Districts of Australia, he got his 24 from nine conversions and two penalty goals and on the same tour he reached his 24 in exactly the same manner. By the end of this tour Piet Visagie, who had begun his international career against France in 1967, had taken his career total of points in the Springbok jersey to 240 from 44 appearances.

THE FIRST INTERNATIONAL

With 202 points from six victories behind them the Springboks went into their first international game against Australia at Sydney on 17th July, 1971. And it turned out to be just a little more difficult than they had anticipated. Hannes Viljoen, then twenty-eight, won his first South African cap in this game and marked the occasion with a try and the other Springbok scorers were Jan Ellis and J. F. Viljoen with a try each, two conversions and a penalty goal by Ian McCallum and a drop goal from Piet Visagie. Australia, who went down by 11-19 had a try from Bob McLean and Arthur McGill kicked two penalty goals and the conversion.

NINETEEN FOR SNYMAN

D. S. L. Snyman of Western Province, on his first Springbok tour in 1971—and as understudy to Piet Visagie at out-half he failed to win an international place during the tour—had his memorable outing at Canberra on 21st July when the South Africans took on Australian Capital Territory. The Springboks romped to a 34-3 victory and Snyman with five conversions, two penalty goals and a drop goal, collected 19 of those 34 points. It was a personal scoring record for him and elevated him into the top ten Springboks who have scored more than 15 points in a tour game.

THE SECOND INTERNATIONAL

The South Africans got it tough when they tackled Australia in the second international of the 1971 tour at Brisbane on 31st July. They got off to a flying start with a penalty goal from Ian McCallum in the third minute and Piet Visagie then put them six points up with a well-executed try. Arthur McGill kicked a penalty for Australia to leave the interval score at 6-3. Midway through the second half Visagie went over for a try but McGill put the Wallabies back into the picture with a neat drop goal. However, shortly before the end Hannes Viljoen had the satisfaction of scoring a try—his second in his first two international appearances—and McCallum wrapped it all up with a conversion to give the Springboks a 14-6 win, their tightest result of the tour.

THE LAST TOUR INTERNATIONAL?

Exactly one week after their second international win, and having routed Queensland County by 45-14 in their midweek game, South Africa played their final game of the 1971 tour against Australia at Sydney and it was never in doubt. Within 15 minutes they were three points up with a try by Piet Visagie and he duly converted. Bob McLean reduced the leeway with a long-range penalty goal for Australia but in a whirlwind end to the first half Cronje went over for a try which Visagie converted and then on the whistle Visagie landed a penalty goal. After that it was one-way traffic and John Ellis with a try which Visagie converted took the South African total to 18 points. Just on the final whistle John Cole got over for a try for Australia—and that ended it all. South Africa had completed their last tour overseas. All the gloomy indications were there, protests, demonstrations, incidents and trouble, to suggest that it would be a long, long time before the Springboks would visit Australia again.

A LONG WAY BACK

With the completion of the South African tour of Australia in 1971, the record between the two countries stood at 28 played and of these South Africa had won 21 to Australia's seven. Only twice in the years since 1933 had Australia managed to win two internationals in succession—in 1963 and 1965. South Africa's greatest domination of the series began with their win at Johannesburg in 1969 and ended with their last international meeting at Sydney in 1971—seven successive victories.

ALMOST A RECORD

With the cancellation of South Africa's tour to New Zealand in 1972—the All-Blacks came to Britain, Ireland and France that season to compensate for the loss of the visit of the Springboks—Grahame Thorne lost the opportunity of setting up what would have been a unique record for All-Blacks and Springboks rugby. He had been New Zealand's top scorer with Brian Lochore's All-Blacks in South Africa in 1970 and during the tour lost his heart to a young lady in South Africa. Shortly after he had returned home with the All-Blacks, he decided to return to South Africa to marry and settle down there. Living in Pretoria, he played rugby with the Northern Transvaal XV and on his displays with them, he became the Springboks first choice at centre for the proposed tour of New Zealand. However, it was called off and Thorne, who had scored 17 tries for the All-Blacks in their tour of South Africa in 1970, did not get the chance of playing against his own country.

SOUTH AFRICA'S RECORD

Since the South Africans made their extremely uneasy debut into international rugby in 1891, they have now played 137 matches against the Lions, New Zealand, Australia, England, Ireland, Scotland, Wales and France. Their record shows that they have won 81, lost 41 and drawn 15. In their 133 games, they have scored 1,605 points and eednccod 1027. This was their record at the start of 1974/75 season.

SPRINGBOK CAPS

From 1891 to the start of the 1974-1975 season, 475 players have worn the jersey of South Africa in either an international game or as a member of a touring side. Those who have won official international caps against the Lions, Australia, New Zealand, England, Ireland, Scotland, France and Wales total 423. South Africa's most capped international is F. C. H. Du Preez (Northern Transvaal), who made his international debut in 1960-1961 and took his total to 38 in 1971 with three appearances against Australia.

AUSTRALIA

THE AUSTRALIANS START

The game of rugby was introduced into Australia as early as 1829 by British settlers but did not become an organised sport until the foundation of the Sydney University Club in 1864 and the famous Wallaroo Club in 1870. In 1875, the Southern Rugby Football Union was founded and this subsequently became the New South Wales Rugby Union which affiliated to the English Rugby Union in 1892. The N.S.W.R.U. continued to govern the game in Australia until the Australian Rugby Union was brought into existence in 1949 with representation on the International Rugby Board.

THE BEGINNING

The first Australians to lift rugby beyond its domestic status were the Sydney club which travelled to New Zealand on a short tour in 1882. They met Auckland in their opening game on 9th September, 1882 and went down by a goal and a try to nil. Subsequently they lost their other games but from the success of this tour began a regular series of fixtures between Australian and New Zealand sides and these continued healthily right up to 1903 when the first official and recognised international game between Australia and New Zealand was played at Sydney on 15th August, 1903. This was a remarkably strong New Zealand side and included Billy Wallace, Dave Gallaher, Jimmy Duncan, George Tyler and Duncan McGregor, all of whom were to become world famous in the All-Blacks tour of Britain, Ireland and France in 1905-1906. Australia were beaten 3-22 in this first international and to Stan Whickham, who was to collect five international caps, went the distinction of scoring his country's first points in international football with a penalty goal.

THE FIRST WIN

Australia began their international games with New Zealand in 1903 and went down 3-22 in the first at Sydney. Two years later, they travelled to New Zealand for the first time and again managed to score three points against the New Zealanders 14. In 1907, however, the series between the two countries settled down to a more permanent pattern with the New Zealanders touring in Australia and playing three international games, two of which they won by 26-6, 14-5 and drawing the third at Sydney by 5-5. The New Zealanders returned again to Australia in 1910 and won their first international by 6-0. However, in the second game at Sydney, they crashed 0-11 and this marked the first victory by Australia in international rugby. The New Zealanders took more than ample revenge by trouncing the Australians 28-13 in the third and final international that year. In all between 1903 and 1929, there were 17 international meetings between Australia and New Zealand with Australia winning five, losing 17 and drawing one. Australia scored 128 points in these 17 games and conceded 239. Then in 1931, the Bledisoe Cup for competition between the two countries came into being.

FOR AND AGAINST

B. I. Swannell, an English forward from Northampton wound up his rugby career by playing against and for Australia. A member of the Lions of 1899, led by the Reverend M. Mullineux, which toured in Australia he appeared in the international games against Australia and then, taking a liking to the country, he made up his mind to settle down there. He turned out regularly for New South Wales and in 1905 won his one and only cap for Australia against New Zealand.

THE FAMOUS "DALLY"

Henry "Dally" Messenger played just the one official international for Australia, against New Zealand in 1907, but this extraordinary personality from New South Wales was to become one of his country's most memorable personalities of rugby. And he finished off his career with the unusual distindtion of playing both rugby union and rugby league for Australia . . . and also of playing rugby league with New Zealand. In 1908, when New Zealand decided to send a rugby league team to tour in England, they found themselves short of a few players and sent out an SOS to "Dally", who was one of the founders of the new code in Australia. He had just switched over to the league code and jumped at the chance of going to England, particularly as he had been cold-shouldered for the Wallabies tour of Britain and Ireland that year. He made his first appearance in Britain as a member of the New Zealand rugby league side and when he returned to Britain two years later, he was a member of the Australian rugby league team. Messenger, one of the most prolific scorers of his time, died in 1959.

THE GREAT ADVENTURE

Between 1903 and 1907, Australia played five international games against New Zealand and won four and drew the fifth. Then in 1908, they set off on their first great adventure in rugby—an ambitious tour of England and Wales and the United States of America. And they were to be quite a surprise packet for the British, who at the time had the distinctly false impression that rugby in Australia was in a class much below that of the rest of the rugby-playing world. The Australians played 34 games on their tour, won 28, lost five and scored 495 points while conceding 149. Their most decisive win of the tour in England and Wales was their 37-3 defeat of Cheshire and their worst beating was by 5-16 to Midland Counties. Only in one game did they fail to score and that was in their 0-6 defeat by Swansea. In the England-Wales portion of the tour, the Australians record was; played 31, lost five, drew one, with 438 points for and 146 against. Top scorer of the Australian side, which was captained by H. M. Moran of New South Wales was Charles "Boxer" Russell with 72 points from 24 tries.

DEATH OF A MASCOT

No touring side ever brought a more unusual mascot with them than the 1908-1909 Australian side. Their prized possession was a carpet snake, rejoicing in the name of "Bertie", which they brought all the way with them from Australia. As long as he was with them, they felt they could beat anyone. Sadly, however, on their visit to play Llanelli, the same "Bertie" suddenly said goodbye to the world and there were more than veiled suggestions from the Australians that some unkindly Welshmen had been the cause of his unexpected demise. As it happened their luck disappeared with the death of the snake. They lost their first game of the tour to Llanelli and, subsequently, when they turned out against Wales in their first international game at Cardiff Arms Park on

12th December, 1908, they went down again, this time by 6-9. However, things picked up a little after that and by the time they faced England in their second international at Blackheath on 9th January, 1909, they were in somewhat better form. With Charlie "Boxer" Russell, playing a magnificent game at wing-threequarter and tremendous work in the pack from Pat McCue, Charlie Hammond and Jim Gavin, they beat England by 9-3, three tries to a try. This was an historic victory for Australia in international rugby. It was their first win on foreign soil.

A SIGNIFICANT TRIUMPH

The 1908-1909 Australian side played the opening game of their tour against Devon and won by the convincing margin of 24-3. They followed this by beating Gloucester 16-0 and then they took on Cornwall at Camborne and won by the wide margin of 18-5. Three weeks later they were to meet Cornwall again and the result of this game was to give the Australians a significant status in the history of world rugby. They became Olympic champions. This second meeting was at the Olympic Stadium, Shepherd's Bush, London and Cornwall, as county champions of the previous season, were nominated by the English Rugby Union Committee to represent the United Kingdom against the Australians. They were to go down to an even worse beating. The papers, and the Olympic reports of the 1908 Olympic Games do not record the Australian scorers but they took the lead in the first five minutes, were 10 points up in 20 minutes and then, according to the reports—"by good following up and remarkable speed outside they scored pretty much as they liked on somewhat slippery ground in dull and rather dark weather". The final score was 32-3 for the Australians. The men who took Olympic gold medals home to Australia were: P. Carmichael, C. Russell, D. B. Carroll, J. Hickey, F. Bede-Smith, C. McKivatt, A. J. McCabe, T. Griffin, J. Barnett, P. McCue, I. Middleton, T. Richards, M. McArthur, C. McMurtrie and R. R. Craig.

A PROFITABLE STAY OVER

T. J. Richards, one of Australia's great international forwards of the 1908-1909 tour of Britain and Ireland, was born of English parents in Queensland, Australia and when the tour in Britain had finished he took some time off to visit relations in Bristol. He enjoyed his stay so much there that he decided to take a job and spend some time in England. Naturally, he turned out with the local club in Bristol and that paid a rich dividend in 1910 when he was invited to tour with the Lions in South Africa, and thus, of course, became the first Australian international to play on a touring side from these islands. Richards also won an Olympic gold medal with Australia in the Games at London in 1908.

NOT HERE, YOU DON'T

S. A. Middletown of New South Wales who was to win three caps for Australia against New Zealand and one against England, went back home after the 1908-1909 tour of Britain and Ireland with his first cap, an Olympic gold medal—and another striking "first" in rugby history. Against Oxford University, a game which the tourists won by 19-3, he was warned by the referee, Mr A. O. Jones, for an early offence and after he had been caught striking one of the Oxford forwards in a line-out, he was given his marching orders. He was the first member of a touring party, the first player wearing an international jersey to be sent to the line in either Britain or Ireland.

A LONG TIME AROUND

Wing-threequarter Danny Carroll, who toured with the 1908-1909 Australian side in Britain, won his only international cap of that tour against Wales at Cardiff Arms Park on Saturday, 8th December, 1908 but he went back home to Australia with a prized possession—an Olympic gold medal. He was on the Australian side which beat the United Kingdom, represented by Cornwall, in the Olympic final at Shepherd's Bush in London. Subsequently he went out of favour with the Australian selectors and did not appear on the sides which played three international games against New Zealand in 1910. However he stepped back into the picture again in 1912, when he was named to travel with Australia to play in one of history's most unusual international games. This was against America in California in 1912 and for which the Australians were awarded official caps. Carroll enjoyed America so much that he decided to settle down there. He did, however, continue to play rugby while studying at Stanford University and following the Olympic trials of 1920, he was named on the United States squad which travelled to Antwerp for the seventh Olympic Games. At the time, he was reckoned to be close to forty years of age but for all that he was still a magnificent forward and as the accounts of the time report—"the guiding and wise head of a sometimes impetuous Yankee side". They reached the final, shocked the French by winning it and so Danny Carroll, son of an Irish emigrant to Australia, wound up his career with a second Olympic gold medal. For many years afterwards, he was one of the game's most able administrators in California.

THE BROTHERS BURGE

The first brothers to play international rugby with Australia were the Burges of New South Wales. Peter and Andrew both played on the Australian side which met New Zealand in 1907 and subsequently toured with the first Wallabies in Britain and Ireland in 1908-1909, who crowned an outstanding trip by winning the Olympic title in rugby at the London Olympic Games. Peter Burge later turned to Rugby League and came back to Britain in 1911-12 to tour with the Australian "Kangaroos" Rugby League side. Another brother, Frank, also played rugby league and was on the Australian side which toured in England in 1921-1922.

TROUBLE AT HOME

The 1908-1909 Australians travelled home through America and finished off their tour by beating The California All-Stars 17-0, California University by 27-0 and Stanford University by 13-3. Then it was back to Australia and straight into a conflict that has ever since prevented Australia from becoming a really major power in world rugby. Two years earlier, following a dispute over expenses for injured players rugby league had been introduced into New South Wales and Queensland and the union game lost one of its greatest personalities when the famous "Dally" Messenger decided to change over to the League code. Following the return home of the 1908-1909 side, no fewer than 14 of them switched over to the professional game and gradually but inexorably the union game became confined to a few areas, notably New South Wales. Several of the 1908-1909 tourists including F. Burge, R. R. Craig, C. Maxwell and P. A. McCue were to return to England to play international rugby league with Australia.

THE WARATAHS

Australia were invited to make a second tour to Europe in 1927-1928, this one to embrace Britain, Ireland and France. Unfortunately with rugby union in Australia then almost exclusively confined to New South Wales, the invitation had to be declined. New South Wales, however, then decided to go it alone. They made the tour and as things happened they turned out to be one of the most popular and exciting sides to visit these islands. Under the captaincy of A. C. "Johnny" Wallace, who had already been capped by Scotland in 1924, 1925 and 1926, but who was never to win a cap for Australia, they played 31 matches, won 24, lost five, drew two and scored 432 points and conceded 207. The extraordinary feature of this tour was that they played five games of international status, against Ireland, Wales, Scotland, England and France and all those who played against them for four of these countries, Ireland, England, Scotland and Wales, were awarded official international caps. The New South Wales players however were not honoured with Australian caps and their only reward were state caps. The "Waratahs", as they were to be universally known, opened their "international" campaign by beating Ireland 5-3, a goal to a penalty goal, at Lansdowne Road, Dublin on Saturday, 12th November, 1927 and then went on to score their most impressive victory of the tour by decisively beating Wales at Cardiff Arms Park on Saturday, 26th November, 1927 by 18-8, three goals and a try to a goal and a try. On 17th December, 1927 they lost 8-10 to Scotland at Murrayfield and went down to England at Twickenham on 7th January, 1928 by 8-18. The first side to beat them on the tour were Oxford University and they finished their tour with a scoreless draw against London at Twickenham.

AND WHO WAS HE?

The "Waratahs" captivated everyone with their exciting approach to rugby during the 1927-1928 tour and they also won tremendous acclaim for the remarkable clean way in which they played every game.

But there was one tiny blot on their record and, perhaps in view of all the good things they had shown, no one really wanted to pinpoint the culprit. It happened during the game against Cardiff at Cardiff Arms Park which brought one of the finest scores ever seen at the ground. Tom Lawton had scored first for the "Waratahs" and his try was converted by Jim Ford who then dropped a goal to put the tourists nine points up. B. O. Male, with two penalty goals for Cardiff reduced the leeway and then Gabe Jones shot over for a try to level the scoring. At this point, following a dust-up in the forward exchanges, one of the New South Wales forwards was sent to the line and the newspaper accounts of the game, with a certain discretion, did not divulge his name. But even with 14 men, the "Waratahs" struck back for an epic victory. Cyril Towers went over for a try which was not converted and then seconds from the end with a move that began on their own line near the right corner, the ball was swept right across to the opposite wing, then back again to the left and then finally back to the right again before their second row forward H. F. Woods heaved himself over the Cardiff line to give them a 15-9 victory. During the entire move, not one Cardiff man had been able to get in a tackle or an intercept. Their reception, leaving the field, according to their captain "Johnny" Wallace, was the finest they received throughout the whole tour. But the mystery of who was sent to the line was kept discreetly quiet for some time. He was, in fact, Jim Ford, whose offence was that he repeatedly queried the decisions of the referee, Mr S. J. Huntley.

A CLEAN SWEEP

In the last series of international games before the introduction of the Bledisoe Cup in 1931, the Australians brought off one of the most memorable feats in their rugby history. In their three-match series in 1929 during the All-Blacks tour of Australia, they slammed New Zealand in all three international games. Tommy Lawton, who had been the Waratahs' top scorer with 104 points during their tour of Britain, Ireland and France in 1927-1928, was the genius who engineered the destruction of the All-Blacks in this 1929 tour. In the first international at Sydney, before a crowd of 40,000, Lawton kicked the first points of the game with a superb penalty goal but the All-Blacks forged ahead with a 50 yards penalty goal from the great George Nepia and then with a try from C. J. Oliver which Nepia converted. However, just before half-time Lawton put over a second penalty goal to leave the half-time score at 8-6 in favour of the All-Blacks. Early in the second half G. C. Gordon put Australia ahead with a try and that was how it ended with the score 9-8 to Australia. This was Australia's first win over New Zealand since 1913. And, of course there was better to come.

THREE-IN-A-ROW

The second international game of 1929 was played at Brisbane and Australia were dealt a sore blow early in the first half when Charlie Oliver was badly gashed on the head and had to leave the field. But with 14 men, led in glorious fashion by Whiley Breckenridge, Wild Bill Cerutti, Pete Judd and Eddie Bonis, Australia played a remarkable game. Lawton kicked a penalty shortly before the end of the first half to level the scoring and then in a one-sided second half George McGhie, Otto Crossman and Ernie Ford galloped over for tries to shatter the All-Blacks. Lawton kicked a second penalty and also converted a try to leave the final score at 17-9 for Australia. This win marked the first time that Australia had beaten the All-Blacks in successive games.

THE HAT-TRICK

Australia and New Zealand returned to Sydney to the third and final international game of the All-Blacks 1929 tour and their meeting pulled in one of the greatest crowds that had ever witnessed a rugby match in Australia. And the crowd had plenty to cheer about in a second half that saw the Wallabies strike back from what appeared to be certain defeat. It was all New Zealand from the start. Within a matter of minutes R. G. Williams went storming through the Australian backline for a magnificent try and three minutes after that J. C. Stringfellow intercepted a pass in the middle of the field and raced all the way to ground the ball between the posts. H. T. Lilburne added the conversion and New Zealand were eight points up. B. A. Grenside added a further try and Lilburne converted and the All-Blacks had 13 points on the scoreboard. But one Tommy Lawton was still there behind the Australian scrum and gradually he changed the pattern of the game. He kicked two penalty goals and then Cyril Towers dropped a glorious goal to make the score 13-9. Towers then put John Ford over for a try in the corner and now there was only a point in it. But time was running away and there was less than four minutes to go. Then, Lawton sparked off a great movement that swept Australia into one last desperate attack and it was finished off by their captain Sid King who dived over at the corner to put Australia ahead for the first time. Lawton missed the conversion but it did not matter. For the first time in the history of their rugby, Australia had brought off a hat-trick of wins over New Zealand and for the first time in their history, New Zealand had lost three international games in succession.

WHERE WAS THE DONOR?

Australia and New Zealand met for the first time for the Bledisoe Cup at Eden Park, Auckland on Saturday, 12th September, 1931—and this was the first time that a full Australian team had been in New Zealand since 1913. Unfortunately neither the Bledisoe Cup nor the man who presented it, Lord Bledisoe, was present on that historic day. The New Zealand Governor-General was caught up in another engagement and at that particular stage, the trophy had neither been designed nor made. However the match went on without both. And New Zealand, after a fierce battle became the first holders of the trophy which, of course, they did not receive until sometime later. Australia opened up at a fierce pace and raced into a lead of 13 points with two tries from Cyril Towers and another from D. L. Cowper, two of which were converted by Dr Alec Ross. But New Zealand gradually whittled away at their lead and early in the second half, following tries from G. F. Hart and N. Ball, R. G. Bush kicked four penalty goals and that plus his conversion of one of the tries gave the All-Blacks victory by 20-11. Since 1931 Australia and New Zealand have met on 44 occasions for the Bledisoe Cup, 25 times in New Zealand and 19 in Australia. Of the 44 games, Australia have won eight, drawn two and New Zealand have won 34.

A NEW ADVENTURE

Under the leadership of Dr Alec Ross, the Australians broke new ground in their rugby history in 1933 by undertaking a full tour of South Africa. And it was a tour that began badly for them. They won their opening games against Natal and Western Transvaal and then went down to three successive defeats by Rand Town, Pretoria and Griqualand West. On the evidence of these defeats, the Wallabies prospects of beating South Africa in any of the five international games looked depressingly remote. By the end of the tour, the Australians had played 18 matches, won 12, lost 10 and drawn one. The points total was 299 points and they conceded 195. Leading the way in their scoring charts was centre-threequarter D. L. Cowper, with 34 points, compiled from four tries, nine conversions and a drop goal. Their top try scorer was wing-threequarter J. D. Kelaher with 9. The Australians were unfortunate in that Alec Ross had to have an emergency appendix operation shortly after arrival in South Africa and he was unable to play until the final international game. Syd Malcolm, the scrum-half and regarded as one of the best of his time, went down with injury early in the tour and he was forced to miss the first three international games.

THE FIRST INTERNATIONAL

Danie Craven had the honour of scoring South Africa's first points against Australia in their first international game at Newlands. He slipped over for a try after three minutes and Gerry Brand, playing on the wing, put the Springboks into a half-time lead of 6-0. Fredie Bergh sent South Africa further ahead with a try early in the second half and after Ron Bulman had kicked a penalty goal for the Wallabies, the Springboks came striking back with another try from Bergh and Bennie Osler completed the afternoon with a try which Gerry Brand converted for a 17-3 win. Following this, the second international game to be played at Durban promised to be another runaway win for the Springboks.

A RUDE SHOCK

Bennie Osler captained South Africa in their second international match against Australia at Kingsmead, Durban in 1933 and, on the evidence of what had happened in the first international, the South Africans decided to open up the game and run with the ball at every chance. Even Osler, noted for his tactical touch-kicking, was under orders to let the ball out. And so the Springboks did—and they wound up with a rude and salutary shock. "Wild Bill" Cerutti, one of the legendary hard men of Australian rugby, smashed his way over for a try and Gordon Sturtridge added a second. Ron Bulman converted both tries, then kicked a penalty goal and Australia led at half-time by 13-6, with South Africa's scores coming from a try by F. W. Waring and a penalty goal by Gerry Brand. Bob Loudon and W. G. Bennett scored two more tries for the Australians in the second half. Bulman converted Bennett's try and the final score was 21-6 for the Wallabies. To this day, that result on 22nd July, 1933, stands as Australia's record win over South Africa.

BACK TO NORMAL

The Springboks reverted to their traditional style of play for the third and fourth international games against the Australians during the 1933 tour and won both handily. In the third at Ellis Park, Johannesburg, Bob Louw gave them an early lead with a try, Freddie Turner added a second and Gerry Brand converted to put them into an 8-0 lead. Bennie Osler dropped his almost inevitable goal in the second half and D. L. Dowper took the bare look off the scoreboard with a try for Australia to leave the final score at 12-3. The fourth international at Port Elizabeth was even more decisive for the Springboks. Jimmy White gave them an early try which Osler converted and in the second half Fanie Louw with a try and Gerry Brand with a penalty goal sent South Africa away to an 11-0 victory. The series had now been won by South Africa; all that remained was the academic exercise of the fifth and last international match at Springbok Park, Bloemfontein. This, in fact, was to be the first and as it transpired the last international game to be played at Springbok Park.

A FINAL FLOURISH

With the series already lost at 1-3, Australia had little to lose in the fifth and final international other than a fading prestige. So they decided to gamble on a fast, open running game and it paid handsome dividends. D. L. Cowper dropped a quick goal, Jack Kelaher tore over for a try and Jack Stegall added another which Alec Ross, back after his operation, converted with a great kick from close to the touch-line. Australia were 12-0 up. Gerry Brand with a drop goal from close to 55 yards brought the score to 12-4 but the Australian lock-forward O. L. Bridle galloped over for a fine try and Australia had won their second international game in South Africa. It was to be 30 years before the Wallabies again managed to beat the Springboks in two games of an international series. With this closing international of 1933, the immortal Bennie Osler, then thirty-one, said good-bye to his illustrious international rugby career. In his seventeen international appearances he had scored 46 points for South Africa. In his 30 Springbok appearances in all tour games, including the internationals, his points total was 108. Osler, still remembered as one of the legendary heroes of South African rugby, died in April, 1962 at the age of sixty.

THE FIRST VICTORY

Australia won the Bledisoe Cup for the first time in 1934, with a resounding win by 25-11 over New Zealand in the first international game at Sydney and a 3-3 draw in the second international game also at Sydney. With over 40,000 supporters to urge them on at Sydney on 11th August, Australia made hard work of containing the All-Blacks in a titanic first half. Jackie Hore opened the scoring for New Zealand with a try after 10 minutes but this was promptly cancelled out by a try for Australia from Cyril Towers. A. Knight of Auckland, whose only international appearance for New Zealand this was to be, got over for the second New Zealand try, which was converted by A. J. Collins. S. S. Max added another try but Jim McLean came back with a penalty goal to leave the Wallabies trailing by 6-11 at the break. Surprisingly New Zealand failed to score again. The Australians took over completely. Alec Ross kicked three penalty goals for a 15-11 lead. Then O. L. Bridle went over for a try which Ross converted and shortly before the end Cyril Towers went in for a try and again Ross was on the mark with the conversion. Alec Ross's 13 points in this international was a record for an Australian in a meeting with New Zealand. The second international at Sydney a fortnight later was a dull and tedious stalemate, R. B. Loudon of New South Wales scored a try for Australia and J. Hore of Otago replied in the second half with a try and that was that. Australia had won the Bledisoe Cup for the first time. Two years later, however, the All-Blacks took it back by winning 11-6 at Wellington and by the decisive margin of 38-13 at Dunedin. That 25 points margin was to represent Australia's worst defeat by New Zealand right up to 1972.

LUCKY THIRTEEN

Prop-forward William Cerutty, known throughout his rugby career as "Wild Bill" began his career as a soccer player but decided early on that it was much too mild a game for him. He switched over to rugby and during his great career that ended with the outbreak of the Second World War, he put up the astonishing record of playing 16 times for Australia, 47 times for New South Wales and 247 top-class club games. He toured with the Australians in South Africa in 1933 and made two tours of New Zealand and made his final international appearance against Philip Nel's Springboks of 1937. But Cerutty is remembered most for a certain superstition. Throughout his career and in every game that he ever played he always insisted on wearing the No 13 jersey. On quite a few occasions he threatened not to play when it was suggested to him that he should wear a different number. He eventually retired from club football in 1948 when he was approaching forty.

THEY DIDN'T EVEN PLAY A MATCH

Under the managership of Dr Walter F. Matthews and under the captaincy of Vincent Wilson of Queensland, the second fully representative Australian side to undertake a tour of Britain and Ireland, arrived in England in August, 1939. They were due to play 28 games, 14 in England, eight in Wales, four in Scotland and two in Ireland. Unfortunately, they were to be the touring side that never even played a game. Their only consolation was a walk around the famous ground of Twickenham. With the declaration of the Second World War, the tour was called off and just as soon as suitable arrangements could be made, the Australian party turned around and made their way sadly home. Eighteen of the 29 players had already been capped for Australia but for nine of the remaining 11, the possibility of playing for their country disappeared with the cancellation of this tour. V. M. Nicholson, B. J. Porter, L. H. Smith, D. Carrick, B. B. Oxenham, S. Y. Bissett,

G. A. Prearson, J. E. Turnbull and A. W. Barr, all of whom stood a chance of winning caps during the 1939 tour, were never again to get the chance of playing for their country. Of the 29 players, only Bill McLean was still around when the next Australian tour to Britain and Ireland was made in 1947-1948—and even then he was unlucky again. In his first game at Twickenham against the Combined Services, he broke his leg just two minutes from time and was out of action for the remainder of the tour.

EVERYONE WANTED HIM

Charles Eastes was just 21 when he was picked to tour with Australia in New Zealand in 1946 and a year later he was an automatic selection for the Wallaby side to tour in Britain, Ireland and France. But for Eastes, who was to win only six caps for Australia, this was a tragic tour. He fractured his arm in the 12th game against Newport and that put him out of contention for the rest of the tour. But he had done more than enough, as top try scorer, to attract the attention of both Leeds and Wigan, who tried very hard to get him to switch over to Rugby League. They, however, were not the only ones in the hunt. The famous Los Angeles Rams were also chasing him to play American football! Eastes, described as one of the most elegant runners in the game, resisted all the offers and returned home to become a top official with the Australian Rugby Union. His last appearance with a touring side was in 1969 when he managed the Wallaby side in South Africa.

ONLY SIX DEFEATS

The 1947-48 Australian touring side finished off their ambitious tour of Britain, Ireland, France and the United States by winning 35 of their 41 match programme and in the process ran up 712 points while conceding 276. Their biggest margin of victory in Britain and Ireland was the 49-0 win over Northumberland and Durham and subsequently they equalled this in the United States by beating Leyland University by 59-10. Their worst defeat by 3-11 by Cardiff in the fifth game of the tour and after that they went on an unbeaten streak of 15 wins before going down 8-9 to Lancashire and Cheshire. Their other four defeats were to Wales by 0-6, London Counties 8-14, Barbarians 6-9 and France 6-13. In only one of their 41 games did they fail to score and that was against Wales.

CHANGED OVER

Ken Kearney, who played in seven internationals for Australia and was one of their top forwards in the tour of Britain, Ireland and France in 1947-1948, had the distinction of representing Australia in both the union and rugby codes. Kearney, who played with Sydney R.U. Club won his first caps against the All-Blacks on his display, became a first choice selection as hooker for the 1947-1948 tourists. In 1948, however, he turned professional and went on to win another 25 caps for Australia, 22 of them in succession. After a spell with the Leeds club in England, he returned home to Australia but was back again that year with the touring Australian "Kangaroos" and in England, he managed to achieve a dubious record. In the game against Halifax, Kearney was sent off and became the first Australian rugby league player to be suspended in Britain.

NOT A TRY!

The 1947-1948 Australians opened up their international campaign with a 16-7 win over Scotland at Murrayfield and the significant feature of the game was that Scotland's scores came from a penalty goal and a dropped goal. The Australians then moved to Lansdowne Road, Dublin, won easily by 16-3 and again the only score against them came from a penalty goal. They lost 0-6 to Wales at Cardiff Arms Park but both of Wales's scores came from penalty goals. They finished their international tour of the four home countries with an 11-0 win over England at Twickenham and thus finished with the remarkable record of not having their line crossed in any of the four games. Unfortunately, this proud record was to go by the board when they faced up to France at Colombes Stadium. France won by 13-6 and in the process went over for three tries, two from Guy Basquet and the other from Michel Pomathios.

THE FIRST BARBARIANS GAME

The 1947-1948 Australians were more than directly responsible for the regular games which now take place between touring sides and the famous Barbarians. Towards the end of their tour, when it became a little embarrassingly obvious that the Australians would need some extra money to finish off their tour in Canada and the United States, the four Home Unions with the assistance of the Cardiff Club and the Barbarians staged a special match at Cardiff Arms Park between the Australians and the Barbarians with the express purpose of raising cash. This game, which the Barbarians won by 9-6 was a resounding success and was, of course, the forerunner of the great games which have since taken place between the Barbarians and touring sides from overseas.

FOR AND AGAINST

Doug Keller, whose solid forward play throughout the tour, made him one of the memorable successes of the 1947-1948 Australian touring side, wound up his international career with the unusual record of playing against Scotland . . . and also for Scotland. Indeed, he had the further distinction of playing for two different countries against Ireland, England, Wales and France! Keller, who won his first international cap for Australia against New Zealand in 1947, played for his country in the five tour internationals of the 1947-1948 trip to Britain, Ireland and France. He remained on in England at the end of the tour and joined London-Scottish and in 1949 was selected to play for Scotland in the four internationals against England, Wales, Ireland and France. The following year he won three further international caps for Scotland against Ireland, Wales and France. In all he won 13 international caps—six for Australia and seven for Scotland.

VICTORY IN NEW ZEALAND

Under the captaincy of Trevor Allan, Australia were to make a memorable tour of New Zealand in 1949. They played 12 games, lost only one in somewhat controversial circumstances and best of all, they won the two international games and won back the Bledisoe Cup. On 3rd September, 1949, they took on New Zealand at Wellington and won by 11-6. Colin Windon opened the scoring for the Wallabies with a try and R. L. Garner added a second which was converted by R. M. Cawsey and another try from Garner left the Australians in an 11-0 lead at the interval. J. W. Kelly of Auckland kicked a penalty goal for New Zealand in the second half and their final score, a try, came from G. J. T. Moore late in the game. Three weeks later at Eden Park, Auckland, H. J. Solomon got the Australians off to a winning start with a try and Colin Windon added a second. New Zealand tore back into the game and with just two minutes to go the score stood at 11-9 in Australia's favour but New Zealand were now firmly on top and storming the Australian line unceasingly. Then in a sudden desperate breakaway N. A. Emery went surging away for a shock Australian try between the posts. To crown an historic afternoon, Australia's captain Trevor Allan took the conversion and gave the Wallabies a 16-9 win—and the Bledisoe Cup. It was the first time in the 46 years of their meetings that Australia had won two games in succession over the All-Blacks in New Zealand. Two years later, however, the Bledisoe Cup was to return to New Zealand and it is still there to this day.

ON THE GO

It is a long way from the Sydney rugby ground to Colombes Stadium in Paris and a long time, too, from 1932 to 1948. But G. M. Cooke, a towering Australian forward covered both in his extraordinary international career. He made his international debut for the Wallabies at Sydney in 1932 against New Zealand and was on the losing side in a 17-22 defeat. He won three internationals that year against the All-Blacks, collected another three the following year in Australia's three games against the Springboks and then dropped out of sight, and one might have assumed that his international career was over. But the remarkable Cooke turned up again in 1946 to play against New Zealand, held his place to play against the All-Blacks the following year and won his place on the Australian team to tour in Britain, Ireland and France in 1947-1948. He played in all five internationals on the tour, against England, Ireland, Scotland, Wales and France. Then he finally said goodbye. He collected his 13th international cap at Colombes Stadium—and it was a 6-13 defeat for the Wallabies—but when he walked off that field he had set a record for international rugby. No one before and no one since has played international rugby over a period of 17 seasons!

TWICE IN HIS CAREER

Australia lost only one game of their 1949 tour of New Zealand— against West Coast Buller at Greymouth. And this was quite an extraordinary and explosive game which was eventually won by 15-17 by the New Zealand side. Things began on more than a mildly bad note when the referee marched into the Australian dressing room before the game and warned the Australian international forward Dave Brockhoff. He told him straight out that he would not tolerate any over-zealous play in the forward exchanges. The unfortunate part of it all was that this warning was issued in front of the entire Australian side. What transpired, of course, was inevitable. Brockhoff was sent off but as he was leaving the field the referee made it known to him that his sending off was just a "temporary" matter. As soon as Brockhoff had cooled down, he could come back on again. Fifteen minutes later, Colin Windon, one of Australia's most famous forwards, also got marching orders. But, as in the case of Brockhoff, it was just for a "cooling off" period. Both of them eventually returned to the game but by then all the damage had been done and the final exchanges in the game were not gentle. For Windon this sending off was somewhat historic. Two years earlier, while wearing the Australian international jersey during the tour of Britain, Ireland and France in 1947-1948 he had also been sent off in the tourists' 6-4 win over Llanelli. Windon's punishment for that first offence was that he missed the next three games of the tour against London Counties, Cambridge University and the combined Hants and Sussex side.

TWENTY YEARS LATER

Exactly 20 years after their first adventure to South Africa, the Australians came back in 1953 to play a 27-matches programme under the captaincy of a twenty-three-year old Sydney University medical student, John Solomon. The 1953 Wallabies won 16 of their 27 games, lost 10 and drew one and set a record for a touring side in South Africa by scoring 450 points. Unfortunately they also set a record by conceding a record number of points for a touring side of 416 points. Tom Sweeney, their full back, was the Wallabies top points scorer with 67 points from 20 conversions and nine drop goals and George Horsley led the way in the matter of try-scoring with 14. Their greatest win of the tour was the 50-12 rout of Western Transvaal and their worst defeat was 3-25 by South Africa in the opening international game at Johannesburg.

THE SPRINGBOKS IN WHITE

Since they had appeared in South Africa, Australia had changed their national colour to green and so for the first international game at Ellis Park, the Springboks appeared in the unusual garb of all-white. And the change of colours certainly brought them a satisfactory and rewarding afternoon. Tom Sweeney kicked a penalty goal for Australia and that was their lot. In return Salty du Rand, Hansie Oelofse, Tjol Lategan, Hennie Muller and Hannes Marais scored tries for South Africa and to complete the rout, Marais also kicked one conversion and a penalty goal and Johnny Buchler dropped a goal and also kicked a conversion. It was a record win for South Africa, a record defeat for Australia and both were to stand until 1961.

DOWN THEY WENT

Going into the second international game against Australia in 1953, South Africa were in the happy position of having not lost an international game since 1938 and had won 10 internationals on the trot against all of the major countries. On the result of the first international against Australia, the money on them to win was odds on, particularly as the Wallabies had been trounced 5-24 by Southern Universities in their final warm-up game for this international. And the early stages of this game did not look too promising for the Wallabies. After 11 minutes the Springboks were eight points up with a try from du Rand, converted by Marais and a try from Ochse. The Australian winger Eddie Stapleton made it 8-3 but Chris Koch went barging over for a try to leave South Africa 11-3 ahead at the break. Within three minutes of the re-start Oelofse put Van Wyk in for a simple try to make it 14-3 and that looked to be the end of Australia. Five minutes later, however, Kevin Cross got in for a try and Colbert converted it and the scoreboard looked a little more respectable at 14-8. Australia had the misfortune to lose their captain John Solomon at this stage but shortly after he had returned the Wallabies tore down the field and B. B. Johnstone scored a shock try. Stapleton with a soaring kick from the touch-line converted and the score was 14-13 and so it remained right into injury time. With 60 seconds to go, Australia struck again in a dramatic finish. Garth Jones took a pass just outside his own "25" and raced 75 yards along the wing and then swung in to ground the ball between the posts. Jones was still on the ground, exhausted from his sensational run, when Ray Colbert put over the conversion to give Australia an 18-14 victory. After 15 years, South Africa's great unbeaten run had finally come to an end.

TWO WALLABY DEFEATS

Australia had their tails up after their sensational victory at Newlands and had high hopes of squaring the series in the third international at Durban. But they were never in with a chance. South Africa with tries, from Dolf Bekker and D. Rossouw, both converted by I. J. Rens, put 10 points on the scoreboard by half-time and Jaap Bekker and Van Wyk with tries, one converted by Rens, gave them a final total of 18 points. Australia's scores came from a try by Cross which was converted by Ray Colbert and John Solomon kicked a penalty goal. The final international at Port Elizabeth was even more decisive. I. J. Rens became one of the exclusive band of South African internationals to go into double figures for an international game with 13 points from two penalty goals, a drop goal and two conversions and Buchler with a drop goal and Koch and Ochse with tries brought the Springbok total to 22 points. Eddie Stapleton with a try and H. S. Barker with two penalty goals provided Australia with their nine points. In the four international games South Africa had registered 79 points, which is still the highest total ever recorded in a series of international games between Australia and South Africa. With Australia's total added to this, the 117 points also remains as the highest aggregate for a series of international games between the two countries.

THE 1957-1958 WALLABIES

Bob Davidson's 1957-1958 Australian touring side came perilously close to losing more matches than they won. In their tour of Britain, Ireland, France, Canada and Japan, they played a total of 36 games and lost 16 of them. They won 17 and drew three and scored 348 points while conceding 258. After winning their opening game over Southern Counties by 29-5, they crashed 6-12 to Oxford University in their second and also went down in the third by 3-13 to Cambridge University. From there on their form was inexplicably erratic and, after losing all five internationals to Wales, Ireland, England, Scotland and France, they suffered the final indignity by losing 8-11 to British Columbia in Canada. In Britain, Ireland and France, their best win was the 29-5 defeat of Southern Counties and in their final game of the tour against Meiji University in Japan, they won by 55-3. Their worst defeat by 0-19 to France at Colombes Stadium, Paris. Their most durable player was Terry Curley who played in 34 of the 36 games and Jim Lenehan and the captain Bob Davidson both appeared in 32 games.

THE TOP SCORER

Nineteen year old Jim Lenehan was one of the surprise choices for the 1957-1958 Australian touring side. At the time he was the No 2 full-back to Terry Curley in New South Wales and when he was named for the tour, it was generally accepted that his main function would be to act as Curley's understudy during the trip to Britain, Ireland, France, Canada and Japan. Curley was then regarded as the top full-back in Australia and there seemed little likelihood that he would lose his place for the international games. Unfortunately he struck bad form early in the tour and was moved into the threequarter line and young Lenehan was given his chance at full-back. By the end of the tour he had taken over completely as the No 1 full-back and as such he was to remain for many years after in Australian rugby. By the time he ended his international career against Ireland in 1967 he had won 24 caps for his country and had also become one of Australia's most prolific scorers. During the 1957-1958 tour, he was top points scorer with 117 for the 32 games in which he played.

THE END OF HIS CAREER

Jim Phipps, one of two brothers to play for Australia—both he and Bob Phipps toured against the All-Blacks in 1955—had 11 international caps to his credit when he was named to play with the Australian side to tour Britain, Ireland and France in 1957-1958. This was to be a tragic tour for him. In the ninth game of the tour, against a Combined Glasgow-Edinburgh side, he broke his leg and that ruled him out of the five international games and for the rest of the tour. Unfortunately, it was to have an even worse effect. On his return to Australia, he tried to play club football, but his injured leg kept coming against him and after a few months he was forced to retire completely from rugby.

TURNED OVER

In his all too short rugby union career, Australia's Arthur Summons had the honour of representing his country on 10 occasions against Ireland, England, Scotland, Wales, New Zealand, the New Zealand Maoris and the Lions—all within two years. Then at the age of twenty-three in 1959, and like so many top Australians, he switched over to Rugby League, the game he had played at college before turning to the union code. Eventually he became captain of the "Kangaroos" and in 1962 a glorious try, for which he ran the entire length of the field, prevented the British touring side from winning all three Test games in Australia for the first time.

DESMOND CONNOR

Saturday, 22nd July, 1961 at Eden Park, Auckland marked two historic firsts. It was the first time France had met the All-Blacks in New Zealand . . . and it was the first international appearance in the All-Blacks jersey for one Desmond Connor. And Connor's debut for New Zealand was a sensational event. From that day he was to go on to win 12 international caps for New Zealand, three against France, seven against Australia and two against England—and he was never to be on a losing side. Impressive, yes . . . but on that day he made his debut for New Zealand, the same Des Connor had already played 12 international games of rugby for his native Australia and had been on the losing side in eleven of those games. A native of Brisbane, Connor, regarded as one of the game's most memorable scrum-halves, toured with the 1957-1958 Wallabies in Britain, Ireland and France and this was the sad tour in which Australia were "white-washed" in all five international games. Subsequently Connor played for Australia against the British Lions and against New Zealand and had 12 Australian caps in his collection before he started collecting his second twelve with New Zealand. He had the unique distinction playing for Australia on three occasions against New Zealand and of playing on seven occasions for New Zealand against Australia. His record, of course of playing 12 times each for two countries in international rugby has never been equalled. Connor, subsequently, returned home to Australia and was coach to the Wallaby side that toured in South Africa in 1969—and that, unfortunately, was another "white-wash" for the tourists. They were soundly beaten in all four international games with the Springboks.

THE 1961 TOUR

Under the leadership of Ken Catchpole, who was to win 23 international caps for his country, Australia made a short tour to South Africa in 1961 in which they played six matches, including two internationals. They won three games, lost two, drew one and scored 90 points while conceding 80. Their top scorer was out-half J. Dowse with 35 points from four conversions, eight penalty goals and a drop goal. Mike Cleary, one of Australia's top sprinters, was their top try scorer with five tries. The tour was unusual that Catchpole made his international debut as captain of Australia and that the two Thornett brothers, John and Dick appeared together for the first time in an Australian side against one of the major countries.

A RECORD CRASH

Ken Catchpole's debut as captain of Australia against South Africa at Ellis Park, Johannesburg on Saturday, 5th July, 1961 was depressingly memorable for him. With Hennie Van Zyl becoming the fourth South African to score three tries in an international game, the Springboks tore the Wallabies apart and cruised away to a 28-3 victory. That result still remains in the record books as the worst defeat ever suffered by an Australian international side at the hands of South Africa.

STILL OUT OF LUCK

The Australians wound up their short tour of South Africa in 1961 with yet another defeat by the Springboks at Port Elizabeth, this time on the score of 23-11 and the main feature worth recording of that game was the fact that South Africa's Keith Oxlee, destined to become one of his country's most prolific scorers, wound up with a personal total of 14 points from a try, a conversion and three penalty goals, which at the time moved him into joint second place in South Africa's individual scoring in an international game. With this defeat Australia had now failed to defeat South Africa since 1953 and had gone six successive meetings without a win.

A SAD START

Stewart Boyce played his first representative game of rugby for Northern New South Wales against the touring All-Blacks of 1962 and was handed the task of marking the All-Blacks flyer Ron Heeps at wing-threequarter. And the young Boyce could hardly have had a more trying afternoon. Ron Heeps ran over for eight tries—still a world record by a player on a tour—and New Zealand won by the astronomical score of 103-0. Boyce, however, survived that dreadful ordeal, joined his brother Jim on the Australian side that year and, of course, went on to become one of his country's greatest wing-threequarters over the next five seasons.

THORNETT'S MEN

The 1963 Australians to tour in South Africa finished with a poor record in their games against the provincial sides. Of the 20 they played they won 13, lost 6 and drew one and scored 274 points and conceded 183. Despite that their record in the four international games was distinctly impressive and a sobering surprise for the South Africans. They won two, lost two, and scored 29 points while giving away 50. The full record of the side was: played 24, won 15, lost eight, drew one, for a total of 303 points, with 233 conceded. Their top points scorer was full-back P. F. Ryan with 79 points from three tries, 11 conversions and 16 penalty goals. Wing-threequarter J. S. Boyce led the way in try scoring with seven. Captain of the Australians was John Thornett, who was making his third tour to South Africa and the manager was R. E. M. McLaughlin, who had been capped for Australia against New Zealand in 1936.

THE END OF THE LINE

The 1963 Australian tourists went down 6-12 to Western Province and 8-14 to Orange Free State in their final preparations for the fourth and final international match against South Africa at the Boet Erasmus Stadium in Port Elizabeth. And their performance in that final international showed unhappily that the rigours of a long tour had finally caught up with them. The Australians made a gallant fight of things for most of the way but in the final stages they were caught for pace and stamina and in the end were overwhelmed. Keith Oxlee, back in favour, kicked the South Africans into a three points lead with a penalty goal early on but Terry Casey levelled almost immediately with another penalty goal. Phil Hawthorne then, with a splendid drop goal, put the Wallabies into a 6-3 lead. Tiny Naude with a huge penalty from 50 yards brought the sides level again and that was how it stayed until 10 minutes from time. Then the Australians cracked. Oxlee kicked a penalty goal, Abie Malan went in for a try and Oxlee duly obliged with the conversion. Naude and Gainsford added further tries, Oxlee converted the last and with those two points took his all-time South African record to 73 points in international games.

INTO THE LEAD

Australia slumped again after their international victory over South Africa and on the Saturday preceding the third international at Johannesburg, they were soundly beaten by 12-5 by the Junior Springboks. For this third international, the South African selectors wielded their axe in no uncertain fashion and among the heads to roll was that of Keith Oxlee. In all there were eight changes, but they did not make any difference. Nelie Smith, who had replaced Oxlee gave the Springboks the lead with a penalty goal after 50 seconds but the Australians rallied rapidly and a 55 yards drop goal followed by a penalty goal, both from the foot of Terry Casey put the Wallabies into a 6-3 lead at half-time. Smith brought South Africa back on level terms with a second penalty goal early in the second half. J. L. Williams then put the Wallabies ahead with a try, the only one of the game and Casey duly kicked a difficult conversion to bring his total for the game to eight points. Just a few minutes later, however, Nelie Smith took over as the top scorer of the game with his third penalty goal. Smith had joined the exclusive band of those who had kicked all his country's points in an international debut. Unfortunately his nine points were not enough and for the first time in the history of the meetings between the two countries, Australia had won two international games in a row.

A FIRST DEFEAT

Australia's string of defeats by South Africa moved to a dismal seven in a row when they met at Pretoria in the opening international game of the 1963 tour. They started with a disadvantage in that just prior to the game it was discovered that scrum-half Ken Catchpole had broken a bone in his hand in the previous week's 14-5 win over Transvaal and was unable to play. His place went to Kevin McMullen and unfortunately, he failed to strike up a happy partnership with Phil Hawthorne at half-back. Certainly they had no answer to South Africa's Keith Oxlee, who began this game with a total of 53 points in his international appearances for the Springboks. All he needed from this game was four points to equal the twenty-five-year old international individual record held by Gerry Brand. It took Oxlee just 19 minutes to edge the record with a penalty goal and this was followed by a try from Cilliers to put South Africa into a 6-0 lead at half-time. Australia cut the leeway midway through the second half with a try from McMullen, but two minutes later Tommy Bedford went over for a South African try. With the conversion Oxlee took his total to 58 points in international games and to a new South African record. Just before the end he kicked a penalty goal to leave the record at 61.

A WIN AT LAST

After seven successive defeats by South Africa since 1953, Australia made the break-through at Newlands in the second international game of the 1963 tour. It was also the first defeat for South Africa in 16 international games. The South Africans opened the scoring with a penalty try—the only one ever awarded in a series of games between the two countries. The referee ruled that Tommy Bedford had been deliberately obstructed by the Australian centre B. J. Elwood as he went running in to follow up a short kick ahead by Jan Engelbrecht. Keith Oxlee converted to take his record to 63 points in international games. Australia, however, came back just before half-time with a try from Boyce and just on the whistle Hawthorne kicked a penalty to put the Wallabies into a 6-5 lead. There was just the one score in the second half. Terry Casey kicked a penalty goal for Australia. This was Australia's fourth victory over South Africa since 1933.

BAD START—WORSE FINISH

John Thornett's 1966-1967 Australian touring side which played 34 games in Britain, Ireland and France wound up with almost as bad a record as the previous touring side of 1957-1958. Of the 34 games, they won 16, lost 15 and drew three and scored 348 points while conceding 324. The tour got off on a sad note when the Australians were beaten 14-17 by North-East Counties and ended in Britain and Ireland on an even sadder note when the Wallabies lost five games in succession before defeating the Barbarians by 17-11. Their greatest margin of victory was their 27-6 defeat of Southern Counties and the worst of their 15 defeats was their 0-13 result against South of Scotland. Three members of the side, Jim Lenehan, John Thornett and Tony Miller were making their second tour of Europe with the Wallabies. They had also played on Bob Davidson's touring side of 1957-1958 and thus joined the legendary Nick Shehadie in the record books. Shehadie had toured with the Australians of 1947-1948 and had returned again with Davidson's tourists in 1957-1958.

SENT HOME

With their opening defeat by North-East Counties followed by a somewhat uneasy win by 12-9 over Midland Counties, the exploits of the 1966-1967 Australian tourists remained purely a sports pages item. Then, with their third game against Oxford University, the Wallabies became front-page news. Their hooker Ross Cullen was alleged to have bitten the ear of the Irish international prop forward Ollie Waldron in a set scrum—and for that he was sent back home to Australia. It was a sad ending to the tour for Cullen, who became the first player in the history of all touring sides to Britain since 1905 to be sent home for a reason other than injury.

A DAY TO REMEMBER

With a somewhat fortunate 3-3 draw against Newport, an 8-9 defeat by Swansea and a 3-12 beating by the combined Pontypool-Cross Keys-Newbridge side, the 1966-1967 Australians went to Cardiff Arms Park on Saturday, 3rd December, 1966 to open their international campaign against Wales. All the signs were there that they could anticipate a thorough hiding. And it looked that way shortly after the start when Haydn Morgan opened the scoring with a good try. Australia, however, came level with a snap drop goal by Phil Hawthorne and then Jim Lenehan put them in front with a long-range penalty goal. Terry

Price, however, cancelled that out with a fine penalty goal from 40 yards out. Then Lenehan stepped back into the picture again. Joining into a back movement he streaked through the Welsh defences to score a try at the corner. His conversion attempt, unfortunately, rebounded from the posts. But Australia went further in front when Alan Cardy danced his way over for a try and this time Hawthorne was dead on the mark with the conversion. In a storming finish John Dawes scored a try for Wales and Terry Price converted but it was too late then. Australia were in front by 14-11 and they held out to the end for an historic victory. For this marked the first time in 60 years that Australia had beaten Wales in an international rugby game.

ALMOST LEVEL

Following their tremendous and somewhat unexpected win over Wales, John Thornett's 1966-1967 Australians headed for Murrayfield to take on Scotland and were beaten by 11-5. Then came a rousing win by 23-11 over England at Twickenham but their luck ran out again against Ireland at Lansdowne Road, where they were defeated 8-15. Then it was on to Paris and Colombes Stadium, where Australia had never won an international game. And again their was a defeat, their third in Paris, with the score 20-14 to the exuberant Frenchmen. This, in fact, was their fourth international meeting with France—they had also met in Sydney in 1961—and with this victory France took their points total against the Wallabies to 67 while conceding 28 points. Of the five countries in the International Championship France was now the only one with an unbeaten record against Australia.

HAWTHORNE'S RECORD

Australia's tour of Britain, Ireland and France in 1967 was not a distinguished one but two of their better days were against Wales whom they beat by 14-11 and against England who crashed to the Wallabies at Twickenham by 11-23. And that was an afternoon to remember for the twenty-three-year old Australian outhalf Phil Hawthorne, who after winning 21 caps for his country, later joined the St George's Rugby League Club for a fee of 30,000 Australian dollars. That afternoon at Twickenham in 1967, with the Wallabies well on top all the way, Hawthorne marched into the history books by dropping three superb goals. And so he joined Pierre Albaladejo of France who up to that afternoon had been the only man to drop three goals in an international game. To this day, they are the only two players to achieve nine points from drop goals in international games.

SAD AND HAPPY

To celebrate the 75th Jubilee of the New Zealand Rugby Union, the Australians made a special trip to Athletic Park, Wellington in 1967 to take on the All-Blacks. For Tony Miller, Australia's great forward, it turned out to be a sad and happy afternoon. Australia went down by 9-29, one of the severest beatings they had taken from New Zealand up to that time and the game also marked Miller's final appearance for his country. He had won his first cap for Australia against Fiji in 1952 and with this latest game against New Zealand he had carried his total to 41 which was then an all-time record for Australia. But on that afternoon he was also thirty-seven and that made him the oldest player to play in an international game for Australia. His span of 15 years in international rugby is also outstanding. Miller, one of the game's most durable players, made tours with Australia to Britain, Ireland and France in 1957-58 and 1966-1967, to South Africa in 1953 and 1961 and to New Zealand in 1952, 1955 and 1967. His Australian record of 41 caps was passed in 1971 by Peter Johnson. Miller continued to play club rugby with Manley in Sydney but finally ended his career at the age of forty-three.

SHORT BUT NOT SWEET

The first Australian side to make a short tour in Europe arrived in Ireland in October, 1968 under the captaincy of Paul Johnstone. And it was to be a short and bitter tour. They lost to the Combined Irish Universities side by 3-9 at Ravenhill, Belfast, then went south to Musgrave Park, Cork where they perked up more than a little by beating the Irish Universities by 15-3. Then came the first international game against Ireland at Lansdowne Road and this was to give the Irish their fourth successive win over Australia. by 10-3. Ireland took an early lead with a try by Barry Bresnihan which was converted by Tom

Kiernan and although John Ballesty reduced the lead with a try for the Wallabies, Ireland's No 8 Ken Goodall tidied it all up with a try midway through the second half with a try which Kiernan converted. The Australians then departed for Scotland and had a fair win over Scottish Districts by 14-9 at Hughenden near Glasgow, but on Saturday, they faced Scotland at Murrayfield and crashed to another defeat. Andy Hinshelwood opened the scoring for Scotland with a try and with two penalty goals by Colin Blaikie they led 9-3 at half-time to Australia's only score, a penalty goal by John Brass. That, in fact, was how it ended. Despite tremendous pressure by the Scots in the second half, they failed to score again. This marked Scotland's third successive win over the Australians since 1958.

WAS IT . . . . OR WAS IT NOT?

The one international game the Australians will never forget is the last-second defeat by the All-Blacks at Ballymore Stadium, Brisbane, on Saturday 22nd June, 1968. With less than 90 seconds to go, they were leading 18-14 and it seemed that the New Zealander's unbeaten record of four years was gone. Then came tragedy and controversy. The All-Black Bill Davis kicked ahead towards the Australian line and as he made to follow it up, he was tackled by the Australian centre Barry Honan. The ball went over the Australian line and was touched down by full-back Arthur McGill. Unfortunately, Mr Kevin Crowe had blown the whistle and had run between the posts to signal a penalty try. Honan's tackle, by his decision, had been a late one. That changed the score to 18-17 and with the final kick of the game New Zealand's full-back Fergie McCormick got the conversion for a shock 19-18 win for the All-Blacks. The controversy raged on and on after that game and a subsequent film showing of the incident indicated that Honan's tackle had not been late and had been fair. But the referee's decision was final and the arguments remain to this day. But for that penalty try, New Zealand's long unbeaten record would have gone and Australia would have won their finest international hour against the all-conquering All-Blacks, led by Brian Lochore.

GREG DAVIS'S WALLABIES

Gregory Victor Davis, born and raised in New Zealand, led Australia on their 26 match tour of South Africa in 1969 and landed himself

with the unhappy distinction of captaining the side in the four international games that were lost by a margin of 76 points to 31. This was
the first time Australia had lost a series of four international games in
South Africa. In all Greg Davis's Wallabies played 26 games, won 15,
lost 11, drew none and scored 465 points while conceding 353. John
Ballesty was their most successful points scorer with 89 points from four
tries, 16 conversions, 12 penalty goals and three drop goals. S. O.
Knight, centre threequarter led the try scoring with 11. Their biggest
win was 37-6 over North-West Cape and their most decisive beating
was by South Africa in the first international by 11-30 at Johannesburg.

VISAGIE'S AFTERNOON

The 1969 Australians were totally outclassed and routed in their first
international game against the Springboks at Ellis Park and down 6-19
at half-time were eventually beaten by 11-30. This was a game that
belonged to the Springbok out-half Piet Visagie, who landed exactly
half of South Africa's total with his boot. He kicked three penalty
goals and three conversions. The South African tries came from yds
Nomis with two, Mannetjies Roux, Piet Greylint and Jan Ellis and all
Australia could offer in return were two penalty goals and a conversion
by Rupert Rosenblum and a try by Terry Foreman. With his 15 points
Visagie joined Aaron "Okey" Geffin in the international individual
scoring list for South Africa, just a point behind Keith Oxlee who set
the all-time mark in 1962 with his 16 points against the Lions at
Bloemfontein.

A RECORD EQUALLED

Apart from the fact that wing-threequarter Jan Engelbrecht was making
his 33rd international appearance for South Africa and thus equalling
the all-time record of the time set by John Gainsford, the second
international between the Australians and the Springboks in the 1969
tour was not a memorable affair. Without ever stretching themselves
to full tilt, the Springboks galloped away to an easy victory which was
marked by two tries from Engelbrecht which, incidentally, also took
him to the top of the South African try scoring list of all time to join
John Gainsford. Both of them, having played 33 international games,

still remain as the top men with eight tries each in South Africa's scoring lists since 1891. Piet Visagie collected a further 10 points to his international collection with a try, a penalty goal and two converts. For Australia John Ballesty had the distinction of kicking all of his country's points with three penalty goals.

VISAGIE MOVES ON

For the second time in an international during the Australians 1969 tour of South Africa John Ballesty was responsible for all of his country's points, but this time, in the third international against the Springboks at Newlands, his contribution came to just three points, from a penalty goal. As against that Piet Visagie was right in form for South Africa. Early on he raced in for a try, which he then converted and with a penalty goal he put the Springboks into a lead of 8-0. Ballesty then kicked his penalty goal but Jan Ellis ran in for a try and that was that. Visagie, with 79 points to his credit at the end of this game needed only another nine points to equal the all-time South African individual international scoring total then held by Keith Oxlee with 88 points.

A SAD ENDING

The Australian touring side to South Africa in 1969 brought their international campaign to a sad ending at Bloemfontein and wound up their trip by losing all four international games. This time the margin was 19-8 for South Africa and once again John Ballesty was the Wallabies top scorer in the game with five points, a penalty goal and a conversion of Steve Knight's try. But almost all the interest in this game centered on the 26-year old Piet Visagie, playing in his 14th international game for South Africa. With the score at 14-8 with barely minutes to go, Visagie had scored eight points and had closed to within a point of Keith Oxlee's all-time record. Then with a blazing burst of speed Eben Oliver went racing in for a South African try. So, with the very last kick of the game, Visagie had the chance to smash the record. It was quite an extraordinary moment. Hardly a sound could be heard as Visagie made his mark, lined up the ball and then moved back to take the kick. Then the uproar began as his kick, rising high and straight, passed between the posts. He had scored his 89th point in international appearances for South Africa and was the new record holder in a list of Springboks going right back to 1891.

TWENTY FOUR FATEFUL DAYS

Greg Davis led his Australian side to a short tour of France in 1971 and in a crowded programme which encompassed eight matches, including two full internationals in 24 days, the Wallabies came out with a slight edge in the final honours. They won four of the eight games and scored 110 points while conceding 101, and each country won an international game. The Australians had their best win in the opening game against a Regional XV at Lille where they won by 28-12 and took their worst beating in the seventh game at Bayonne where they were beaten by another Regional XV by 13-25. Their top scorer was Jim McLean with 35 points and he also had the distinction of scoring 16 points in their first game with two tries and four conversions.

A STORMY ENDING

In their warm-up for the first international game against France at Toulouse on 20th November, 1971, the Australians beat a Regional XV at Lille by 28-12, lost to a second Regional XV at Limoges by 9-6, lost to a Regional XV at Strasbourg 6-7, beat a Regional XV at Grenoble by 12-3 and three days before the international game beat a Regional XV at Toulon by 20-9. And this international game was to be rough and fiery. Australia's captain Greg Davis came in for some extremely heavy punishment and following the game had to enter hospital for an emergency operation on his nose which had been broken by a punch. Following the game the Australians had to have a police escort from their dressing rooms to the team coach. The match itself was quite extraordinary and at one stage it looked as though the French were going to run away to an overwhelming victory. With tries from Betranne and Skrela and a penalty goal by Villepreux, they led the Wallabies by 11 points in the first half. Gradually, however, the Australians fought back and with two tries from David l'Estrange, one converted by Arthur McGill, they closed the gap to a point. Then they moved into the lead with a penalty goal from Jim McLean and it was at this stage that matters began to get just a little out of hand. The Australians, however, took as good as they got and held out for their first international win on French soil.

ALL SQUARE

Four days after their first international win in France, the touring Australians went down to a shattering defeat by 13-25 against a Regional XV at Bayonne. Three days later, they headed for Colombes Stadium, Paris on Saturday, 27th November, to try for their first win at French headquarters. But it was not to be. France's full-back Pierre Villepreux was in his most elegant kicking form and he knocked over four penalty goals and converted Bofelli's try. All that Australia could offer in return were the three penalty goals, two kicked by Jim McLean and the other by Arthur McGill. But, even in defeat, there was to be a moment of history for one of Australia's great heroes, hooker Paul Johnston. With this appearance, his 42nd in the front row, he became Australia's most capped player. The previous record-holder had been the durable Tony Miller with 41. As it happened, this was also to be Johnston's goodbye to international rugby after a career that had begun in 1959 with his first cap against the Lions.

A RECORD FIFTH

When Peter Sullivan led the 1973 tourists on their short tour to Wales and England, the trip brought a new record for full-back Arthur McGill and scrum-half John Hipwell. For both, this visit to Britain marked their fifth tour overseas. Unfortunately, like so many of the previous Australian tours it was not to be a rewarding one. They played eight matches, won two, drew one, lost five and conceded more points than they scored. Their total was 85 points for and 131 against. In the opening game against South-Eastern Counties at Bournemouth they scraped home by 17-15 but three days later at Bath they went down 14-15 to South and South-West. On 31st October, they were well beaten by 11-19 at Newport by East Wales but then came up with a good result by holding Swansea to an 11-11 draw at St Helen's. On 6th November, they beat West Wales 18-13 at Aberavon and in their final game against a provincial side, the North of England at Gosforth on 12th November, they went down by 13-16.

A RECORD FOR WALES

Australia's first international of the 1973 short tour, at Cardiff Arms Park on Saturday, 10th November, 1973 was never more than a good training outing for Wales, who won just as they pleased. Australia were out of the hunt right from the start, were well-beaten up front and had no answer at all to a well-drilled and smooth moving Welsh pack-line. By the time it was over Phil Bennett with four penalty goals, Dave Morris, T. G. R. Davies and R. W. Windsor with a try each had taken Wales to a 24-0 win, their most decisive in the history of the meetings between the two countries. Windsor, winning his first inter-national cap, had the satisfaction of scoring in his debut for Wales and the only other noteworthy feature of a one-sided game was that Gareth Edwards, the Welsh captain, who was winning his 32nd cap for his country at scrum-half, had to go off with injury and was replaced by Clive Shell who had been Edward's patient understudy for some time at that stage.

DOWN TO ENGLAND

England brought in one new cap, David Roughley of Liverpool for the final game of the Australian's short tour at Twickenham on 17th November, 1973 and the only feature of another lop-sided encounter was that it gave England the proud honour of having defeated South Africa, New Zealand and Australia, all within the space of 18 months. For Australia it was another sad afternoon. Russell Fairfax, their New South Wales full-back, kicked a penalty goal and that was the only score they managed to put on the scoreboard. Against that England with tries from Tony Neary, Andy Ripley and Alan Old and two penalty goals and a conversion from Peter Rossborough ran up a total of 20 points. It was Australia's worst-ever defeat by England.

FIVE FOR FAIRFAX

Australia's full-back Russell Fairfax wound up on the losing side in the Wallabies international game against France on 25th June, 1972 at Brisbane and equalled his country's record for kicking penalty goals in an international game. He put over five to join his countryman Arthur McGill, who had previously achieved five penalty goals against

New Zealand also at Brisbane in 1968. Fairfax, however, kicked all his side's points in their 15-16 defeat by France but McGill got his 15 in Australia's defeat, 18-19 by New Zealand.

THE FIRST FAMILY

The three Thornett brothers can probably claim to be Australia's first family in rugby history. Dick was the oldest, with Ken the middle brother and John the youngest. Dick, also an Australian waterpolo international, won his first cap for his country with three games against Fiji and followed this with two more against South Africa and one against France. He finished with five international caps against New Zealand in 1962 and a year later he decided to change over to rugby league with Parramatta. John Thornett, surely one of the greatest personalities of Australian rugby made his debut against New Zealand in 1955, and by the time he played his final international game against France at Colombes Stadium, Paris, in 1967, he had added 37 international caps to the family collection. Ken, unfortunately never played rugby union with Australia. He was spotted by rugby league scouts when he was still at school and eventually wound up in England with the Leeds club. But like his other brothers he did play internationally for Australia. In all he was to represent his country in 12 international games against France, Britain, New Zealand and South Africa. Between them the three Thornett brothers, in both union and league, represented Australia on a record 60 occasions.

THE CENTURY UP

At the start of the 1973-1974 season, Australia were just one away from a century of defeats in their international games against the major countries. Their short tour of England and Wales, in which they lost both international games to Wales and England took them over the 100 mark. Australia have a particularly dismal record against New Zealand, South Africa, England, Ireland, Scotland, Wales, France and the Lions and have, at one time or another, been defeated by all eight. They have played 138 international games—and their games against America, Fiji and the Maoris are excluded although caps are awarded for them—and of these they have won only 30, have lost 103 and have drawn five. This was their international record at the start of the 1974-1975 season.

THE TRUE BROTHERS

Sets of brothers have studded the history of international rugby football for over 100 years but a real bit of "brother" history was created when Australia took on New Zealand at Dunedin at Carisbrook Stadium on Saturday, 8th August, 1964. The two Boyce brothers were in the Australian side and it marked the first time they had come together on an Australian side. Stewart Boyce was the first of the two to win international honours for his country and had made his debut against the All-Blacks in 1962. Unfortunately he was not available for the tour to South Africa the following year and it was on this tour that his brother Jim became Australia's top wing-threequarter. But they were both picked for that international against New Zealand in 1964 and occupied the two wing-threequarter positions . . . and that was historic. It was the first and still the only time that twin brothers have played together in international rugby.

LIKE GRANDPA!

D. G. McLean was a member of the first Australian side to tour in New Zealand and, apart from his great displays there, he came back home with the honour of having scored Australia's first try in international rugby—and it was in fact the only score the Wallabies made in that first game. And D. G. McLean had quite a few promising sons, notably Douglas McLean who won five caps for Australia against South Africa and New Zealand between 1933 and 1936 and Bill, who won two caps against the Maoris in 1946 and against New Zealand in 1947. And he had a grandson, too, who was to follow his two uncles and grandfather into the Australian side. Jim McLean who won his first cap for Australia against South Africa and who, of course, is still a current international, is the grandson of the immortal D. J. McLean, the first man to score for Australia. And for better measure, Jim McLean's brother, twenty year-old Paul, won his first Australian cap against New Zealand in the summer of 1974.

JOHNSON LEADS

Australia's hooker Peter Johnson (New South Wales) who made his international debut in 1959 is his country's most capped player with 42 appearances—one ahead of Tony Miller, whose international career lasted from 1952 to 1967. Caps have been awarded in Australia for appearances against the Lions, New Zealand, South Africa, England, Scotland, Ireland, Wales, France, the Maoris, Fiji and America. At the start of the 1974-1975 season, 469 players had been capped for Australia.

WHAT THEY SAID

MORE THAN RUGBY

When the New Zealanders wound up their 1963-64 tour of Britain, Ireland and France with a scintillating 36-3 win over the Barbarians at Cardiff Arms Park, no one summed up their final exciting flourish better than writer Andrew Mulligan, the former Irish scrum-half, who wrote; "It was a champagne farewell. As soon as they relaxed, they were irresistible. It was as if they suddenly tasted the full elation of fulfilment. They carried rugby to a super-plane and when they walked back from the goal line with the Welsh crowd chanting, 'More, More', they experienced a sensation that they did not know existed in rugby. They being the All-Blacks, of course . . . There was no hoax. No promises to play open rugby, no defiant victory. Simply a magnificent best performance for the last night, with curtain calls and all. This was more than rugby. It was theatre."

SEND HIM OFF

Ireland's most endearing rugby character of the period between the two World Wars was the inimitable "Jammie" Clinch and Sean Diffley in his *The Men in Green* recalls some of his exploits; "In all Jammie played seven times against Wales and one of his most treasured memories is of trotting on to the field at Cardiff before the start of the match to hear a local voice coming loud and clear from the terraces; 'Send the bastard off' . . . He returned to Dublin some years ago to a rather lively retirement, playing golf, following Wanderers and Ireland and enriching the folklore of rugby with his outrageously hyperbolic yarns told in a deep rumbling drawl . . . That drawl is used to excellent effect in his account of the France-Ireland match in Paris in 1927 where the French according to Jammie were a bit rough. That means they were probably playing just slightly short of berserk which they were wont to do in those less enlightened days. The late W. F. "Horsey" Browne who died when only 29 was apparently aghast that the French forwards should so forget themselves and play so roughly in front of their own president. At half-time Horsey called his cohorts together and exhorted them that no matter what the provocation they were to resist all ideas of retaliation. No matter what the French did, explained Horsey, the Irish should be determined to uphold their honour and play like gentlemen. Whereupon, Jammie Clinch demanded that the referee should be requested to delay the restart on the grounds that, 'I don't know anything about playing like a gentleman and I would need a lot of quick briefing on the subject.'"

THE GLOBULAR MASS

Rugby, according to the late Sir Montague Shearman, was not a very entertaining sport in its early days. In the Badminton Library Book of Football, published in 1899, Shearman, one of the game's first historians, wrote; "We may begin by saying, we hope without offence, that the early matches at the Rugby game were very dull affairs, and that it is only very slowly and tentatively that the Rugby Union rules and styles of play have been altered so as to render skill of more avail than force in the settlement of matches. Rather more than twenty years ago, I saw a shoving match between rival teams of Scotchmen and Englishmen, which was dignified by the name of an 'international match'. A quarter of a hundred of heavyweights appeared to be leaning up against each other for periods of five minutes or thereabouts, while occasionally the ball became accidentally disentangled from the solid globe of scrummagers and the remaining players then had some interesting bursts of play between themselves while the globular mass gradually dissolved."

SUCH CHEEK!

Charles Wray Palliser, the representative in England of the New Zealand Rugby Union during the 1905 All-Blacks tour in Britain, Ireland and France, discovered before the party arrived in England that one or two people firmly believed that the New Zealanders were stepping out of their class and above their station in attempting to play the best clubs and counties in England! Writing shortly after the tour began, he said; "I shall never forget that bleak and gloomy morning when I turned out

433

" HE SAYS IT'S THE ONLY WAY HE
CAN EXPRESS HIS PASSION "

at 3.00 a.m. with an expectant heart to board the tender and welcome to Old England, the rugger players from the land of the white cloud, who had come on so audacious an errand. 'What! New Zealand coming to play against the clubs and counties of England! Well, was there ever such cheek ?'. This remark was made to me by a football acquaintance and what was I to expect after that? For it had never occurred to me to look upon the venture in that light. I dread to consider what this candid friend's remark would have been had I further enlightened him to the fact that not only were these daring Colonials to play clubs and counties, but they were also prepared to tackle such bodies as united England, Ireland, Scotland and Wales." His friend's belief, however, was quite general. Indeed, after the All-Blacks had routed Devon by 55 points to 4 in the first game at Exeter on 16th September, 1905, one newspaper, on getting the result, refused to credit it and, in fact, gave the result, Devon 55, New Zealand 4. The doubters, however, were effectively converted by the New Zealanders after their sixth game, by which time they had walloped Devon, Cornwall, Bristol, Northampton, Leicester and Middlesex with a total of 231 points. In those six games only one drop goal had been scored against them!

PARSIMONY

Scotland came within five minutes of becoming the first side to beat the all-conquering All-Blacks of 1905-1906 when they met in their first international game at Inverleith on 18th November, 1905. At that stage Scotland led by 7-6 but then when victory seemed to be certain the All-Blacks threequarter G. W. Smith shot over for a try and with the last move of the game, W. Cunningham added the final touch with another try. F. T. Prall, the great Scottish rugby writer of the time, duly extolled the Scots for their display but devoted far more space to the Scottish Rugby Union in his report of the proceedings. "No caps were given to the Scottish XV"—he wrote—" and this display of parsimony has been adversely commented on on both sides of the Border. It seems that when the fixture was arranged, the Scottish Rugby Union authorities, doubting the drawing properties of the New Zealanders, refused to give the required guarantee of £200 and, instead, decided to let them take the whole of the gate, minus expenses. As the receipts from the match amounted to over £1,000, there was considerable soreness in official circles at missing such a grand opportunity of swelling the Union coffers. Hence, it is stated, the determination not to award caps to the Scottish XV." It would appear, however that the Scottish Rugby Union later had a change of heart. All those who played for Scotland on that afternoon are now listed among Scotland's international players.

THEY SMOKED TOO!

One can only wonder at what would happen, nowadays, to the members of a New Zealand international side—or, for that matter, to the members of any international rugby side—if they were to lend their names and their fame to a newspaper advertisement . . . and to an advertisement for cigarettes at that. Things, however, were not quite so strict in the old days. After the All-Blacks conquering tour of Britain, Ireland and France in 1905-1906, a picture of the team appeared in a large newspaper advertisement, extolling the goodness of B.D.V. cigarettes. And the advertisement carried a message from C. M. Dixon, the manager of the New Zealand side—"The New Zealand team think B.D.V. cigarettes are a very excellent smoke and they have been greatly appreciated by the members." In addition to the testimonial, the advertisement also carried a little poem.

> "The All-Blacks from over the seas
> have won most of their matches with ease
> But it's pleasing to learn
> they were conquered in turn
> by the famed cigarettes B.D.V's".

Just for the record, a packet of 20 cost sixpence!

AN ALL-BLACK GEM

Although the remark has been credited to quite a few famous New Zealand international players over the years, no one now recalls the name of the first All-Black to say it. It has, however, become part of New Zealand's rugby lore; "There are two things I abominate—nagging wives and kicking threequarters".

FRANCE'S RUGBY PRIEST

As far as rugby is involved, France's most celebrated priest is the Abbé Henri Pistre, whose passionate love of the game and whose glorious writing on rugby, has enriched sport in France. His most famous and most quoted piece concerns a certain referee. "His perfumed luggage included a tiny hunting horn (presumably in place of a whistle) but not the lorgnette indispensable to one so short-sighted. At a welcoming hostelry, he refreshed himself after his long journey and bright-eyed and rosy-cheeked, stepped confidently on to the field, to be greeted with cries of 'Scoundrel! Knave! Hooligan! Bandit! Give us victory or tonight we'll hang you on a lamp-post'. Terrified, the sounder of the hunting horn lost control. His lofty brow sank almost to the ground as though he were looking for daisies or butter-cups in the December slush . . . His brain box was as empty as the purse of a mendicant . . . I have till now stubbornly defended referees. I have stood by the short-sighted, the short of breath, the clumsy, the unlucky and the partial . . . I cannot support the stupid".

WHY BURY IT?

And again from the Abbé Henri Pistre, after a drab England-France game which ended in a 3-3 draw . . . "We don't go to stadiums to see the ball systematically buried. What are undertakers for?" Later when France beat Ireland at Colombes Stadium by 23-6, he wrote; "It was gay. A fig for those who called it mad. When our rugby, rid of its old inferiority complex, spreads its wings in the spring sunshine, may we not call it joyful? Why give its young and smiling face a monocle?"

AND THE DRIVER, TOO

Ireland's Tony O'Reilly made quite unusual rugby history by writing a special article for the England v Ireland programme at Twickenham in 1970—and then finding out less than 24 hours before the game that he had been recalled to the Irish side after a lapse of seven years. O'Reilly turned up for training at the Honourable Artillery Ground on the Friday evening in a chauffeur-driven limousine, which occasioned more than a little comment in the following morning's papers. Some time later 'OReilly recalled that fateful last game he played against England . . . "I found myself at the last moment reduced to bravery. A long English footrush was terminated when—quite out of character —I dived at the feet of the English pack. As I was emerging from momentary unconsciousness, I heard a loud and let me confess Irish voice shouting from the popular terrace, 'and kick his bloody chauffeur while you're at it.'"

ON THE WRONG FEET

After the "Battle of Arms Park" in which the Springboks beat Cardiff 13-0, during the 1960-1961 tour, Vivian Jenkins, writing in the *Sunday Times,* had no doubts at all but that it had been a battle. "The H. Bomb holds no terrors after this. The South Africans beat Cardiff all right by two goals and a penalty goal to nil and, indeed, more than beat them. They mangled them, reduced them to pulp, heroically though the Welsh side resisted. But, as for pleasing the Welsh spectators, the tourists took off on as many wrong feet as the proverbial centipede."

DO IT YOURSELF

Amadée Domenech, the gigantic prop-forward who won 22 caps for his country, recalls his experience with the legendary Jean Prat in England's defeat by France at Twickenham in 1955; "Jean was a great player and a fine leader but he kept a special eye on me and crazed me with commands. Stand here, stand there, get him, get out of the way, run, stop, pass it, hold it, grab it, punch it, kick it . . . we were attacking and Jean was ordering me and only me it seemed, what to do. Then the ball came to me just as Jean standing a few yards away, yelled at me louder than ever. So I flung it at his head, shouting, 'See what you can do with it'. He caught it neatly and scored a lovely drop goal." Prat, who was captain that afternoon, dropped two goals in the 16-9 win.

VERY QUIETLY

Paul MacWeeney of the *Irish Times*, known throughout the world for his rugby writings, is also renowned as a glorious story-teller. Unfortunately the written word can never never give even the remotest hint of the impact with which he delivers those stories in his most appealing accent. He tells one of G. W. E. Mitchell, the Edinburgh Wanderers forward who won his first cap against New Zealand in 1967 at Murrayfield—and realised that he had been handed the job of looking after the gigantic Colin Meads in the line-outs. After the game, he told his colleagues that at the first line-out Meads, using the well-known All-Black technique of showing who was boss, told him in no uncertain manner what he intended to do to him. "And what did you say to Meads,"—the team-mates asked. He paused for a moment and then said; "I told him straight out to - - - - off " . . . and then Mitchell added—"but I did it very, very quietly".

FOR SCOTLAND

The Springbok utility player of the 1951-1952 tour was Stephanus Viviers, better known as "Basie", who in his 14 games, alternated between full-back and centre-threequarter and also appeared at scrum-half. Regarded as the great wit of the side, he was asked at the end of the tour for his opinion on the toughest game of the tour. Viviers, who had watched the international game against Scotland, had no hesitation in answering, "Scotland," and then, after a slight pause, —"For Scotland."

UNIFORMED RIOT

What does rugby football look like to the outsider? One American reporter, having seen the England v Wales game of 1974, wrote the following in *Newsweek* magazine on 25th March, 1974; "To the uninitiated, it resembles a uniformed riot more than a sport born at a school for English aristocrats. Heads swathed in surgical tape, limbs streaming with mire if not blood, two packs of grown men lock arms in a bizarrely brutal dance, flailing with their legs at a distended leather bag. On the edges of this fray lurk other, more nimble combatants, waiting to snatch up the ball and convey it downfield through lumbering legions of defenders whose chief objective seems to be to shorten the ball carrier's life span".

TWO IN ONE GRAVE

The All-Blacks captain in 1905-1906, Dave Gallaher, was constantly in trouble with referees who, in many cases refused to accept his interpretation of the "rover" forward in rugby. He accepted all their decisions with dignity and never complained but there is a story told that on a certain afternoon some years later when he was walking through a cemetery with another old All-Black, they saw a headstone with the inscription—"Here lies the body of ————. He was a famous referee and an honest man." Gallaher is reputed to have smiled and said gently—"It must be the first time they have ever buried two men in the one grave".

TO DO OR DIE

To play for Wales at rugby! What greater honour could there be for a Welshman? The deep and dedicated fervour for every Welshman to the game is perhaps typified best by Clive Rowlands, one of the country's memorable scrum-halves of the 1960s. Later the Welsh coach and a Lions selector, Rowlands made it clear that more than 100 per cent effort should be the first essential of any man wearing the Welsh jersey. "I believe that if you are proud to play for Wales, then you should be prepared to die for Wales,"—he said.

THE GOLDEN-HAIRED APOLLO

Ronnie Poulton, who was later to become Ronnie Poulton-Palmer when he joined the family business of Huntley and Palmer, made 17 appearances in the English threequarter line between 1909 and 1914 and wound up his international career with a total of 28 points from eight tries and a drop goal. Poulton-Palmer, who was to die in the first World War in 1915 at the age of twenty-five, became one of the legendary heroes of English rugby and he had no more ardent admirer than the late A. A. Thomson, whose book *Rugger my Pleasure* remains as one of the classic publications on the game. Writing of Poulton-Palmer, he said: "For me and forever, the most dazzling figure on the rugger field will be that of Ronald Poulton, the golden-haired Apollo, who clove through the enemy ranks as Galahad's good blade clove the

casques of men. There never was and never will be another like him . . .
When you saw Poulton flying through a defensive gap that had not
been there a split second before, you instantly had the feeling that the
opposition did not really exist. He went through a ruck of players as
the prince in some fairy tale might pass by a touch of his magic sword
through a castle wall. He would move with his rhythmic stride towards
a waiting full-back, and hey presto, Poulton was over the line and the
unhappy back was clutching the air . . . He has some of the swift,
shining quality of a rapier . . . I shall, of course, remember him, tall,
slender of limb, delicately poised as a ballet dancer, his football boots
might have been dancing shoes. His fair hair streamed in the wind
and his build was the tapering build of the ideal athlete, sturdy of
shoulder, slim at the waist and below . . . A beautiful player, a character
of the highest integrity, one of the loveliest and best . . ., he might have
stood as the symbol of Rupert Brooke's generation, of the golden
young men who died faithfully and fearlessly in a war where much that
was of value beyond price in an imperfect world perished too."

A THICK SKIN

Frank Potter-Irwin, a vice-President of the English Rugby Union in
1925, was one of the most famous referees of his time and on one
occasion was invited to give the prime requisites for taking charge of a
game. His reply was brief. "Quickness of decision, an aptitude for
seeing ahead, firmness, an agreeable manner, a capability for keeping
up with the game, a clear head, control of the players, an insight into
character, self-effacement, courage of conviction . . . and above all,
a thick skin. And never, if you wish to have a happy and peaceful life,
write on the subject of refereeing."

AN AVALANCHE

Dr Jacques Dufourcq of Stade Bordelais Universitaire de France, was
one of the first great players in French rugby and won five caps prior
to the First World War. And he never forgot his first one, which was
France's first ever international, against New Zealand in 1906 on New
Year's Day, 1906. France were beaten 8-38 and over 50 years later when
Dr Dufourcq looked back on that game, he said; "They were formid-
able. I remember the match largely as a series of black avalanches".

I HOPE NOT

On the eve of England's international game against the touring South Africans of 1931-1932, Carl Aarvold, the English captain, was making his leave after a function for both teams. As he was making his way to the door, a former English international came to him and wished him the best on the morrow. "All the luck in the world to you tomorrow, Aarvold"—he said—"May be the better team win". Aarvold looked at him and said . . . "I hope not".

YOU'RE BORING

The Welsh referee, Merion Joseph, speaking at a dinner in Wales, told the following story against himself. Not very long before that he had been refereeing one of Ireland's International games at Lansdowne Road and one of the first things he did was to watch the two front rows. He wanted to be sure that there would not be any trouble. A special warning had been given to all international referees at the time to keep an extra-special watch out for "boring" by the prop-forwards onto the opposing hookers. Sometime during the first half Mr Joseph blew sharply on his whistle and signalled out Phil O'Callaghan in Ireland's front row. "O'Callaghan,"—he said—"You're boring." He was quite taken aback with O'Callaghan's most unexpected reply—"You're not so bloody exciting yourself."

THE HYPHEN!

Tony O'Reilly, capped 29 times for Ireland between 1955 and 1970, tells the following story about Mick English, who represented Ireland on 16 occasions. "The pity is today that you will not be seeing the former Irish fly half, Michael Anthony Francis English, in action. Straight from '*The Experiences of an Irish R.M.*', it has been rightly said that he would gladly sell you a spavined horse for £25 and make you feel under a compliment to him. Michael was marking that 'Eligint Englisman', J. P. Horrocks-Taylor in a closely fought game at Twickenham. England won a narrow victory 8-6 through a last minute Horrocks-Taylor try. English, the most resolute of tacklers, had for once missed him. A court-martial was held in the dressing rooms afterwards. 'There I was,' he said, 'with 50,000 pairs of hostile eyes fastened on me. I went for the tackle, the Horrocks went one way, the Taylor went the other and I was left holding his bloody hyphen.'''

AS MOTIONLESS

Sir J. H. A. MacDonald, speaking at the Jubilee dinner of the Edinburgh Academicals Rugby Football Club in 1908, suggested that very few of those present at the dinner had ever seen one of the "real scrums" of early rugby. "Had they ever seen a haycock that was put up when the hay was wet and the smoke or steam was rising from it? That was just like a scrum in those days . . . and it was just about as motionless."

THE BEST TO LEAVE

All-Black Jim Parker, who toured with Cliff Porter's "Invincibles" of 1924-1925 and who made three full international appearances against Ireland, Wales and England, was asked on one famous occasion to name the best side that ever left the shores of New Zealand. His reply has now gone into history . . . "The 1937 Springboks"—he said.

ONLY TO EAT

E. H. D. Sewell, one of the game's great historians gives his advice on rugby captaincy in his book *Rugby Football Today*, which was published in 1931; "The very best leadership of all is Silent Example . . . two of the most memorable captains were the late Dave Gallaher of the All-Blacks team, that of 1905, and that stolid old Boer pastor Paul Roos of the South African team of 1906. It is said that not even when he was penalised off the earth in the Welsh match at Cardiff did Gallaher make a remark. While for four months Roos only opened his mouth to eat and to make a telling speech at the Rugby Union dinner at the end of the tour."

GET A DOUBLE-DECKER

The famous story which went the rounds in Wales after Keith Jarrett had scored his 19 points in the Welsh defeat of England by 34-21 at Cardiff Arms Park in 1967 is recalled by David Watkins, the Welsh out-half that afternoon, in his book, *The David Watkins Story*. Watkins, who won 21 caps for Wales before turning to Rugby League, writes; "Keith Jarrett turned up at a bus stop for the last bus to Newport which had left 10 minutes before. A conductor and a driver came past. 'The last bus to Newport has gone,' they said, 'and you won't get another one tonight'. 'Oh dear,—said Jarrett—'That means I'm stranded.' The conductor looked at him; 'It's Keith Jarrett, isn't it? The 19 points against England today.' Jarrett admitted that was right so the conductor told him, 'Hang on there. We'll get a bus to run you home'. They disappeared and came back with a bus. Jarrett was about to get on board when an inspector came up and addressed his two men. 'Now where the hell do you think you are going with that bus?' They explained: 'It's Keith Jarrett—19 points against England today—and he has missed his last bus. We're going to take him home.' The inspector told them: 'Put it back, get him a double-decker. He might want to smoke on his way home.' "

PURE RECREATION

The French wing-threequarter Adolphe Jaureguy, who won 26 international caps between 1920 and 1929 ,was passionately devoted to the game of rugby. At the end of the 1920s, when the prospects of a break between France and the other four countries in the International Championship became depressingly stronger, he said; "I can understand British wishes to keep so noble a game out of the rolling mill into which some of the new sports methods would draw it. If the day comes when only one game is played as pure recreation, that game will be rugby."

THE BREATHALYSER

Ireland's Tony O'Reilly recalls the game against Wales at Cardiff Arms Park in 1957; "The teams were quite indistinguishable midway through the second half. The referee finally asked the Welsh team to leave the field and fortify themselves with clean jerseys. They fortified themselves with more than that and on their return their breath would have turned the Irish jerseys back to their natural green. It seemed a sort of early version of the breathalyser. I need hardly add that they won easily."

NO HAKA!

Writing in *The Winter Men*, one of the wonderful series of rugby books written by Wallace Reyburn, the author talks of the Seventh All-Blacks; . . . "When the All-Blacks trotted out on to the field for their first match at Gloucester, the crowd sensed that something was wrong but couldn't quite put their finger on it. Then as the team lined up for the kick-off, they realised what it was—the All-Blacks were not going to do a haka. Perhaps they hadn't time to rehearse it. A buzz of disappointment went around the ground. Probably they'd get going with it in the next match or so. But they didn't. The shattering news was announced that the All-Blacks had abandoned the haka. A trivial matter? Not at all. The haka was a tradition going back over more than half a century, part of the All-Black image, a little touch that put them thoughtfully apart from other touring sides. . . A New Zealander by birth I had always in the past done some national gloating whenever the All-Blacks were mentioned. When rugbymen here talked of touring teams, they dismissed the Wallabies as Aussie roughnecks. The Springboks—well, we know what the feeling about them is. But the All-Blacks—ah, that was different. I always felt a glow of pride when Britishers talked about the All-Blacks. They were popular . . . Now, however, we had this new contingent and from the outset, they seemed determined in a single tour to wreck the good name their predecessors had built up over a period of 60 years . . ."

OVER-COACHING

U. A. Titley, one of the beloved scribes of rugby and co-author with Ross McWhirter of the *Centenary History of the Rugby Football Union*, told the following in a programme article in 1970 . . . "One lovely Mediterranean afternoon during the siege of Malta in 1942, I was walking up a hill after a sea bathe interrupted by bombs when I was joined by a cheerful little Maltese urchin who said, 'Good morning, Charlie—you'. It was rather an unusual greeting but in the interests of accuracy, I had to point out first that it was not morning, secondly that my name was not Charlie and that in any case he had no right to use such an obscene verb at his age. Giving me an angelic look, he said, 'Good morning Charlie —— you' and I suddenly realised that this was his entire knowledge of English. I have known over-coached rugger teams like that small boy."

AN ORIGINAL

The Irish have had a memorable succession of outstanding full-backs, from George Stack, who captained Ireland in their first international in 1875 to Tom Kiernan who finished his international career in 1973 with a then world record number of 54 caps, all in the full-back position. But, perhaps no Irish full-back is remembered with more affection than the late Ernie Crawford, who won the first of his 30 caps in 1920. In his *History of the Lansdowne Football Club*, Garry Redmond, whose passionate love of rugby is eloquently evident in all his writing, says; "Ernie Crawford, coming back from the war, was of a new generation. He was an original for he came into senior football relatively late in playing terms. He was just 27 when he was first capped, yet built an unforgettable international fame when many players are coming to their close. He was original, too, in that while still a player, he involved himself in the politics as it were of rugby administration, and, in fact was frequently at daggers drawn with Jack Coffey and most of the Alickadoos, particularly for his missionary zeal on behalf of Sunday football—how prophetic he was, taking scratch sides all over the place to encourage rugby outside Dublin—and in the 1930 campaign which he moved in Lansdowne for a reduction in the ex-officio influence of past presidents of the I.R.F.U. and Ernie was always, right through his late years, as President of Lansdowne, of the Union, as Irish selector, a player's man. His exploits on the field are countless; from turning his back on French opponents to disconcert them or giving the Colombes crowd—in long anticipation of Harvey Smith's more demotic gesture—a provocative New Year's greeting by tying a sprig of mistletoe to the backside of his breeches or doing the old fox in the Cardiff match . . . On the field his tactical judgement in reading a game was acknowledged as superb and he had the capacity to lift the men in front of him to special effort. He was a great full-back, arguably one of the greatest; not a long kick but seldom missing catch or touch and a marvellous tackler . . . In many ways he was a larger-than-life figure whose memory lives wherever there is rugby. He looked strangely old fashioned on the field, for he always played with the collar of his jersey fully buttoned up . . . Extraordinary."

OUT OF SHAPE

From Terry McLean, one of the most gifted of all rugby writers . . . "Good teams have bad days and bad teams have good days and when

" GOSH! DAI, YOU'RE RIGHT — HIS INJURY _IS_ MORE THAN TRIVIAL !"

you try to arrive at a firm judgement, everything becomes higgledy-piggledy. Which after all is rugby football—what sensible man would ever play a sport wherein the main object of contention, the ball, was out of shape anyway?"

. . . . . .

And from McLean again, after the French tour of New Zealand in 1961 had yielded a vast profit of £68,000. . . . "Money no longer grows on trees in New Zealand. It grows on rugby fields."

THE TABLECLOTH

The late Jock Wemyss, one of the beloved characters of Scottish rugby, who won the first of his Scottish caps in 1914 and the seventh in 1922, had a delightful sense of humour and one of the best stories told by him and about him was of a famous Barbarians game in Wales. On the eve of the match, the great B. H. "Jyka" Travers, the Australian, who was to lead the Barbarians in this game, worked out on a table cloth, for Wemyss's benefit, of how the game could be won. Travers, one of the great theorists of rugby, plotted out an elaborate drawing on the tablecloth to show how the Barbarians could get away to a fine start with a surprise try in the first minute. The surprise try was scored but, unfortunately not by the Barbarians! The Welsh scrum-half got the ball from the first scrum, shot around on the blind side and scampered over for a try. Travers, who at the time happened to be standing close to Wemyss who was acting as touch-judge, turned to the Scottish international and asked somewhat plaintively as to what had gone wrong. Wemyss looked at him and said rather dryly—"Nothing . . . except that you forgot your bloody tablecloth."

A NOTE TO CRITICS

Marcel Puget ended a most unusual international career with France with the record of having played his first game against Italy in 1961 and then disappearing from the international scene until 1966 when he won his first two official caps against Ireland and Scotland. His only other appearance in the International championship was in the last game of his career against England in 1969. Yet, in between he had played five times against South Africa and three times against New Zealand! Puget, who was noted for his turn of phrase had this to say on one occasion about the commentators of rugby; "Critics should remember that we have to play as circumstances make us play . . . not as they or we ourselves would like to play."

EVERY LOOSE HEAD

Norman Mair, who won four caps for Scotland in 1951 against England, Ireland, Wales and France and who, nowadays, is one of the game's most erudite commentators, wrote once of Frank Laidlaw, the Scottish hooker from 1965 to 1971; "To Frank Laidlaw, every lost loose head is a personal bereavement."

NOT A WORD

At a time in French rugby when there had been considerable publicity over some fighting that had marred a major game, Rene Crabos, who was capped 15 times for France between 1920 and 1924 and had by then become President of the French Rugby Federation was asked for his views on the tremendous publicity which had been showered on this particular game. He gave them with typical Gallic philosophy. "One big match, one little fight, stories in every newspaper. Five hundred little matches, without a fight, not a word."

THE SPECIALISTS

Writing in *Mid Olympique* in 1956, Adolphe Jaureguy, one of France's most famous players of the 1920s gave his views of the age of specialisation in rugby; "Talk of specialist prop-forwards, of right-hand props and left-hand props, amuses me. As though an international prop should not be able to play equally well left or right! Talk of third row forwards not being able to play in the second row is also amusing. I know nothing of forward play, you say? That's possible. But I don't believe in those mysteries of the scrum the technicians talk so much about. Loose scrums, tight scrums, and lineouts are very important but they are less complicated than some say. In my opinion, forwards should be able to play anywhere on the pack and as I give first importance to speed and mobility, I think the ideal pack would be composed of eight wing-forwards."

DEAD SLOW

Towards the end of his great career which brought him 41 international caps for Australia from 1952 to 1967, prop forward Tony Miller was asked about his pace. His answer was brief and to the point . . . "Dead slow and stop."

TERROR!

Among the 12,000 spectators who watched the All-Blacks win their 26th successive game of the 1905-1906 tour by crushing Cheshire at Birkenhead Park on 9th December, 1905, was Henry Eagles, one of the first great northern England players to turn professional. He was duly impressed with the New Zealanders but writing afterwards in the *Daily Mail,* he claimed that the All-Blacks had struck terror into the Cheshire ranks; "The Colonials, I am afraid, though they delighted the spectators, struck something like terror into the Cheshire men when they chanted their Maori war-cry, which is such an unique feature, before the game—that is if, if the look of astonishment on the faces of some of the players may be taken as a criterion, or after the exhibition given by G. Tomes at full-back, for he was decidedly nervous all through and fumbled the oval in shocking fashion."

FAULTY SIGHT?

Right at the end of Wales's game with Ireland at Balmoral, Belfast on Saturday, 12th March, 1904, the Scottish referee disallowed a late Welsh try on the grounds that a forward pass had been made. And that try would have given Wales a 15-14 win. As it was they wound up with a 12-14 defeat. The Welsh critics were anything but kind to the same referee, Mr Crawford Findlay in their later comments. "Dromio", one of the best writers of the time was perhaps the kindest. He said;

"It was the referee who beat us. Perhaps Crawford Findlay suffered from a physical obliquity of vision, perhaps he could not really see whether a pass was right or wrong. At Leicester earlier in the season under exactly the same circumstances, he disallowed a try which would have given Wales victory over England. Shall we say that his eyes were not quick enough to see that Dick Jones coming up at full speed could take a correct pass and be in front of the man who gave it in the fifth of a second?"

"LE SERGENT GALLAHER"

Alex Potter, an Englishman living in Paris, has written on the French rugby scene for almost 50 years, and with Georges Duthen, produced one of the great books on the game—*The Rise of French Rugby*. One of his favourite stories is about Dave Gallaher, the Irishman, who led the New Zealanders on their first tour of Britain, Ireland and France in 1905-1906.

"There is a French trawler named 'Le Sergent Gallaher' after the captain of the All-Blacks. A firm at La Rochelle, on France's West Coast, decided to build a fleet of trawlers and name them after famous rugby players. The first was the 'Yves du Manoir', so called after the legendary fly-half of that name, who was killed in 1928 at the age of 23 while flying a military plane. There is a statue of him, probably the only statue in the world to a rugby player, at Colombes Stadium, Paris. 'Le Sergent Gallaher' was the second in the fleet. It is a small craft, 119 tons, and its builders told me—'We could not help being deeply impressed by the name of Dave Gallaher, who was killed in Flanders, when leading a section of Foreign Colonial troops not many years after he had led the famous All-Blacks in France.' "

NOR FORGIVEN EITHER

R. B. Walkington (N.I.F.C.) was Ireland's first full-back in rugby and was, in fact, the first Irishman to win 10 international caps. Unfortunately he missed one extremely vital kick in his career—and Jacques MacCarthy, the first of Ireland's famous rugby writers, never forgot that omission. Writing later in Marshall's *Football—the Rugby Union Game,* he said: "R. B. Walkington always affected a coolness which he never really felt and often in attempting to demonstrate his confidence allowed himself to be charged down. He was also inclined to run too much but during his time he was unquestionably the best full-back we had. His failure to convert Cuppaidge's try—the first gained by Ireland—will never be forgotten . . . nor forgiven, either!"

THE COMPLETE CENTRE

In the Rugby Football Annual of 1938-1939, an obituary, signed "D.R.G." paid tribute to Erith Gwyn Nicholls who had died during the previous 12 months. "By common consent he was one of the very greatest centre threequarters who ever played the rugby union game. Born in 1875, he was given his first chance in the Cardiff side in 1894 —as a full-back. He played three times in that position and then took up the position with which he is always associated. From 1896 to 1906, he played regularly for Cardiff and Wales, being capped 26 times. He captained his club from 1898 to 1901 and Wales on very many occasions, the most famous being when Wales beat New Zealand in that historic game at Cardiff when the All-Blacks sustained their first defeat. Here was the complete centre if there ever was one. Others may have been more spectacular and others may have scored many more points, by tries or goals. But if the perfect centre is the one who realises that he is primarily one of the backs and above all one who has a wing outside him and still can use his own skill to score when his opponents are caught napping, then Nicholls indeed was the perfect centre. Big, fairly fast, a magnificent kick, a grand giver and timer of passes and with an uncanny eye for an opening, he was the cynosure of all eyes for years, wherever he played . . . So gone now is a great friend but as always, he shall be my beau ideal of a centre threequarter."

NOT A GLIMPSE

The late Scottish international Jock Wemyss had a tremendous admiration for Ireland's Ned Crichton of Trinity who won 15 caps for his country between 1920 and 1925; "In my time I regarded Ned Crichton as enormous. Whenever I greeted him and asked how he was his invariable reply was 'I'm immense'. He certainly was and a wonderful shield. I remember playing with him for the Barbarians. We were in the second row against Cardiff whose very tough forwards played a most anxious game. As I was no apprentice then, I quickly decided that the sensible thing to do was to shelter behind the large and jovial Ned and not a Cardiff player got a glimpse of me during the game."

A FIFTH TIME

Ireland ended 15 years of frustration at Twickenham on Saturday, 8th February, 1964 with a sensational win over England by 18-5. *The Times* reported the game on Monday morning; "Ireland finished their scoring with the last kick of the match on Saturday—a dramatic end to a thrilling contest which the visitors won by three goals and a try to a goal. Immediately there was a wild surge of Hibernian spectators on to the field to mob their heroes and to savour noisily and utterly justifiably, their first victory over England at Twickenham since 1948 and only their fifth there since the ground opened . . . Old men cackled wheezily in their joy at memories revived, the young sat wide-eyed and rather incredulous, but both were blissfully happy. Two teams living dangerously on taking risks was a stirring, virile sight. Moreover they supported a view always held there, that it is people and not laws that make rugby football, that the approach is in the mind and not in the book and that two venturesome sides, but it must be both, can cock a snook with a mania for constant tinkering with the rules."

THE GREATEST

J. B. G. Thomas, whose love affair with Welsh and world rugby has produced a stream of over 20 magnificent books on the game, paid his tribute to John Dawes Lions of 1971 in *The Roaring Lions*. . . . The whistle went for time and it was all over. The Lions had won their first series in New Zealand and had become the first Lions side in the twentieth century to win a major series abroad . . . It was a magical moment. A triumph for team work and coaching; for the blending of pace and skill in a disciplined approach without the loss of flair. In the end it was flair and confidence that carried the Lions through and the amazing kicking prowess of Barry John. Yet the Lions could not have succeeded without Willie John McBride and his forwards who surprised the world with their good sense, skill and courage. Thus it was a team victory and 'Witch' Doctor Smith was right. From the final whistle at Auckland to London Airport, it was champagne and more champagne plus a few tears . . . but no side deserved the honour more than the 1971 Lions. They were the greatest!"

THE CHARMED CIRCLE

Terence de Vere White, literary editor of the *Irish Times,* has this to say in the Ireland v Scotland programme of Saturday, 2nd March, 1974 . . . "Great rugby football players—and Michael Gibson has for a long time been in the charmed circle—fall into the category of the grave or the gay. The latter make rugby seem tremendous fun. Gibson is as graceful in action as a swallow on its way home but he is not one of the light-hearted fraternity; rather is he among those who have lent authority to the game. He is essentially an artist; and when he makes a mistake—yes, even Gibson can make mistakes—it is as if Menuhin had for a fraction of a second gone off the note. He corrects himself at once, because he knows much better that you do what has gone wrong. Gibson gets his 47th cap for Ireland today and in doing so he beats the record of his inimitable predecessor Jack Kyle. I am sure that Gibson would be the last to relish any comparison with Kyle to the latter's disadvantage. In any event, I find it more fruitful to bring to mind some of the things they have in common. First of all; to see the name of either in the programme make attendance at the match obligatory. Secondly; even if it was one of his quiet days you held on until the end of the match in lively anticipation that he would produce some transforming magic at the eleventh hour. No team, however good, was Kyle-proof or Gibson-proof. Finally; and this is to be rated high, neither ever fell below a flawless standard of performance. Having seen him play you would trust your life on either. I think you would be right. Neither, I should add ever went in for glamour. Their eyes were always on the ball."

THE WEIRDEST TOUR

Writing on the 1969-1970 tour in Britain and Ireland by South Africa, Chris Laidlaw, the great All-Blacks and Oxford University scrum-half, said; "The weirdest rugby tour in history may not last more than another month. The alien world of Britain is closing in on the Spring-boks in a variety of ways. The political and social implications of the tour are such that the whole of White South Africa is on trial in the dark mud of Britain's rugby fields."

SORO AND MOGA

Two French names will always be remembered by the Irish who saw them turn out at Lansdowne Road in the years after the Second World War—and Edmund van Esbeck, official historian of the Irish Rugby Football Union recalls them; "Today's men, Dauga, Villepreux, Trillo and Lux will have their admirers but for me, fear and respect for French rugby was born on the terraces of Lansdowne Road in 1949 and it came not from the darting thrusts of Prat or the elegance of Dufau but from two massive second row forwards with the easily pronounced names of Soro and Moga . . . remember them? I had read of this prodigious pair's toughness and durability and how they had devoured their opponents. They had left a mark two years earlier and I had not forgotten them. I never will. It was not just bulk, but brain and energy and each ball to the line-out seemed to be marked for them. They were the launching pad for those vibrant attacks from the line out and their huge frames did not so much cover the ground as eat it up. They brought a new concept to line-out play. . . . My respect for French rugby was created by Soro and Moga and I have never lost it. I believe every country has come to respect it."

IN TUNE

Pierre Danos, who won 12 international caps for France between 1958 and 1960, summed up his own prowess on the field rather neatly. "Rugby players are piano shifters or piano players. I'm one of those who gets a tune."

BE FIRM!

Blackheath's Frank Mitchell, who won six caps for England in 1896 and 1897, believed that good tackling was the essence of good rugby. "Hard tackling more than anything else is necessary all through a fifteen"—he said—"And with regard to tackling there is one great and successful method which should always be adopted when in the open. It is known as the Scots schoolboy tackle. Run hard up to your man and when within a few feet down with your head and dive at his buttocks. The head goes to one side of him, you catch him fair and square with your shoulder and your arms go round him. If properly timed you are certain to knock him over like a shot rabbit. It is the most certain of all methods. The one thing you have to remember is that you make sure of getting the ball at the same time. This in the open; at close quarters, e.g., out of touch, take him by the shoulders and pull him down. There need be no roughness; it is only necessary to be firm. The neck is a poor thing and sometimes leads to exhibitions of ill-temper. Why a man should object to being collared by the neck more than anywhere else it is difficult to see but he does object and it is best to leave it alone".

SOME SOUND ADVICE

Mark Sugden, the Englishman who played international rugby for Ireland, had ambitions of making his name as a centre but was brought solidly down to earth one afternoon at College Park in Dublin. "Harry Thrift, a famous wing who played 18 times for Ireland and who was a professor at Trinity, came into the dressing room after one game at College Park and told me I had as much hope of getting an Irish cap as a centre as he had of appearing in the Covent Garden Ballet. He advised me to try scrum-half. From that point everything slipped into place and in that position I remained until I gave up international rugby in 1931." It was, of course, the best of advice. Sugden, who won his first cap against France in 1925, went on to collect 28 caps as Ireland's scrum-half. He remains as the most-capped Irish scrum-half in international rugby.

THE MAN WITH THE SPONGE

One of the unique characters of rugby, according to Hylton Cleaver in his *Sporting Rhapsody*, is the Man with the Sponge. "He has not penetrated into London rugby"—he says—"but in the West of

England, the game would seem strange without him. No one knows how he gets the job. He needs no qualification and he has no rivals but he is profoundly jealous of his powers. The Man with the Sponge is singular because no club, however rich, has two such servants. The reason he has never set foot on Twickenham's turf is that when a man is hurt in London rugby, the game proceeds with unabated zeal until it is remarked by some analytical participant that one side appears to be one short. This observant individual draws the attention of the referee to an anomaly and after a careful search the missing figure is detected lying outstretched on the field of play. Those who are nearest inspect him with aloof disfavour and a certain impatience. Those farthest away seize the opportunity to talk like women at gates, with hands on hips. No medical attention is bestowed upon this weakling while he stays on the field. So if he appears to be in dire need of it, he is dragged to the touchline like a horse from the bull-ring, where one or two inquisitive spectators gather around and somebody lays a coat upon him, more in relief than respect, having got tired of carrying it long ago."

JUST A BRUISE

The average New Zealander's unflinching belief in the indestructibility of Colin "Pinetree" Meads was never more evident than when the gigantic second row forward was injured during the 1970 tour of South Africa. In the opening minutes of the All-Blacks 24-3 win over Eastern Transvaal on 8th July, Meads broke his arm but played on for 20 minutes before going to the sideline for examination and treatment. Following the game he went to hospital where the arm was put in plaster from bicep right down to his fingers and the first news suggested that he might be out of action for the remainder of the tour. But when this news reached New Zealand, no one really believed it and, in fact, one Christchurch orthopaedic surgeon was quotd in his local paper as saying that Meads could play if he could stand the pain. "If he is stoical enough,"—he added—"he can treat it as a bruise and get on with the game." As it was, Meads, with a guard to protect his arm, returned to the All-Blacks side for their 36-6 win over the South-Western Districts on 12th August.

DEAD ON THE MARK

Georges Lane, the French captain was dead on the mark with his final sporting prediction of the year 1909. On the eve of the international game against Wales at St Helen's, he was asked just before midnight to give his opinion on the outcome of the game. After giving the matter some thought, he said—"I think Wales will win by 35 points." And, of course, the Welsh duly obliged the following afternoon by beating France, 49-14. This score still stands as the record aggregate between the two countries.

THE ROUGHEST EVER

For reasons best known to themselves, the great Welsh forward Percy Jones and Dr Billy Tyrrell decided to liven up the proceedings in the Ireland v Wales at Belfast in 1914 and their private confrontation eventually led to what has been described as the "roughest ever" in international rugby football. In his *Rugby Recollections,* the famous Welsh historian, W. J. T. Collins, recalls the game. "Percy Jones and his Irish challenger had their private scrap. They watched each other, followed each other. If either of them got the ball, his rival did his utmost to out him. And when the ball was far away, if they got within reach of each other, they carried on their feud as if the chief purpose of the game was to secure a personal triumph. It was not to be supposed that all the other forwards would let the scrap remain private. Perhaps half of them played football, the others let themselves go with unrestrained roughness. The referee, a Scotsman, simply ignored it. Many of the fierce exchanges took place when his attention was engaged elsewhere. With the ball away in the hands of the threequarters, gentlemen in red and green jerseys, who had been carrying on pleasant private conversations in the scrummage or breathing threatenings and slaughters raised their heads and looked for someone with whom to continue the argument. But enough happened under the very nose of the referee and in full view of the Press to justify the ordering off of half a dozen players. Scores of times men were tackled and flung to the ground when they were yards from the ball, frequently blows were exchanged, there were times when the game was more like a free fight than scientific rugby football. But this must be said—it was not malicious or bad-tempered."

HEAVILY IN DEBT

Asked for his philosophy of rugby, France's durable hooker Rene Benesis, who won his first cap against Wales in 1969, summed up his great love for the game with the answer; "I am heavily indebted to rugby. It has opened many doors for me and widened my horizons. It has given me many friends and taught me a thing or two about human nature. I pay my debt to it in 80 minute instalments by playing with all my heart and hoping that I will never betray the game's true spirit."

DO IT PROPERLY

In the 18th match of their 1963-1964 tour of Britain, Ireland and France, New Zealand took on Wales at Cardiff Arms Park and within two minutes, the Welsh crowd got their first sample of Don Clarke's prodigious kicking. Wales were penalised close to the right touch line and the New Zealand full-back had a shot at goal from 57 yards out. It was close. The ball struck the tip of the right post and dropped back into play. A minute later Wales were penalised again, this time on the left touchline and about the same distance out. Clarke tried again and this time his soaring kick struck the left upright and again came back into play. Wales gave away another penalty a minute later, this time on their own "25", dead straight in front of their own posts. There was hardly a sound in the ground as Clarke placed the ball and then went back to kick. Suddenly, piercing the silence, came the distinctive voice of a Welsh supporter; "Stop showing off. Plant the bloody ball between the posts". Clarke duly obliged and New Zealand eventually went on to beat Wales by 6-0.

NEARLY ALL THE VOTES

After the 9-9 draw between Ireland and England at Lansdowne Road in 1953, the great R. C. Robertson-Glasgow, writing in *The Observer* said of Jack Kyle; "You may loudly and publicly prefer Napoleon Bonaparte to Julius Caesar, Helen of Troy to the local Beauty Queen or even Disraeli to Gladstone and your hearers will just wag a head, say 'too true' or even go to sleep. But, if Euclid-like, you seek to prove in writing that one stand-off half is greater than another stand-off half, there are plenty who will be reaching for the fountain-pen or the shillelagh. So let's seek safety by saying that Kyle is on the shortest list of the great. To parody a line from that corpulent old Roman wiseacre, Horace, 'He wins pretty nearly all the votes who mixes the serviceable with the brilliant' . . . It doesn't worry him that a few sometimes have said, 'Kyle is not the player he was.' After all, people have been known to speak disrespectfully of the Equator."

JUST TRY!

International games between Ireland and Wales have never been the most gentle of affairs—and Ireland's scrum-half Mark Sugden (1925-1931) certainly subscribes to that view. "The matches against Wales were more serious and more robust affairs"—he recalls—"Before one such game I looked in to the Welsh dressing room and said to Dai Parker, a good friend of mine; 'I hope we will have a good game, Dai'. His response was; 'Just try lying on the ball, boyo and I will break every bloody rib in your body.' "

TOO TIRED

Wing-threequarter Andy Handcock (Northampton) won only three international caps for England but against Scotland at Twickenham in 1965, he did more than enough to ensure a lasting fame in the history of the game. In this Calcutta Cup game, Scotland led 3-0 right up to the last minute. Then 15 yards out from the English line, Handcock picked up a pass and breaking through the tackles of several Scottish players, he set off on a long sprint through the mud of Twickenham. With the Scots pouring after him, he ran 95 yards to score one of the most memorable tries in modern football. Afterwards he recalled it; "I was puffed enough when I started. I did not think for a second that there was the likelihood of a try. I was too far back and the going was too heavy. It became a matter of simply going on. All I can remember was the line when I got near it. It became very blurred. I threw myself across. I had no feeling of elation. I was too tired." And what he most certainly did not hear in that moment of crossing the line was the English supporter who screamed at him—"Under the posts, for God's sake."

I KICKED YOU!

On the morning after Ireland's victory over Wales by a goal and a try to a try at Lansdowne Road in 1896, the two Irish forwards, Charles V. Rooke and Harry Lindsay went for a walk with the Welsh half-back, Llewellyn Lloyd. The match on the previous day, like most Ireland v Wales games had been a pretty robust one and Lindsay later wrote of one particular remark that Rooke made to Lloyd during the course of their walk near Dublin Bay. "It's by the grace of God that you're alive today, Lloyd. When I couldn't kick the ball, I kicked you." Rooke, who won 19 caps for Ireland between 1891 and 1897 is nowadays credited with the distinction of inventing wing-forward play as it is known today.

THE BARBARIAN MOTTO

Although he was one of the great forwards of the 1890s, Walter J. Carey (Oxford University and the Barbarians) was never capped for England. He was, however, selected on the Lions side for the tour of South Africa in 1896 and had the consolation of playing against South Africa in a Test game. He liked South Africa so much that he eventually returned there to settle down and subsequently became Bishop of Bloemfontein. Perhaps his greatest contribution to the history of rugby is the motto he coined for the Barbarians; "Rugby is a game for gentlemen of all classes but never for a poor sportsman of any class."

A WHISTLING FANTASIA

The 1905-1906 New Zealanders duly won the 14th game of their tour with an 11-0 margin over Surrey at Richmond on 1st November, 1905. But the lasting memory of the game was not the All-Blacks supremacy but the irritating performance by the referee. Writing in the *Daily Mail* report of the proceedings, the famous rugby writer J. A. Buttery said; "Over 10,000 people, many of them ladies, made their way from various parts of the metropolis to see the All-Blacks that everybody is talking about. They expected to see some wonderful football but they had reckoned without one factor—the referee. This gentleman—a Londoner and a member of the Rugby Union Committee—was evidently under the impression that everybody had come to hear him perform on the whistle and as he was in charge of the stage, so to speak, he was enabled to indulge his fancy to his heart's content. The finest artists are said to shut their eyes when whistling their hardest and judged on that hypothesis, the referee must have had his eyes closed on and off for the greater part of the game. The fantasia commenced in the first minute and continued, with brief intervals for respiration, throughout the game. As one of the rules of rugby is that you may not kick or handle the ball while the whistle is blowing, it is obvious that there was very little actual football. Directly someone got the ball and there was a prospect of a bit of play worth seeing, the referee would recommence his fascinating solo. A Scottish young lady, whose first football match this was and evidently with literary recollections of the efficacy of the pibroch, asked her escort, after one All-Blacks movement had been stopped at the referee's musical behest—'Why aren't the New Zealanders allowed to have a man to whistle for them, too?' . . . At the end of these games there is usually a rush for the jersey of the man who has scored so that it may be kept as a trophy. On this occasion there was a wild scramble for the referee's whistle."

THE NAME STUCK

The first international side to leave South Africa to play abroad was the party which toured in Britain, Ireland and France in 1906-1907. And it was at this time that the South Africans became known as the Springboks. How this came about was subsequently told by J. C. Cardin, their team manager on that tour. "The fact is that the Springbok as a badge existed when my team left South Africa and here is proof positive. We landed at Southampton on the evening of September 20, 1906 and from the *Daily Mail* of September 20, I took this paragraph. 'The team's colours will be myrtle green jerseys with gold collar. They will wear dark blue shorts and dark blue stockings and the jerseys will have embroidered on them, in multi-coloured silk on the left breast, a Springbok—a small African antelope which is as typical of Africa as the kangaroo is of Australia'. Now to the adoption of the name. No uniforms or blazers had been provided and we were a motley turn out at practice at Richmond. That evening, I pointed out to members of the team that the British Press would more than likely invent some funny name for us if we did not invent one for ourselves. We, thereupon, agreed to call ourselves the Springboks. I remember this distinctly for Paul Roos, the captain, reminded us that Springbokken was the correct plural. However, the *Daily Mail,* after our first practice called us the Springboks and the name stuck."

BEAUTY IN THE PRESS BOX!

Applications for Press tickets for international rugby games are always more than a mild headache for the unfortunate man appointed to distribute the same tickets. And Press tickets have, more than once, posed an entertaining problem at French international games. Alex Potter, one of the truly great historians of rugby recalls; "For the international matches, applications come in expectant shoals from all manners of publications, including a few dealing with agriculture, the cinema or even with women's underwear. Four ravishing pin-up girls used to be seen in the Press stand, distributing smiles right and left, making no notes and occasionally remarking, among themselves, on the muscular development of this or that prop forward or the Apollonian aspect of this or that threequarter. About the play, or the significance of the occasion, not a word. They were, it transpired, mannequins employed on journalistic work for a fashion magazine. How they got their Press tickets we do not know. But though technically trespassing, they were never asked to leave. We don't know what would have happened in New Zealand. We do know there never breathed a Frenchman who would have been ungallant enough to turn them out, they were so beautiful and seemed so charming, so innocent. It was all very irregular and very disturbing."

AND DEAF AS WELL

No one enjoys a rugby story more than Mitchel Cogley, the *Irish Independent* sports editor, who has been writing with a deep affection about the game for almost 40 years. In his son's *Yearbook of Rugby* for 1971-1972, he tells: "Everybody has his own favourite referee story and I think mine is about the fellow who had been refereeing in all grades for about 30 years and then decided to call it a day. His last match was something of an occasion and afterwards in the club bar he made the rather startling disclosure that he had never sent a player off. 'Surely,' someone said, 'there must have been occasions when you should have done so? The referee replied that he supposed so but now he was glad he had not. And then he was asked; 'What was the nearest you ever got to sending a man off?' 'No doubt about that,'—said the referee with a glint in his eye. 'It was a Metropolitan Cup match a good few years ago. This fellow, a wing-forward was at it from the start, obstructing, jersey-pulling, late tackling, the lot. Eventually after he had given away half a dozen penalties I called him over and told him if I caught him again I would have to take very serious action. As he walked away, I heard him make a very rude remark, so I whistled him back and said: 'What did you say?' He turned to his rather embarrassed team-mates and then said: 'What did I tell you? The bastard is deaf as well'. I came very close to sending him off.' "